BREAKOUT TRADING
Made Easy

BREAKOUT TRADING
Made Easy

Maximize Your Profits with
Simple Price Action Strategies

SUNIL GURJAR

JAICO PUBLISHING HOUSE

Ahmedabad Bangalore Chennai
Delhi Hyderabad Kolkata Mumbai

Published by Jaico Publishing House
A-2 Jash Chambers, 7-A Sir Phirozshah Mehta Road
Fort, Mumbai - 400 001
jaicopub@jaicobooks.com
www.jaicobooks.com

BREAKOUT TRADING MADE EASY
ISBN 978-81-19153-98-5

First Jaico Impression: 2024
Eighth Jaico Impression: 2024

Page design and layout by Inosoft Systems, Delhi

Contents

1. Introduction to Breakout Trading   1

2. Types of Breakout Trading   11

3. Trend Analysis   45

4. Gap Analysis   54

5. Chart Patterns   65

6. Breakout Trading Strategies   155

7. Chartmojo Candidates for Breakout Trading   175

8. Risk Management and Position Sizing   193

9. Trading Psychology   198

10. Trading Journal   201

11. Trailing Stop-Loss   205

12. Case Studies   209

Conclusion   378

1

Introduction to Breakout Trading

As a trader, I have been using classical chart patterns since the beginning of my trading journey which has given me the edge to not only grow my capital multiple times, but also preserve my capital during static market conditions. This is the only strategy which has statistically beaten all other types of trading strategies in the market. It stands out because it enables traders to ride the big trends in the market with defined limited losses. Your mantra when it comes to trading breakouts should be to try to spot a real price trend early and get on it, as it offers bigger potential returns on your trades.

However, if you are new to trading, this is often easier said than done. It requires practice to know the difference between a real breakout and a fake one. Setting smart price goals and stop-losses (the price at which our analysis goes wrong and we need to exit the trade, to prevent losses) is also not an easy task. To do this, you will need to know the basic rules and strategies of breakout trading which we will discuss in the subsequent chapters.

To understand breakout trading better, we need to be clear about certain concepts which are used in it. Let's take a look at different types of markets to understand the different conditions which may prevail in the market while we are doing breakout trading.

A price series that continually closes either higher or lower (on average over a defined number of periods) is said to be trending. An upward trending market is one that may fluctuate up and down but on average tends to close periodically higher. A downward trending market ends periodically lower regardless of interim moves. Securities in any asset class tend to show trending behaviour of some kind.

A sideways market consists of relatively horizontal price movements that occur when the forces of supply and demand are nearly equal for some period of time. This typically occurs during a period of consolidation before the price continues a prior trend or reverses into a new trend.

A ranging market is a market where the security prices move back and forth between a price range of a high price level and a low price level. The highest price level is formed with a resistance line, whereas the lowest price level is formed with a support line.

Support and Resistance

A stock trader's most essential (and challenging) task is predicting the securities future price. It's impossible to reliably predict when prices will rise (or fall).

As a consequence, the idea of support and resistance provides a decent framework for making sense of price fluctuations. Trends may be recognised and trading choices can be made with the aid of support and resistance levels.

A support or resistance level is established when the price activity of a market reverses and changes direction, putting behind a market peak or trough (swing point: a turning point price in the past).

What is a breakout?

A breakout is a potential trading opportunity that occurs when an asset's price climbs above or falls below a resistance level (explained in chapter 2) on increasing volume of a security. This happens when the price of a stock moves outside the defined support or resistance level, chart patterns, trend line, moving average, with increasing volume (all discussed later in the book). When the stock price breaks over resistance, a breakout trader will enter a bullish long position (wherein they trade for a longer period of time and buy the security at a lower price then sell it at a higher price), and when the stock price breaks below support, a breakout trader will enter a bearish short position (wherein they trade for a short period and sell the security at a higher price then buy it at a lower price).

Breakouts are frequently connected with chart patterns such as triangles, flags, wedges, and head-and-shoulders, trend line, moving average and so on. These breakouts occur when the price moves consistently, resulting in well-defined support and/ or resistance levels. Traders then keep an eye on these levels for breakouts. If the price breaks above resistance, they may initiate long positions, if the price breaks below support, they may establish short positions.

Breakout trading is a trading method that seeks to enter a breakout trade as soon as the price breaks out of its range. It is a way for market participants to take a position in the early stages of a trend.

As Jim Rogers, renowned American investor and financial commentator, said,

"I just wait until there is money lying in the corner, and all
I have to do is go over there and pick it up. I do nothing
in the meantime."

Similarly, in breakout trading, unless we see a breakout,
we should not take any long or short positions. Traders seek
high momentum, and the breakout is the indication to enter
a trade and profit from the subsequent market action.

When you've executed a breakout plan, know when to
reduce your losses and re-evaluate the scenario if the breakout
fails (which will be explained later in this chapter).

What are real and fake breakouts?

A real breakout happens when the price goes through an
indicated level of support or resistance with momentum to
continue in that direction. A failed breakout happens when the
price goes through an indicated level of support or resistance
but lacks the momentum to continue in that direction.
However, some traders try to build positions in the breakout
direction when a breakout happens. They may choose to close
those trades if the breakout fails.

Breakout tactics are among the first that novice traders either
learn or feel compelled to use. The goal of a breakout strategy
is to profit from a large price movement once an obvious chart
pattern breakout has formed, such as a breakout from a range
or a triangle.

Although trading breakouts may be profitable, traders should
be prepared to encounter several false breakouts, in which the
price first moves outside the pattern before reversing back
within. This is a message from the market. If false breakouts
are persistent then it is a source of frustration and you should
definitely wait for distinct breakout opportunities before you
take any entries.

Knowing when a false-break is likely to happen requires discipline and a little 'gut-feel,' and you never truly know 'for sure' until one has occurred. However, we can look for some traits that differentiate a fake breakout from a real breakout which I have mentioned below.

Features of a genuine breakout strong candles body

- strong volume with breakout
- significant support and resistance
- breakout in line with long-term trends
- low volume before the breakout is a good sign
- tight closing build-up (consolidation) right before the breakout

These are the basic principles of breakout trading, if you use them well while trading then it might increase your odds of being on the right side of the trade.

Case Study: Real Breakout

Image 1.1 depicts the daily chart of Tata Elxsi which shows all the characteristics of a real breakout. The stock had good volume with a strong breakout candle. It also had a strong prior uptrend which signifies momentum in the security.

Always remember, if the breakout is real then the stock will never appear below the breakout candle provided that the breakout candle is strong.

A genuine breakout should fulfill all the criteria for a strong candle body

- strong volume with breakout (yes)
- significant support and resistance (yes)

TATA ELXSI, 1D, NSE O2980.00 H3050.00 L2835.00 C2861.20 −88.60 (−3.00%)
Vol 1.461M

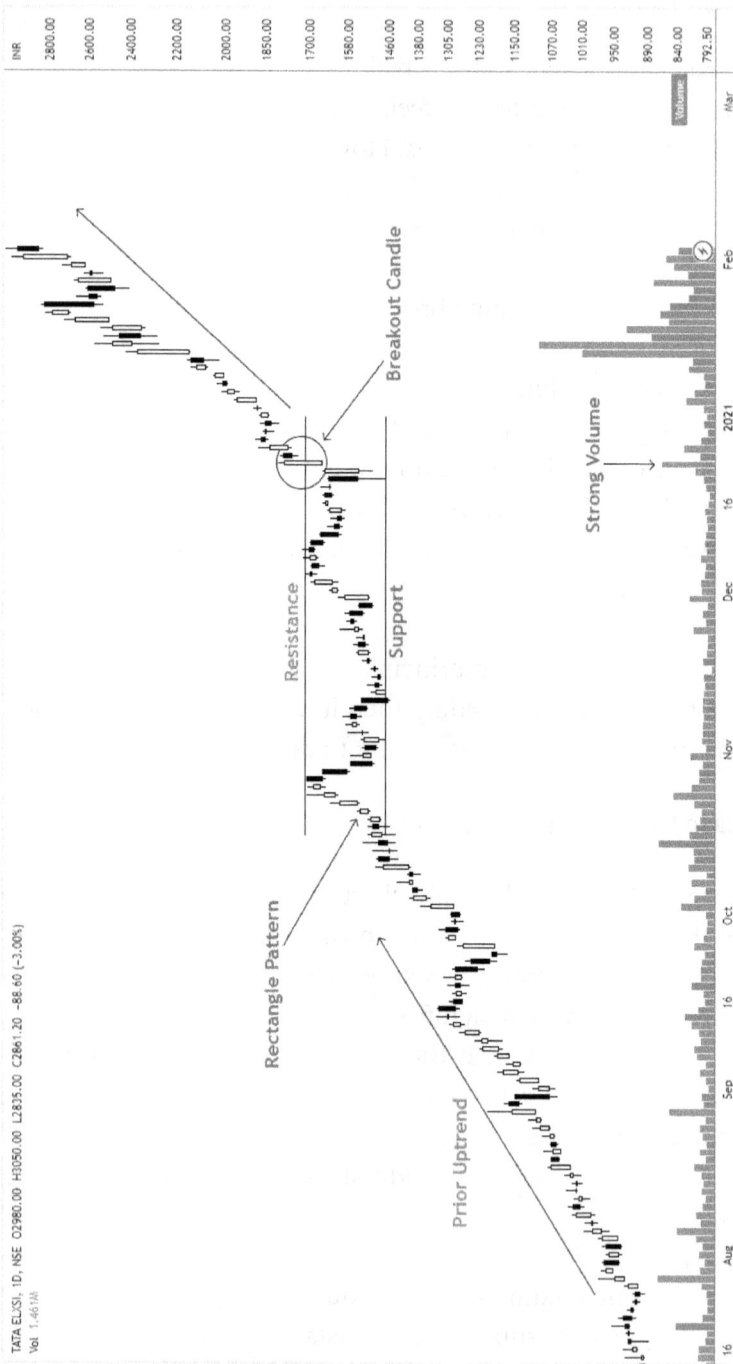

Image 1.1: Real breakout

- breakout in line with long-term trends (yes)
- low volume before the breakout is a good sign (yes)
- tight closing build-up right before the breakout (no)

If the stock has a tight closing build-up (TCB), that is, a tight consolidation or range, then it would be a more positive sign as it signifies that the weak hands got out. Sometimes, if the TCB is very tight then it becomes easier to place the stop-loss just below it.

Case Study: Fake Out Candle/Signal

Image 1.2 shows the daily chart of Hindustan Unilever Limited (HUL). This stock did not display most of the characteristics of a real breakout. It did not have a strong volume. However, the breakout candle was decent. But the subsequent candle turned bearish and the breakout turned fake. The stock did have a strong prior uptrend which signifies momentum in the security.

The stock with these characteristics should be avoided as it is bound to hit stop-loss. If you didn't put a stop-loss then you will have to suffer a lot as you can see that the price drifted down from Rs 1,780 all the way down to Rs 1,500.

Pro Tip: Never trade without entering the stop-loss in the trading system. Trade with price-based or technical analysis-based stop-loss to prevent losses.

You can also notice the big candlestick pattern that formed around the breakout zone suggesting a bearish sign and with strong volume bars (signalling pessimism on the stock price).

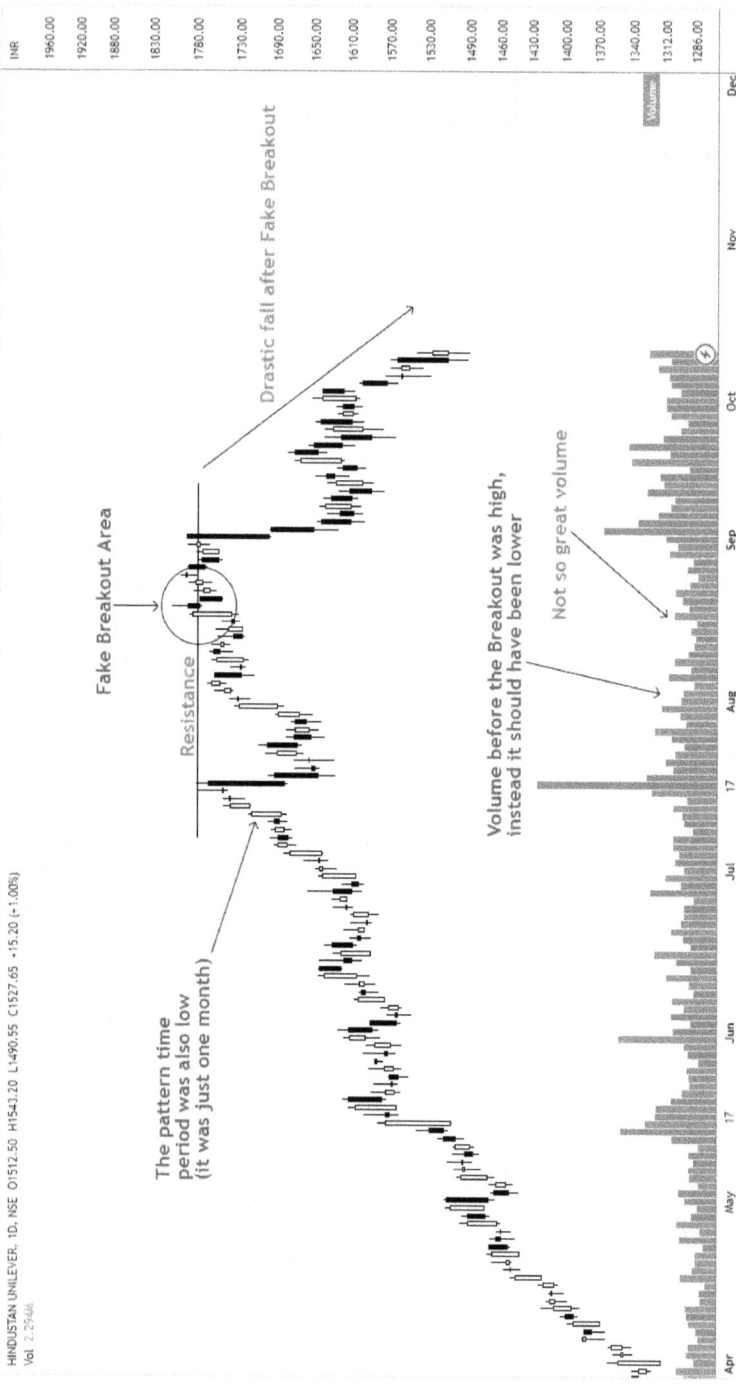

Image 1.2: Fake out candle/signal

Why is this important?

People are not habituated to putting a stop-loss. They end up losing a big chunk of their entire trading capital and blow up the trading account.

Case Study: Fake Breakout

The daily chart of City Union Bank in image 1.3 shows most of the characteristics of a real breakout. The stock did have a decent volume (above average). The breakout candle was also a wide range candle making it ideal for taking a trade. However, the stock gave a fake signal. It went beyond the stop-loss (placed at the breakout candle's low point (or the recent swing low) which was just lower than the breakout candle.

This is a case where many will get stuck if they have not put a stop-loss and suffer capital erosion.

In this type of situation, book the loss, as the stock reaches stop-loss and look for another opportunity.

The best breakout traders say—I myself have experienced this throughout my trading journey—if a trade is going to work, the market will tell you almost right away. If the breakout is real then the price should never go below the breakout candle. Always remember that the best or the strongest breakout will be one which has a tight base (TCB) just before the breakout occurs.

If there's a significant level to break, consider a breakout. The more a price hits support/resistance/trend line/chart patterns/moving average, the more legitimate the level. Channels, triangles, flags and many more patterns can help identify breaking points. Critical levels are difficult to breach. A breach of this magnitude will have far-reaching effects.

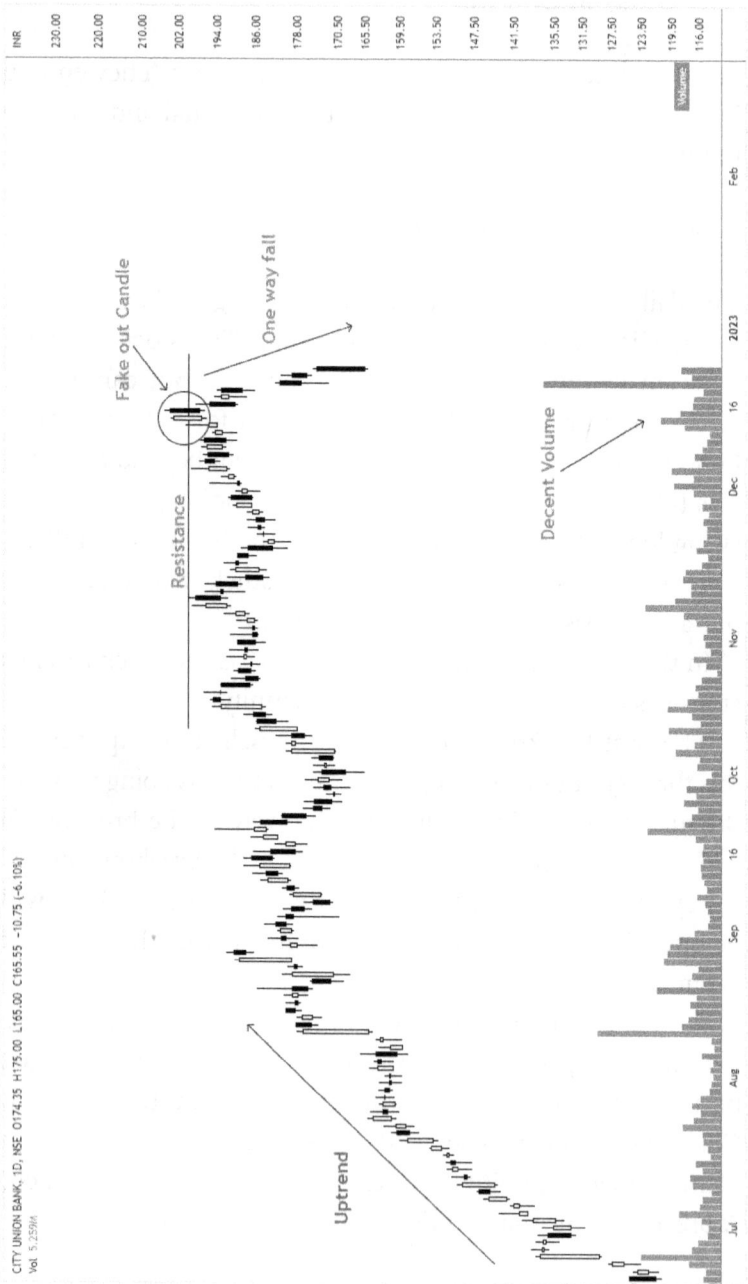

Chart_mojo published on TradingView.com, Dec 25, 2022 21:58 UTC+5:30

CITY UNION BANK, 1D, NSE O174.35 H175.00 L165.00 C165.55 -10.75 (-6.10%)

Vol 5.25M

INR

Uptrend

Resistance

Fake out Candle

One way fall

Decent Volume

Volume

Image 1.3: Fake breakout

2

Types of Breakout Trading

In this chapter we will be talking about different breakout techniques as given below:

Support and Resistance

Support and resistance are two of the most important pillars in technical analysis. If a trader doesn't doesn't understand how they form and what they mean, it can really slow down their technical progress. However, worry not, I will explain everything about this in a greater detail later in the text.

A support or resistance level is established when the price activity of a market reverses and changes direction, putting behind a market peak or trough (swing point: a turning point price in the past). Support and resistance levels may carve out trading ranges, as seen in image 2.1, and they can also be observed in trending markets when a market retraces and leaves swing points behind. Simply put, support and resistance can be spotted in ranging and trending market as well. Let's look at both the examples.

Support and resistance in a sideways market

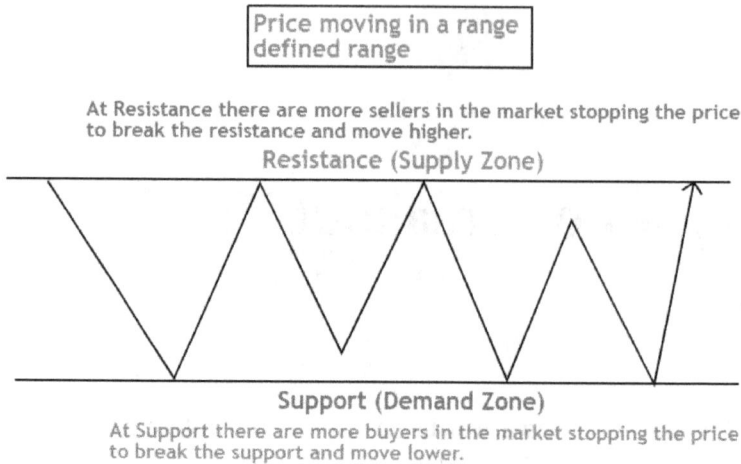

```
Price moving in a range
defined range
```

At Resistance there are more sellers in the market stopping the price
to break the resistance and move higher.

Resistance (Supply Zone)

Support (Demand Zone)

At Support there are more buyers in the market stopping the price
to break the support and move lower.

Image 2.1: Support and resistance in a sideways market

Case Study: The graphic shows the monthly chart for Tata
Steel in a ranging market.

*Example of support and resistance in a ranging
market*

Image 2.2 shows the monthly chart of Tata Steel indicating a
ranging market from 2007 to 2021. Traders who usually do
reversal trading buys at support and sell at resistance. However,
one should remember that while doing breakout trading, we
will only buy the security once it breaches the resistance and
take a short position once the security breaks the support zone.

The price action in this chart indicates that bulls and bears
are confused and fighting with each other. Whoever wins will
have the liberty to move the price in their direction as they
would have defeated the counter party. Therefore, you see
a breakout happening and watch the price moving in one
direction.

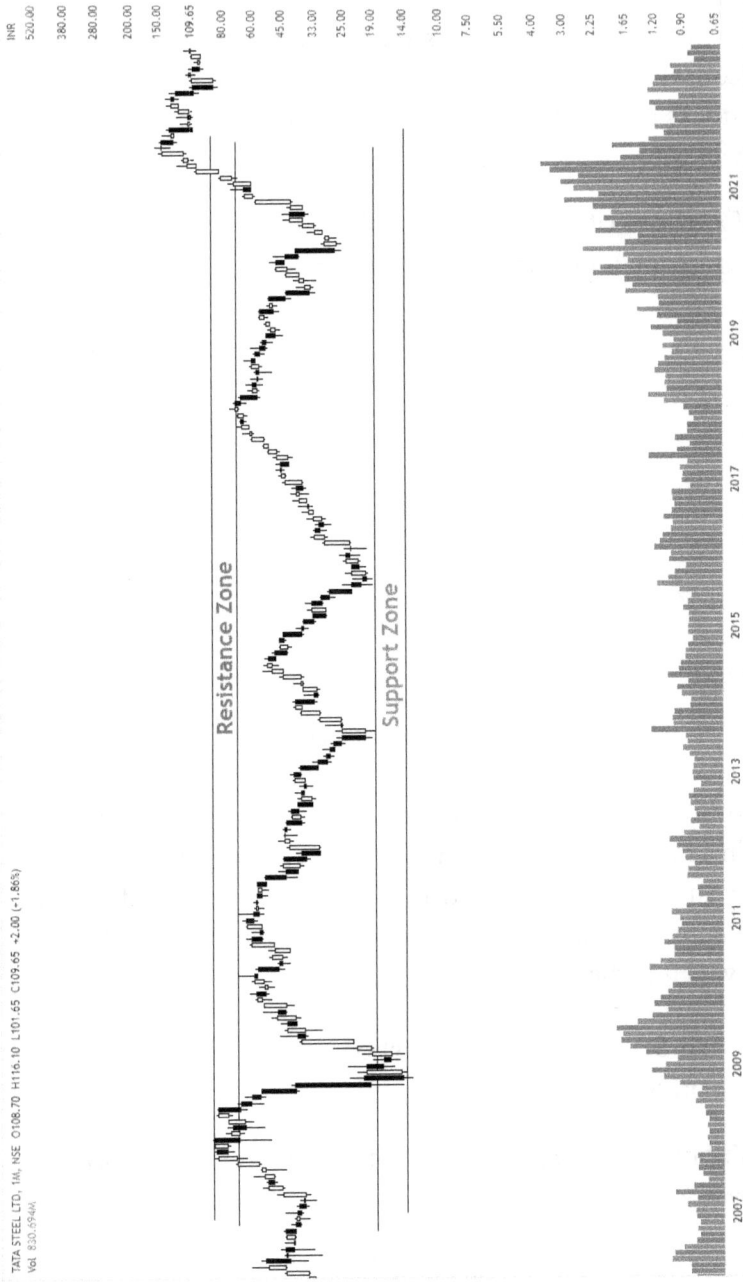

Image 2.2: Tata Steel (ranging market)

Scan charts and find stocks which are going through a consolidation phase and keep them on the radar. Once these stocks move out of their resistance zone or support zone, you will get to see a move either way.

Example of Support support and Resistance resistance in a trending market

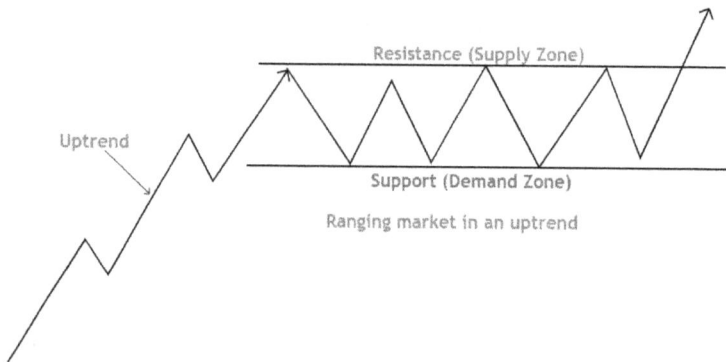

Image 2.3: Support and resistance in a trending market

By looking at image 2.3 you can see the support and resistance in a ranging market in an uptrend. Let us look at a few practical examples to understand these in a more detailed manner. Remember, the same is applicable for a downtrend as well (which is the opposite of an uptrend).

Case Study: The graphic shows the State Bank of India monthly chart.

Example of support and resistance in a trending market

Image 2.4 shows a ranging market in an uptrend. We can take a long position once we see the resistance zone breaking towards upside. As we can see from the chart, the long-term

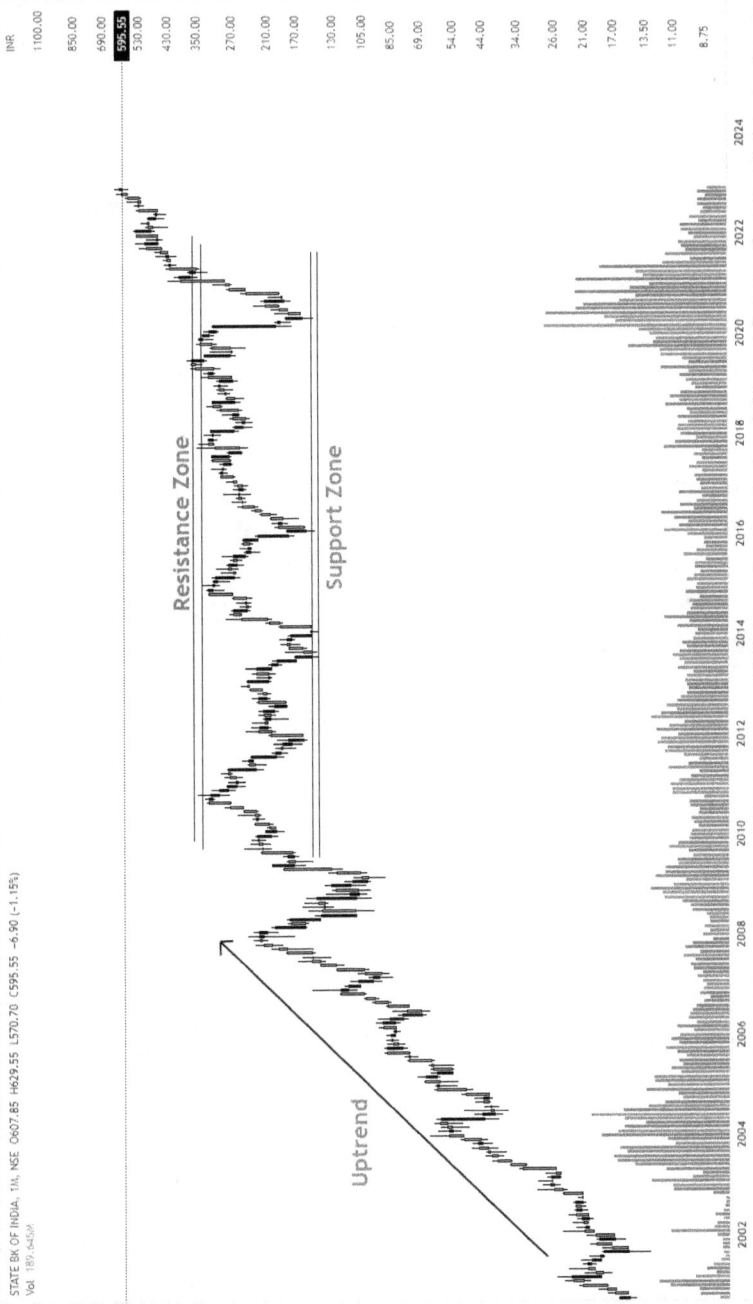

STATE BK OF INDIA, 1M, NSE O607.85 H629.55 L570.70 C595.55 -6.90 (-1.15%)
Vol 189.645M

Resistance Zone

Support Zone

Uptrend

INR

1100.00
850.00
690.00
595.55
530.00
430.00
350.00
270.00
210.00
170.00
130.00
105.00
85.00
69.00
54.00
44.00
34.00
26.00
21.00
17.00
13.50
11.00
8.75

2002 2004 2006 2008 2010 2012 2014 2016 2018 2020 2022 2024

Image 2.4: State Bank of India (ranging market in an uptrend).

view is looking good and the stock has been in an uptrend for a long period of time.

Support

Support is a level where a price movement in a downward direction stops for a while. In theory, support is when a lot of buyers come into the market and surpass the sellers. In short, when demand is higher than supply, prices go up. This stops a price drop or makes it turn around and go up.

A break below support suggests that individuals are prepared to sell at a new level. When support is broken, it is common for a new support level to be established at a lower price point. This is when we take the trade on short side and benefit from it.

A widely held belief is that the when the support is formed, a trader usually buys at support and intends to sell at resistance which is the part of reversal trading.

However, here we are talking about breakout trading so we will not do reversal trading and only take the short-biased trade when support is taken out on the downside.

Another opportunity is when we see a downtrend. So when the trends forms, we can take a short biased trade, keeping in mind that lower lows and lower highs are created (a downtrend).

Pro Tip: Never ever take a short position in an up-trending market. There are only two scenarios where we can take a short position:

1. A short position in a ranging market when the support is broken.
2. A short position in a down trending market when the support is breached.

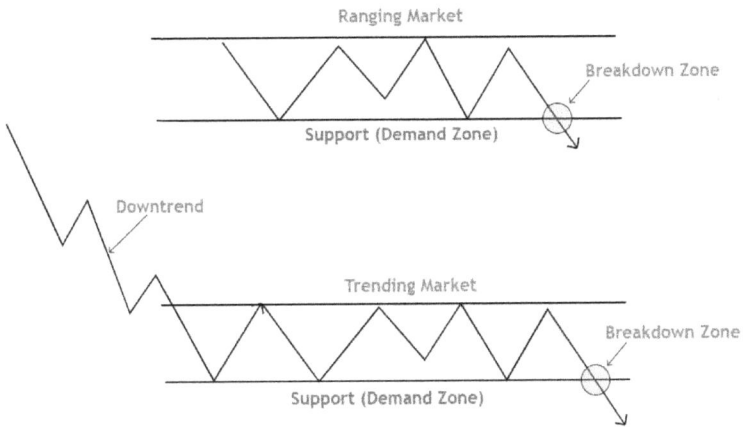

Image 2.5: (a) A short position in a ranging market when the support is broken (top image); (b) A short position in a down trending market when the support is breached (bottom image).

Case Study: The graphic shows the IRB Infrastructure chart.

Example of short position in a ranging market.

Image 2.6 is the weekly chart of IRB Iinfrastructure Developers Ltd. indicating a ranging market from September 2014 to September 2018. As we can see in the chart, it is an environment wherein the stock ranges between support and resistance and shows a breakdown from the support zone. It will be prudent to take a short position once the breakdown pattern is confirmed, and ride the downside move.

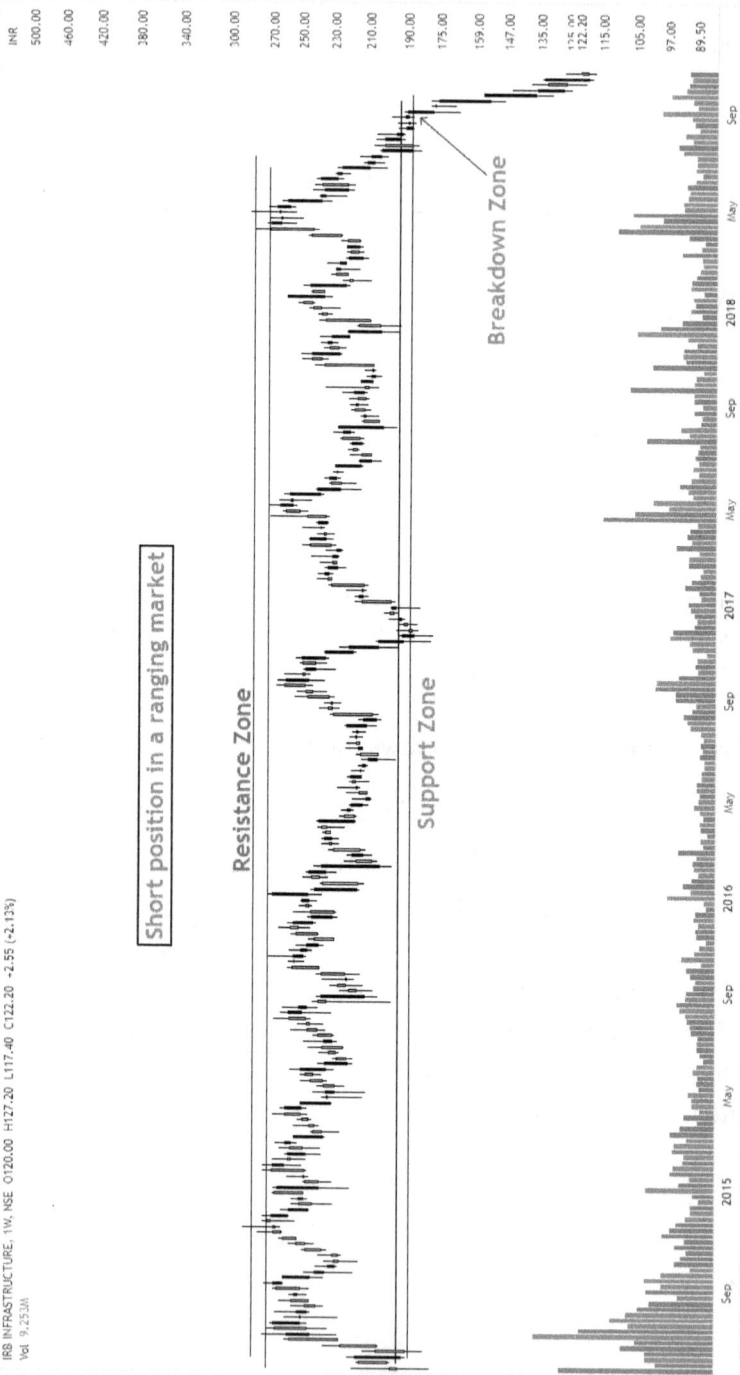

IRB INFRASTRUCTURE, 1W, NSE O120.00 H127.20 L117.40 C122.20 -2.55 (-2.13%)
Vol 9,253M

Short position in a ranging market

Resistance Zone

Support Zone

Breakdown Zone

Image 2.6: Weekly chart of IRB Infrastructure Developers Ltd. indicating a ranging market.

Case Study: The graphic shows the daily chart for BASF India.

Example of short position in a trending market.

Image 2.7 shows the daily chart of BASF India indicating a down trending market from November 2018 to October 2019.

As we can see in the chart that, the stock ranges between support and resistance in the downtrend and shows a breakdown from the support zone indicating bearishness towards downside. It will be prudent to take a short position once the breakdown was is conformed confirmed from with a rectangle pattern and ride the downside move as the price started starts drifting lower.

Resistance

Resistance is totally opposite to support. At the resistance level, selling pressure is believed to be strong enough to prevent the price from rising further. The rationale for opposition is that more sellers than purchasers have joined the market.

So we will only trade on resistance breakout and take a long position when we take a trade.

When the resistance barrier is broken, a new resistance level is formed at a higher level. This is when we take the trade on the long side and benefit from it.

A common belief is that the when the resistance is formed on the price chart, the trader usually sells at resistance and intends to buy at support (which is the part of reversal trading).

Here, we are talking about breakout trading so we will not do reversal trading and only take the long-biased trade when resistance is taken out on the upside.

When an uptrend forms, we can take a long-biased trade (based on our understanding of the prevalent market

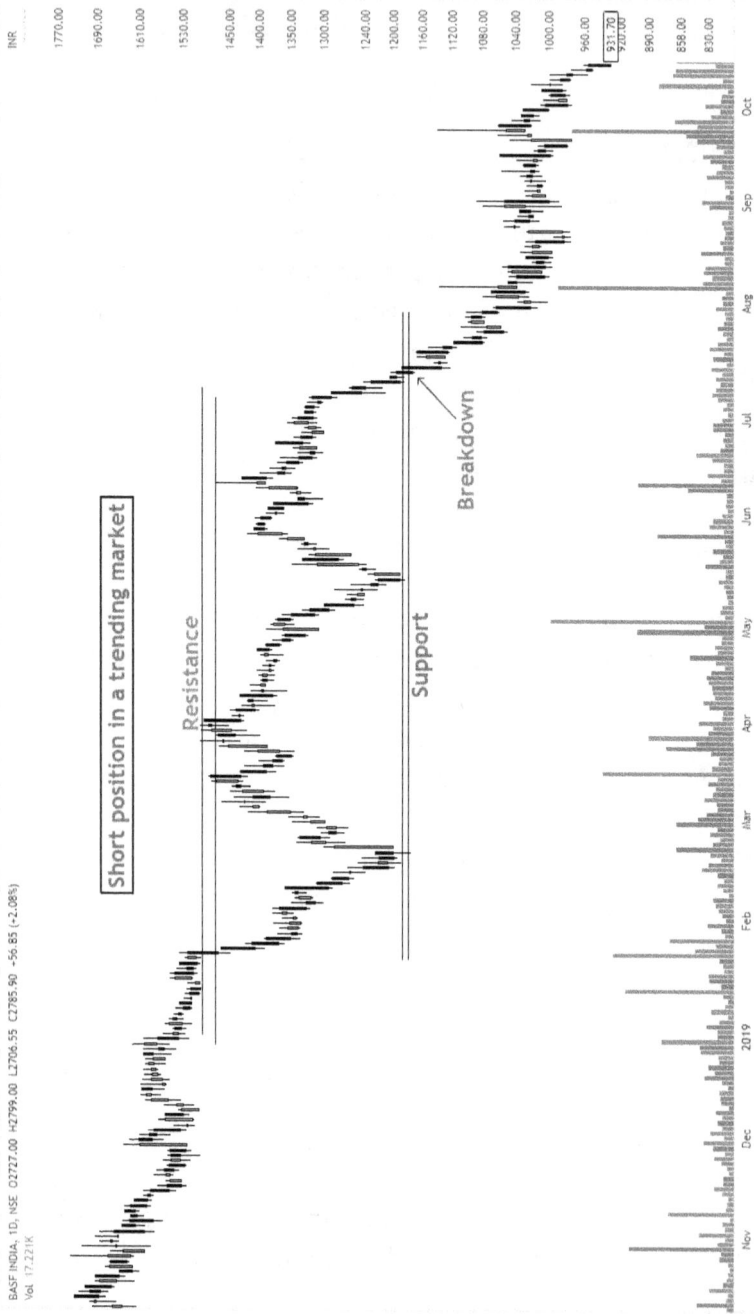

Image 2.7: Daily chart of BASF India indicating a down trending market.

conditions), keeping in mind that higher highs and higher lows are created on the chart (an uptrend).

> **Pro Tip**: Never ever take a long position in a down-trending market. There are only two scenarios where we can take a long position:
>
> 1. A long position in a ranging market when the resistance is broken.
> 2. A long position in an up-trending market when the resistance is breached.

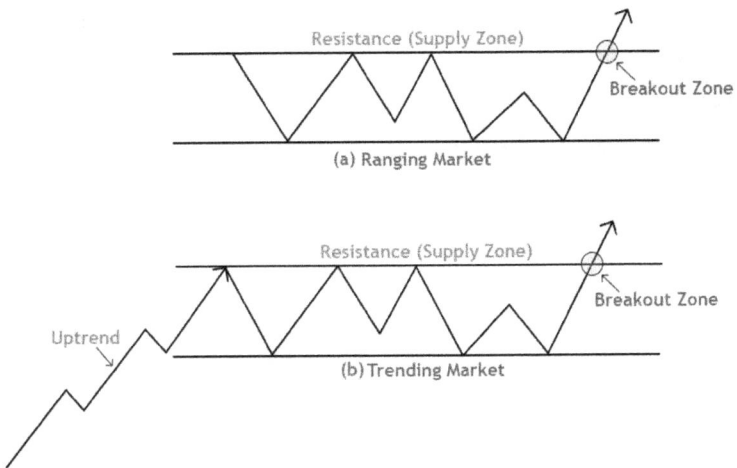

Image 2.8: (a) A long position in a ranging market when the resistance is broken; (b) A long position in an up-trending market when the resistance is breached.

Image 2.8 shows two examples wherein the first example one is of a ranging market which breaks through resistance on upper band of the sideways trend.

The second example shows a ranging market in an uptrend which breaches through the resistance on the higher band.

Case Study: The graphic shows the JSW Steel monthly chart.

Example of long position in ranging market

Image 2.9 shows the monthly chart of JSW Steel Ltd. indicating a ranging market from 2007 to 2018. Traders who usually do reversal trading buy at support and sell at resistance. However, one should remember that while doing breakout trading we will only buy the security once it breaches the resistance and take a short position once the security breaks the support zone.

In this chart, the stock showed a breakout towards the upside with a small bullish candle. In this case, the breakout candle was small so here we can put a stop-loss at the previous candle low which is marked with a line just below the candle low point and the encircled area.

JSW STEEL LTD, 1M, NSE O399.30 H427.55 L374.20 C381.65 -14.70 (-3.71%)
Vol 146.294M

Long position in ranging market

Breakout

Stop Loss

Resistance

Support Zone

440.00
340.00
260.00
200.00
147.80
125.65
110.00
85.00
65.00
49.00
37.00
29.00
21.00
16.00
12.00
9.50
7.50
5.75
4.50

2006 2008 2010 2012 2014 2016 2018 2020

TradingView

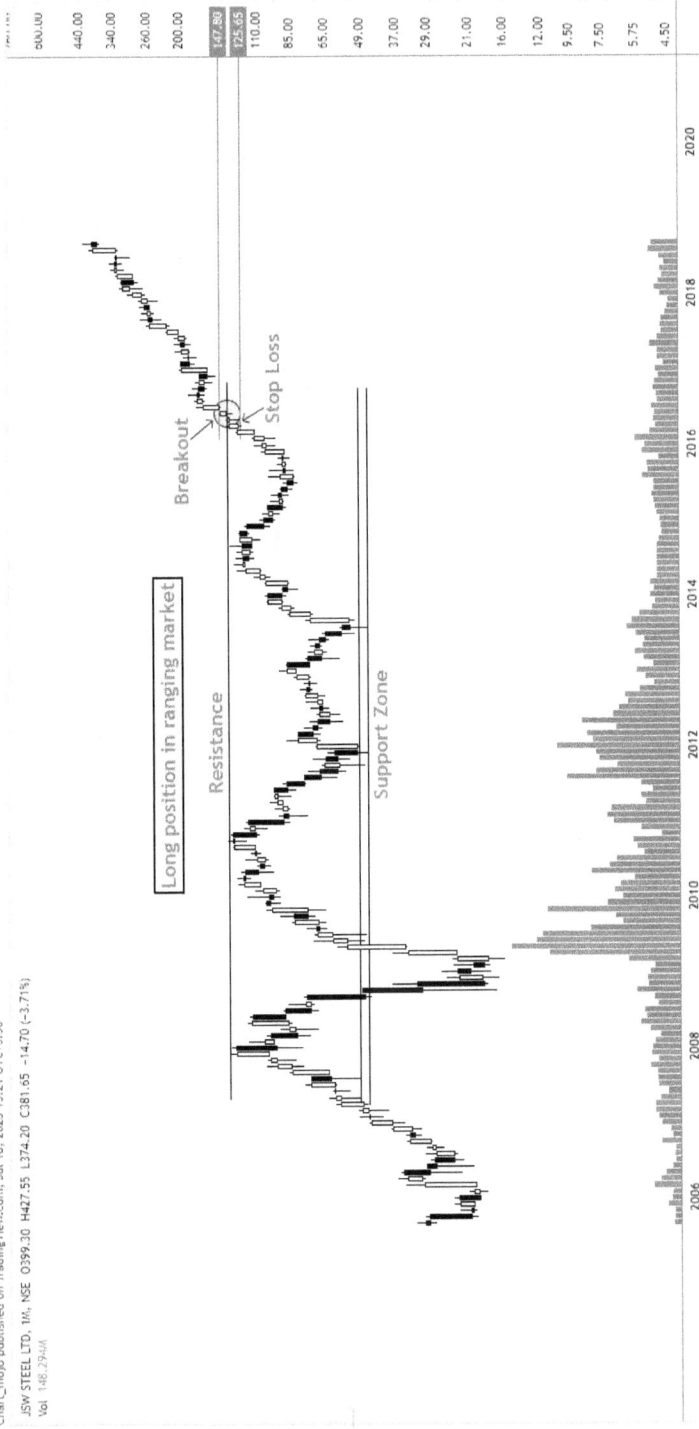

Image 2.9: JSW Steel Ltd. (ranging market from 2007 to 2018)

Case Study: The graphic shows the AU Small Finance chart.

Example of a long position in a ranging market

Image 2.10 is the weekly chart of Action and Urgency (AU) Small Finance Bank. The stock went into a sideways market. Then it showed a decent breakout towards upside, indicating a bullish momentum. This example shows us that we should always take a position towards long side, when the security is in a sideways phase (ranging market) and the breakout happens above the resistance line.

Once the breakout happened with a strong breakout candle, the price marched towards the higher side and showed a good move.

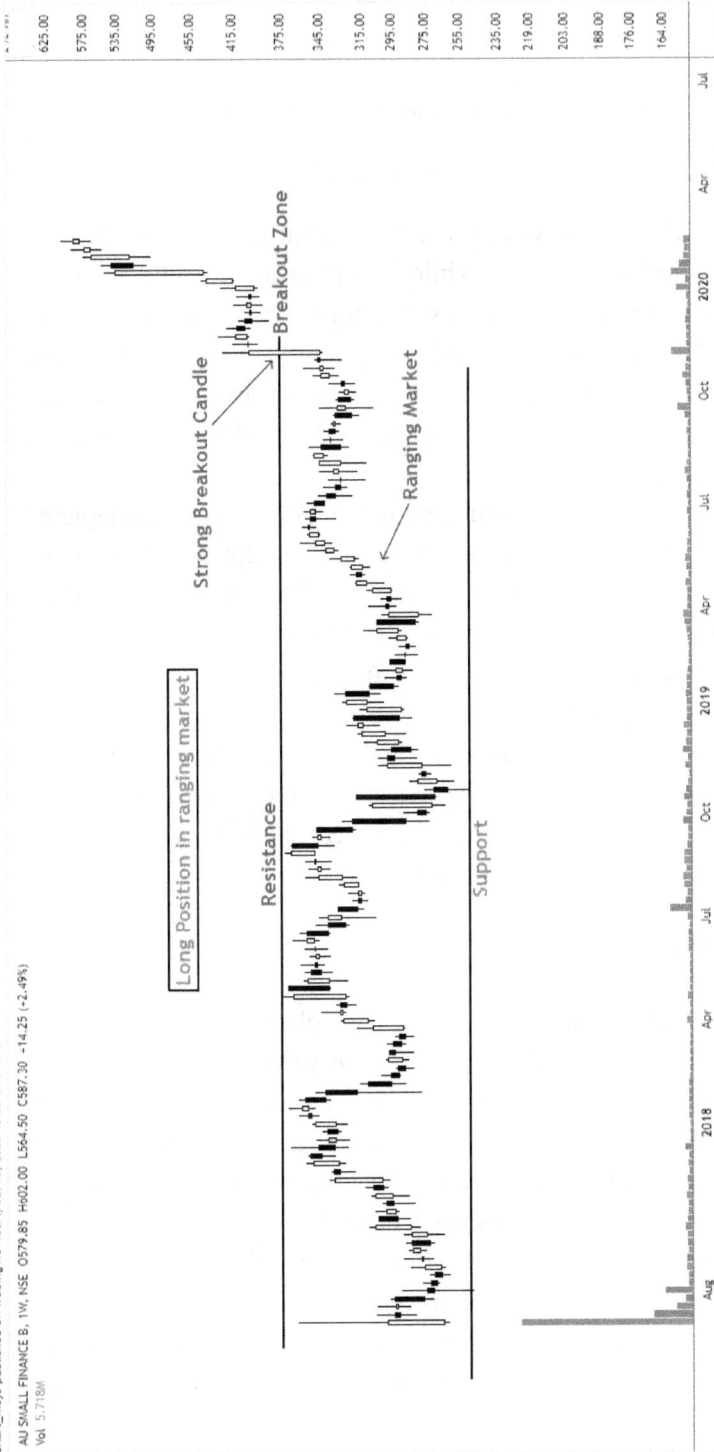

Image 2.10: Weekly chart of Action and Urgency (AU) Small Finance Bank.

Case Study: The graphic shows the Astral Ltd chart.

Example of long position in trending market

Image 2.11 is the weekly chart of Astral Ltd. The stock went into a sideways phase while it was in an uptrend. Then it showed a wide range breakout (depicted by the bigger body candle) towards upside, indicating a bullish momentum. The breakout happened with a strong momentum and then the price never fell below the bigger body candle as it was a real breakout.

The breakout happened with a strong volume (as depicted by the big volume bar in the chart). As the pattern formed, the volume went through a dry up phase indicating that no more sellers were interested in selling this security.

While establishing support and resistance levels is not a precise science, it is critical to grasp what they signify, how they operate, and, most importantly, how to apply them. Finding and graphing support and resistance level patterns on your own may be tricky, but when applied correctly, they can help you set up more winning trades.

Chart Patterns

Chart patterns are lines and shapes placed onto price charts to aid in the prediction of future price movements such as breakouts and reversals. They comprise a fundamental technical analysis tool that allows traders to leverage previous price movements to forecast likely future market moves.

Chart patterns often show when a trend is going up or going down. or changing from going up to going down. A chart pattern is a recognizable arrangement of price changes that can be found by looking at a series of trend lines or curves. Here, we are going to take a bird's eye view of continuation

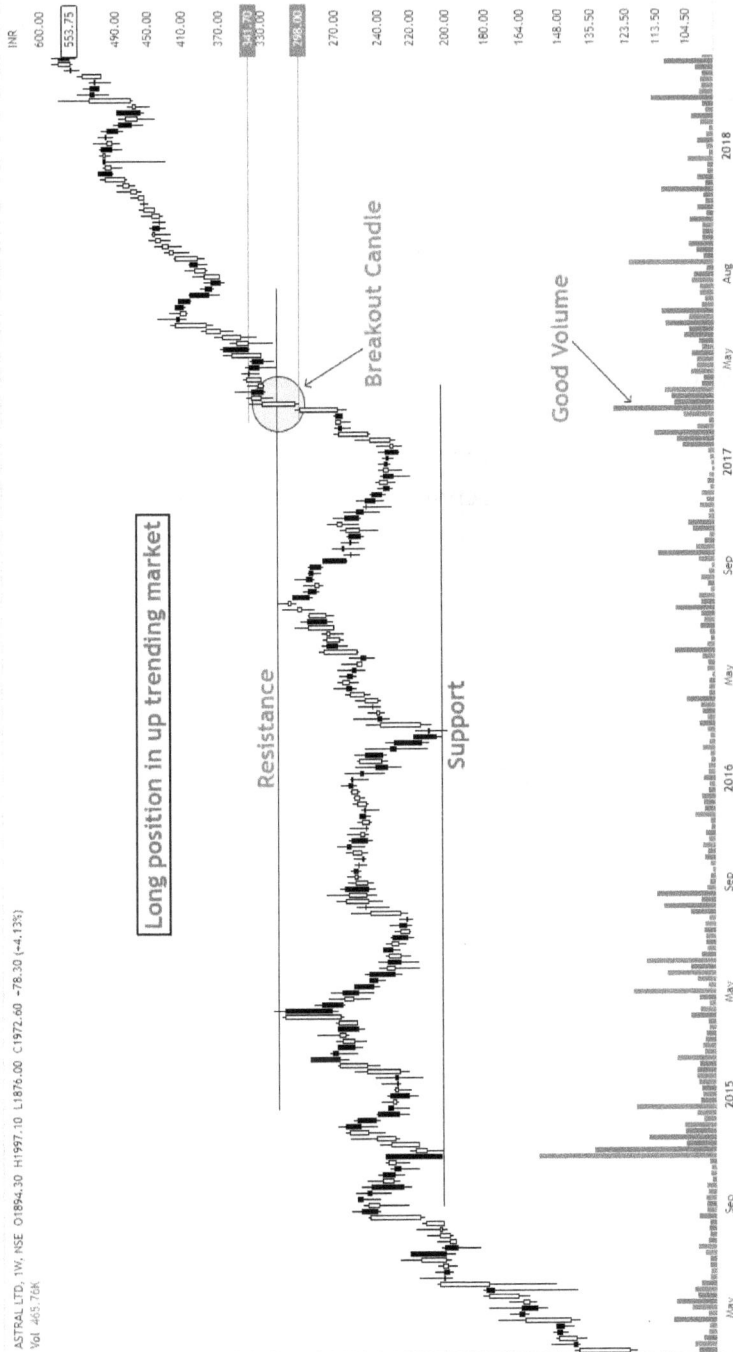

Image 2.11: Weekly chart of Astral Ltd.

and reversal pattern. We will learn all this in greater detail in dedicated chapters of chart patterns.

There are two types of chart patterns

- Continuation chart pattern
- Reversal chart pattern

Continuation Chart Pattern

Continuation patterns show that a stock or index's current price trend is likely to go on. It happens in the middle of a trend and shows that the trend will continue after the pattern ends. Triangles, flags, pennants, and rectangles are all common continuation patterns.

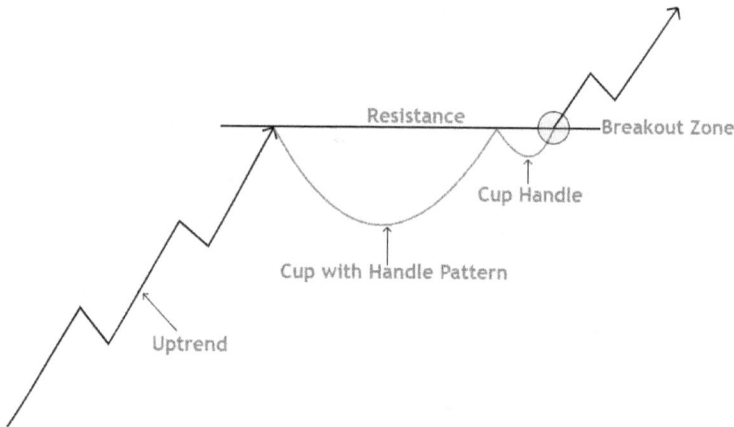

Image 2.12: Continuation chart pattern

The image shows a graphical representation of a continuation pattern (cup and handle pattern).

Case Study: Practical cup and handle pattern (continuation chart pattern)

Image 2.13 shows the daily chart of Tata Elxsi with a continuation pattern. The stock was in a strong uptrend and we can see that the cup with handle pattern formed midway. It showed a strong breakout trend with a robust volume spurt indicating bullishness.

Reversal Chart Pattern

Reversal patterns could mean that either the bulls or the bears have lost control and that a change in trend is coming soon. This is an indication that the current trend will end and the price will move in a different direction (bull or bear).

A trading reversal occurs when the trend direction of stocks or traded assets turns or reverses. When traders see a reversal pattern, they take it as a signal to consider exiting their transaction as the trading environment may have changed. A reversal pattern also initiates fresh transactions, resulting in the start of a new trend.

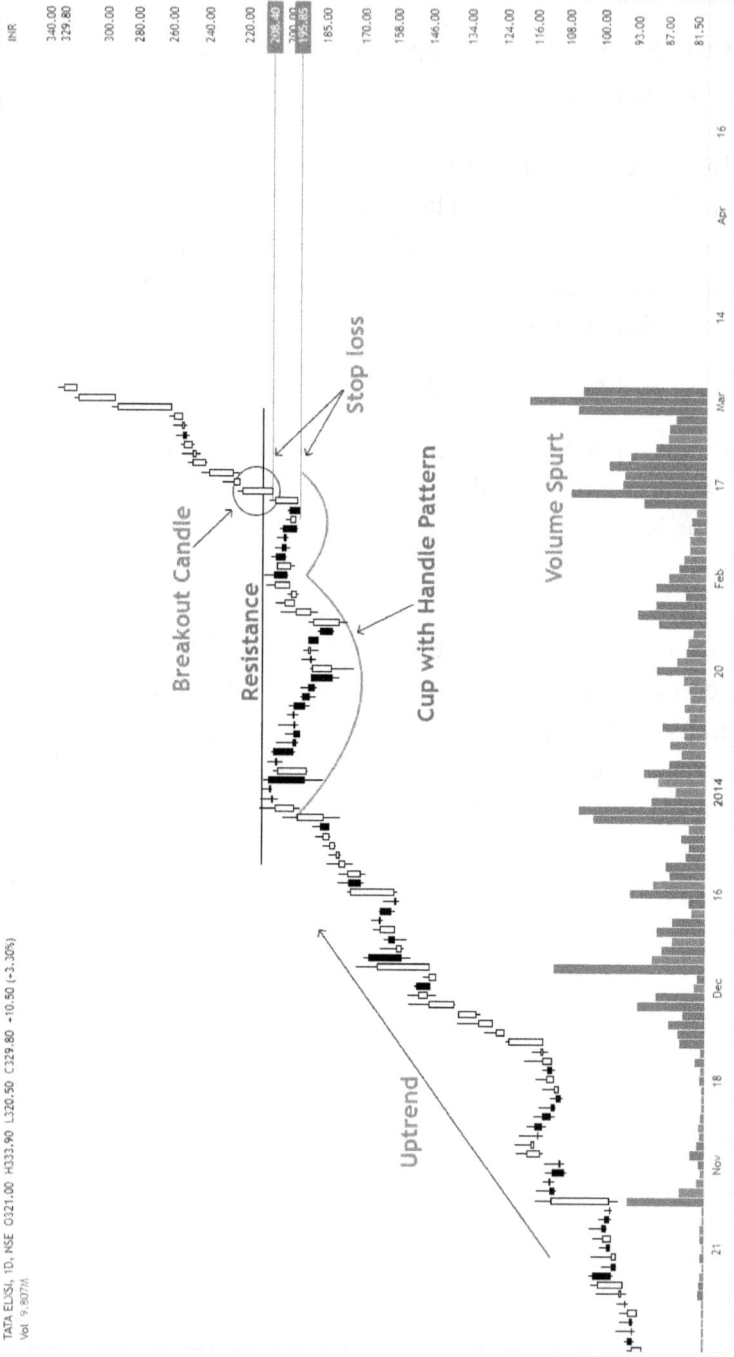

Chartmojos published on TradingView.com, Dec 27, 2022 15:47 UTC+5:30

TATA ELXSI, 1D, NSE O321.00 H333.90 L320.50 C329.80 -10.50 (-3.30%)
Vol 9.807M

Breakout Candle

Stop loss

Resistance

Cup with Handle Pattern

Volume Spurt

Uptrend

Image 2.13: Tata Elxsi (continuation pattern)

Example of a reversal pattern (double bottom)

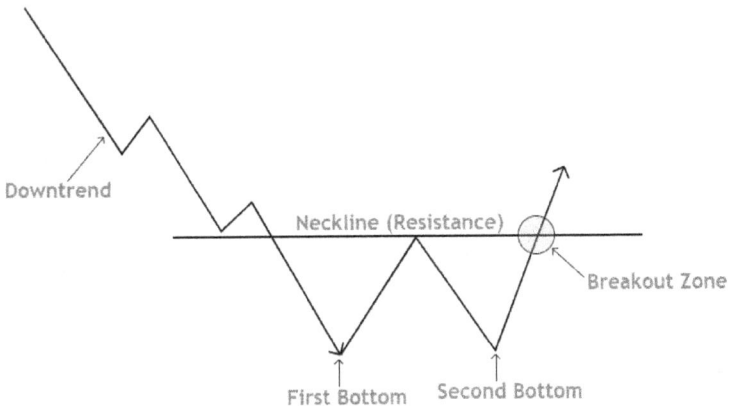

Image 2.14: Reversal pattern (double bottom)

Case Study: Practical double bottom (reversal chart pattern).

In image 2.15, the daily chart of Lakshmi Machine shows a trend reversal pattern. The stock was in a downtrend followed by an uptrend. We can see that the trend reversal pattern formed (double bottom) and showed a strong breakout with increasing volume indicating bullishness in the stock.

Trend line breakout

Trend lines, as the name suggests, are lines that can be drawn along a trend to show either support or resistance, depending on the direction of the trend. Think of them as the diagonal versions of support and resistance in the horizontal plane.

Trend lines are used by traders to link a sequence of prices on a chart. The resultant line is then utilised to provide the trader with a solid indication of the direction in which the value of a stock may change.

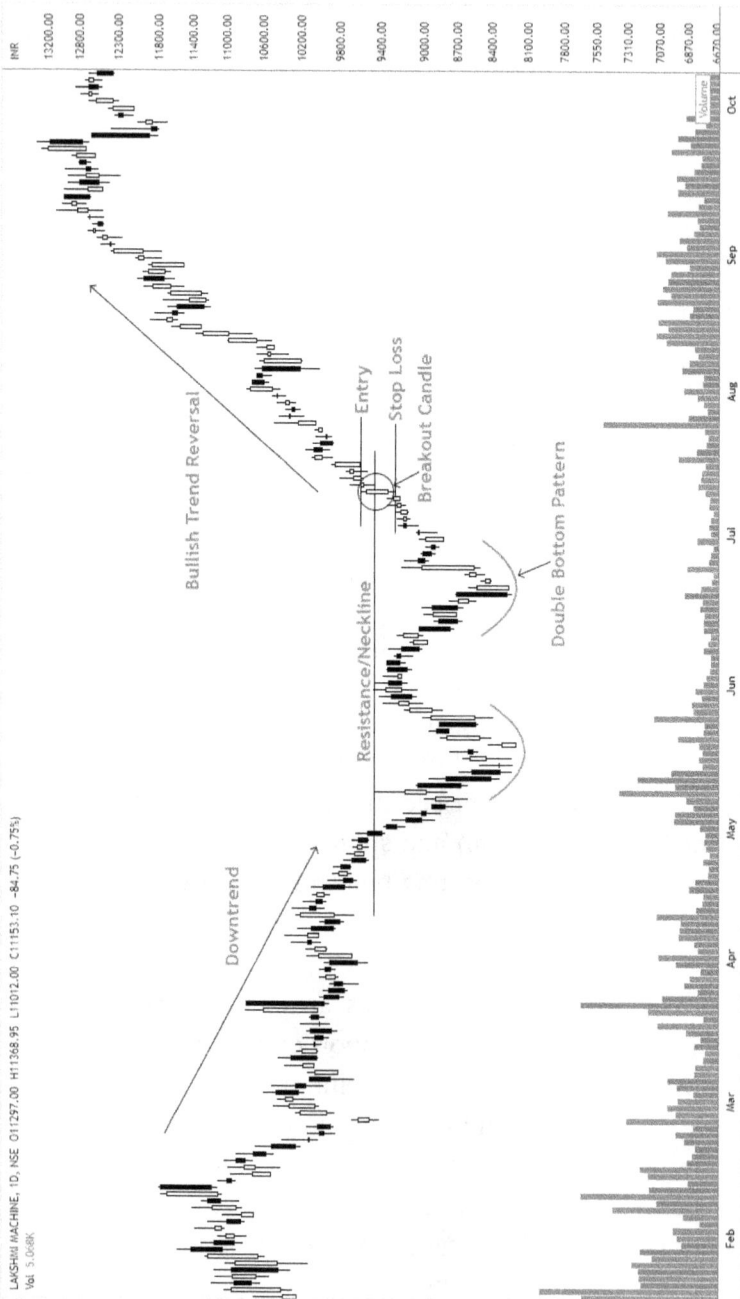

Chart_mojo published on TradingView.com, Jan 21, 2023 13:42 UTC+5:30
LAKSHMI MACHINE, 1D, NSE O11297.00 H11368.95 L11012.00 C11153.10 −84.75 (−0.75%)
Vol 5.048K

Downtrend

Resistance/Neckline

Bullish Trend Reversal

Entry

Stop Loss

Breakout Candle

Double Bottom Pattern

Volume

Image 2.15: Daily chart of Lakshmi Machine with a trend reversal pattern.

A broken trend line is a technical indicator of an imminent trend reversal. If low volume follows the break of a trend line rather than high volume, the signal is weaker and less powerful. So always remember that the trend line breakout should happen with strong volume which will signify the change in the trend.

There are three very important things you need to know about drawing trend lines that work.

1. Start with higher time periods for the most reliable trend lines.
2. Most trend lines will overlap a candle's high or low, but it's vital to acquire as many touches as possible without breaking through a candle.
3. Don't try to make a trend line fit, because if it doesn't fit the chart, it is not valid and it shouldn't be on your chart.

How to draw a trend line on your device

To start a trend line, you need to select the major swing low and drag the selected trend line tool towards upside for rising trend line and drag towards downside for falling trend lines. You need at least two points in the selected security. Once you have found the second high or low, you can draw your trend line.

Let's examine a trend line that was formed during an upswing.

Case Study: Practical trend line during an uptrend.

The chart in image 2.16 is the weekly chart of Vodafone Idea Ltd. which has formed a rising trend line. The chart shows that the stock was in a strong uptrend and formed higher highs and higher lows indicating an uptrend, once the stock breached the rising trend line. It indicated that the trend changed and one should have taken a position at the breakdown zone.

Remember, in a trend line breakout technique always take a trading position at the critical zone (breakout/breakdown). In this case, take a short position as there was a breakdown indicating a downside bias.

Let's now examine a trend line that was drawn during a downtrend.

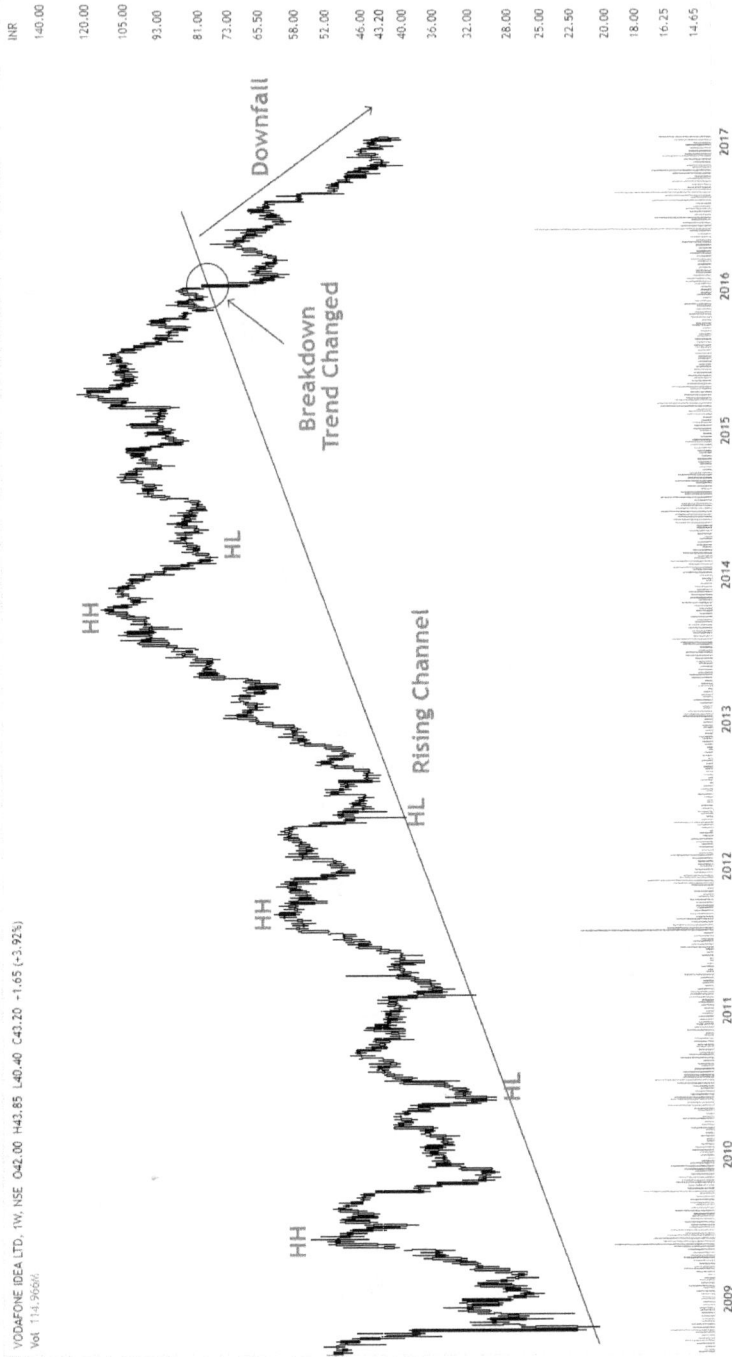

Image 2.16: Weekly chart of Vodafone Idea Ltd.

Case Study: Practical trend line during a downtrend.

Image 2.17 is the daily chart of HCL Technologies Ltd. which shows a falling trend line. It shows that the stock was in a strong downtrend and formed lower lows and lower highs indicating a downtrend, once the stock breached the falling trend line, it indicated the change in trend from downward to upward and one should take a bullish position at the breakout zone.

Always remember, in the trend line breakout technique, take a trading position at the critical zone (breakout/breakdown). In this case, take a long position as the there was a breakout indicating upside bias.

You can also notice that once the breakout occurred, the price trended higher and showed a huge upside on the stock.

Moving Average Breakout

Moving average (MA) is a technical analysis indicator used to assist smoothing out price data by calculating a continually updated average price. A rising moving average suggests an uptrend, while a falling moving average indicates a decline.

There are two types of moving averages

- Simple moving average
- Exponential moving average (EMA)

We will use the exponential moving averages as they give more weightage to the recent price data.

The length of the trend you capture will be determined by changing lengths of the prevailing market trend. A lengthier moving average allows you to ride longer-term trends. But the trade-off is that a lot of unrealized profit is lost. A shorter

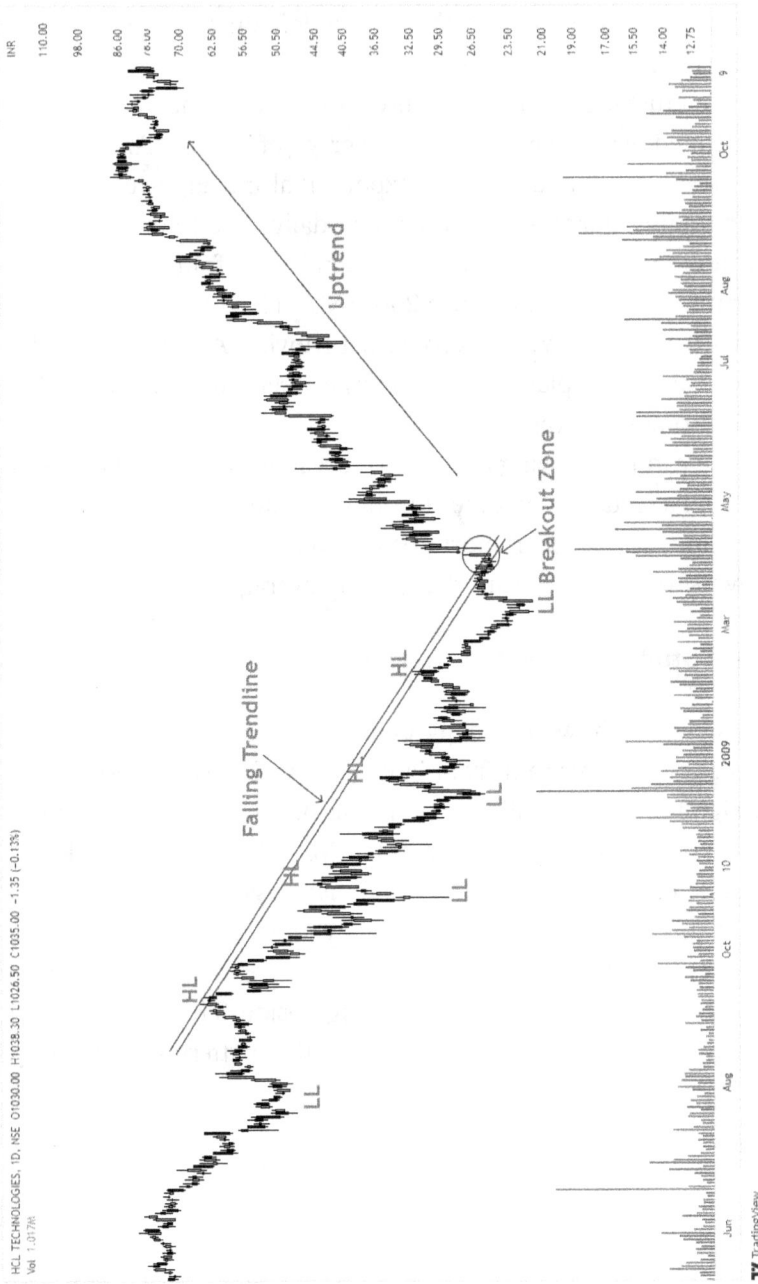

HCL TECHNOLOGIES, 1D, NSE O1030.00 H1038.30 L1026.50 C1035.00 −1.35 (−0.13%)
Vol 1.017M

INR

110.00
98.00
86.00
76.00
70.00
62.50
56.50
50.50
44.50
40.50
36.50
32.50
29.50
26.50
23.50
21.00
19.00
17.00
15.50
14.00
12.75

Uptrend

Falling Trendline

LL Breakout Zone

HL

LL

2009

Jun Aug Oct 10 Oct 2009 Mar May Jul Aug Oct 9

TradingView

Image 2.17: Daily chart of HCL Technologies Ltd. which shows a falling trend line.

moving average reduces the profits left on the table while increasing the whipsaw(noise).

We must first trade in the direction of the trend. The trend is defined using a single moving average of 200-EMA. We will utilise a 21, 50 and 200-day exponential moving average for our trading purposes while using a daily time frame. Always remember that while using a weekly time frame for trend identification we cannot use 200-EMA. Here, we will have to use 40-WEMA (Week Exponential Moving Average) instead because the big players in the market prefer to buy the stock above one year average.

We can use moving average for breakout trading when the price of a security penetrates through the moving average. Then we can take a long or short position on the basis of upside or downside breakout from the moving average.

Case Study: A 200-EMA Breakout

Image 2.18 shows the daily chart of Jindal Stainless which has shown a breakout from 200-EMA with a strong volume. It signifies strong bullishness as the breakout occurred with a classical chart pattern and 200-EMA. So, in a way, it is a double conformation for the potential upside.

In this chart, the stock was already in a strong uptrend and this breakout occurred in the prevailing direction of trend which qualifies that it will be a strong upside. The pattern also resembled the bullish basing continuation pattern which gave further conformation for the upside.

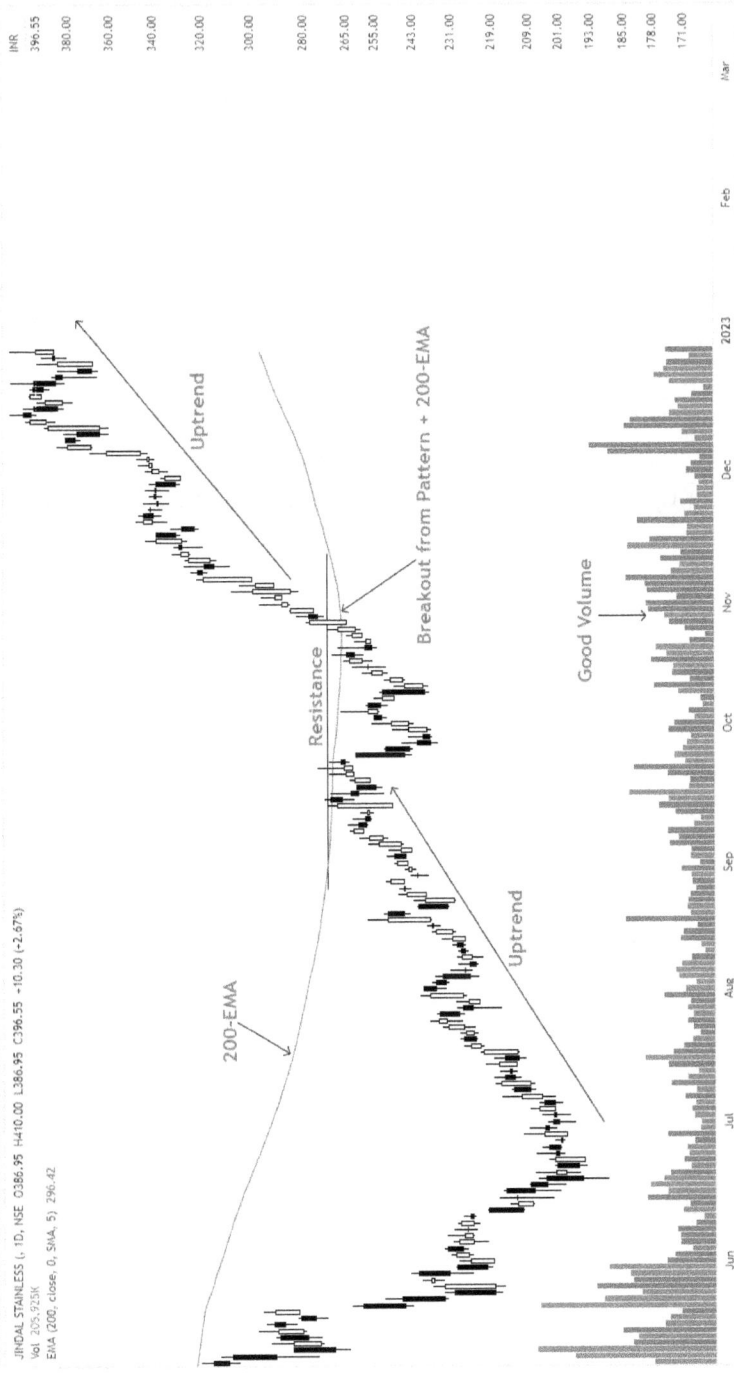

Chartmojos published on TradingView.com, Dec 28, 2022 15:31 UTC+5:30
JINDAL STAINLESS (, 1D, NSE O386.95 H410.00 L386.95 C396.55 -10.30 (-2.67%)
Vol 205,925K
EMA (200, close, 0, SMA, 5) 296.42

Image 2.18: Daily chart for Jindal Stainless Ltd. (a 200-EMA breakout).

Case Study: A 50-EMA Breakout

Image 2.19 is the daily chart of Jindal Stainless Ltd. which shows a breakout from 50-EMA with a strong volume. The chart signifies strong bullishness as the breakout occurred with a classical continuation chart pattern (falling wedge) and 50-EMA. So, in a way, it is a double confirmation for the pending upside.

In this chart, the stock was already in a strong uptrend, trading well above 50-EMA. This breakout occurred in the prevailing direction of trend which qualifies that it will be a strong upside. The pattern also resembled the falling wedge pattern (continuation pattern) which further confirmed that the price will continue to be bullish.

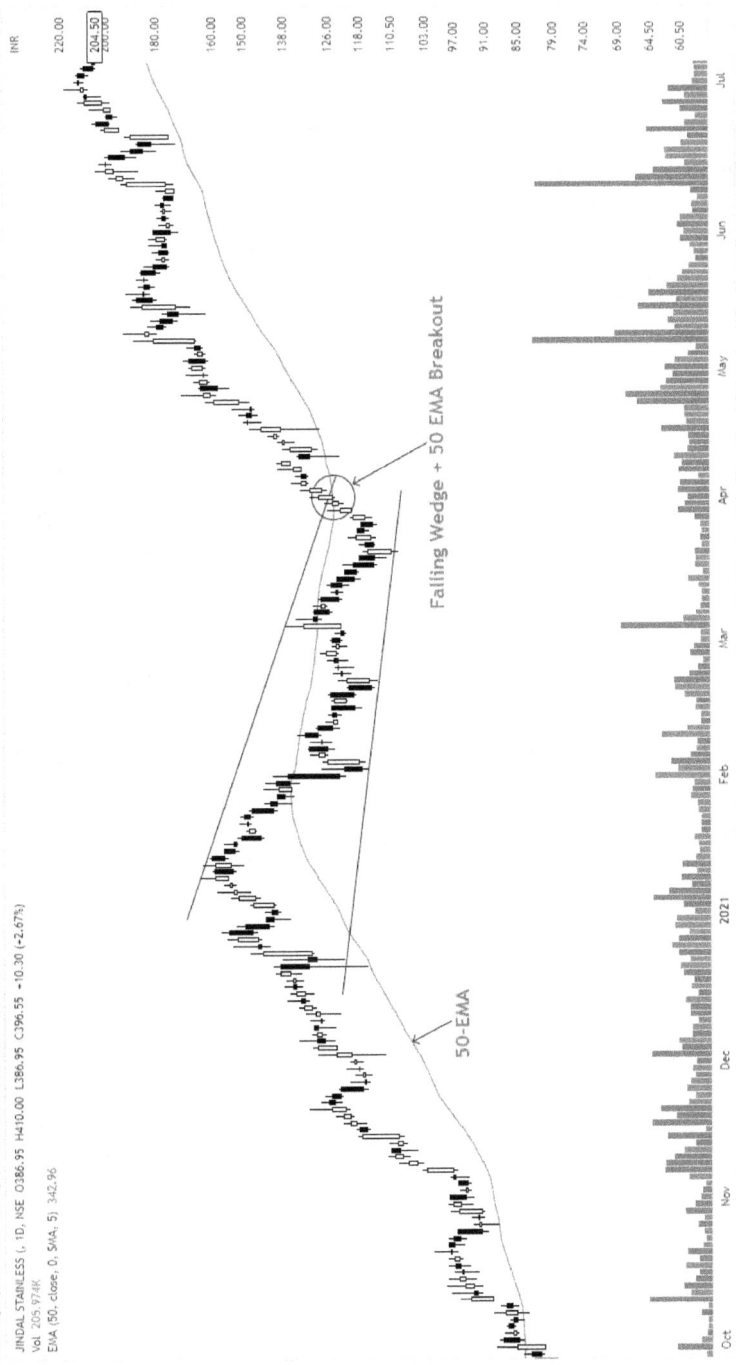

Image 2.19: Daily chart of Jindal Stainless Ltd. (a 50-EMA breakout).

Case Study: A 50-EMA breakdown

The daily chart of Balaji Amines Ltd. in image 2.20 shows a breakdown from 50-EMA with strong volume. The chart signifies strong bearishness as the breakout occurred with a classical reversal chart pattern (symmetrical triangle) and 50-EMA, so in a way it is a double confirmation for the pending downside.

Case Study: A 21-EMA Breakout

This is the daily chart of Just Dial showing a breakout from 21-EMA with strong volume. The chart signifies strong bullishness as the breakout occurred with a classical continuation chart pattern (symmetrical triangle) and 21-EMA, so in a way it is a double confirmation for the potential upside.

In this chart, the stock was already in a strong uptrend, trading well above 21-EMA most of the time and this breakout occurred in the prevailing direction of trends. This signifies that it will be a strong upside. The pattern also resembles a symmetrical triangle (continuation pattern) which provides further confirmation for the upside.

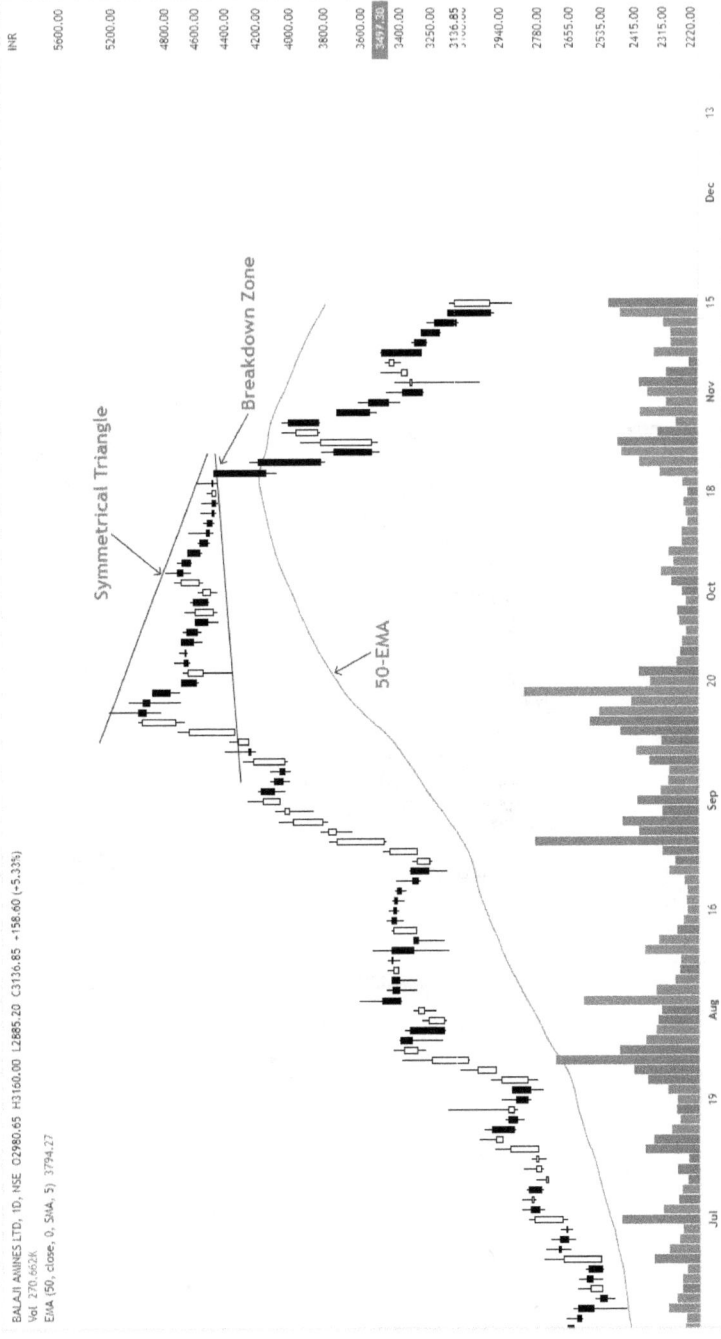

Chartmojos published on TradingView.com, Dec 28, 2022 16:12 UTC+5:30

BALAJI AMINES LTD, 1D, NSE O2980.85 H3160.00 L2885.20 C3136.85 -158.60 (-5.33%)
Vol 270.662K
EMA (50, close, 0, SMA, 5) 3794.27

Symmetrical Triangle

Breakdown Zone

50-EMA

Image 2.20: Daily chart of Balaji Amines Ltd. (a 50-EMA breakdown).

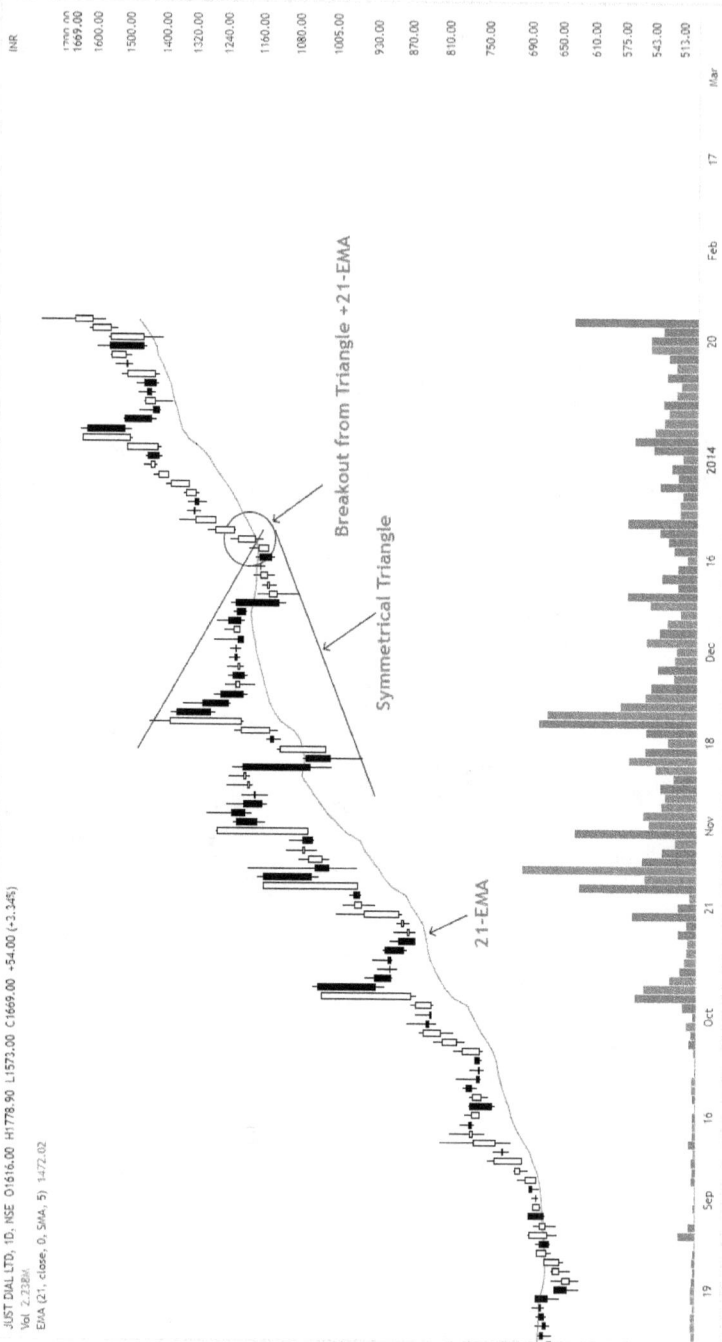

Image 2.21: Daily chart of Just Dial showing a breakout from 21-EMA.

3

Trend Analysis

The goal of a technical analyst is to anticipate the direction of the market trend. As they say "the trend is your friend". As a technical trader, look at how prices have changed in the past to figure out how the market is moving. So, decide what to do with a stock or any security (stock, commodity, currency) based on what you learn. This is why it's so important to understand market trends.

A securities trend is the direction in which its price is trending. Share prices often rise or fall in response to positive or negative market sentiment. They never move in a straight line since stock values might be volatile in the near term. To interpret stock price swings as a trend, traders must evaluate a specific period of time.

Trend analysis is a strategy for estimating the path of market movements by analysing past data. Thus, using this trend analysis strategy, traders may attempt to anticipate whether a growing market will continue to develop or not. It is a form of technical analysis that assists traders in determining a security's current price patterns. It is often used as an indication to aid traders in deciding whether to purchase or sell.

Types of trends

- Uptrend
- Downtrend
- Sideways trend

Uptrend

A rising trend or uptrend represents the price movement of a stock, index, or other financial instrument when the general direction is upward. Thus, the market is bullish.

Uptrends are defined by increasing data points, such as rising swing highs and rising swing lows. This construction of higher lows and higher highs is referred to as an up trending market.

In an uptrend, a trader will look for a long opportunity as the uptrend continues towards the higher side.

Example of uptrend

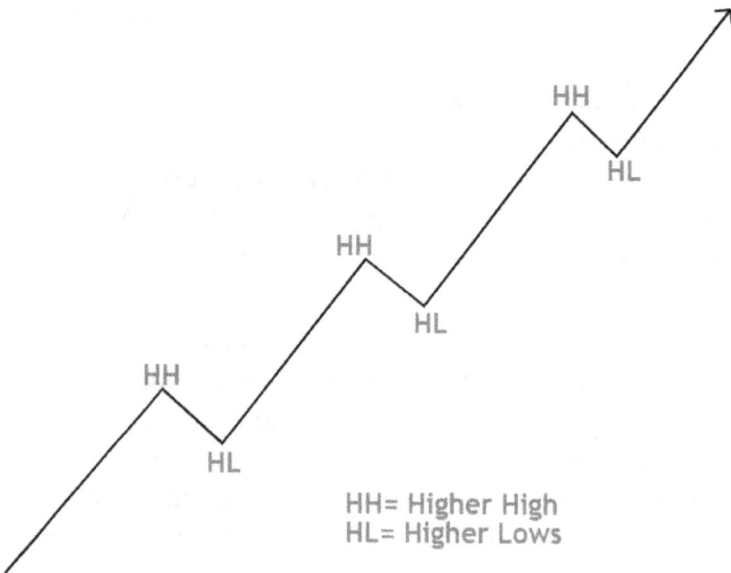

Image 3.1: Uptrend with higher highs and higher lows

Image 3.1 is a graphical representation of an uptrend with higher highs and higher lows marked at every swing top and bottom.

Case Study: Uptrend

Image 3.2 is the monthly chart of Abbott India Ltd. The stock has formed an uptrend with higher highs and higher lows marked at every swing top and bottom.

This image clearly shows that if the security is trending upside, then trade on the long side. In an uptrend, the higher peaks (rising leg) will be larger than the trough (counter trend).

The only time when profit booking happens leading the stock to move sideways is when the stock is going through a sideways phase. Once the stock breaches the resistance of that consolidation, it starts moving towards the higher side again as people who missed the leg up last time would also enter the market and new buyers will push the price higher.

Downtrend

Likewise, a market that continually builds a structure of lower lows and lower highs is referred to as a market with a downward trend.

This signifies that traders are confident that the stock price or any security will go down even more. Traders use every small rise in the price of a stock to sell some of the shares they already own. At these prices, no one buys anything else. Even if the price of the stock has gone down a lot, you shouldn't buy it. This is especially true if you are a short-term trader.

In a downtrend, a trader will look for a shorting opportunity (bearish position) as the downtrend continues towards the lower side.

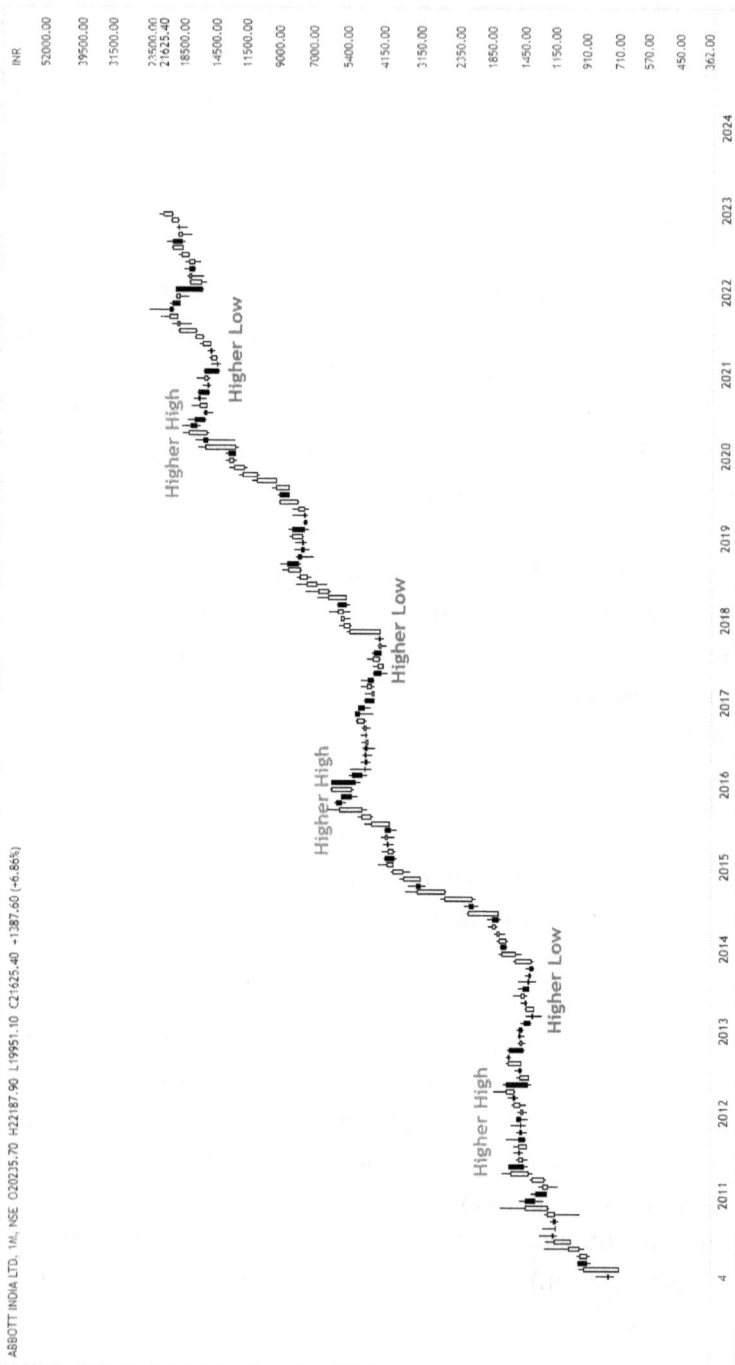

ABBOTT INDIA LTD, 1M, NSE O20235.70 H22187.90 L19951.10 C21625.40 −1387.60 (−6.86%)

Higher High

Higher High

Higher High

Higher Low

Higher Low

Higher Low

Image 3.2: Monthly chart of Abbott India Ltd. showing an uptrend.

Example of downtrend

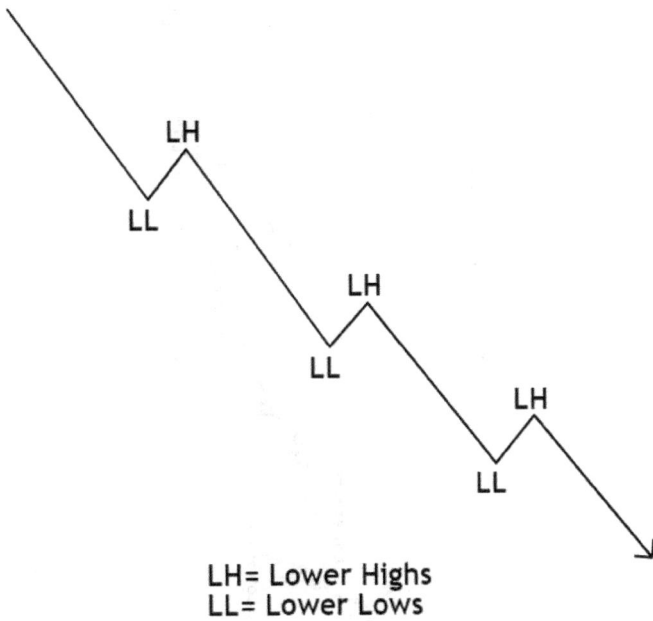

LH= Lower Highs
LL= Lower Lows

Image 3.3: Lower highs and lower lows in a downtrend

A graphical representation of a downtrend with lower highs and lower lows marked at every swing top and bottom is shown in image 3.3.

Case Study: Downtrend

Image 3.4 shows the daily chart of Bajaj Consumer Care Ltd. The stock has formed a downtrend with lower lows and lower highs marked at every swing top and bottom.

This image clearly shows that if the security is trending downside, then trade on the short side as we can see that in a downtrend, the lower peaks will be larger than troughs (counter trend).

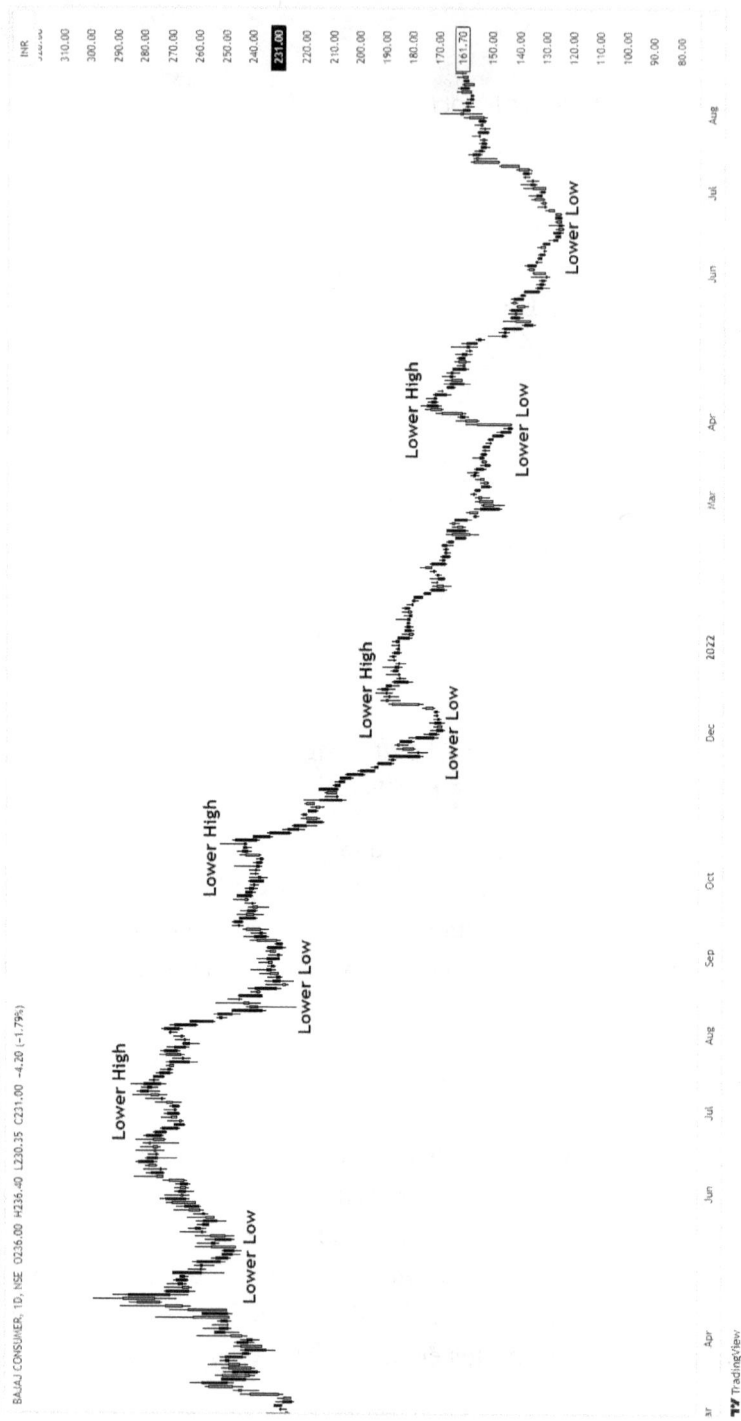

Image 3.4: Daily chart of Bajaj Consumer Care Ltd. showing a downtrend.

Sideways Trend

A stock moves sideways when it doesn't move much in either direction for a long time. Peaks and troughs stay the same, and there are no big changes to help you decide whether to buy a stock or not.

However, once any of the ranges is broken, take a trading position based on the conditions. If the breakout is on the resistance side, then take a long position. Likewise, if the support is broken, then take a short position on the respective security.

Example of sideways trend

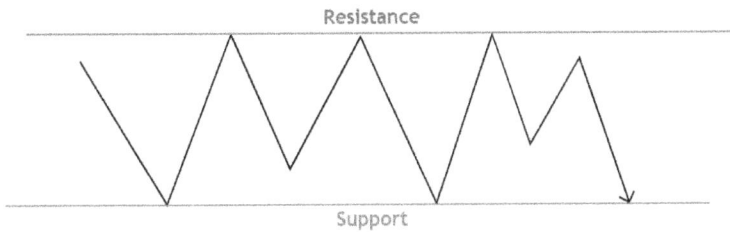

Image 3.5: Sideways trend with equal lows and equal highs

A graphical representation of a sideways trend with higher highs and higher lows marked at every swing top and bottom is shown in image 3.5.

Case Study: Practical sideways trend

Image 3.6 is the daily chart of Bharti Airtel Ltd. The stock shows a sideways trend from 2007 to 2020 with equal lows and equal highs marked at every swing top and bottom.

BHARTI AIRTEL LTD, 1M, NSE O484.30 H558.35 L474.40 C513.85 -26.55 (-5.45%)

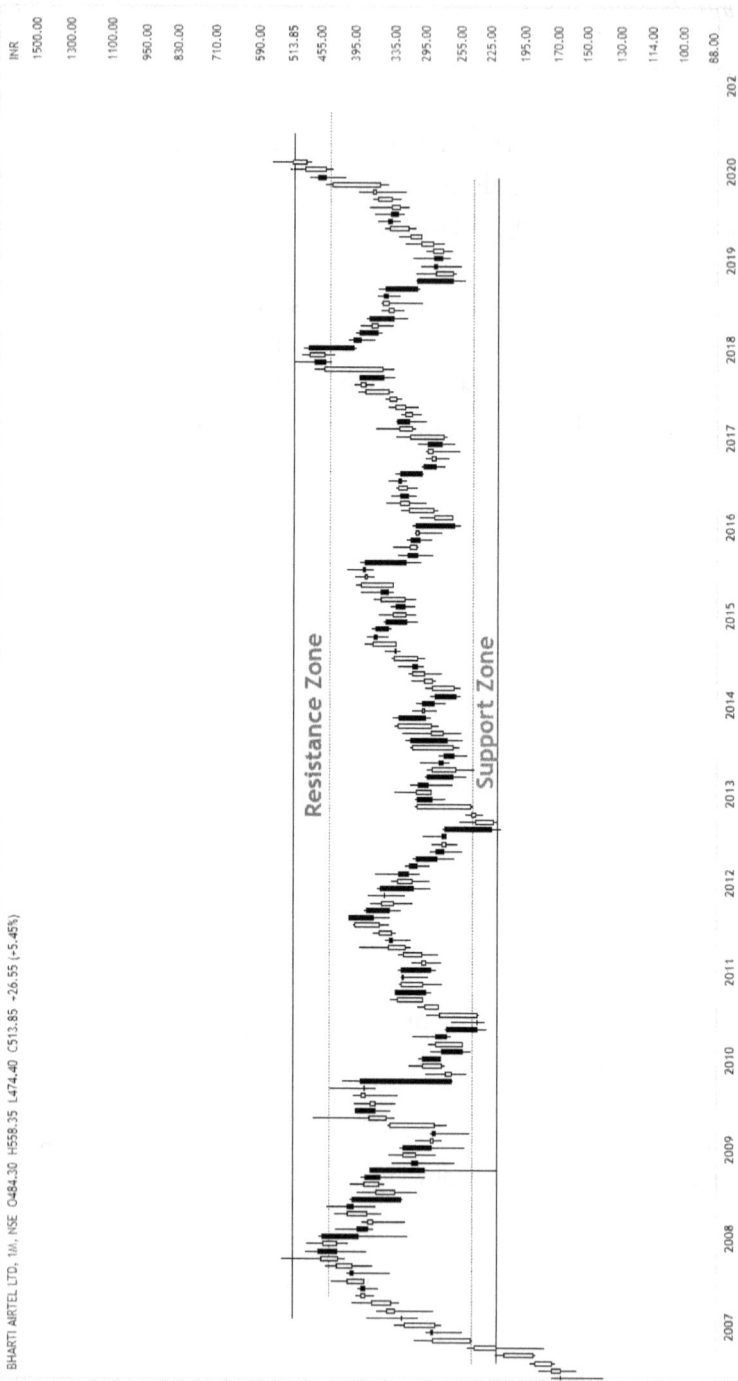

Image 3.6: Monthly chart of Bharti Airtel Ltd. showing a sideways trend.

Image 3.6 clearly shows that if the security is trending sideways, then trade on the short side if the breakdown happens. If the breach happens on the higher side (breakout) then trade on the long side.

4

Gap Analysis

Gap analysis is important to know the reason why a particular stock moved up or down when the next trading session opened. If the stock price moves up (gap up) creating a gap, it means people are impatient to buy. If the stock price moves down (gap down) creating a gap, it means people are impatient to sell. This could also occur during smaller timeframes. The different types are explained below:

Types of Gaps

- Common gaps
- Breakaway gaps
- Runaway gaps
- Exhaustion gaps

Common gaps

The common gap, also known as a trade gap or an area gap, is generally uneventful. In reality, they may be generated by a security declaring ex-dividend during a period of low trading activity. These gaps are frequent, and they generally close fast.

"Getting filled" suggests that price movement in the future (a few days to a few weeks) normally retraces at least to the previous day before the gap. This is sometimes referred to as 'closing the gap'.

A common gap usually arises in a trading range or congestion region, reinforcing the stock's seeming lack of interest at the moment. This is often amplified by low trade volume. Being aware of these types of gaps is beneficial, but it is doubtful that they will result in trading opportunities.

Case Study: Common gaps

Image 4.1 is the daily chart of Infosys Ltd. which shows a practical example of common gaps from May 2022 to December 2022.

One has to keep in mind that these common gaps do not generate any trading opportunity and one has to stay away from stocks which have a formation of common gaps.

Breakaway gaps

Breakaway gaps are the ones that are most fun. They happen when a price moves out of its trading range or congestion area. Before you can understand gaps, you need to know how market congestion works.

A congestion area is just a range of prices where the market has been trading for a while, usually a few weeks. From below, it's usually hard to get near the top of the congestion area. When coming from above, the area near the bottom of the congestion area is also a support. To get out of these areas, the market needs to be excited (either a lot more buyers than sellers or a lot more sellers than buyers).

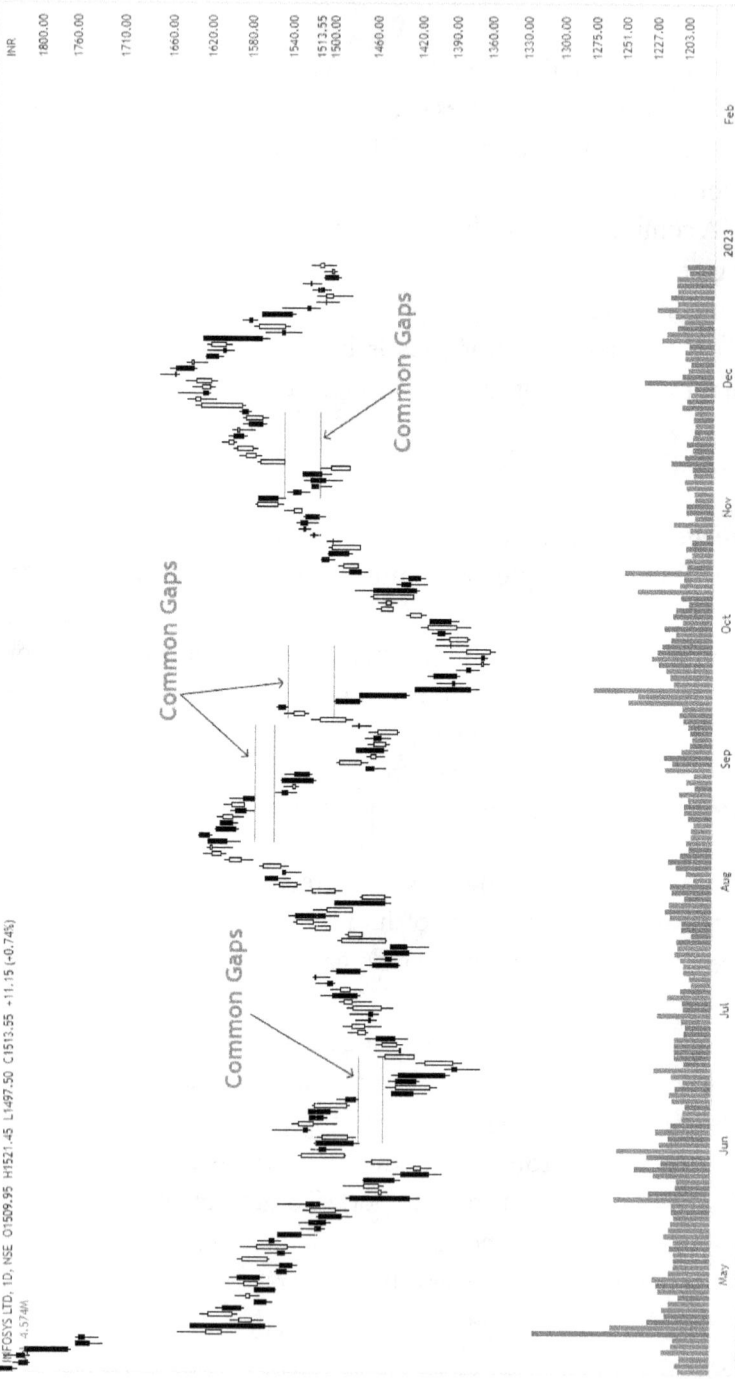

Image 4.1: Daily chart of Infosys Ltd. showing common gaps.

Trading volume should increase a lot, not only because people are more excited, but also because many people have positions on the wrong side of the breakout and need to cover or sell them. It would be better if there is high average volume after the gap. This means that the new direction of the market has a chance of sticking around.

If the breakout goes up, the point of breakout becomes the new support. If the breakout goes down, the point of breakdown becomes the new resistance. Don't fall into the trap of thinking that this kind of gap will be filled soon—if it's linked to a lot of volume, it could take a while. Go with the fact that the stock has started moving in a different direction and trade accordingly.

Case Study: Breakaway Gap

The daily chart of Navin Flourine International Ltd. in image 4.2 shows a practical example of breakaway gaps and indicates a strong upside after the breakout occurred with a decent gap.

If trading gaps are connected well to chart patterns, that's a good sign. For example, if an ascending triangle suddenly has a gap to the upside, this can be a much better trade than a gap without a chart pattern which has breakaway gap at the breakout zone. Head and shoulders continuation is usually bullish because it has a flat top and a rounding bottom. Image 4.2 shows a head and shoulders continuation with a breakaway gap to the upside, which is what you would expect from an ascending triangle.

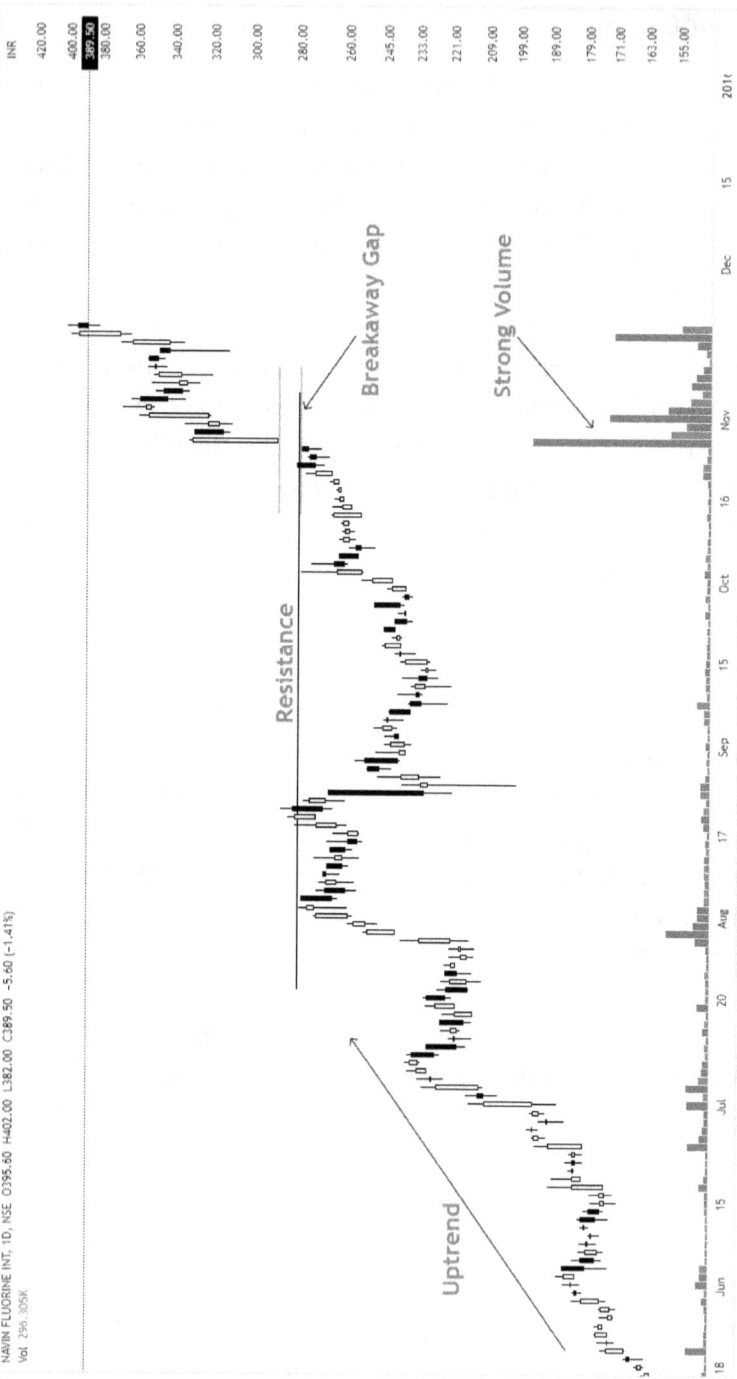

Image 4.2: Daily chart of Navin Flourine International Ltd. showing breakaway gaps.

Runaway gaps

Runaway gaps or 'measuring gaps' are caused by buyers showing a strong tendency to purchase the stock. Runaway gaps to the upside usually occur because traders didn't get in at the start of the uptrend, and while waiting for a price retracement (pullback), decided it wasn't going to happen. Suddenly, more people want to buy the stock, and the price jumps up from where it was the day before.

Case Study: Runaway Gaps

Image 4.3 is the daily chart of Balaji Amines Ltd. which has formed runaway gaps. When traders see this kind of a runaway gap, they are almost in a state of panic. Also, a good uptrend can have gaps called 'runaway gaps', which are caused by big news stories that make people interested in the stock again making them buy more of it.

Look at image 4.3 to see how the volume went up a lot during and after the runaway gap.

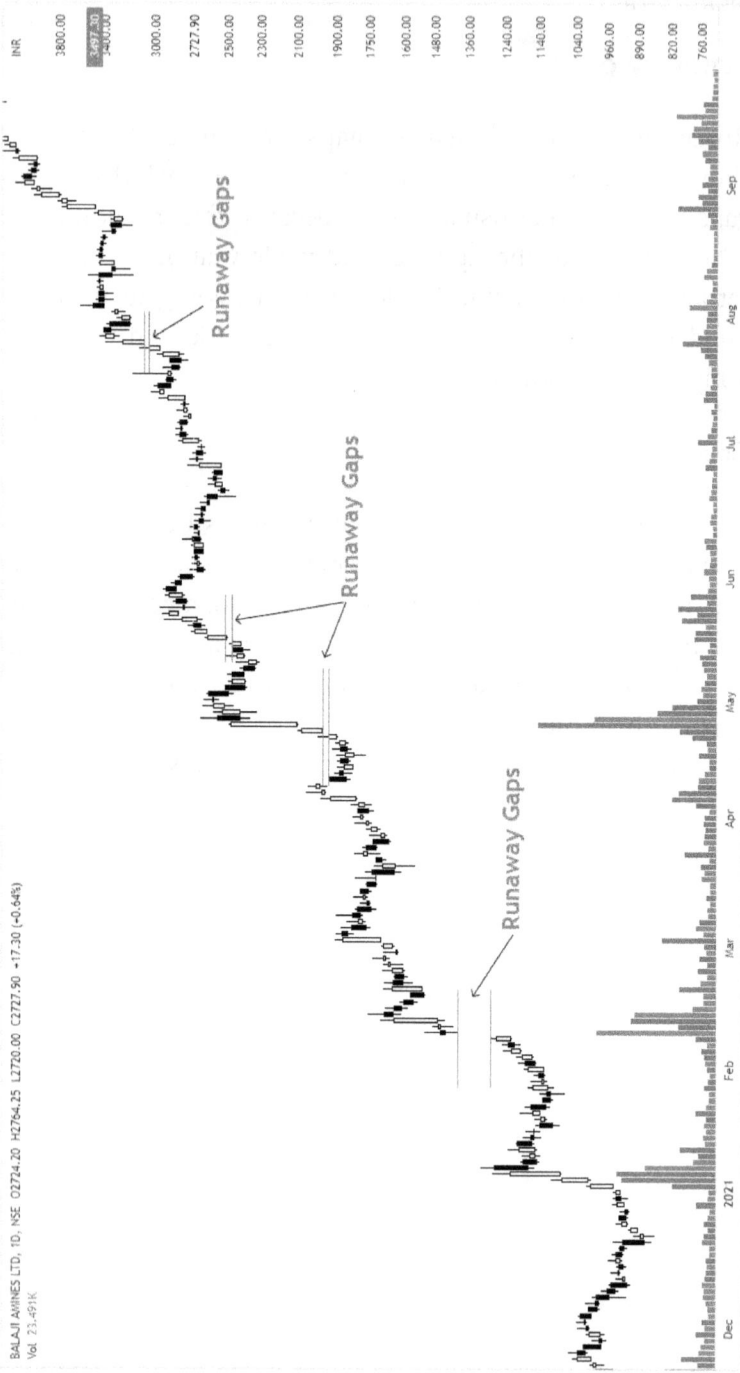

Image 4.3: Daily chart of Balaji Amines Ltd. showing runaway gaps.

Case Study: Runaway Gaps

Image 4.4 is the daily chart of Oil and Natural Gas Corporation Ltd. which depicts runaway gaps. Remember that runaway gaps may occur during downtrends as well. Typically, this indicates that the buying pressure is way higher than the selling pressure.

Runaway gaps are also called measuring gaps. It is hard to find examples that fit this meaning, but it is a way to figure out how long a trend will last. The idea is that the measurement gap will be visible in the middle of the move, or about halfway through.

Exhaustion Gaps

Exhaustion gaps occur when a good uptrend or downtrend is about to end. They are often the first sign of the move coming to an end. These are easy to spot because there is a big difference between the price at the end of the day before and the price when the market opens the next day. It is easy to mistake them for runaway gaps if you don't pay attention to how large the gap is. Additionally, see the price over the next few days to whether it is continuing or reversing.

As prices begin to rise again, the resulting supply shortages are soon filled. When they occur during a bull market, buyers get overexcited and the stock price skyrockets. Enormous volumes cause prices to spike in a 'gap', but then investors sell for huge profits and trading volume drops to nothing. There is a dramatic decline in prices and reversal in trend.

As prices reverse their trend, exhaustion gaps are quickly filled. Similarly, if they occur during a bull run, bullish excitement overcomes trading, and traders can't get enough of that stock. Prices spike rapidly, followed by massive profit

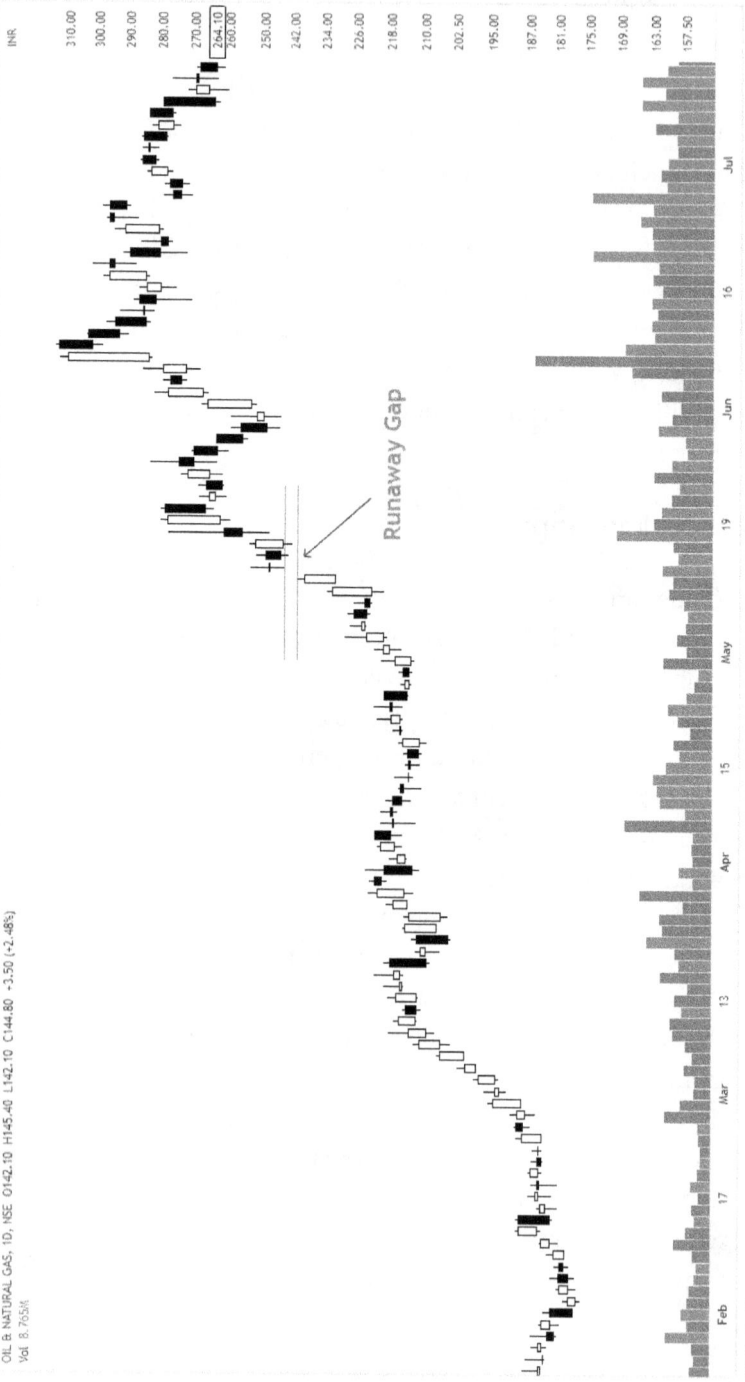

Image 4.4: Daily chart of Oil and Natural Gas Corporation Ltd. showing runaway gaps.

taking and a complete absence of demand for the stock. Prices come down, and the trend changes significantly.

Case Study: Exhaustion Gaps

The daily chart of Mangalore Refinery and Petrochemicals Ltd. in image 4.5 shows an example of exhaustion gaps. It indicates a strong reversal occurred after the breakout, with a decent gap with rising volume, and gets filled soon after the exhaustion gap.

MANGALORE REF &PET, 1D, NSE O54.30 H55.90 L54.20 C54.90 +1.15 (+2.14%)
Vol 2.379M

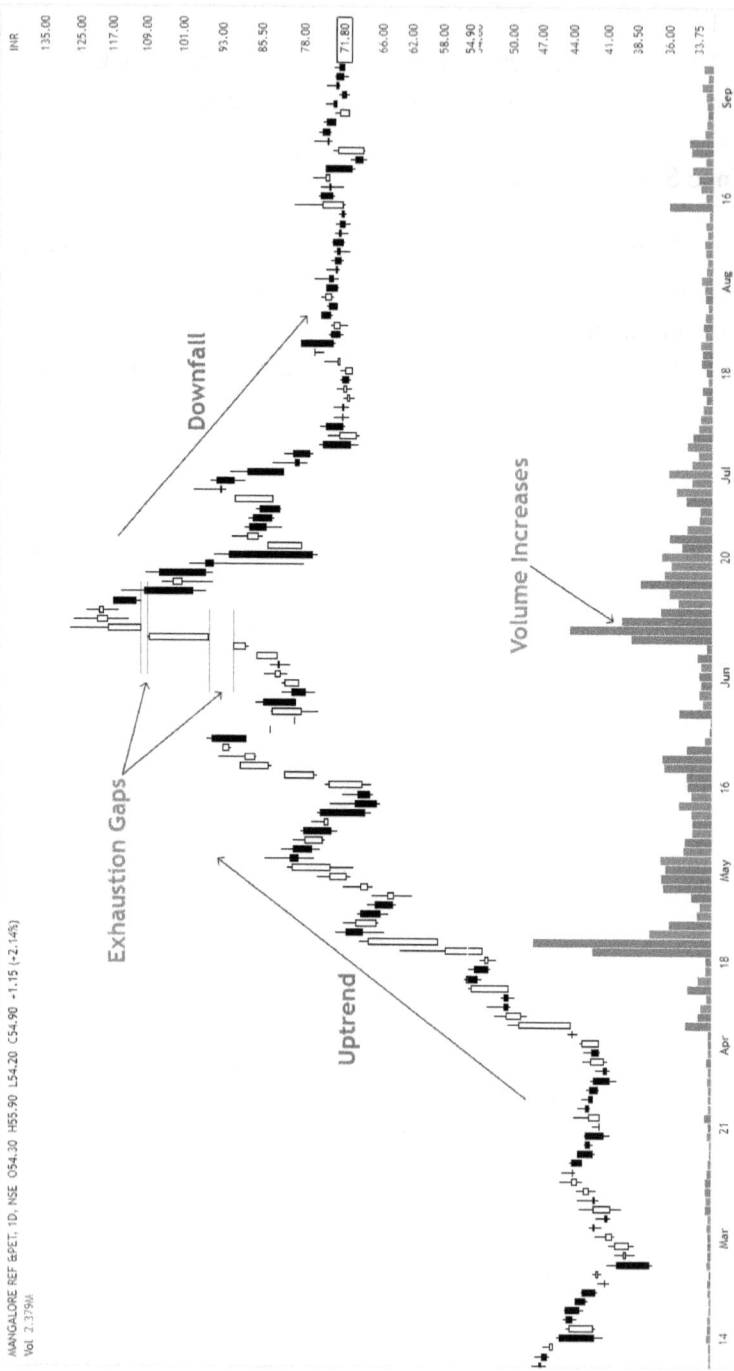

Image 4.5: Daily chart of Mangalore Refinery and Petrochemicals Ltd. showing exhaustion gaps.

5

Chart Patterns

A chart pattern is a collection of trend lines or curves that graphically represent price movement. Chart patterns are used in technical analysis to identify trends in the price movement of an asset. They are changes in the price of a financial asset that happen naturally and are caused by a number of things, including how people act.

Do keep in mind, the ability to accurately understand chart patterns requires practice and dedication.

How does a chart pattern work?

Chart patterns work across time periods because markets are fractal(in which the parts resemble the whole) so they show recurrent pricing patterns.

Trader psychology drives price movement; therefore these chart patterns work for stocks, bonds, currencies, commodities, cryptocurrencies, and so on.

Technical traders think the price represents market sentiment and fair value. If so, chart patterns should indicate future market action.

Types of Chart Patterns

The two types of chart patterns we will discuss in detail with real life case study examples are continuation chart patterns and reversal chart patterns. The different types of patterns are mentioned below:

- Continuation Chart Pattern
- Reversal Chart Pattern

Ascending Triangle

An ascending triangle pattern is characterized by a flat resistance at the top and an upward slope on the bottom side when the price approaches higher lows. It may indicate fading resistance and an impending breakout to the upside. The ascending triangle pattern is good if the price touches the support line three times and the resistance line twice (or the support line at least twice and the resistance line three times).

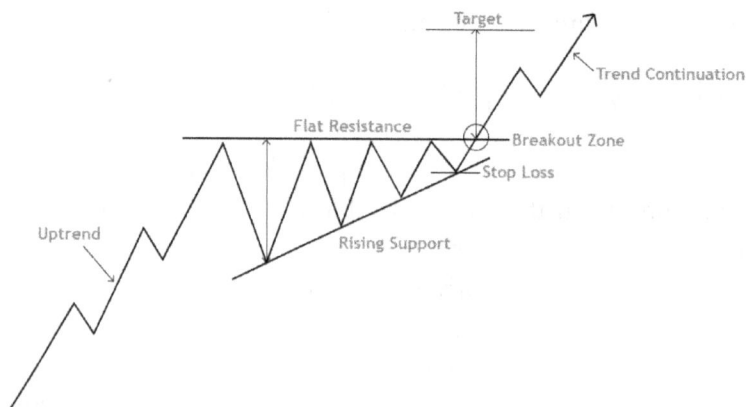

Image 5.1: Ascending triangle chart pattern

Trend: The prevailing trend of the security should be up as it shows that we are going with the trend and indicates upside momentum.

Entry: We will enter the market once the breakout happens from resistance towards upside.

Stop-loss: We will place a stop-loss at the recent swing low or breakout candles low (if the breakout candle is strong).

Profit target: The pattern base at the start of the pattern will be taken as a target from the breakout zone of the pattern.

Volume: If the ascending triangle is forming up with a strong volume then it shows that more market participants are interested in buying the security.

Descending Triangle

The descending triangle is a bearish formation that often forms as a continuation pattern during a downtrend. Descending triangles may sometimes form as reversal patterns towards the conclusion of an upswing, although they are mainly continuation patterns.

A descending triangle is an indication for traders to initiate a short position in anticipation of a breakdown. On a chart, a descending triangle may be identified by drawing trend lines between both the highs and lows.

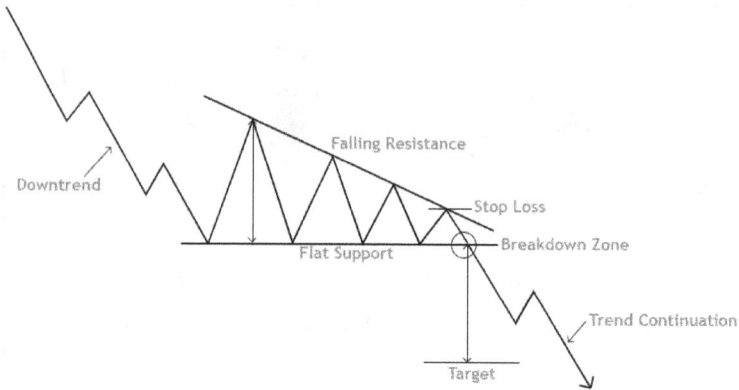

Image 5.2: Descending triangle chart pattern

Trend: The prevailing trend of the security should be down as it shows that we are going with the trend and indicates downward momentum.

Entry: We will enter the market when the breakdown happens from support towards downside.

Stop-loss: Place a stop-loss at the recent swing high or breakdown candles low (if the breakdown candle is strong).

Profit target: The pattern base at the start of the pattern will be taken as target from the breakdown zone of the pattern.

Volume: If the ascending triangle is happening with strong volume, it shows that more market participants are interested in buying the security.

Symmetrical Triangle

Bullish Symmetrical Triangle

A bullish symmetrical triangle is a continuation pattern on the chart. Two converging trend lines that are symmetrical in regard to the diagonal line constitute the pattern.

The first line is a resistance-creating bearish trend line, often known as the 'resistance line of the bullish symmetrical triangle'.

The second line is a bullish trend line that provides support known as the 'support line of the bullish symmetrical triangle'.

A bullish symmetrical triangle is valid if the two lines oscillate effectively. To confirm the pattern, each of these lines must have been touched at least twice.

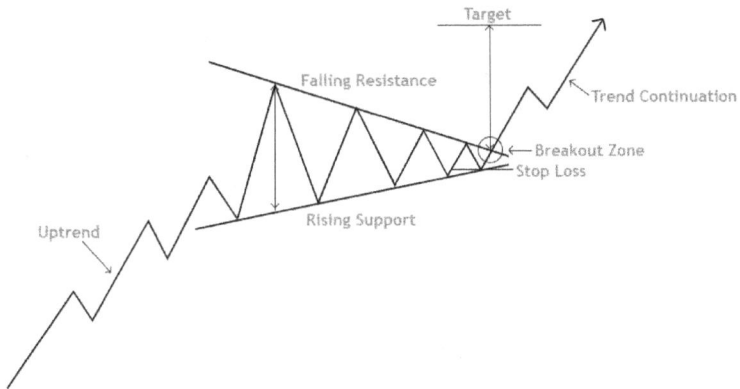

Image 5.3: Bullish continuation symmetrical triangle

Trend: The stock predominant trend should be up, since this demonstrates that we are following the trend and indicates positive momentum.

Entry: We will buy the stock once the price breaks above the falling resistance and gives us a strong breakout towards upside.

Stop-loss: Stop-loss orders for symmetrical triangular patterns are often placed slightly below the breakout point (recent swing low).

Profit target: The price target for a bullish symmetrical triangle is based on the height of the triangle's base at the breakout point (exit from the triangle).

Volume: As the symmetrical triangle length increases and the trading range shrinks, the volume should begin to decline. This refers to the calm before the storm or the consolidation leading up to the breakout.

Bearish Symmetrical Triangle

A bearish symmetrical triangle is a continuation pattern for bearish trends. Two converging trend lines that are symmetrical in regard to the diagonal line constitute the pattern.

The first line is a resistance-creating bearish trend line, commonly known as the 'resistance line of the bearish symmetrical triangle'.

The second line is a positive trend line that provides support known as the 'support line of the bearish symmetrical triangle'.

For a symmetrical triangle to be described as 'bearish', the trend before its creation should have been bearish.

If there is excellent oscillation between the two lines, a bearish symmetrical triangle is valid. To confirm the pattern, at least two touches must have been made on each of these lines.

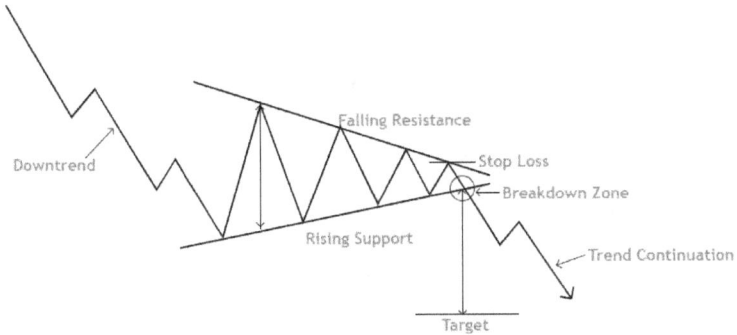

Image 5.4: Bearish symmetrical triangle continuation pattern

Trend: The stock predominant trend should be down, since this demonstrates that we are following the trend and indicates negative momentum.

Entry: We will purchase the stock once the price breaks below the rising support and give us a strong breakdown towards downside.

Stop-loss: Stop-loss orders for symmetrical triangular patterns are often placed slightly above the breakdown point (recent swing high).

Profit target: The price target for a bearish symmetrical triangle is based on the height of the triangle's base at the breakdown point (exit from the triangle).

Volume: As the symmetrical triangle length increases and the trading range shrinks, the volume should begin to decline. This refers to the calm before the storm or the consolidation leading up to the breakdown.

Pennant Pattern

A pennant is a continuation chart pattern that resembles a symmetrical triangle but has distinct properties.

Typically, this chart pattern follows a sharp upward or downward movement. As a result of the time constraint, a pennant has a brief lifespan.

Bullish Pennant Pattern

The bull pennant is a bullish continuation pattern that indicates the continuation of the uptrend after the consolidation phase has ended.

In contrast to the flag, where price movement consolidates between two parallel lines, the pennant consolidates between two converging lines until a breakthrough occurs.

The bullish pennant is a continuation pattern because it tends to help the current uptrend go even higher. In a nutshell, the pennant helps traders figure out what stage the trend is in at the moment.

So, trading the pennant is much easier because the two lines that meet in the middle and the flagpole makes it clear where the trading levels are.

Image 5.5: Bullish pennant continuation pattern

Trend: There should be evidence of a previous trend for a pattern to be considered a continuation pattern. pennants need to show a sharp rise or fall on a lot of volume. This move is usually the first step of a big move forward, and the pennant is just a pause.

Entry: We will enter the market once the price breaks above the falling resistance and shows a strong breakout towards upside.

Stop-loss: Stop-loss orders for bullish pennant patterns are often placed slightly below the breakout point (recent swing low).

Profit target: The length of the flagpole can be used to estimate the advance based on the resistance break of the pennant.

Volume: The uptrend which creates the flagpole should be accompanied by high volume. The buying volume pressure on the resistance breach validates the pattern and increases the chances of continuation.

Bearish Pennant Pattern

The bearish pennant is a bearish continuation pattern that indicates the continuation of the downtrend after the consolidation phase has ended.

In contrast to the flag, where price movement consolidates between two parallel lines, the pennant consolidates between two converging lines until a breakthrough occurs.

The bearish pennant is a continuation pattern because it tends to help the current downtrend go even lower. In a nutshell, the pennant helps traders figure out what stage the trend is in at the moment.

So, trading the pennant is much easier because the two lines that meet in the middle and the flagpole make it clear where the trading levels are.

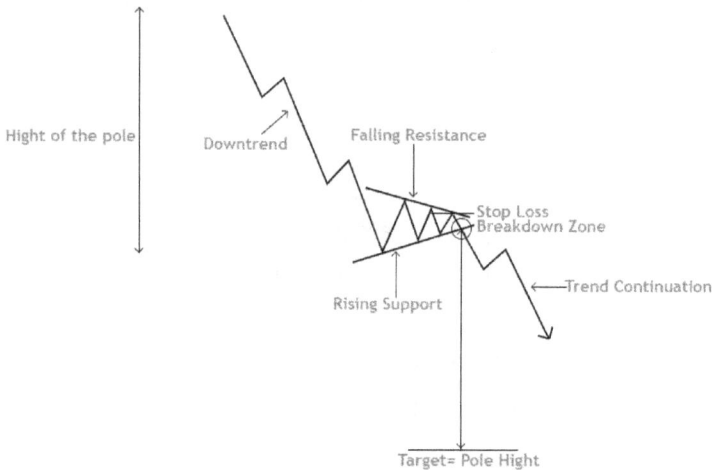

Image 5.6: Bearish pennant continuation pattern

Trend: There should be evidence of a previous trend for a pattern to be considered a continuation pattern. Bearish pennants need to show a sharp fall on a lot of volume. This move is usually the first step of a big move forward, and the pennant is just a pause.

Entry: We will enter the trade once the price breaks below the rising support and give us a strong breakdown towards downside.

Stop-loss: Stop-loss orders for bearish pennant patterns are often placed slightly above the breakdown point (recent swing high).

Profit target: The length of the flagpole can be used to estimate the decline based on the support break of the pennant.

Volume: During the downtrend which creates the flagpole, it should be accompanied by high volume. The selling volume pressure on the support breach validates the pattern and increases the chances of continuation.

Flag Pattern

A flag is a small rectangle that slopes in the opposite direction of the last pattern. If the last move was up, the flag would start to go down. If the move went down, the flag would rise.

Bullish Flag

The bullish flag is a retracement pattern. Retracement is a small movement away from the overall direction of a price. It is temporary in nature and does not reflect a wider market trend. Over a certain period of time the value of an asset may rise or fall overall, but it rarely does so consistently. A retracement pattern helps traders determine the present stage of the trend. As a general trading guideline, it is never advisable to purchase at a random price expecting an extension to the upside; rather, one should wait for a significant resistance to be broken.

Simply put, price movement is constrained by two parallel trend lines (resistance and support) that slant downward.

The flagpole and the flag are what make up a bullish flag. In this way, it looks like a flag on a pole. It's formed when the price moves in a steady uptrend, making higher highs and higher lows. The bull flag looks like the letter F.

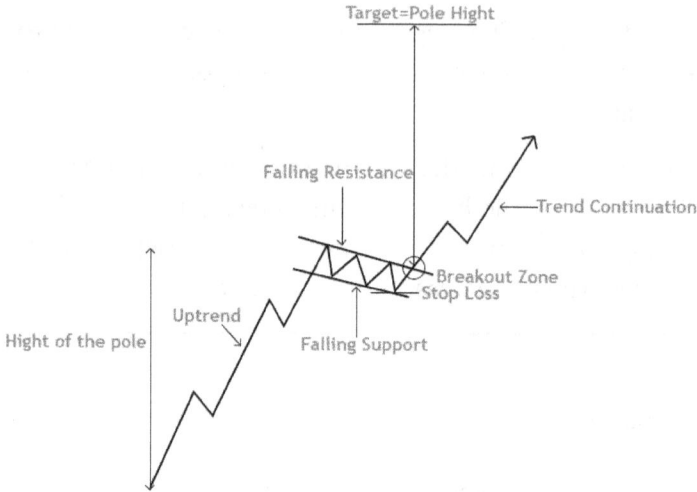

Image 5.7: Bullish flag pattern

Trend: To be considered a bullish flag continuation pattern, there should be evidence of a prior uptrend.

Entry: Traders often anticipate entering a flag the day after the price breaks and closes above the upper parallel trend line (long position).

Stop-loss: Traders anticipate to use the opposite side of a flag pattern as a stop-loss level. For instance, if the upper trend line of the pattern is at Rs 60 per share and the lower trend line is at Rs 50 per share, then it would make sense to put the stop-loss order for a long position below Rs 50 per share.

Profit target: The length of the flagpole can be used to calculate the advance based on the resistance break of the flag.

Volume: The volume should be high throughout the rise or fall of the flagpole. The quick and sharp movement that forms the flagpole is validated by the magnitude of the volume. An increase in volume on the resistance break validates the formation and increases the probability of its continuance.

Bearish Flag

The bearish flag is a retracement pattern. It helps traders determine the present stage of the trend. As a general trading guideline, it is never advisable to purchase at a random price expecting an extension to the upside; rather, one should wait for a significant support to be broken.

Simply put, price movement is constrained by two parallel trend lines (resistance and support) that are slanted showing an uptrend.

The flagpole and the flag are what make up a bearish flag. In this way, it looks like a flag on a pole. It is formed when the price moves in a steady downtrend, making lower highs and lower lows. The bear flag looks like the opposite letter F.

Image 5.8: Bearish flag continuation pattern

Trend: To be considered a bearish flag continuation pattern, there should be evidence of a prior downtrend.

Entry: Traders often anticipate entering a flag the day after the price breaks and closes below the lower parallel trend line which can also be called the rising support line (short position).

Stop-loss: Traders anticipate using the opposite side of a flag pattern as a stop-loss level. For instance, if the upper trend line of the pattern is at Rs 60 per share and the lower trend line is at Rs 50 per share, then it would make sense to put the stop-loss order for a short position above Rs 60 per share.

Profit target: The length of the flagpole can be used to calculate the decline based on the support break of the flag.

Wedge Pattern

A wedge is a price pattern made up of two trend lines that meet in the middle. The two trend lines are made by connecting the price series highs and lows. The lines show that the highs and lows are going up or down at different rates. As the lines get closer together, they look like a wedge. People think that wedge-shaped trend lines can help predict when prices might change direction.

Rising Wedge Pattern

The rising wedge is a bearish pattern that starts out big at the bottom and gets smaller as prices go up and the trading range gets smaller. Rising wedges have a clear upslope and a tendency to go down.

Simply put, a rising wedge is a bearish chart pattern that signals a possible breakdown to the downside.

It is true if the two bullish lines move back and forth in a good way. The line at the top is the resistance line, and the line at the bottom is the support line.

To prove the pattern, each of these lines must have been touched at least twice. If the support line is broken, the pattern is confirmed. Most of the time, this break out is accompanied by high volumes.

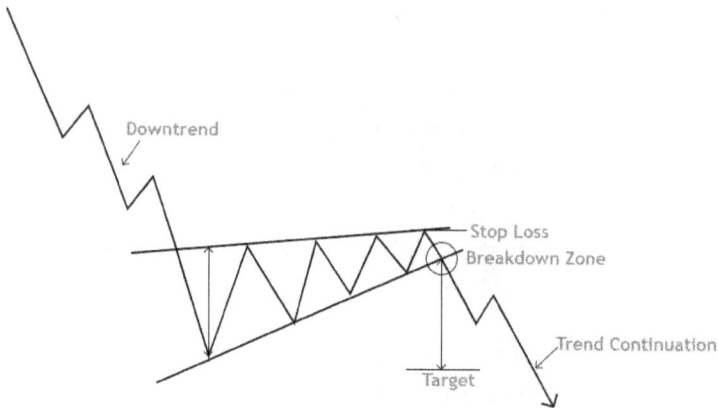

Image 5.9: Rising wedge pattern

Trend: Defining criteria for a reversal pattern include the presence of an existing down trend. A rising wedge may signal a change in trend, either intermediate or long term, and typically occurs over a period of three to six months.

Entry: Once we have a first daily close outside the wedge's territory (below support line), we place a short position.

Stop-loss: Stop-loss orders should be placed inside the wedge's area around the recent swing high (resistance line) since a price move back into the wedge's area would invalidate the pattern.

Profit target: The price goal is the same as the height of the wedge's back (pattern base).

Volume: In an ideal world, as prices go up and the wedge changes, volume will go down. When the support line breaks, a rise in volume can be seen as confirmation that the price is going down.

Falling Wedge Pattern

The falling wedge is a bullish pattern that starts out big at the top and gets smaller as prices go down and the trading range gets smaller. Rising wedges have a clear downside and a tendency to go down.

Simply put, a falling wedge is a bullish chart pattern that signals a possible breakout to the upside.

A falling wedge is true if the two bullish lines move back and forth in a good way. The line at the top is the resistance line, and the line at the bottom is the support line.

To prove the pattern, each of these lines must have been touched at least twice. If the resistance line is broken, the pattern is confirmed. Most of the time, this break out is accompanied by high volumes.

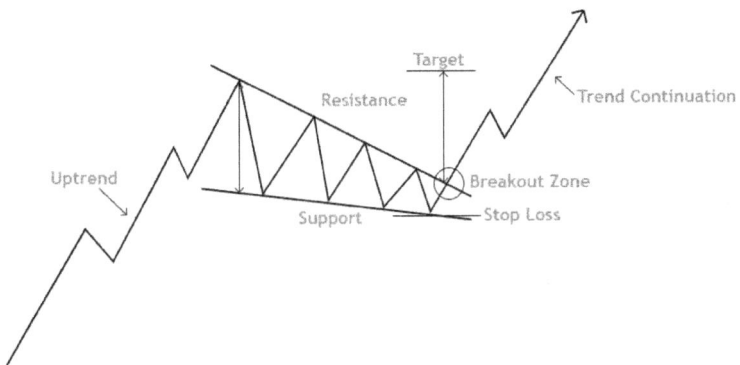

Image 5.10: Falling wedge pattern

Trend: Defining criteria for a reversal pattern include the presence of an existing up trend. A falling wedge may signal a change in trend, either intermediate or long term, and typically occurs over a period of three to six months.

Entry: Once we have a first daily close outside the wedge's territory (above resistance line), we place a long position.

Stop-loss: Stop-loss orders should be placed inside the wedge's area around the recent swing low (support line) since a price move back into the wedge's area would invalidate the pattern.

Profit target: The price goal is the same as the height of the wedge's back (pattern base).

Volume: In an ideal world, as prices go up and the wedge changes, volume will go down. When the resistance line breaks, a rise in volume can be seen as confirmation that the price is going up.

Cup and Handle Pattern

Bullish Continuation Cup and Handle

Cup with handle is a bullish continuation pattern that shows a period of consolidation followed by a breakout. The pattern is made up of two parts: the cup and the handle.

After an advance, the cup takes the shape of a bowl or a bottom that gets rounder. As the cup is formed, a trading range forms on the right side, and the handle comes together. The previous rise will continue if the handle breaks out of its trading range again.

The duration of the cup might vary from one to six months, and on occasion much longer. Ideally, the handle will develop and be finished within one to four weeks.

Image 5.11: Bullish cup and handle pattern

Trend: To qualify as a continuation pattern, there must be a preceding trend. The trend should ideally be a few months old and not very mature. The more mature the trend, the lower the probability that the pattern represents a continuation and the lower the potential for growth.

Entry: The purchase point happens when a stock breaks out or advances above the previous level of resistance (right side of the cup).

Stop-loss: Stop-loss orders for bullish cup and handle patterns are often placed slightly below the breakout point (recent swing low at the handle's bottom area).

Profit target: We can estimate the price objective after the breakout by measuring the distance from the top of the cup to the bottom of the cup and adding that amount to the purchase point.

Volume: When price finally breaks out over the handle's resistance, there should be a significant uptick in volume.

Bearish Continuation Cup and Handle

Cup with handle can also be formed as a bearish continuation pattern that shows a period of consolidation followed by a breakout. The pattern is made up of two parts: the cup and the handle. After a down move, the cup takes the shape of an opposite bowl or a top that gets rounder.

As the cup gets completed, a trading range forms on the right side, and the handle comes together. The previous fall will continue if the handle breaks down from its trading range again.

The duration of the cup might vary from one to six months, and on occasion much longer. Ideally, the handle will develop and complete within one to four weeks.

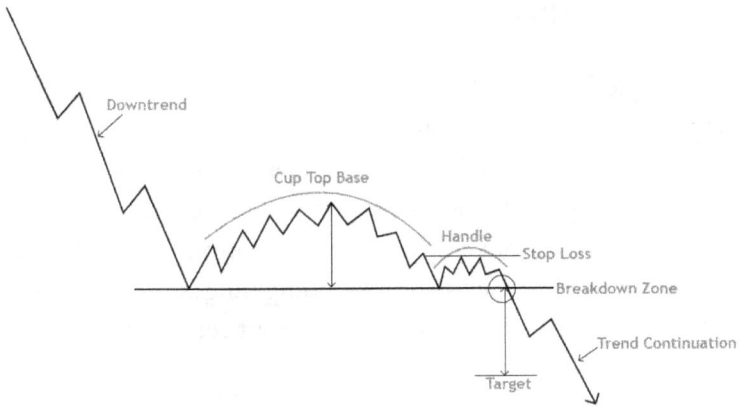

Image 5.12: Bearish Continuation Cup and Handle

Trend: To qualify as a bearish continuation pattern, there must be a preceding down trend. The trend should ideally be a few months old and not very mature. The more mature the trend, the lower the probability that the pattern represents a continuation and the lower the potential for growth.

Entry: The purchase happens when a stock breaks down or declines below its neckline or the level of support.

Stop-loss: Stop-loss orders for bearish cup and handle patterns are often placed slightly above the breakdown point (recent swing high at the handle's top area).

Profit target: We can estimate the price objective after the breakout by measuring the distance from the top of the cup to the bottom of the cup and adding that amount to the purchase point.

Volume: When price finally breaks out over the handle's resistance, there should be a significant uptick in volume.

Rectangle Pattern

A rectangle is a continuation pattern that looks like a trading range. It forms when the trend stops for a while. The pattern is easy to spot because it has two similar highs and two similar lows. The highs and lows can be connected to make two parallel lines that make up the top and bottom of a rectangle. People sometimes use the terms trading ranges, consolidation zones, and congestion areas to talk about rectangles.

Bullish Rectangle

You should usually trade rectangles or box plays as continuation patterns. In this situation, people aren't sure what to do, but usually decide to go with the trend. At the moment, supply and demand seem to be in balance.

Both buyers and sellers seem to be in the same position. The same 'highs' and 'lows' are always put to the test. The market moves back and forth between two clear limits.

As seen in image 5.13, the price climbs in a robust uptrend before beginning to consolidate between temporary support and resistance levels.

It continues to travel sideways, bouncing between these two parallel lines and generating the pattern's box-like shape.

The price then breaks through the top level of resistance and continues its rise.

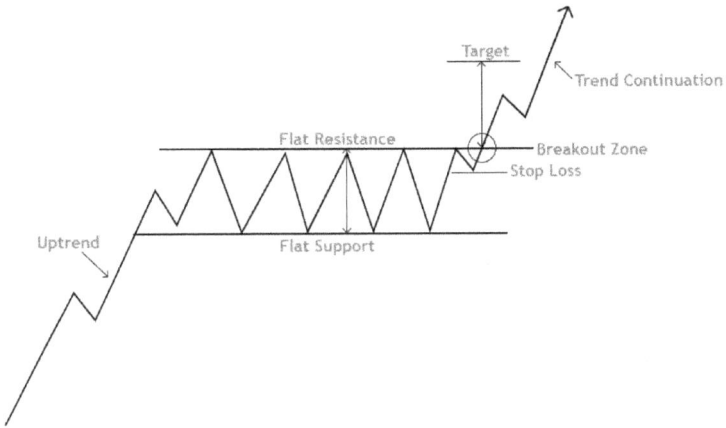

Image 5.13: Bullish rectangle continuation pattern

Trend: To be considered a bullish rectangle continuation pattern, there should be evidence of a prior uptrend.

Entry: As the price action breaks the resistance of a bullish rectangle pattern, buy the stock.

Stop-loss: Set your stop-loss just below the resistance line of the rectangle at the recent swing low (just below the resistance).

Profit target: You can figure out the estimated move by measuring the height of the rectangle and applying that number to the breakout.

Volume: Patterns of volume in rectangles do not follow standard patterns. As a pattern develops, the volume will sometimes go down. At other times, the volume will change as the prices bounce between support and resistance. As the pattern gets older, the volume will rarely go up. If the volume goes down, the best way to confirm a breakout is to look for the breakout to grow with strong volume.

Bearish Rectangle

In image 5.14, supply and demand seem to be in balance.

Both buyers and sellers seem to be in the same position. The same 'highs' and 'lows' are always put to the test. The market moves back and forth between two clear limits.

In this chart, the price climbs in a robust downtrend before beginning to consolidate between temporary support and resistance levels.

It continues to travel sideways, bouncing between these two parallel lines and generating the pattern's box-like shape.

The price then breaks through the bottom level of support and continues its fall.

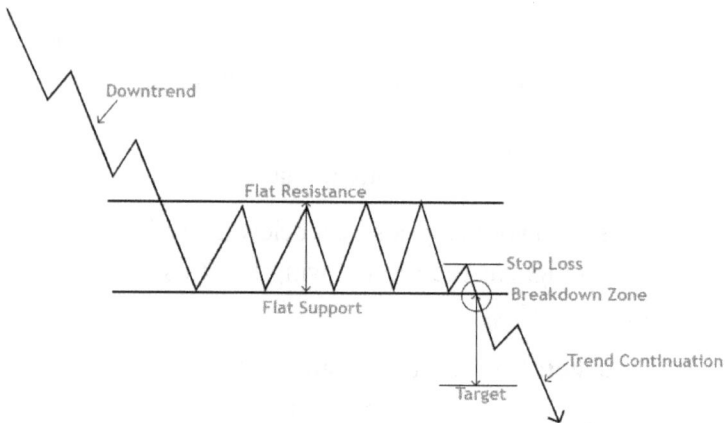

Image 5.14: Bearish rectangle continuation pattern

Trend: To be considered a bearish rectangle continuation pattern, there should be evidence of a prior downtrend.

Entry: Enter the market as the price action breaks through the support level of bearish rectangle pattern.

Stop-loss: Set your stop-loss just above the support line or neckline of the rectangle at the recent swing high (just above the support).

Profit target: You can figure out the estimated move by measuring the height of the rectangle and applying that number to the breakdown towards downside.

Volume: Patterns of volume in rectangles do not follow standard patterns. As a pattern develops, the volume will sometimes go down. At other times, the volume will change as the prices bounce between support and resistance. As the pattern gets older, the volume will rarely go up. If volume goes down, the best way to confirm a breakout is to look for the breakout to grow with strong volume.

Basing Pattern

Bullish Basing

This is a technical analysis chart pattern recognised by price movements that, when graphed, resemble a 'U' shape.

Bullish basing occurs towards the end of extended upward trends and may indicate a price continuation over the long term.

The length of the pattern may need months or even years to develop. Investors should be aware of the probable amount of time required for a complete market rise.

Simply put, the primary objective of spotting the bullish basing pattern is to predict a significant move in price trend from breakout of resistance.

Image 5.15: Bullish basing continuation pattern

Trend: The pattern develops when the price rises and stabilises for a lengthy time, forming a bullish basing; the prevailing trend should be upwards prior to the occurrence of the pattern.

Entry: Enter the market when the pattern's neckline is broken. Look for candle closes above the neckline (for the bullish basing)

Stop-loss: The stop-loss is placed just below the neckline at the recent swing low, when trading the bullish basing.

Profit target: Profit objective is determined by measuring the actual pattern's height and extending that distance from the neckline break.

Volume: When price finally breaks out of resistance, there should be a significant uptick in volume.

Bearish Basing

A bearish basing is a technical analysis chart pattern recognised by price movements that, when graphed, resemble an inverted 'U' shape.

Bearish basing occurs towards the end of extended downward trends and may indicate a price continuation over the long term.

The length of the pattern may need months or even years to develop. Investors should be aware of the probable amount of time required for a complete market decline.

Simply put, the primary objective of spotting the bearish basing pattern is to predict a significant move in price trend from breakdown of support from the breakdown zone towards downside.

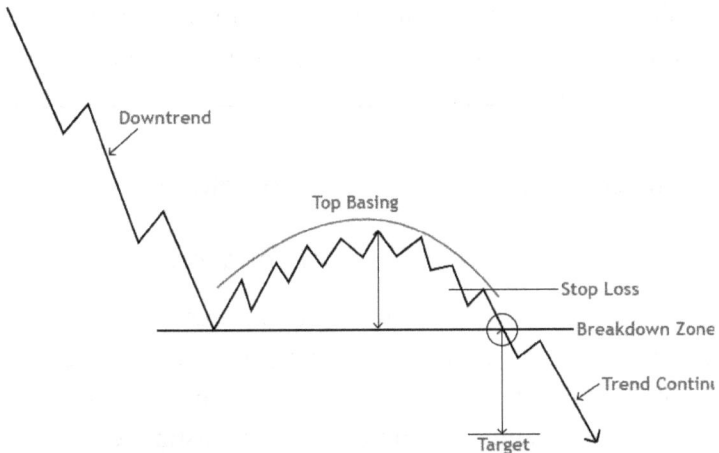

Image 5.16: Bearish basing continuation pattern

Trend: The pattern develops when the price falls and stabilises for a lengthy time, forming a bearish basing; the prevailing trend should be down prior to the occurrence of the pattern.

Entry: Enter the market when the pattern's neckline is broken. Look for candle closes below the neckline (for the bearish basing)

Stop-loss: The stop-loss is placed just above the neckline at the recent swing high, when trading the bearish basing continuation pattern.

Profit target: The profit objective is determined by measuring the actual pattern's height and extending that distance from the neckline break.

Volume: When price finally breaks down from support, there should be a significant uptick in volume.

Head and Shoulder Continuation Pattern

Bullish Head and Shoulder Continuation Pattern

The head and shoulders are one of a series of chart patterns commonly seen as trend-reversing. On closer inspection, however, the head and shoulders may also serve as a continuation. There are some significant distinctions between continuation and reversal patterns, which may help you make profitable trades and prevent losing ones.

Simply put, the head and shoulders pattern may indicate a continuation rather than a reversal, but this function occurs less often. The head and shoulders continuation pattern emerges in a decline, but the inverse head and shoulders pattern shows an upswing, thus you are unlikely to mistake them. The following chart demonstrates a negative continuation pattern.

This continuation pattern arises after a rapid uptrend (or run down). This makes the head and shoulders pattern seem more like a consolidation pattern than a reversal pattern when seen from a broader perspective.

Image 5.17 shows a bullish heads and shoulders continuation which has the same characteristics as reversal. However, heads and shoulders continuation signifies a prevailing trend continuation and reversal head and shoulders indicate trend reversal.

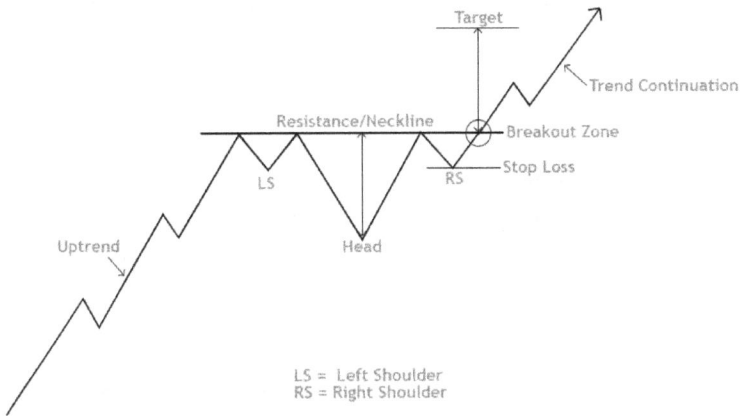

Image 5.17: Bullish head and shoulders continuation pattern

Trend: The prevailing trend of the security should be up as it shows that we are going with the trend and indicates upside momentum.

Entry: We will enter the market once the breakout happens from resistance towards upside.

Stop-loss: We will place a stop-loss at the recent swing low (just below right shoulder) or breakout candles' low (if the breakout candle is strong).

Profit target: After breaking through the neckline resistance, the projected target is found by measuring the distance from the neckline to the bottom of the head. The neckline is then added to this distance to get a price target.

Volume: If the bullish heads and shoulders continuation is forming up with strong volume at the breakout zone then it shows that more market participants are interested in buying the security.

Bearish Head and Shoulders Continuation Pattern

The head and shoulders continuation pattern emerges in a decline, but the inverse head and shoulders pattern shows an upswing, thus you are unlikely to mistake them. The following chart demonstrates a bearish continuation pattern.

This continuation pattern arises after a rapid downtrend (or run down). This makes the head and shoulders pattern seem more like a consolidation pattern than a reversal pattern when seen from a broader perspective.

Image 5.18 shows a bearish head and shoulders continuation which has the same characteristics as reversal. However, head and shoulders continuation signifies prevailing trend continuation and reversal head and shoulders indicate trend reversal.

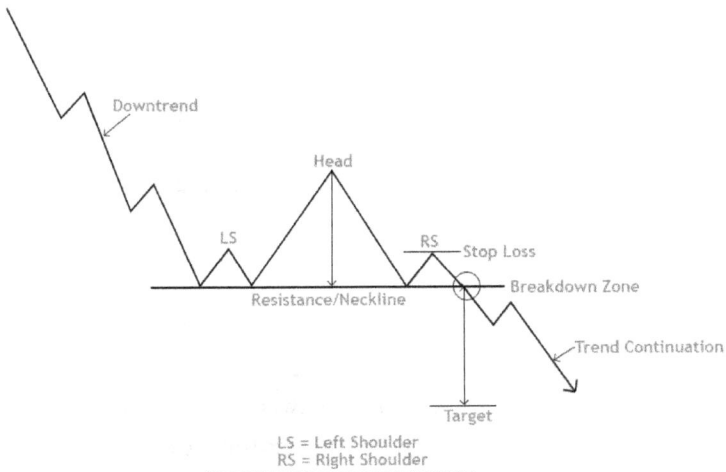

Image 5.18: Bearish head and shoulders continuation pattern

Trend: The prevailing trend of the security should be down as it shows that we are going with the trend and indicates downside momentum.

Entry: We will enter the market once the breakdown occurs with the price moving from support towards downside.

Stop-loss: We will place stop-loss at the recent swing high (just above the right shoulder) or breakdown candles high (if the breakdown candle is strong).

Profit target: After breaking through the neckline support, the projected target is found by measuring the distance from the neckline to the top of the head. The neckline is then added to this distance to get a downside price target.

Volume: If the bearish head and shoulder continuation is forming up with a strong volume at the breakdown zone then it shows that more market participants are interested in a short position in the security.

Descending Broadening Wedge Continuation

A descending broadening wedge continuation is a bullish chart pattern. It is generated by two falling lines that diverge.

If there is excellent oscillation between the two downward lines, a descending broadening wedge continuation is confirmed. The top line represents resistance, while the lower line represents support.

To authenticate the pattern, each of these lines must have been touched at least twice.

If the price line meets the support or resistance at least three times, the line is considered valid.

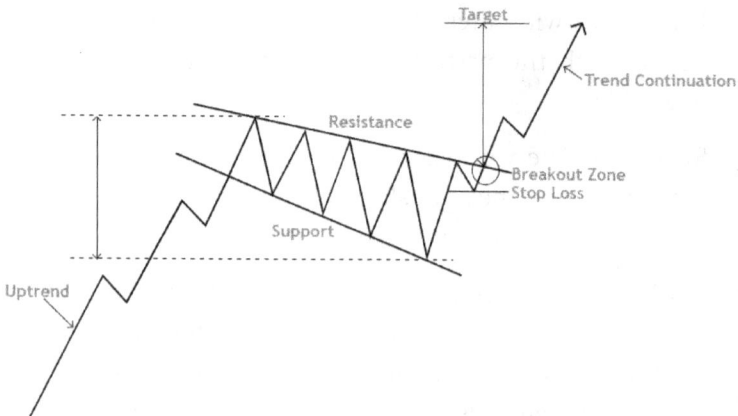

Image 5.19: Descending broadening wedge continuation pattern

Trend: To be considered a descending broadening wedge continuation pattern, there should be evidence of a prior uptrend.

Entry: The entry will be taken as the price action breaks the falling resistance of a bullish continuation pattern.

Stop-loss: Set your stop-loss just below the falling resistance line of the pattern at the recent swing low (just below the resistance).

Profit target: The profit target will be estimated from the pattern top edge swing to the bottom edge of swing (refer to image 5.19) and add the same distance to neckline at the breakout zone.

Volume: When price finally breaks out of falling resistance of the pattern, there should be a significant uptick in volume.

Ascending Broadening Wedge Continuation

An ascending broadening wedge continuation is a bearish chart pattern. It is generated by two rising lines that diverge.

If there is good oscillation between the two upward lines, an ascending broadening wedge continuation is confirmed. The top rising line represents resistance while the lower rising line represents support.

To authenticate the pattern, each of these lines must have been touched at least twice.

If the price line meets the support or resistance at least three times, the line is considered valid.

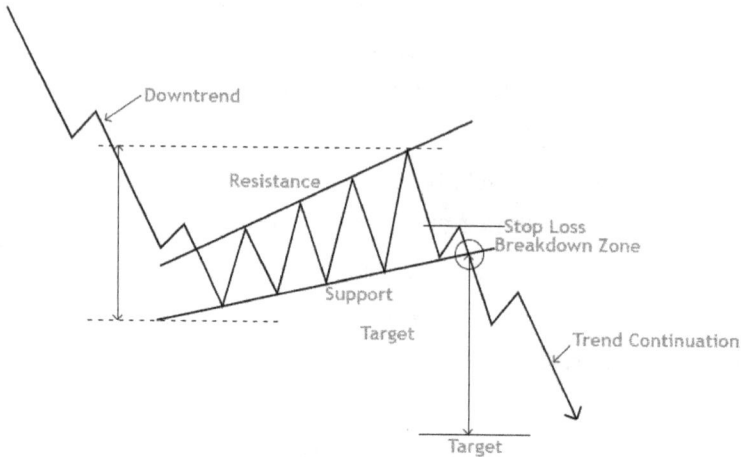

Image 5.20: Ascending broadening wedge continuation pattern

Entry: Enter the market as the price action breaks the rising support of a bearish continuation pattern.

Stop-loss: Set your stop-loss just above the rising support line of the pattern at the recent swing high (just above the support).

Profit target: The profit target will be estimated from the pattern bottom edge swing to top edge of swing (refer to image 5.20) and add the same distance to neckline at the breakdown zone.

Volume: When price finally breaks out of rising support in the pattern, there should be a significant uptick in volume.

Channel

Descending Channel

A trading channel is like a horizontal trading range that has been turned at an angle. While the range trades between fairly well-defined levels of support and resistance over time, the angular channel has lower lows (a descending channel) as price action moves on the chart.

A descending channel pattern is both a continuation and a reversal chart pattern. It depends on how the trade goes.

For example, if you trade within the channel and in the direction of the channel trend, it will act as a continuation chart pattern. If you trade the channel breakout, on the other hand, it will work as a reversal chart pattern.

Image 5.21 shows a pattern called a continuation descending channel pattern.

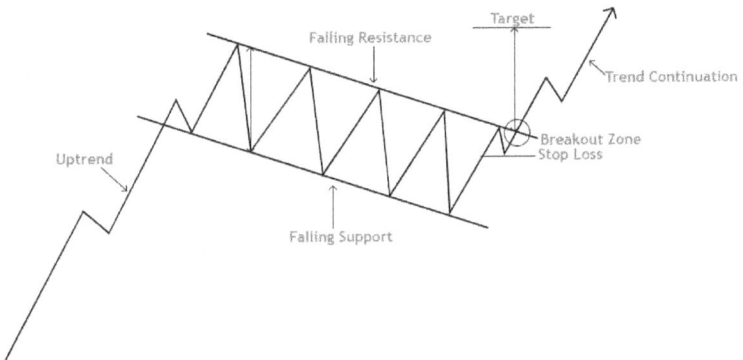

Image 5.21: Continuation descending channel pattern

Trend: The trend prior to the formation of descending channel pattern should be up.

Entry: One should take entry into long position once the stock has breached the upper band of the channel and has closed above it.

Stop-loss: A stop-loss can generally be placed a few rupees below the final swing low that occurred before the breakout.

Profit target: Once the neckline (upper band of channel) of a descending channel is broken, the trader must calculate the distance between the highest and lowest points in the descending channel formation and add it to the breakout point to determine the possible move.

Volume: When price finally breaks out of falling resistance or neckline, there should be a significant uptick in volume.

Ascending Channel

While the range trades between fairly well-defined levels of support and resistance over time, the angular channel has higher highs (an ascending channel) as price action moves on the chart.

An ascending channel pattern is both a continuation and a reversal chart pattern. It depends on how the trade goes.

For example, if you trade within the channel and in the direction of the channel trend, it will act as a continuation chart pattern. If you trade the channel breakout, on the other hand, it will work as a reversal chart pattern.

Image 5.22 shows a pattern called a continuation ascending channel pattern.

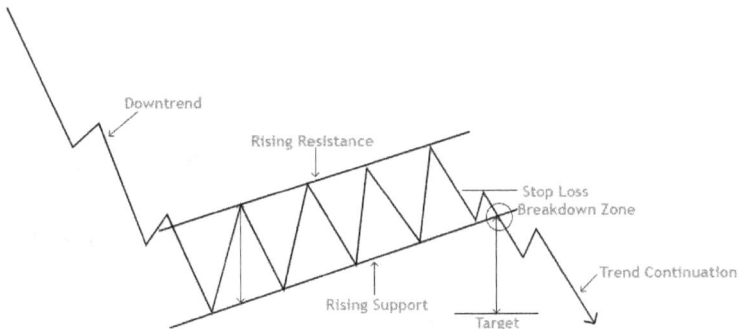

Image 5.22: Ascending channel pattern

Trend: The trend prior to the formation of ascending channel pattern should be up.

Entry: Once the stock has breached the lower band of the channel and has closed below it, enter a short position.

Stop-loss: A stop-loss can generally be placed a few rupees above the final swing high that occurred before the breakdown.

Profit target: Once the neckline (lower band of the channel) of an ascending channel is broken, the trader must calculate the distance between the highest and lowest points in the ascending channel formation and add it to the breakdown point in order to determine the possible move.

Volume: When price finally breaks out of falling resistance or neckline, there should be a significant uptick in volume.

II Reversal Patterns

Chart patterns are studied by technical analysts because they provide a strong indicator of market behaviour. Certain chart patterns can suggest when a trend might reverse direction.

We will focus on reversal patterns and continuation patterns as the two primary chart patterns as we have already discussed continuation patterns in the previous charts.

Reversal patterns imply that a significant trend reversal is occurring. Continuation patterns signal that the trend is only halting briefly for a correction and will likely continue in the same direction as discussed before.

A previous trend is required for the formation of any price pattern. Breaking a key trend line or neckline is often the first warning of an approaching trend reversal or continuance. The longer it takes to complete a pattern and the higher the price variations inside it, the greater the likelihood that the next move will be significant. Reversal patterns need much more time to form than continuation patterns.

Broadening Pattern

Broadening Bottom

A bottom that is broadening is a bullish reversal pattern. The pattern is made by two horizontally symmetric diverging lines. So it is an inverted symmetrical triangle.

Therefore, the oscillations between the two triangle ends become larger. To verify a line, it must be touched at least twice.

According to Thomas N. Bulkowski, a broadening bottom must be confirmed by at least two minor highs and two minor lows.

Broadening bottom develops as a result of a downward trend. It is further subdivided into an upward breakout and a downward breakout, with image 5.23 showing a bullish reversal pattern.

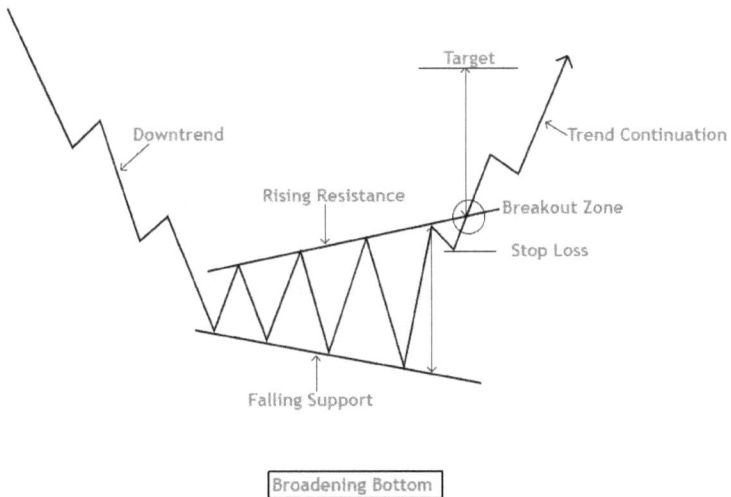

Image 5.23: Broadening bottom reversal pattern

Trend: The trend prior to the formation of broadening bottom pattern should be down.

Entry: One should take entry into long position once the stock has breached the upper band of broadening pattern and has closed above it.

Stop-loss: A stop-loss can generally be placed a few rupees below the final swing low that occurred before the breakout.

Profit target: Once the neckline (upper band of pattern) of a broadening bottom is broken, the trader must calculate the distance between the highest and lowest points of pattern end base (refer to image 5.23) and add it to the breakout point in order to determine the possible up move.

Volume: When price finally breaks out of rising resistance or neckline, there should be a significant uptick in volume.

Broadening Top Reversal Pattern

A top that is broadening is a bearish reversal pattern. The pattern is made by two horizontally symmetric diverging lines. Therefore, it is an inverted symmetrical triangle.

So, the oscillations between the two triangle ends are becoming larger. To verify a line, it must be touched at least twice.

According to Thomas N. Bulkowski, a broadening top must be confirmed by at least two minor highs and two minor lows.

A broadening bottom develops as a result of a downward trend. It is further subdivided into an upward breakout and a downward breakout, with image 5.24 showing a bearish reversal pattern.

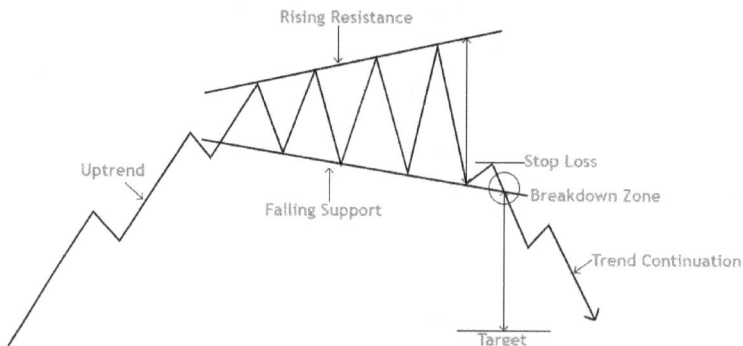

Image 5.24: Broadening top reversal pattern

Trend: The trend prior to the formation of broadening top pattern should be up.

Entry: One should enter a short position once the stock has breached the lower band of broadening pattern and has closed below it.

Stop-loss: A stop-loss can generally be placed a few rupees above the final swing high that occurred before the breakdown.

Profit target: Once the neckline (lower band of a pattern) of a broadening bottom is broken, the trader must calculate the distance between the highest and lowest points of pattern end base (refer to image 5.24) and add it to the breakdown point in order to determine the possible down move.

Volume: When price finally breaks down from falling support or neckline, there should be a significant uptick in volume.

Right-angled Descending Broadening Wedge Reversal Pattern

A right-angled descending broadening wedge is a bullish reversal chart pattern. It is an inverted ascending triangle produced by two diverging lines, the resistance being a horizontal line and the support a bearish downward slope. Therefore, the oscillations between the two triangle ends are becoming larger. To verify a line, it must be tapped at least twice.

The right-angled descending broadening wedge illustrates the increasing worry and uncertainty of traders.

If the chart pattern is not promptly identified, the price changes may look completely random, luring in many traders.

The creation of this pattern must be preceded by a bearish trend.

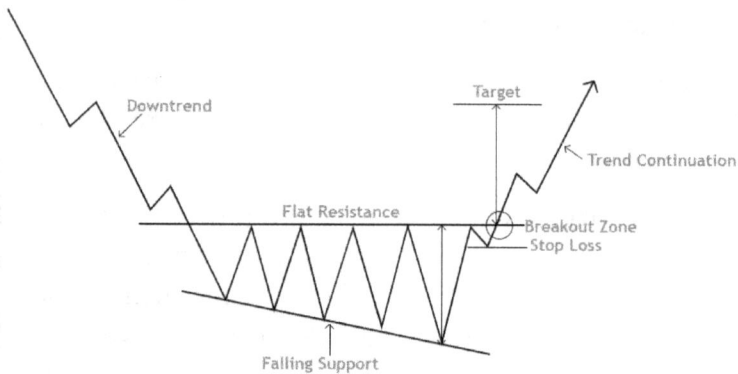

Image 5.25: Right-angled descending broadening wedge pattern

Trend: To be considered a right-angled descending broadening wedge pattern, there should be evidence of a prior downtrend.

Entry: The entry will be taken as the price action breaks the resistance of bullish reversal pattern.

Stop-loss: Set your stop-loss just below the resistance line of the pattern at the recent swing low (just below the resistance).

Profit target: You can figure out the estimated move by measuring the height of the pattern's end base and applying that number to the breakout.

Volume: When the price finally breaks out from the resistance of right-angled descending broadening wedge, there should be a significant uptick in volume.

Right-angled Ascending Broadening Wedge Reversal Pattern

This pattern shows downward reversal. The pattern is made by two diverging lines, the support is a horizontal line and the resistance is a slanting bullish one, therefore it is an inverted descending triangle. So, the oscillations between the two triangle ends become larger. To verify a line, it must be touched at least twice.

A right-angled ascending broadening wedge illustrates the increasing worry and uncertainty of investors.

If the pattern is not identified soon enough, the fluctuations may look completely random, luring in many investors.

The creation of this pattern must be preceded by a bullish trend.

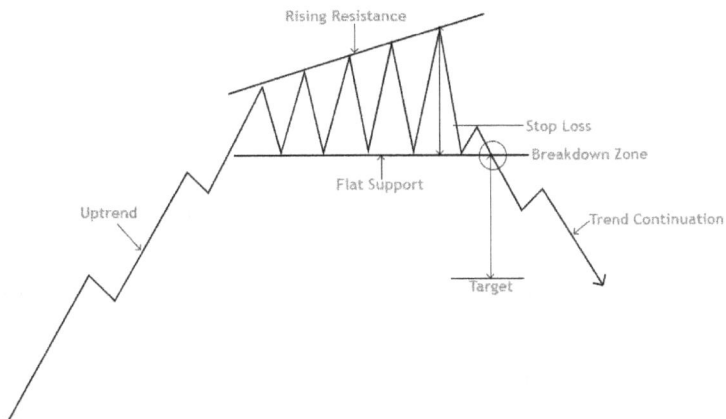

Image 5.26: Right-angled ascending broadening wedge pattern

Trend: To be considered a right-angled ascending broadening wedge pattern, there should be evidence of a prior uptrend.

Entry: As the price action breaks the support of bearish reversal pattern, enter the market.

Stop-loss: Set your stop-loss just above the support line of the pattern at the recent swing high (just above the support).

Profit target: You can figure out the estimated move by measuring the height of the pattern's end base and applying that number to the breakdown towards downside.

Volume: When the price finally breaks down from the support of right-angled ascending broadening wedge, there should be a significant uptick in volume at the time of breakdown.

Descending broadening wedge

A descending broadening wedge is a bullish reversal chart pattern. It is generated by two falling lines that diverge.

If there is excellent oscillation between the two downward lines, a descending widening wedge is confirmed. The top line represents resistance, while the lower line represents support.

To authenticate the pattern, each of these lines must have been touched at least twice.

If the price line meets the support or resistance at least three times, the line is deemed valid.

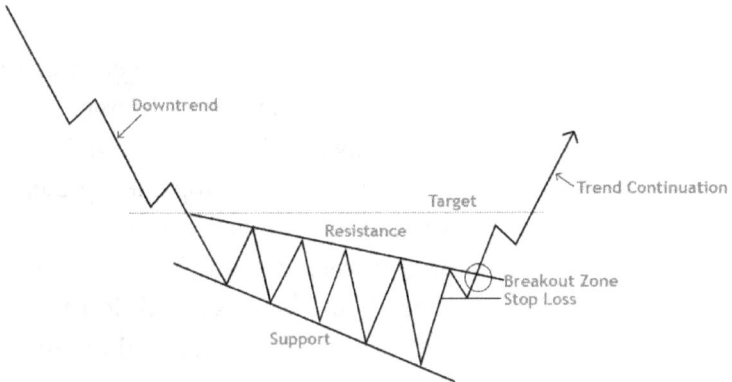

Image 5.27: Descending broadening wedge reversal pattern

Trend: To be considered a descending broadening wedge pattern, there should be evidence of a prior downtrend.

Entry: The entry will be taken as the price action breaks the resistance of bullish reversal pattern.

Stop-loss: Set your stop-loss just below the falling resistance line of the pattern at the recent swing low (just below the resistance).

Profit target: The profit target will be placed at the point where the two lines started broadening from the breakout zone.

Volume: When price finally breaks out of falling resistance of the pattern, there should be a significant uptick in volume.

Ascending broadening wedge

An ascending broadening wedge is a bearish reversal chart pattern. It is generated by two rising lines that diverge.

If there is good oscillation between the two upward lines, a broadening ascending wedge is verified. The top line represents resistance, while the lower line represents support.

To authenticate the pattern, each of these lines must have been touched at least twice. A line is considered 'legitimate' if the price line meets the support or resistance three times or more.

This indicates that the ascending expanding wedge pattern is acceptable if the price strikes the support line at least three times and the resistance line at least twice (or the support line at least twice and the resistance line three times).

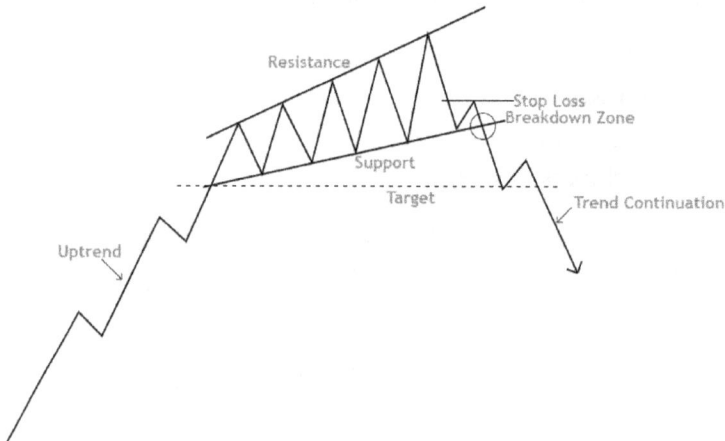

Image 5.28: Ascending broadening wedge reversal pattern

Trend: To be considered an ascending broadening wedge pattern, there should be evidence of a prior uptrend.

Entry: As the price action breaks the rising support line of a bearish reversal pattern, enter the market.

Stop-loss: Set your stop-loss just above the rising support line of the pattern at the recent swing high (just above the resistance).

Profit target: The profit target will be placed at the point where the patterns two lines started broadening from the breakout zone.

Volume: When the price finally breaks out of rising support of the pattern, there should be a significant uptick in volume towards downside.

Bump and Run Reversal Bottom

Thomas Bulkowski identified the bump and run reversal pattern (BARR) when there is a rapid increase or decrease in the price of an asset due to excessive speculation and volume spike.

The formation consists of three phases: the lead-in, the bump, and the run. The premise behind this pattern is that the price will make a short-term retracement back to a crucial level of support or resistance after a big advance in one direction.

The key to successfully trading with this pattern is identifying an entry opportunity once the run phase starts. Consider joining the market when the price breaches the falling trend line that precedes it, (either the falling trend line of the bump phase or larger falling trend line of the pattern).

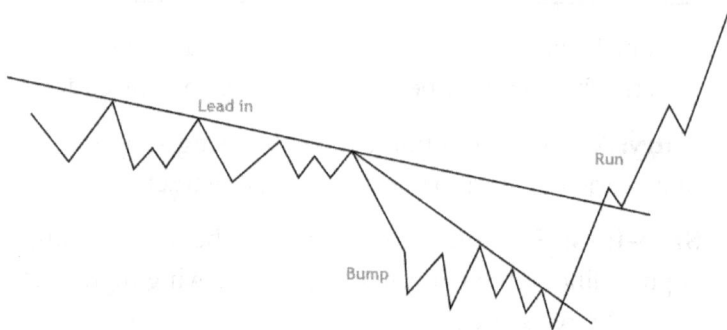

Image 5.29: Bump and run reversal pattern

Trend: To be considered a bump and run reversal pattern, there should be evidence of a prior downtrend.

Entry: As the price action breaks out from the falling resistance, either falling trend line in the bump phase or larger degree trend line of the of bullish reversal pattern, enter the market.

Stop-loss: Set your stop-loss just below the falling resistance line of the pattern at the recent swing low (just below the falling resistance).

Profit target: Your target profit is the height of the bump, and your stop-loss is determined on your risk tolerance. In this case, you may place your stop-loss slightly below your entry point at the recent swing low as mentioned above.

Volume: When price finally breaks out of falling resistance of the pattern, there should be a significant uptick in volume.

Bump and Run Reversal Top

The bump and run reversal pattern formation consists of three phases: the lead-in, the bump, and the run. The premise behind this pattern is that the price will make a short-term retracement back to a crucial level of support or resistance after a big advance in one direction.

The key to successfully trading this pattern is identifying an entry opportunity once the run phase starts. Consider joining the market, that is, taking a short position when the price breaches the rising trend line that precedes it, (either the falling trend line of the bump phase or larger rising trend line of the pattern).

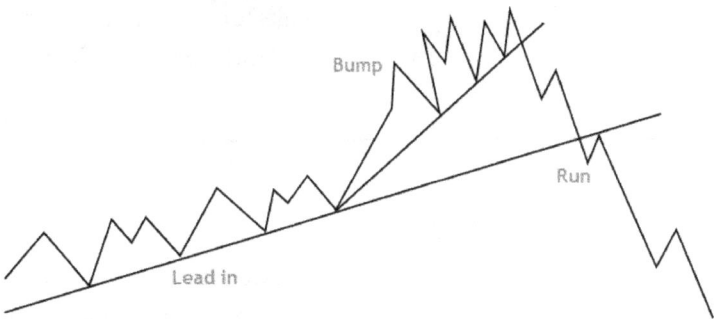

Image 5.30: Bump and run reversal pattern

Trend: To be considered a bump and run reversal pattern, there should be evidence of a prior uptrend.

Entry: As the price action breaks down from the rising resistance, either falling trend line in the bump phase or larger degree trend line of the bullish reversal pattern (where the run phase starts after the breach), enter the market.

Stop-loss: Set your stop-loss just above the rising resistance line of the pattern at the recent swing high (just above the either of the rising resistance).

Profit target: Your target profit is the height of the bump, and your stop-loss is determined by your risk tolerance. In this case, you may place your stop-loss slightly above your entry point at the recent swing high as mentioned above.

Volume: When price finally breaks down from rising resistance in the pattern, there should be a significant uptick in volume.

Cup With Handle Bottom

This is a bullish reversal pattern that shows a period of consolidation followed by a breakout. The pattern is made up of two parts: the cup and the handle. After a decline, the cup takes the shape of a bowl or a bottom that gets rounder.

As the cup is finished, a trading range forms on the right side, and the handle comes together. The trend will reverse if the price breaks out of its trading range around the handle.

The duration of the cup might vary from one to six months, and on occasion, much longer. Ideally, the handle will develop and be finished within one to four weeks.

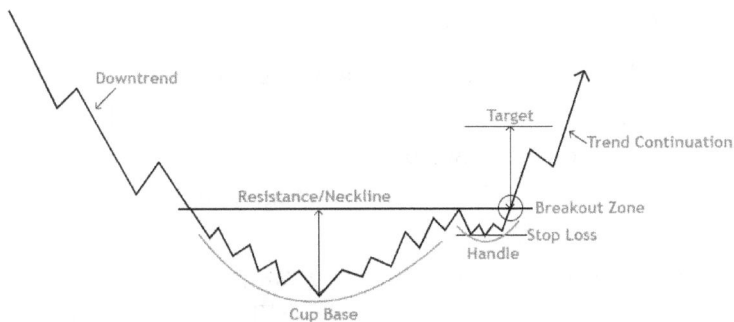

Image: 5.31: Cup with handle bottom pattern

Trend: To qualify as a reversal pattern, there must be a preceding downtrend. The trend should ideally be a few months old and not very mature. The more mature the trend, the lower the probability that the pattern represents a reversal and the lower the potential for upside growth.

Entry: The purchase point happens when a stock breaks out or advances above the level of resistance or neckline.

Stop-loss: Stop-loss orders for bullish cup and handle reversal patterns are often placed slightly below the breakout point (recent swing low in the handle's bottom area).

Profit target: We can estimate the price objective after the breakout by measuring the distance from the top of the cup to the bottom of the cup and adding that amount to the purchase point.

Volume: When price finally breaks out over the handle's resistance, there should be a significant uptick in volume.

Cup With Handle Top

Cup with handle top pattern is a bearish reversal pattern that shows a period of consolidation followed by a breakout. The pattern is made up of two parts: the cup and the handle. After a decline, the cup takes the shape of an inverse bowl or a top that gets rounder.

As the cup is finished, a trading range forms on the right side, and the handle comes together. The trend will reverse if the price breaks out of its trading range around the handle towards downside.

The duration of the cup might vary from one to six months, and on occasion much longer. Ideally, the handle will develop and be finished within one to four weeks.

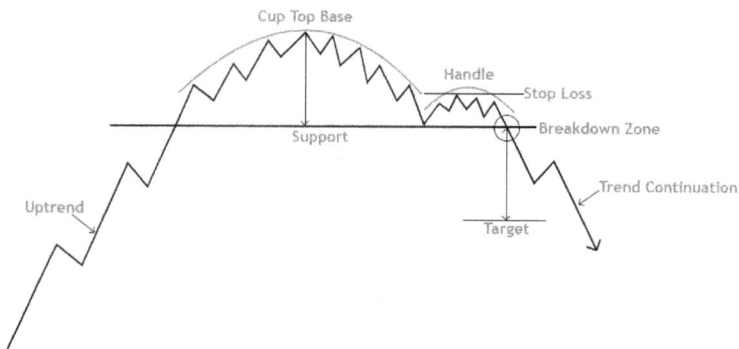

Image 5.32: Cup with handle top pattern

Trend: To qualify as a reversal pattern, there must be a preceding uptrend. The trend should ideally be a few months old and not very mature. The more mature the trend, the lower the probability that the pattern represents a reversal and the lower the potential for downside growth.

Entry: The purchase point happens when a stock breaks down or declines below the level of support or neckline.

Stop-loss: Stop-loss orders for bearish cup and handle reversal patterns are often placed slightly above the breakdown point (recent swing high in the handle's top area).

Profit target: We can estimate the price objective after the breakdown by measuring the distance from the top of the cup to the bottom of the cup and adding that amount to the purchase point.

Volume: When price finally breaks down over the handle's support, there should be a significant uptick in volume.

Rounding Bottom

A rounding bottom is a technical analysis chart pattern recognised by price movements that, when graphed, resemble a 'U' shape.

Rounding bottom occur towards the end of extended downward trends and may indicate a price reversal over the long term.

The length of the pattern may need months or even years to develop. Investors should be aware of the probable amount of time required for a complete market decline.

Simply put, the primary objective of spotting the rounded bottom pattern is to predict a significant change in price trend from downward to upward.

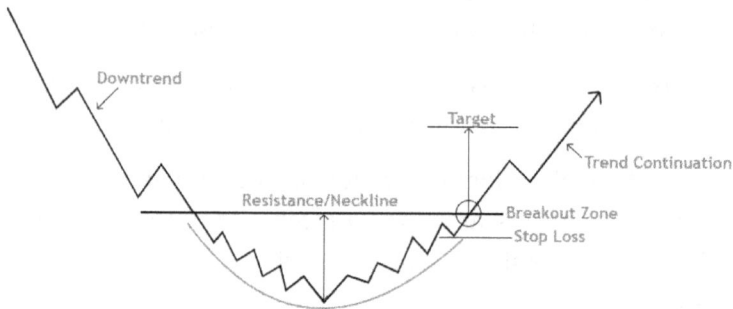

Image 5.33: Rounding bottom pattern

Trend: The pattern develops when the price falls and stabilises over a long period of time, forming a rounded top; the prevailing trend should be downwards prior to the occurrence of the pattern.

Entry: Enter the market when the pattern's neckline is broken. Look for candle closes above the neckline (for the rounded bottom).

Stop-loss: The stop-loss is placed below the neckline at the recent swing low, when trading the rounded bottom.

Profit target: Profit objective is determined by measuring the actual pattern's height and extending that distance from the neckline break.

Volume: When price finally breaks out of resistance, there should be a significant uptick in volume.

Rounding Top

A rounding top is a technical analysis chart pattern recognised by price movements that, when graphed, resemble an upside-down U.

Rounding tops occur towards the end of extended upward trends and may indicate a price reversal over the long term.

The length of the pattern may need months or even years to develop. Investors should be aware of the probable amount of time required for a complete market decline.

Simply put, the primary objective of spotting the rounded top pattern is to predict a significant change in price trend from upward to downward.

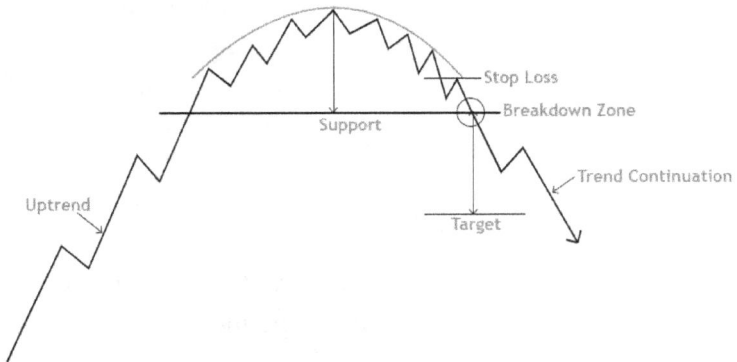

Image 5.34: Rounding top pattern

Trend: The pattern develops when the price rises and stabilises for a long time, forming a rounded bottom; the prevailing trend should be up prior to the occurrence of the pattern.

Entry: Enter the market when the pattern's neckline is broken. Look for candle closes below the neckline (for the rounded top)

Stop-loss: The stop-loss is placed just above the neckline at the recent swing high, when trading the rounded top.

Profit target: Profit objective is determined by measuring the actual pattern's height and extending that distance from the neckline break towards downside.

Volume: When price finally breaks out of support or neckline, there should be a significant uptick in volume.

Head and Shoulder Patterns

Head and Shoulder Bottom

Head and shoulders pattern shows that a trend is about to change. It is one that traders know the most about, which is why they do well with it.

The pattern is the same as a triple bottom in every way except that the second bottom is higher than the first two.

The shoulder is made up of the first and third peaks, which are about the same height. The head is made up of the second peak, which is taller than the shoulder peaks.

In theory, both shoulders should be the same height, and the line of the neck should be straight.

In real life, shoulders aren't always the same height and the neckline can go up or down (depending on the shape of the shoulders in the pattern).

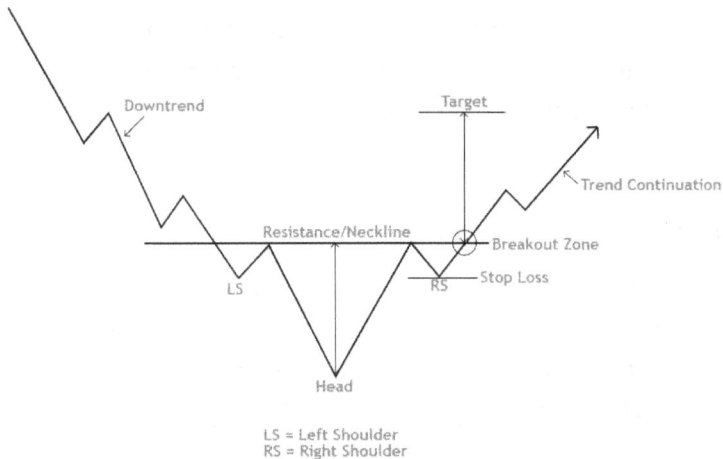

Downtrend

Target

Trend Continuation

Resistance/Neckline

Breakout Zone

LS

RS

Stop Loss

Head

LS = Left Shoulder
RS = Right Shoulder

Image 5.35: Head and shoulders bottom pattern

Trend: For this to be a reversal pattern, it is important to show that there was a downtrend before. A head and shoulders bottom can't happen if there hasn't been a downtrend to reverse.

Entry: The head and shoulders bottom pattern remains incomplete (and the downtrend is not reversed) until the resistance at the neckline is broken. This must occur in a convincing way for a head and shoulders bottom and this is when we take entry.

Stop-loss: Stop-loss should be placed at the right shoulder which will also act as a recent swing low for the stock.

Profit target: After breaking through the neckline resistance, the projected target is found by measuring the distance from the neckline to the bottom of the head. The neckline is then added to this distance to get a price target.

Volume: In the head and shoulders top, volume is important, but in the head and shoulders bottom, it is very important. Without the right increase in volume, any breakout isn't likely to be true.

Head and Shoulders Top

The pattern is the same as a triple top in every way except in this case, the second top is higher than the first two.

The shoulder is made up of the first and third peaks, which are about the same height. The head is made up of the second peak, which is taller than the shoulder peaks.

In theory, both shoulders should be the same height, and the line of the neck should be straight.

In real life, shoulders aren't always the same height and the neckline can go up or down (depending on the shape of the shoulders in the pattern)

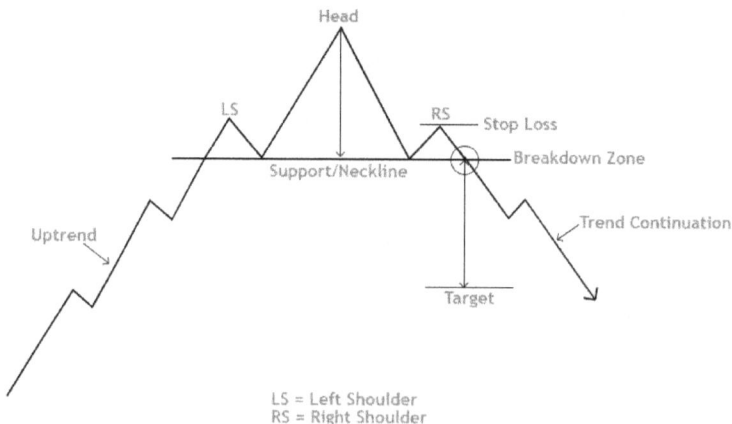

Image 5.36: Head and shoulders top

Trend: For this to be a reversal pattern, it is important to show that there was an uptrend before. A head and shoulders top can't happen if there hasn't been an uptrend to reverse.

Entry: The head and shoulders top pattern remains incomplete (and the uptrend is not reversed) until the support at the neckline is broken. This must occur in a convincing way for a head and shoulders top and this is when we enter into a trade.

Stop-loss: Stop-loss should be placed at the right shoulder which will also act as a recent swing high for the stock.

Profit target: After breaking through the neckline support, the projected target is found by measuring the distance from the neckline to the top of the head. The neckline is then added to this distance to get a price target.

Volume: In the head and shoulders top, volume is important. Without the right increase in volume, any breakout isn't likely to be true.

Complex Head and Shoulder Bottom

Typically, the head and shoulders pattern is a very reliable technical formation indicating a trend reversal in a stock.

The design has four unique components: the left shoulder, the head, the right shoulder, and the neckline. Each of these four components is required for the formation to exist.

Despite the fact that the great majority of head and shoulders formations I've witnessed resemble this one, it is essential for traders to realise that deviations occur.

Multiple or complex head and shoulder shapes describe these structures. These mutations include patterns with two left shoulders and one right shoulder, two right shoulders and two left shoulders, and many heads.

Despite having complex forms, the pattern's fundamental qualities remain the same. When the head and shoulders pattern is identified and the neckline is broken, it typically indicates that the stock price will increase.

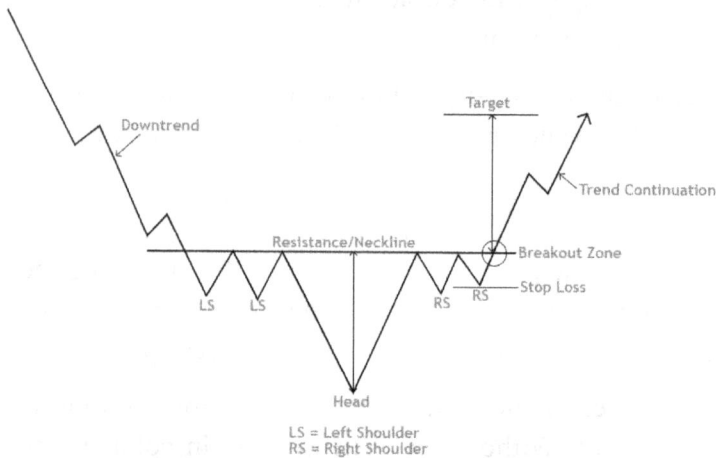

Image 5.37: Complex head and shoulders bottom

Trend: The pattern develops when the price falls and stabilises for a lengthy time, forming a complex head and shoulders bottom pattern; the prevailing trend should be down prior to the occurrence of the pattern.

Entry: Enter the market when the pattern's neckline is broken. Look for candle closes above the neckline.

Stop-loss: The stop-loss is placed just below the neckline at the recent swing low (at the right shoulder bottom), when trading the complex head and shoulder pattern.

Profit target: Profit objective is determined by measuring the actual pattern's height from bottom of the head to the neckline of the pattern and extending that distance from the neckline break toward upside.

Volume: When price finally breaks out of resistance or neckline, there should be a significant uptick in volume.

Complex Head and Shoulders Top

Typically, the head and shoulders pattern is a very reliable technical formation indicating a trend reversal in a stock.

The design has four unique components: the left shoulder, the head, the right shoulder, and the neckline. Each of these four components is required for the formation to exist.

Despite the fact that the great majority of head and shoulders formations I've witnessed resemble this one, it is essential for traders to realise that deviations occur.

Multiple or complex head and shoulder shapes describe these structures. These mutations include patterns with two left shoulders and one right shoulder, two right shoulders and two left shoulders, and many heads.

Despite having complex forms, the pattern's fundamental qualities remain the same. When the head and shoulders pattern is identified and the neckline is broken, it typically indicates that the stock price will decline.

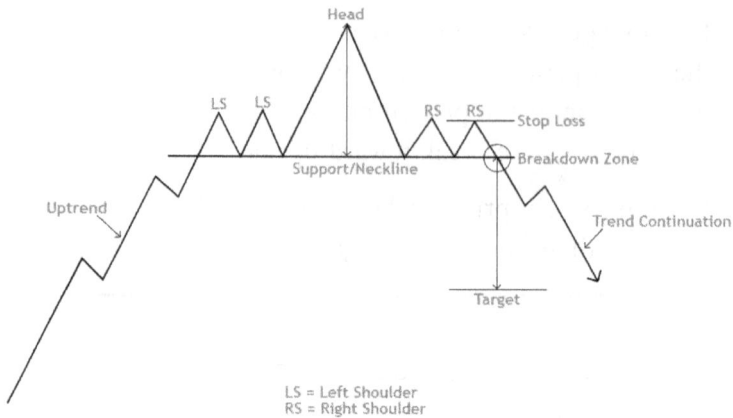

Image 5.38: Complex head and shoulders top

Trend: The pattern develops when the price rises and stabilises for a long time, forming a complex head and shoulder top pattern. The prevailing trend should be up prior to the occurrence of the pattern.

Entry: Enter the market when the pattern's neckline is broken. Look for candle closes below the neckline.

Stop-loss: The stop-loss is placed just above the neckline at the recent swing high (at the right shoulder top), when trading the complex head and shoulder pattern.

Profit target: Profit objective is determined by measuring the actual pattern's height from the top of the head to the neckline of the pattern and extending that distance from the neckline break toward downside.

Volume: When the price finally breaks out of support or neckline, there should be a significant uptick in volume.

Diamond Patterns

Diamond Bottom

A diamond bottom is a bullish chart pattern that reverses the trend.

The bottom of a diamond is made by two symmetrical triangles making a diamond pattern.

A bearish trend needs to precede a diamond bottom. This pattern indicates the end of the selling trend and trader uncertainty.

Volatility and oscillations grow during the first half of the pattern (that is, the symmetric broadening wedge pattern) and subsequently diminish during the second half (that is, in the symmetric triangle).

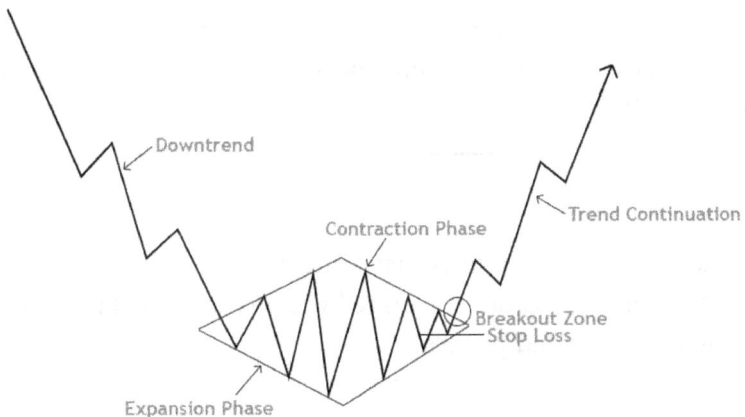

Image 5.39: Diamond bottom pattern

Trend: The trend prior to the formation of a diamond bottom pattern should be downwards.

Entry: One should take entry into long position once the stock has breached the upper band of contraction phase and has closed above it.

Stop-loss: A stop-loss can generally be placed a few rupees below the final swing low that occurred before the breakout.

Profit target: Once the neckline of a diamond formation is broken, the trader must calculate the distance between the highest and lowest points in the diamond formation and add it to the breakout point in order to determine the possible move.

Volume: When the price finally breaks out of resistance or neckline, there should be a significant uptick in volume.

Diamond Top

A diamond top is a bearish chart pattern that reverses the trend.

The top of a diamond is made by two symmetrical triangles making a diamond pattern.

A bullish trend needs to precede a diamond bottom. This pattern indicates the end of the buying trend and trader uncertainty.

Volatility and oscillations grow during the first half of the pattern (that is, the symmetric broadening wedge pattern) and subsequently diminish during the second half that is, in the symmetric triangle).

Diamond top formations only occur at the end of an upswing, while diamond bottom forms occur at the end of a decline.

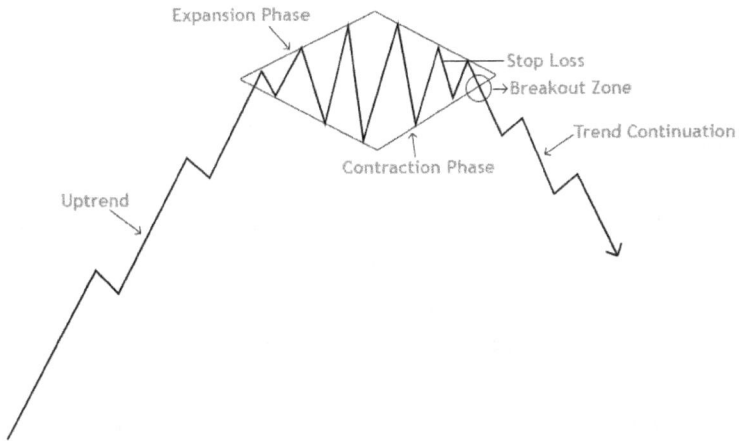

Image 5.40: Diamond top pattern

Trend: The trend prior to the formation of a diamond top pattern should be up.

Entry: One should enter a short position once the stock has breached the lower band of contraction phase and has closed below it.

Stop-loss: A stop-loss can generally be placed a few rupees above the final swing high that occurred before the breakout.

Profit target: Once the neckline of a diamond formation is broken, the trader must calculate the distance between the highest and lowest points in the diamond formation and add it to the breakout point to determine the possible move.

Volume: When price finally breaks out of support or neckline, there should be a significant uptick in volume.

Rectangle Patterns

Rectangle Bottom

You should usually trade rectangle bottom as a reversal pattern. There are situations when people aren't sure what to do, but usually decide to go with the trend and the trend change occurs after the breakout happens through resistance.

Both buyers and sellers seem to be in the same position. The same highs and lows are always put to the test. The market moves back and forth between two clear limits.

As seen in image 5.41, the price climbs in a robust down before beginning to consolidate between temporary support and resistance levels.

It continues to travel sideways, bouncing between these two parallel lines and generating the pattern's box-like shape.

The price then breaks out through the top level of resistance and continues its rise.

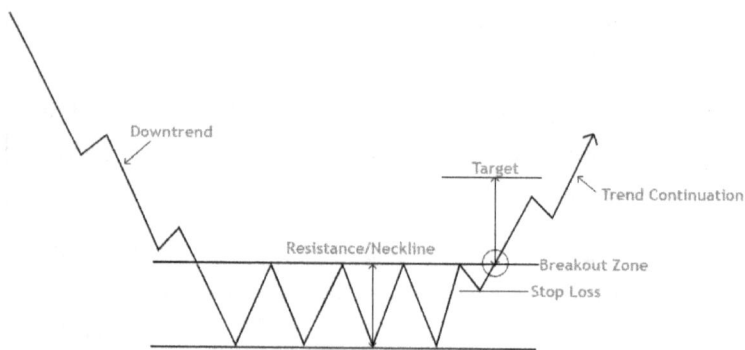

Image 5.41: Rectangle bottom reversal pattern

Trend: To be considered a bullish rectangle reversal pattern, there should be evidence of a prior downtrend.

Entry: As the price action breaks the resistance of bullish reversal rectangle pattern (rectangle bottom), enter the market.

Stop-loss: Set your stop-loss just below the resistance line of the rectangle at the recent swing low (just below the resistance).

Profit target: You can figure out the estimated move by measuring the height of the rectangle and applying that number to the breakout.

Volume: Patterns of volume in rectangles do not follow standard patterns. As a pattern develops, the volume will sometimes go down. On other occasions, the volume will change as the prices bounce between support and resistance. As the pattern gets older, the volume will rarely go up. If volume goes down, the best way to confirm a breakout is to look for a breakout with strong volume.

Rectangle Top

You should usually trade rectangle top as a reversal pattern. In such cases, people usually go with the trend and the trend change occur after the breakout happens through support towards downside.

Both buyers and sellers seem to be in the same position. The same highs and lows are always put to the test. The market moves back and forth between two clear limits.

As seen in image 5.42, the price climbs robustly upwards before beginning to consolidate between temporary support and resistance levels.

It continues to travel sideways, bouncing between these two parallel lines and generating the pattern's box-like shape.

The price then breaks down through the bottom level of support and continues its fall and marks a reversal towards the downside.

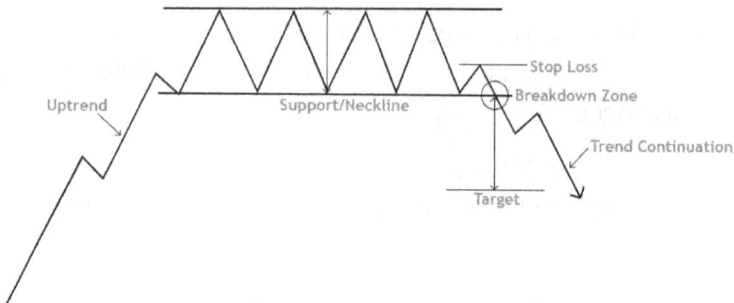

Image 5.42: Rectangle top reversal pattern

Trend: To be considered a bearish rectangle reversal pattern (rectangle top), there should be evidence of a prior uptrend.

Entry: As the price action breaks the support of bearish reversal rectangle pattern (rectangle top), enter the market.

Stop-loss: Set your stop-loss just above the support line of the rectangle at the recent swing high (just above the resistance).

Profit target: You can figure out the estimated move by measuring the height of the rectangle and applying that number to the breakdown.

Volume: Patterns of volume in rectangles do not follow standard patterns. As a pattern develops, the volume will sometimes go down. At times, the volume will change as the prices bounce between support and resistance. As the pattern gets older, the volume will rarely go up. If volume goes down, the best way to confirm a breakdown is to look for the breakdown with strong volume.

Double Bottom Chart Patterns

Double Bottom Adam and Adam

The Adam and Adam double bottom is defined by twin minor lows that seem to be narrow and lengthy, and take a decent amount of time to form the bottom as it is a long-term classical chart pattern.

Prices must close above the highest high between the two bottoms for this to qualify as a legitimate double bottom. This price is known as the breakout or confirmation price.

Observe this pattern during a downward trend. It signals a trend reversal, and a further bullish rise is expected. Due to the twin bottom design, two valleys can be seen. The first Adam has a thin V-shaped bottom, while the second Adam has the same form as the first Adam.

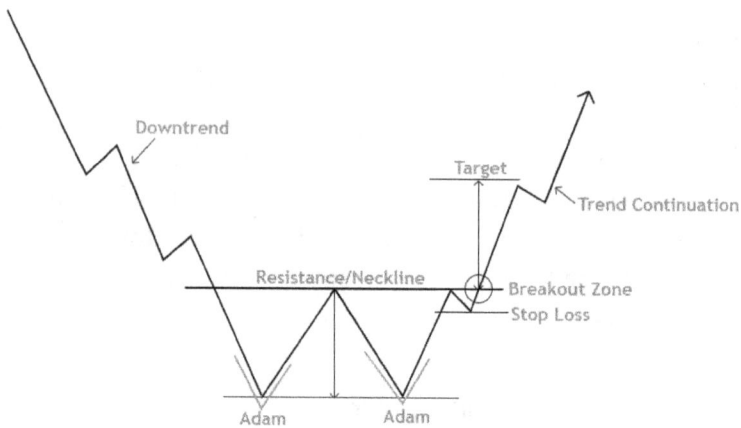

Image 5.43: Adam and Adam double bottom pattern

Trend: The pattern develops when the price falls and stabilises for a lengthy time, forming an Adam and Adam double pattern. The prevailing trend should be down prior to the occurrence of the pattern.

Entry: Enter the long position when the pattern's neckline is broken. Look for candle closes above the neckline.

Stop-loss: The stop-loss is placed just below the neckline at the recent swing low, when trading the Adam and Adam double pattern.

Profit target: Profit objective is determined by measuring the actual pattern's height from top of the neckline to bottom of the double bottom, and extending that distance from the neckline breakout toward upside.

Volume: When price finally breaks out of resistance or neckline, there should be a significant uptick in volume.

Double Bottom Adam and Eve

The double bottom Adam and Eve is defined by twin minor lows (the first one is V-shaped and the second one is rounded in shape) that seem to be narrow and lengthy, and take a decent amount of time to form the bottom as it is a long-term classical chart pattern.

Prices must close above the highest high between the two bottoms for this to qualify as a legitimate double bottom. This price is known as the breakout or confirmation price.

Observe this pattern during a downward trend. It signals a trend reversal, and a further bullish rise is expected. Due to the twin bottom design, two valleys can be seen. The first Adam has a thin, V-shaped bottom, while the second Eve is wider and more rounded in shape.

Image 5.44: Double bottom Adam and Eve

Trend: The pattern develops when the price falls and stabilises for a long time, forming an Adam and Eve double bottom. The prevailing trend should be down prior to the occurrence of the pattern.

Entry: Enter the long position when the pattern's neckline is broken. Look for candle closes above the neckline.

Stop-loss: The stop-loss is placed just below the neckline at the recent swing low, when trading the Adam and Eve double bottom pattern.

Profit target: Profit objective is determined by measuring the actual pattern's height from top of the neckline to bottom of the double bottom, and extending that distance from the neckline breakout toward upside.

Volume: When price finally breaks out of resistance or neckline, there should be a significant uptick in volume.

Double Bottom Eve and Adam

The Eve and Adam double bottom is defined by twin minor lows (first one is rounded in shape and second one is V-shaped) that seem to be narrow and lengthy, and take a significant amount of time to form the bottom as it is a long-term classical chart pattern.

Prices must close above the highest high between the two bottoms for this to qualify as a legitimate double bottom. This price is known as the breakout or confirmation price.

Observe this pattern during a downward trend. It signals a trend reversal, and a further bullish rise is expected. Due to the twin bottom design, two valleys can be seen. The first Eve is wider and more rounded like U shape, while the second Adam has a thin V-shaped bottom.

Image 5.45: Double Bottom Eve and Adam

Trend: The pattern develops when the price falls and stabilises for a lengthy period, forming an Eve and Adam double bottom. The prevailing trend should be down prior to the occurrence of the pattern.

Entry: Enter the long position when the pattern's neckline is broken. Look for candle closes above the neckline.

Stop-loss: The stop-loss is placed just below the neckline at the recent swing low, when trading the Eve and Adam double bottom pattern.

Profit target: Profit objective is determined by measuring the actual pattern's height from top of the neckline to bottom of the double bottom, and extending that distance from the neckline breakout toward upside.

Volume: When price finally breaks out of resistance or neckline, there should be a significant uptick in volume.

Eve and Eve Double Bottom

The Eve and Eve double bottom is defined by twin minor lows (first one is rounded in shape and second one is also rounded in shape) that seem to be narrow and lengthy, and take some time to form the bottom as it is a long-term classical chart pattern.

Prices must close above the highest high between the two bottoms for this to qualify as a legitimate double bottom. This price is known as the breakout or confirmation price.

Observe this pattern during a downward trend. It signals a trend reversal, and a further bullish rise is expected. Due to the twin bottom design, two valleys can be seen. The first Eve is wider and more rounded, while the second Eve also has the same shape like a rounded one.

Image 5.46: Double bottom Eve and Eve

Trend: The pattern develops when the price falls and stabilises for a long time, forming an Eve and Eve double bottom. The prevailing trend should be down prior to the occurrence of the pattern.

Entry: Enter the long position when the pattern's neckline is broken. Look for candle closes above the neckline.

Stop-loss: The stop-loss is placed just below the neckline at the recent swing low, when trading the Eve and Eve double bottom pattern.

Profit target: The profit objective is determined by measuring the actual pattern's height from the top of the neckline to bottom of the double bottom, and extending that distance from the neckline breakout toward upside.

Volume: When price finally breaks out of resistance or neckline, there should be a significant uptick in volume.

Double Top Chart Patterns

Adam and Adam Double Top

The Adam and Adam double top is defined by twin minor highs that seem to be narrow and lengthy, and take a decent amount of time to form the top as it is a long-term classical chart pattern.

Prices must close below the lowest low between the two tops for this to qualify as a legitimate double bottom. This price is known as the breakdown or confirmation price.

Observe this pattern during an upward trend. It signals a trend reversal, and a further bearish fall is expected. Due to the twin top design, two peaks can be seen. The first Adam has a thin A-shaped top, while the second Adam has the same form as the first Adam.

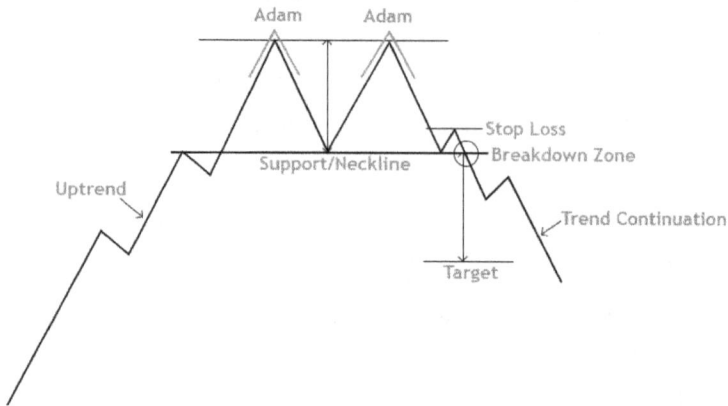

Image 5.47: Adam and Adam double top

Trend: The pattern develops when the price rises and stabilises for a long time, forming an Adam and Adam double top. The prevailing trend should be up, prior to the occurrence of the pattern.

Entry: Enter the short position when the pattern's neckline is broken. Look for candle closes below the neckline.

Stop-loss: The stop-loss is placed just above the neckline at the recent swing high, when trading the Adam and Adam double top pattern.

Profit target: The profit objective is determined by measuring the actual pattern's height from bottom of the neckline to top of the double top, and extending that distance from the neckline breakdown toward the downside.

Volume: When price of support or neckline finally breaks down, there should be a significant uptick in volume.

Adam and Eve Double Top

The Adam and Eve double top is defined by twin minor highs that seem to be narrow and lengthy, and take a decent amount of time to form the top as it is a long-term classical chart pattern.

Prices must close below the lowest low between the two tops for this to qualify as a legitimate double bottom. This price is known as the breakdown or confirmation price.

Observe this pattern during an upward trend. It signals a trend reversal, and a further bearish fall is expected. Due to the twin top design, two peaks can be seen. The first Adam has a thin A-shaped top, while the second Eve has an inverted U shape.

Image 5.48: Adam and Eve double top

Trend: The pattern develops when the price rises and stabilises for a long time, forming an Adam and Eve double top. The prevailing trend should be up, prior to the occurrence of the pattern.

Entry: Enter the short position when the pattern's neckline is broken. Look for candle closes below the neckline.

Stop-loss: The stop-loss is placed just above the neckline at the recent swing high, when trading the Adam and Eve double top pattern.

Profit target: The profit objective is determined by measuring the actual pattern's height from bottom of the neckline to the top of the double top, and extending that distance from the neckline breakdown toward downside.

Volume: When price of the support or neckline finally breaks down, there should be a significant uptick in volume.

Eve and Adam Double Top

The Eve and Adam double top is defined by twin minor highs that seem to be narrow and lengthy, and take a decent amount of time to form the top as it is the long-term classical chart pattern.

Prices must close below the lowest low between the two tops for this to qualify as a legitimate double bottom. This price is known as the breakdown or confirmation price.

Observe this pattern during an upward trend. It signals a trend reversal, and a further bearish fall is expected. Due to the twin top design, two peaks can be seen. The first Eve has the inverted U shape, while the second Eve has a thin A-shaped top.

Image 5.49: Eve and Adam double top

Trend: The pattern develops when the price rises and stabilises for a long time, forming an Eve and Adam double top. The prevailing trend should be up prior to the occurrence of the pattern.

Entry: Enter the short position when the pattern's neckline is broken. Look for candle closes below the neckline.

Stop-loss: The stop-loss is placed just above the neckline at the recent swing high, when trading the Eve and Adam double pattern.

Profit target: The profit objective is determined by measuring the actual pattern's height from bottom of the neckline to top of the double top, and extending that distance from the neckline breakdown toward downside.

Volume: When price of support or neckline finally breaks down, there should be a significant uptick in volume.

Eve and Eve Double Top

The Eve and Eve double top is defined by twin minor highs that seem to be narrow and lengthy, and take a decent amount of time to form the top as it is a long-term classical chart pattern.

Prices must close below the lowest low between the two tops for this to qualify as a legitimate double bottom. This price is known as the breakdown or confirmation price.

Observe this pattern during an upward trend. It signals a trend reversal, and a further bearish fall is expected. Due to the twin top design, two peaks can be seen. The first Eve has a thin A-shaped top, while the second Eve has the same form like the first top.

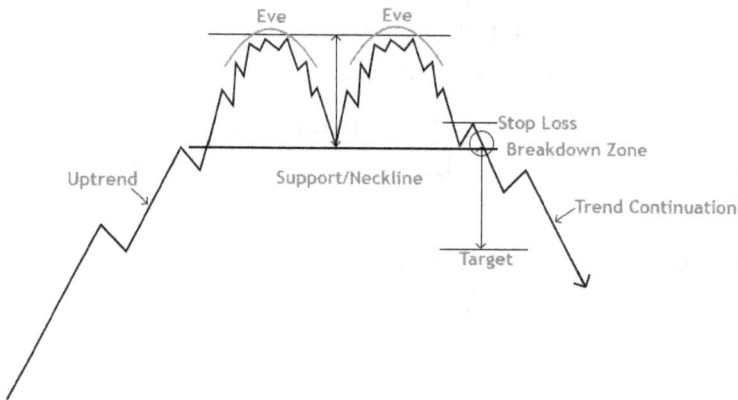

Image 5.50: Eve and Eve double top

Trend: The pattern develops when the price rises and stabilises for a long time, forming an Eve and Eve double top. The prevailing trend should be up prior to the occurrence of the pattern.

Entry: Enter the short position when the pattern's neckline is broken. Look for candle closes below the neckline.

Stop-loss: The stop-loss is placed just above the neckline at the recent swing high, when trading the Eve and Eve double top pattern.

Profit target: The profit objective is determined by measuring the actual pattern's height from bottom of the neckline to top of the double top, and extending that distance from the neckline breakdown toward the downside.

Volume: When price of support or neckline finally breaks down, there should be a significant uptick in volume.

Triple Bottom

The WV-shaped triple trough or triple bottom is a bullish chart pattern. The succession of three troughs indicates solid support. This is an indication of a potential reversal.

For the triple bottom in image 5.51, the support zone permits three price recoveries. The neckline of the pattern is created by the higher of the two bullish peaks. The price thus makes a first comeback and then returns to the support line. Typically, the size of the two troughs is same (as seen in image 5.51), although it is possible for the first trough to be smaller than the subsequent two.

Simply put, there are three lows that are the same, and then there is a break above resistance. Most of the time, these major reversal patterns take three to six months to form.

Image 5.51: Triple bottom reversal pattern

Trend: For any reversal pattern to work, there should already be a trend to change. For the triple bottom reversal to happen, there should be a clear downtrend.

Entry: As the price action breaks the resistance of bullish reversal triple top pattern, enter the market.

Stop-loss: A stop-loss can generally be placed a few rupees below the final swing low that occurred just before the breakout (recent swing low).

Profit target: The distance between the resistance break and lows may be measured and added to the resistance break to calculate a price target. The longer a pattern persists, the greater the significance of its final breakout.

Volume: Typically, as the triple bottom reversal develops, volume levels decrease. Occasionally, the volume rises around the lows. After the third low, an increase in volume on the advance and at the resistance breakout significantly strengthens the pattern's validity.

Triple Top

The MA-shaped triple peak or triple top is a bearish chart pattern. The succession of three peaks indicates solid resistance. This is an indication of a potential reversal towards downside.

For the triple top (image 5.52), the resistance zone permits three price recoveries. The neckline of the pattern is created by the lower of the two bearish troughs. The price thus makes a first comeback and then returns to the resistance line. Typically, the size of the two peaks is same (as seen in image 5.52), although it is possible for the first peak to be smaller than the subsequent two.

Simply put, there are three highs that are the same, and then there is a break below support. Most of the time, these major reversal patterns take three to six months to form.

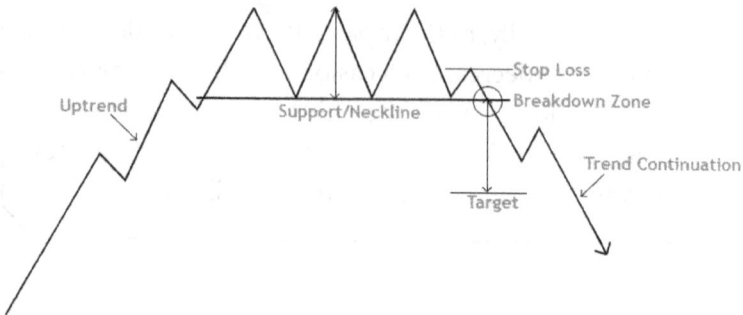

Image 5.52: Triple top reversal pattern

Trend: For any reversal pattern to work, there should already be a trend to change. For the triple bottom reversal to happen, there should be a clear uptrend.

Entry: The entry will be taken as the price action breaks the support of bearish reversal triple top pattern.

Stop-loss: A stop-loss can generally be placed a few rupees above the final swing high that occurred just before the breakdown (recent swing high).

Profit target: The distance between the resistance break and lows may be measured and added to the resistance break to calculate a price target. The longer a pattern persists, the greater the significance of its final breakout.

Volume: Typically, as the triple top reversal develops, volume levels decrease. Occasionally, the volume rises around the lows. After the third low, an increase in volume on the advance and at the support breakdown significantly strengthens the pattern's validity.

Island Bottom Reversal

An island reversal is a reversal pattern formed by two gaps and price movement between the gaps. These gaps indicate that the island reversal represents a quick and quick change in direction. Despite their rarity, island reversals are significant patterns that need our attention.

The secret lies in the alignment of the gaps. Observe that a bullish island reversal consists of a gap down followed by a gap up. Hence, the phrase 'island reversal' is obtained from the overlap of these price action gaps. The island that is located above the gaps will be referred to as a bullish island reversal.

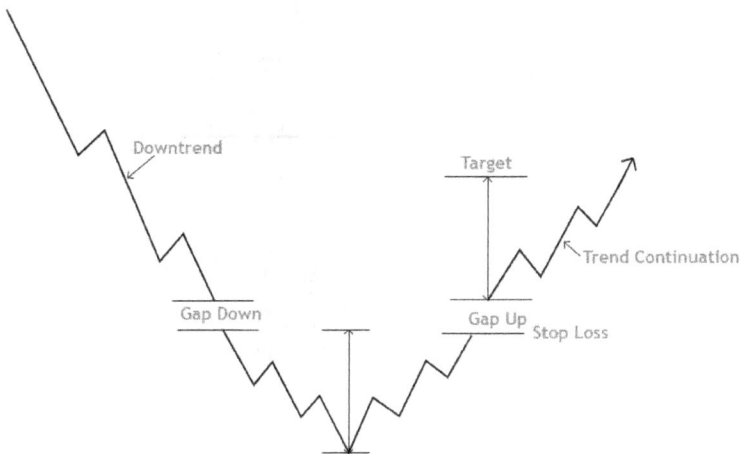

Image 5.53: Island bottom reversal pattern

Trend: To be considered a bullish reversal pattern, there should be evidence of a prior downtrend.

Entry: As the price action gaps down and creates a gap towards downside, enter the market.

Stop-loss: Set your stop-loss as the last price before the gap down was created (refer to image 5.53).

Profit target: You can figure out the estimated move by measuring the height of the island bottom reversal and applying that number to open price after the gap down was created.

Volume: Patterns of volume in island bottom reversal follow standard patterns. As a pattern develops, the volume will increase.

Island Top Reversal

An island reversal is a reversal pattern formed by two gaps and price movement between the gaps. These gaps indicate that the island reversal represents a quick change in direction. Despite their rarity, island reversals are significant patterns that need our attention.

The secret lies in the alignment of the gaps. Observe that a bullish island reversal consists of a gap up followed by a gap down.

Hence, the term 'island reversal' is obtained from the overlap of these price action gaps. The island that is located below the gaps will be referred to as a bearish island reversal.

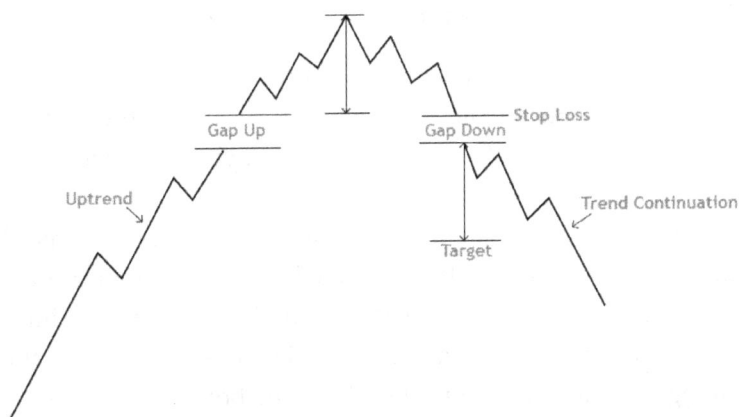

Image 5.54: Island top reversal pattern

Trend: To be considered a bearish reversal pattern, there should be evidence of a prior uptrend.

Entry: As the price action gaps down and create a gap towards downside, enter the market.

Stop-loss: Set your stop-loss as last price before the gap down was created (refer to image 5.54).

Profit target: You can figure out the estimated move by measuring the height of the island top reversal and applying that number to open price after the gap was created.

Volume: Patterns of volume in island top reversal follow standard patterns. As a pattern develops, the volume will increase.

Falling Wedge Reversal

The falling wedge can also occur as reversal pattern that starts out big and gets smaller as prices go down and the trading range gets smaller. Rising wedges have a clear downside and create a bullish reversal pattern.

Simply put, a falling wedge reversal is a bullish trend reversal chart pattern that signals a possible breakout to the upside.

A falling wedge reversal is true if the two bearish lines move back and forth in a good way. The line at the top is the falling resistance line, and the line at the bottom is the falling support line.

To prove the pattern, each of these lines must have been touched at least twice. If the resistance line is broken, the pattern is confirmed for sure. Most of the time, this break out is accompanied by high volumes.

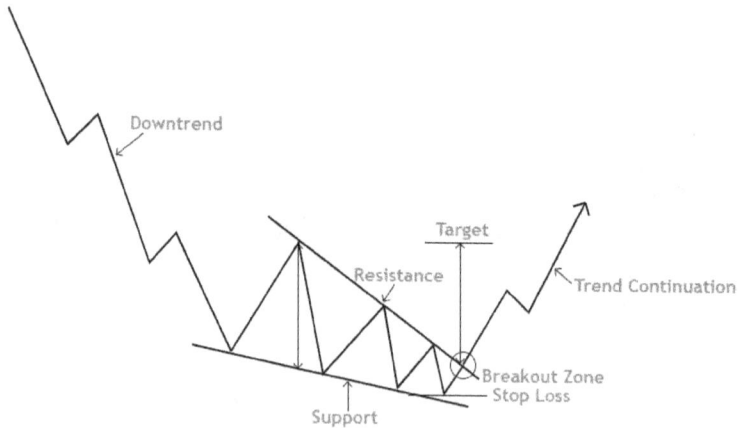

Image 5.55: Falling wedge reversal pattern

Trend: The trend prior to the formation of falling wedge reversal pattern should be down.

Entry: One should enter the long position once the stock has breached the upper falling band of contraction phase and has closed above it.

Stop-loss: A stop-loss can generally be placed a few rupees below the final swing low that occurred before the breakout.

Profit target: Once the neckline of a falling wedge reversal formation is broken, the trader must calculate the distance between the highest and lowest points in the pattern formation and add it to the breakout point in order to determine the possible down move.

Volume: When price finally breaks out of falling resistance or neckline, there should be a significant uptick in volume.

Rising Wedge Reversal

The rising wedge pattern is a bearish trend reversal pattern which starts out big at the start and gets smaller as prices go up and the trading range gets smaller. Falling wedges have a clear upside and form a bearish reversal pattern.

Simply put, a rising wedge reversal is a bearish trend reversal chart pattern that signals a possible breakdown to the downside.

A rising wedge reversal is true if the two bullish lines move back and forth in a good way. The line at the top is the rising resistance line, and the line at the bottom is the rising support line.

To prove the pattern, each of these lines must have been touched at least twice. If the rising support line is broken, the pattern is confirmed for sure. Most of the time, this break out is accompanied by high volumes.

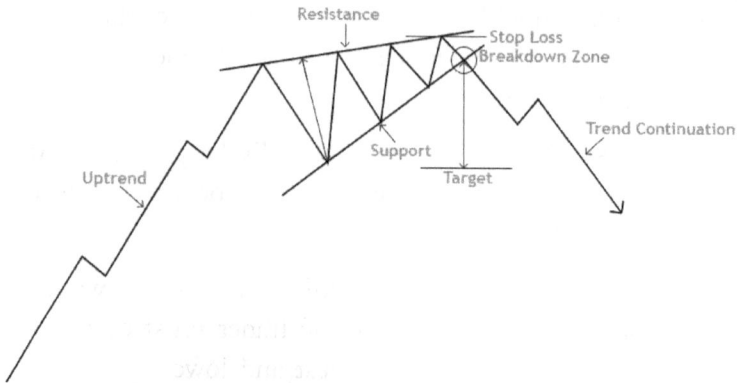

Image 5.56: Rising wedge reversal pattern

Trend: The trend prior to the formation of a rising wedge reversal pattern should be up.

Entry: One should take entry into short position once the stock has breached the lower rising band of contraction phase and has closed below it.

Stop-loss: A stop-loss can generally be placed a few rupees above the final swing high that occurred before the breakdown.

Profit target: Once the neckline of a rising wedge reversal formation is broken, the trader must calculate the distance between the highest and lowest points in the rising wedge reversal formation and add it to the breakdown point in order to determine the possible down move.

Volume: When price of rising support or neckline finally breaks down, there should be a significant uptick in volume.

6

Breakout Trading Strategies

B reakout trading is a strategy that looks for areas or levels that a stock hasn't been able to move above or beyond. Traders who use this strategy are called breakout traders. They wait for the prices of these stocks to go up. When the price of a stock goes above a point where it has been stuck for a while, this is called a breakout.

When a stock's price has stayed the same for a long time, many traders switch their attention to other securities with more active price changes. They do this because they want their trades to be profitable faster.

For a breakout strategy to work, traders have to be patient and wait for a security to move a bit above a level it has been at for a while which is called a neckline. The neckline is a level of support or resistance found on any chart pattern that is used by traders to determine strategic areas to place orders.

A number of experts in breakout trading use technical analysis to find patterns and trends in prices. For example, a breakout trader looks for times when the price of a security has not moved above or below a certain price range. After that, they make a trade in the direction of a breakout to try to make money by placing bets that the price will continue to move in the same direction.

The breakout trading strategies which I use for trading are mentioned below:

ATH Breakout

ATH stands for 'all-time high' and refers to the highest price a stock has ever hit on a certain exchange. For instance, if a stock goes public (IPO) for Rs 100 per share, increases to Rs 200 per share, and then falls to Rs 150 per share over time, the all-time high share price for the XYZ firm was Rs 200.

As mentioned earlier, all-time high is the highest point or price peak that a company's stock has ever reached. When security is at its best, resistance gets broken through.

Let's say a company makes huge profits quickly and often. If that's the case, traders are more likely to buy its stocks because they think the company will keep doing well in the future.

How can you trade stocks at all-time highs?

Classify breakout progress: To assess the stock's uptrend or downturn, classify the breakout's development. Track the stock for a few weeks and compare it to its previous price action. This will show how powerful or weak the stock is, which can help you trade.

Review pattern structure: Examine the breakout pattern. Examine past trading patterns to find the breakout pattern. Determine how long to keep the stock by analysing its triangle, flag, or double top/bottom pattern.

Identify resistance levels: Find resistance at fresh highs. This will help you set stop-loss and profit targets. Find these resistance levels using your breakout analysis to see where the price may reverse or continue its trend.

Determine a stop-loss price: Find your stop-loss 'protection price'. If the stock falls, sell it at this stage. This helps us know the pattern failure area which will protect our downside potential if we are taking a long position. For a short position trade, we will put the stop-loss above our support level.

Take entry into the position: Once all the conditions satisfy your buying criteria then take a position for the stock.

Remember the above-mentioned method and steps apply to all the breakout trading strategies. All the stocks should qualify above-mentioned rules or steps.

Examples of ATH breakouts signalling the beginning of a fresh massive upswing.

Case Study: Example of ATH Breakout.

Image 6.1 shows the weekly chart of NBCC Ltd. (formerly known as National Buildings Construction Corporation) forming a bullish basing continuation pattern. The trend continuation pattern forms from January 2013 to April 2014. The stock consolidated below the horizontal resistance and made up the huge round in the form of bullish basing. Then it gave a strong breakout from the pattern neckline or resistance at the breakout zone which was ATH for the stock.

Also notice the very strong pattern breakout candle which is a very good sign that the trend will continue.

We will place a buy order once the breakout occurs from the trend continuation chart pattern, and stop-loss will be placed just below the pattern breakout candle, which is also shown in the chart with the tagging of stop-loss and entry point. Moreover, I also mentioned where the breakout zone is for clarity on the chart.

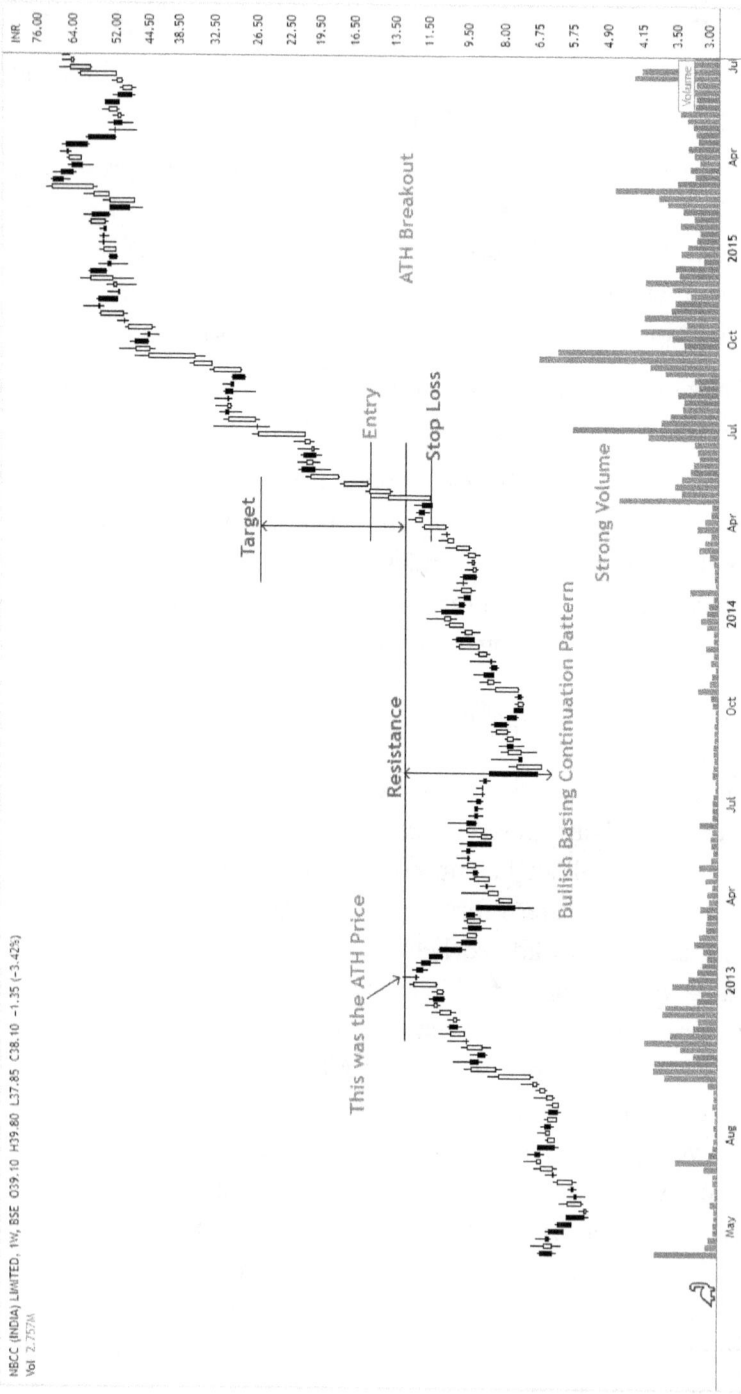

Image 6.1: Weekly chart of NBCC Ltd. showing an ATH Breakout.

The stock went up by huge margins after the breakout candle occurred and it started rising from the price of around Rs 16 all the way up to Rs 64 from the breakout zone.

52-week high breakout

"The share price is reaching a new 52-week high. Is this a good time to purchase it?" This is a frequent query that has been posed to me.

The fundamentals of the 52-week method may be applied to any asset or market due to their simplicity and accessibility. It involves using the highest price point during the last year as a significant signal.

Instead of using a price peak as a signal to exit a position in order to lock in gains, the 52-week high process involves entering or expanding a position.

Excitingly, a great deal of research has been conducted over the years, and the majority of it indicates that greater momentum occurs in equities achieving 52-week highs.

The 52-week high price explains a substantial amount of momentum trading's earnings. We find that proximity to the 52-week high is a more accurate indicator of future returns than previous returns.

Enter a long trade with a tight stop-loss below the recent swing bottom or the low of a wide range breakout candle when the bigger trend restarts. Most of these breakouts occur during the first hour of trading, so remain watchful throughout that time frame.

Examples of 52-Week high breakouts signalling the beginning of a fresh massive upswing are provided below.

Case Study: 52-Week High Breakout

Image 6.2 shows the weekly chart of Mazagon Dock Ship Building Ltd. forming a bullish basing continuation pattern. The trend continuation pattern formed from March 2022 to September 2022. The stock was below the horizontal resistance and made up the huge round in the form of bullish basing. Then it showed a strong breakout from the pattern neckline or resistance at the breakout zone which is where 52-week high breakout occurred.

We can also notice the very strong pattern breakout candle which is a very good sign for trend continuation.

You can also see that I have pointed out the 52-week low and 52-week high and once the price breached 52-week high, then the price moved only towards the upside.

We place a buy order when the breakout occurs from the trend continuation chart pattern, and stop-loss will be placed just below the pattern breakout candle which is also shown in the image. Moreover, I have also pointed out where the breakout zone is and where the 52-weeks high took place.

Stock went up by huge margins after the breakout candle occurred and it started rising from the price of around Rs 355 all the way up to Rs 930 from the breakout zone.

5-10% near 52-week high

The fundamentals of the 5-10% near to 52-week high method may be applied to any asset or market due to simplicity and accessibility.

It involves using the highest price point during the last year as a significant signal and then scanning for stocks which are trading near the 52-week high in the range of 5% to 10%.

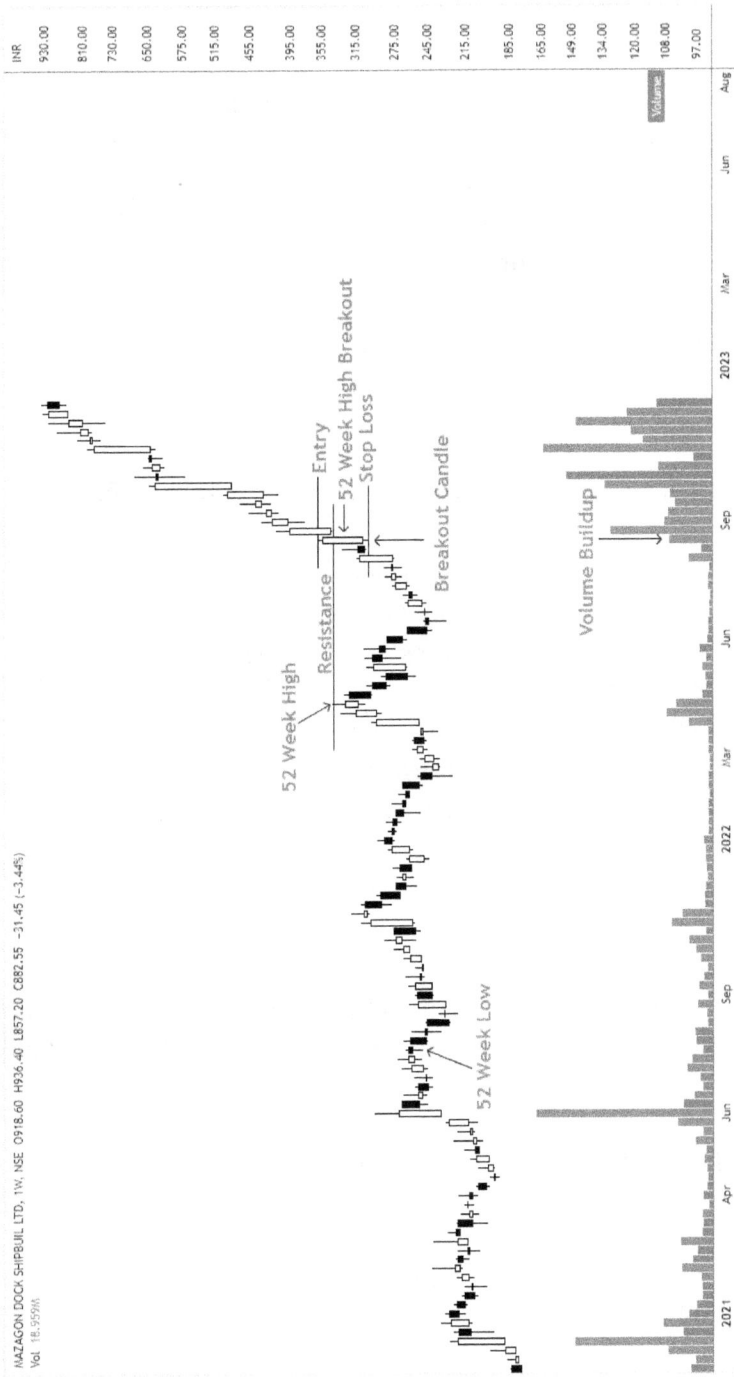

Image 6.2: Weekly chart of Mazagon Dock Ship Building Ltd. showing a 52-Week high breakout

The stocks which are trading near 52-week high signify that they have stock momentum and will continue towards upside. If the stock forms any chart pattern, and breakout happens then there will be huge upside.

The 5–10% near 52-week high price explains a substantial amount of momentum trading. We find that proximity to the 5–10% near 52-week high is a more accurate indicator of a potential upside continuation.

Case Study: 5-10% near 52-week high.

Image 6.3 is the daily chart of Bharat Electronics Ltd. forming a lengthy symmetrical triangle continuation pattern. The trend continuation pattern formed from May 2014 to August 2022. One can also see in the image that the stock was just 9% away from a 52-week high. It consolidated between the falling resistance and rising support and then showed a strong breakout from the pattern neckline or falling resistance.

Notice that the very strong breakout candle occurs at the breakout zone which is a very good sign for trend continuation.

Place a buy order once the breakout occurs from the trend continuation chart pattern, and stop-loss should be placed just below the pattern breakout candle which is also shown in the chart with the stop-loss and entry point.

The stock went up by huge margins after the breakout candle occurred and it started rising from the price of around Rs 82 all the way up to over Rs 108 in a very short span of time.

Multiyear resistance breakout trading

Among traders, buying a breakout of a resistance level is a common technique. Occasionally, the resistance level is at the top of a multiyear trading range. A stock that breaches a multiyear resistance level may see a substantial upswing.

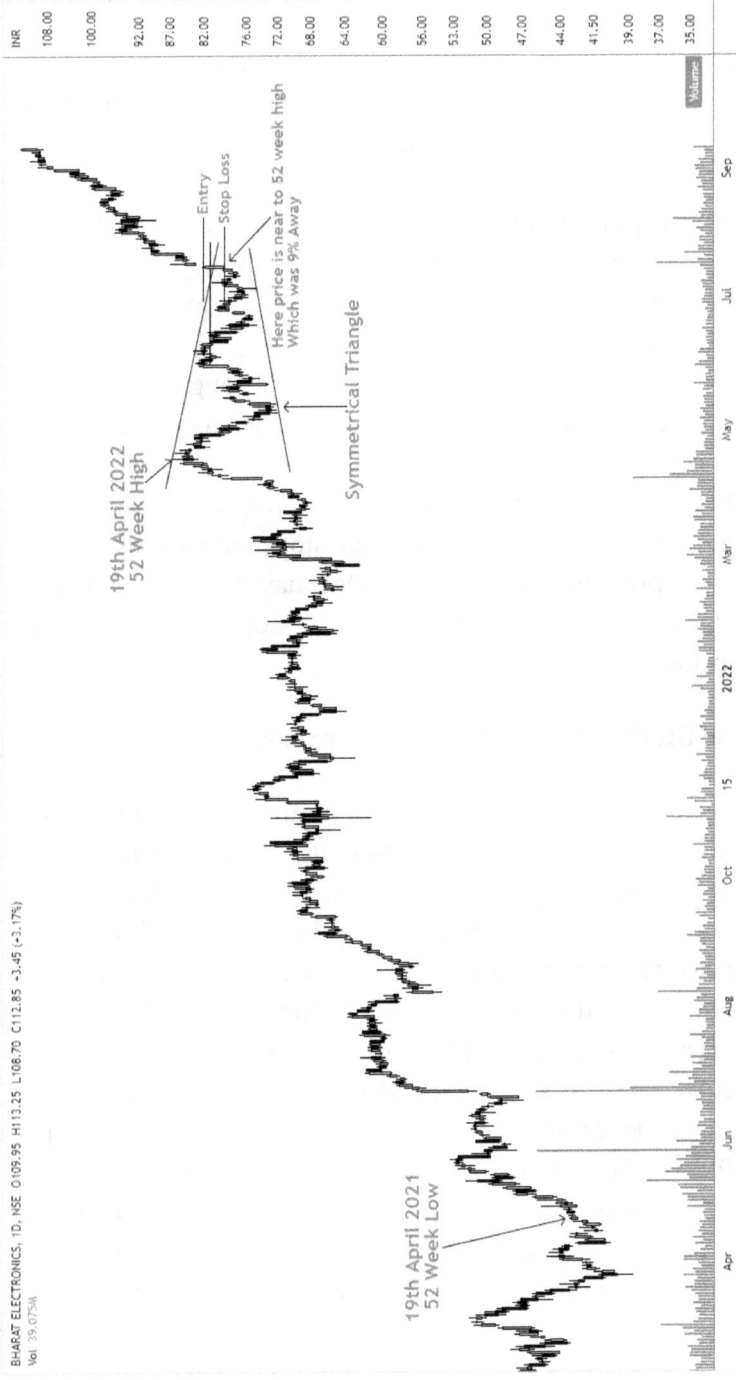

Chart_mojo published on TradingView.com, Jan 21, 2023 17:33 UTC+5:30

BHARAT ELECTRONICS, 1D, NSE O109.95 H113.25 L108.70 C112.85 +3.45 (+3.17%)
Vol 39.075M

INR

108.00
100.00
92.00
87.00
82.00
76.00
72.00
68.00
64.00
60.00
56.00
53.00
50.00
47.00
44.00
41.50
39.00
37.00
35.00

Entry
Stop Loss

Here price is near to 52 week high
Which was 9% Away

19th April 2022
52 Week High

Symmetrical Triangle

19th April 2021
52 Week Low

Volume

Apr   Jun   Aug   Oct   15   2022   Mar   May   Jul   Sep

Image 6.3: Daily chart of Bharat Electronics Ltd. showing 5-10% near 52-week high.

Even better if the stock's resistance level is at its all-time high since there is no overhead resistance. Everyone who owns the stock will essentially profit. After a breakthrough, the following movement might be large.

These potentially big movements are better suited to patient traders than to short-term traders. By applying trading techniques to a long-term chart, a trader may boost the likelihood of a winning trade.

Generally, it is advisable to examine a longer-term chart so that the trader may determine how the stock has moved in the past.

For trading reasons, both the initial stop and trailing stop should be relatively generous. If the stops are too close to the present price movement, the trader may exit early. We will discuss this in the chapter on initial stop-loss and trailing stop-loss.

Case Study: Multiyear resistance breakout trading.

Image 6.4 shows the monthly chart of Amara Raja Battery Ltd. forming a lengthy continuation pattern. The trend continuation pattern formed from 2009 to 2012. The stock consolidated below the horizontal resistance and then showed a strong breakout from the multiyear resistance neckline or resistance.

Notice that the stock had a very strong uptrend (shown with rising arrow and uptrend). Then, a very strong breakout candle occurred which is a very good sign for trend continuation towards higher side.

Place a buy order once the breakout occurs from the trend continuation chart pattern, and stop-loss will be placed just below the pattern breakout candle which is also shown in the chart with the tagging of stop-loss and entry point.

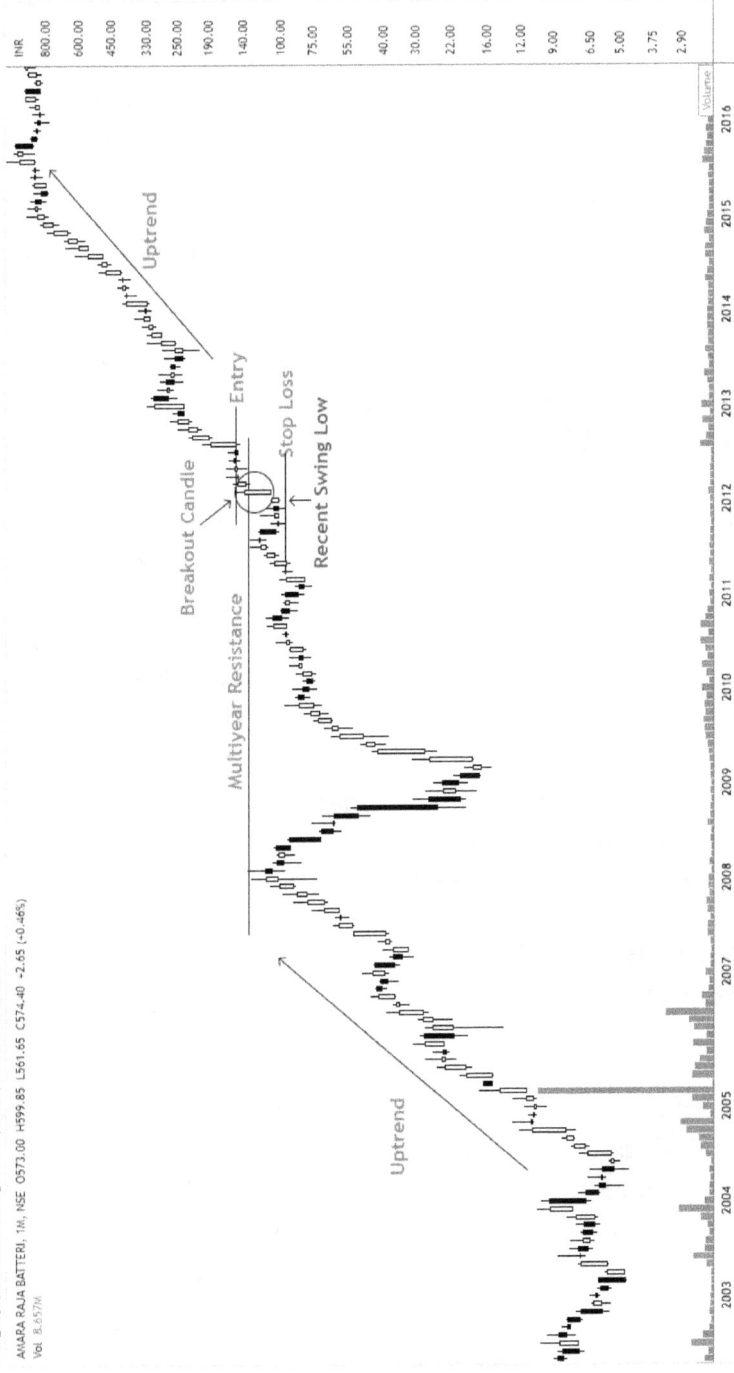

Image 6.4: Amara Raja Battery Ltd. showing multiyear resistance breakout trading.

The stock went up by huge margins after the breakout candle occurred and it started rising from the price of around Rs 150 all the way up to a whopping over Rs 800 with most of the candlestick being bullish after the breakout.

Case Study: Multiyear Resistance Breakout Trading.

Image 6.5 shows the daily chart of Sudarshan Chemical Industries Ltd. forming a lengthy rectangle continuation pattern. The trend continuation pattern formed from October 2014 to July 2016. The stock consolidated between the horizontal resistance and support and then showed a strong breakout from the high pattern neckline or resistance.

We can also notice the very strong breakout candle which is a very good sign for trend continuation.

We will place a buy order once the breakout occurs from the trend continuation chart pattern, and stop-loss will be placed just below the pattern breakout candle which is also shown in the chart with the tagging of stop-loss and entry point.

The stock went up by huge margins after the breakout candle occurred and it started rising from the price of around Rs 165 all the way up to Rs 475 in a very short span of time.

Moving Average Breakout with Chart Pattern Breakout

First, we need to trade in the direction of the trend. We define the trend using a single moving average. For our purpose we'll use a 200-day exponential moving average.

The above-mentioned trading strategy involves buying a stock when it is forming up a chart pattern and simultaneously shows a breakout from the key moving average.

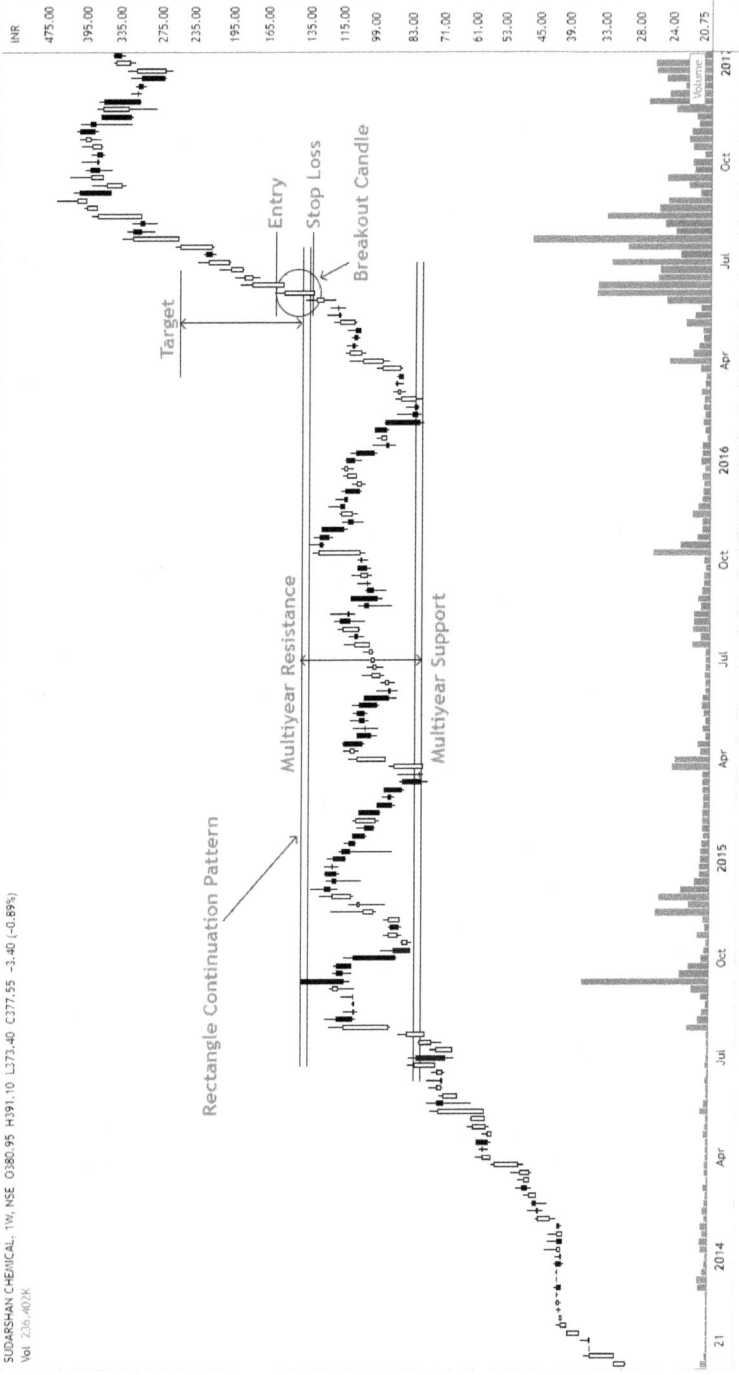

Chart_mojo published on TradingView.com, Jan 21, 2023 17:20 UTC+5:30

SUDARSHAN CHEMICAL. 1W, NSE O380.95 H391.10 L373.40 C377.55 −3.40 (−0.89%)
Vol 236.402K

Rectangle Continuation Pattern

Multiyear Resistance

Multiyear Support

Target

Entry

Stop Loss

Breakout Candle

Image 6.5: Sudarshan Chemical Industries Ltd. showing multiyear resistance breakout trading.

As the stock is forming up, any bullish chart pattern indicates upside potential and if it breaks through the resistance of the pattern with moving average breakout will be a good signal to enter the stock.

This strategy has double the advantage as the confirmation is taken from a chart pattern breakout with moving average breakout which further gives the upside momentum to the security.

Case Study: Moving average breakout with chart pattern breakout.

Image 6.6 shows the daily chart of L&T Finance Holdings Ltd. The chart shows a sideways chart pattern (consolidation phase) after the end of the downtrend. The stock consolidated below 200 EMA and the price took resistance a few times. After facing supply from resistance zone two times, the stock breached the resistance, moving together. and gave a strong bullish signal for the upside.

You can also notice in the chart that I have mentioned where the trend turned into a downtrend and into uptrend when price action crossed the long term (trend identification moving average 200-EMA).

Place a buy order once the breakout occurs from the resistance and long-term moving average (200-EMA) and place a stop-loss just below the resistance breakout candle which is also shown in the chart.

This stock went up drastically after the breakout candle and it started rising from the price of around Rs 71 to all the way up to over Rs 112 in a very short span of time.

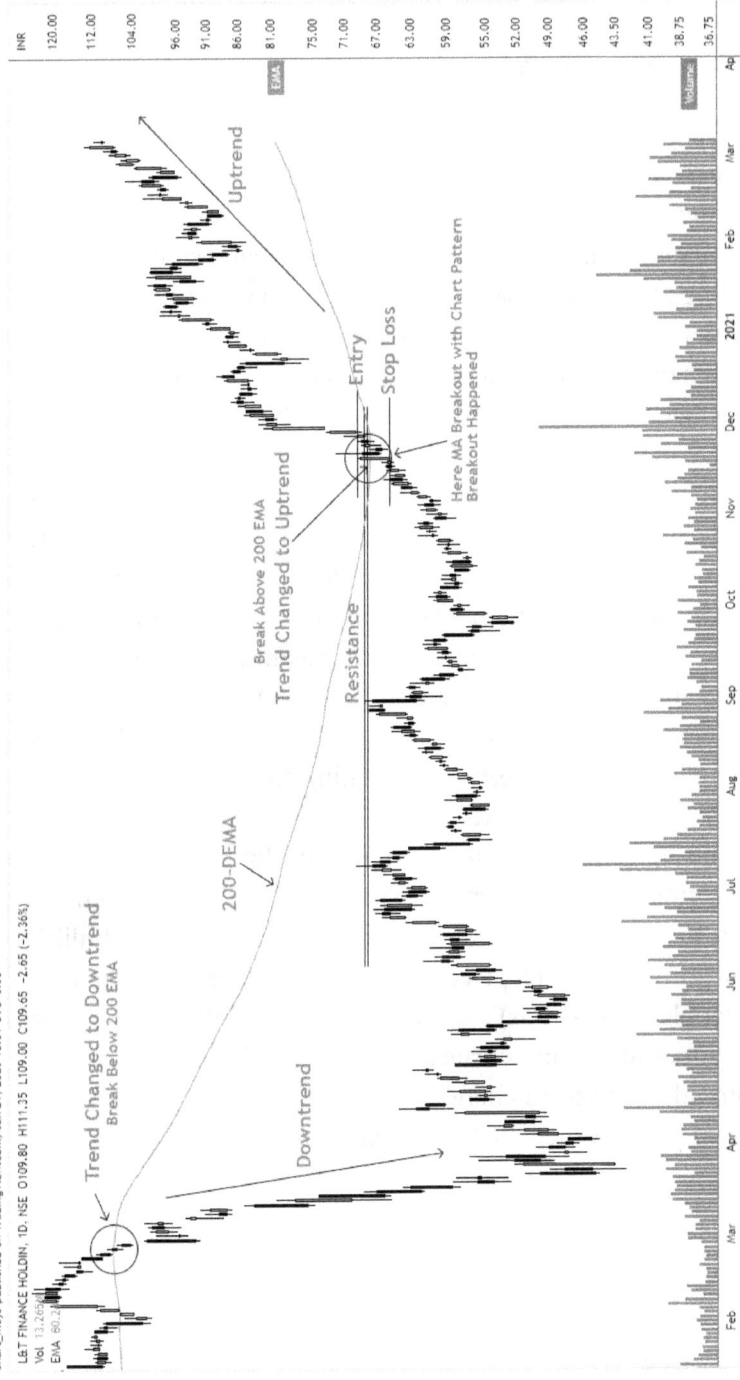

Image 6.6: Daily chart of L&T Finance Holdings Ltd. showing moving average breakout with chart pattern breakout

Darvas Box Theory

The Darvas Box Theory is a trading method developed by Nicolas Darvas that picks companies based on highs and volume.

Darvas trading method involved purchasing stocks that are trading at new highs and drawing a box around the previous highs and lows to determine the entry point and stop-loss order placement. A stock is deemed to be in a Darvas box when the price action rises above the prior high but then falls back to a price that is close to the previous high.

The Darvas box idea is not bound to a certain time period; the boxes are produced by drawing a line between the recent highs and lows of the time period being used by the trader.

Darvas boxes are a very simple indication made by drawing a line between the minimum and maximum values. As the highs and lows get updated over time, you will see increasing or decreasing boxes. The Darvas box hypothesis advocates only trading rising boxes and updating stop-loss orders using the highs of the breached boxes.

The uptrend seems to be supported by a strong volume indicating that big players are also accumulating this security.

In this breakout trading technique, we tend to take bullish positions once the price has breached the resistance of rectangle (Darvas box) pattern. Keep in mind that as the price continues to rise and create another rectangle formation in the uptrend, we need to change the stop-loss to the recent swing low of the newly created rectangle formation (see image 6.7).

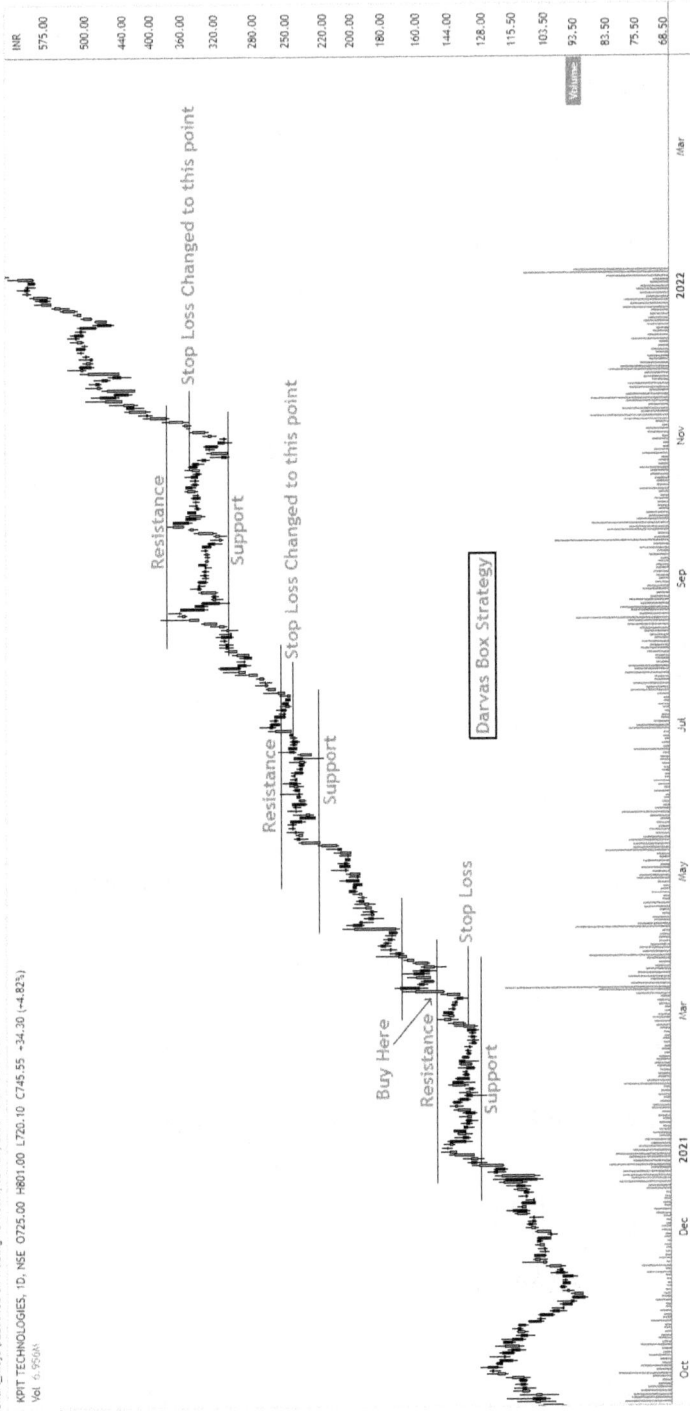

Image 6.7: KPIT Technologies Ltd. chart showing Darvas box. It shows the higher highs and higher lows price action which indicates a strong momentum in the prevailing trend.

High Compression Squeeze

The Bollinger band indicator is an excellent method for determining the volatility of any trading asset. Using an upper band and lower band separated by the number of standard deviations (often 2) from the centre moving average (typically the 20-period moving average), we may determine when an instrument is trading at an extreme price and when volatility has risen or reduced.

The breakout method will use the Bollinger band 'squeeze' to inform traders of a contracting market. We soon see a breakout trading opportunity resulting from compression.

One of the primary features of a Bollinger band is that it narrows when price volatility reduces, resulting in price movement within a narrow range. It is known as the 'Bollinger band squeeze'.

The element we are searching for is the highlighted squeeze area—when the Bollinger bands contract. Since we do not know when the squeeze will occur, we must constantly monitor our charts for this component of the system.

Once the Bollinger bands begin to squeeze, we know that a breakthrough to the upside or downside will soon occur. The issue is that we do not know when it will occur.

In addition, we do not know in which direction the breach will occur.

You may watch market activity to trade any directional move resulting from the Bollinger band squeeze, or you can trade in the direction of the prevalent trend. I would recommend trading in the prevailing trend.

Case Study: High Compression Squeeze.

Image 6.8 shows the daily chart of Whirlpool India Ltd forming up a symmetrical triangle in high compression squeeze with

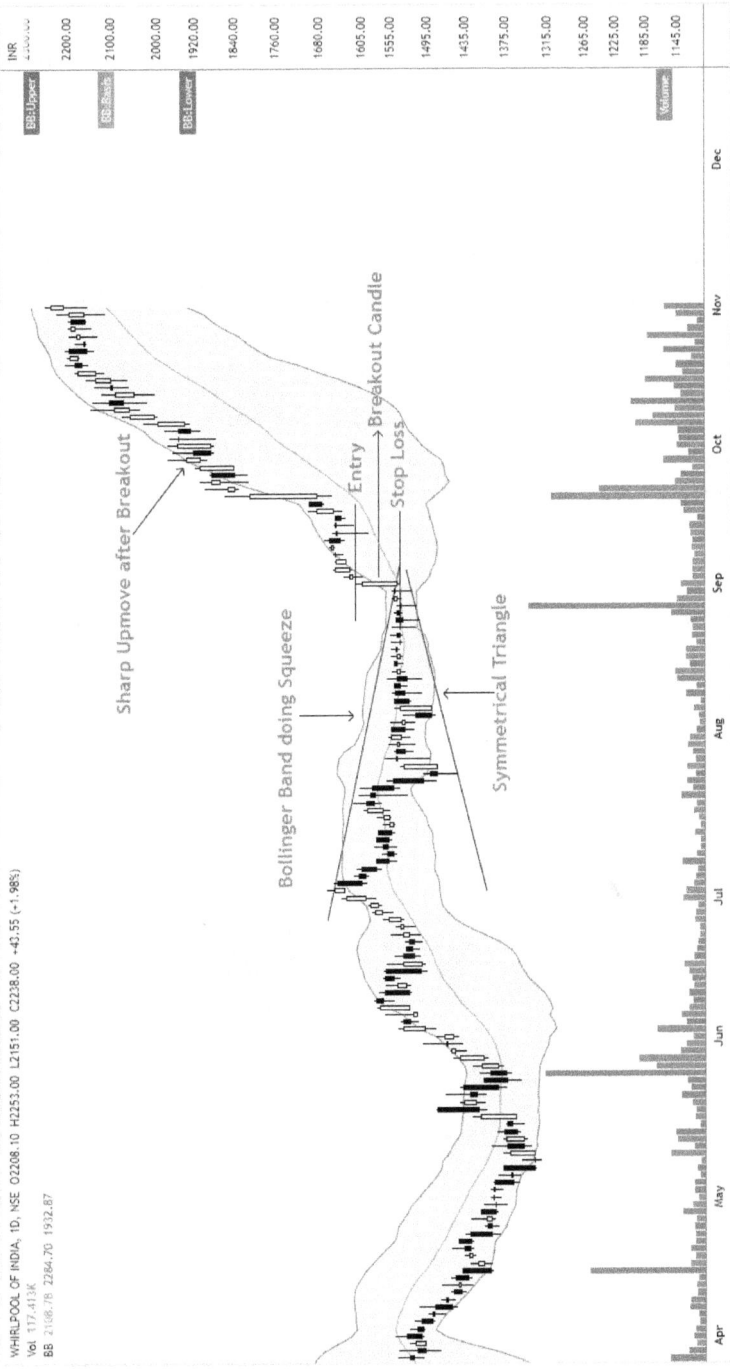

Image 6.8: Daily chart of Whirlpool India Ltd. showing high compression squeeze with Bollinger band

Bollinger band. The stock contracted between the falling resistance and rising support and then showed a strong breakout from the high compression squeeze. We can also notice the very tight range just before the breakout which indicates that it is due for breakout.

Place a buy order once the breakout occurs from the continuation pattern, and the stop-loss just below the pattern breakout candle which is also shown in the chart with the tagging of stop-loss and entry point.

The stock went up drastically after the breakout candle and it started rising from the price of around Rs 1600 to all the way up to over Rs 2200 in a very short span of time.

7

Chartmojo Candidates for Breakout Trading

Chartmojo candidates are those stocks which I trade personally and have simplified all the stock movements and given specific names to those stock movements for myself as well as for the people who wish to trade the same stocks.

I have given a name to every type of stock movements. If the stock is trading just near its resistance then I will call that stock as breakout soon because I like that stock and it might show breakout in the days to come. Likewise, I have these five types of Chartmojo candidates which I have been trading and making money from the market.

Following are the Chartmojo candidates:

- Breakout stock
- Breakout soon stock
- Breakout retest
- Squeeze stocks
- Reversal stocks

Breakout candidate

Breakout candidate includes those which have shown a clear breakout from resistance of any chart pattern and indicate a strong momentum for potential upside.

The traders who do breakout trading will like breakout candidates because the stock has already shown a strong breakout (which should happen with strong volume and will benefit the traders most).

One should always be aware of the fact that the structure of the breakout should be towards upside if trading a bullish pattern and if the structure is towards downside then traders should be trading a bearish pattern.

Chartmojo breakout candidates will give best rewards if you take care of your stop-losses, whenever you trade a breakout candidate. Enter the position only if the confirmation candles appear above the breakout candidate.

Case Study: High Breakout Candidate

Image 7.1 shows the daily chart of Page Industries Ltd. First, the stock was in an uptrend and formed a cup and handle continuation pattern. Once the pattern ended, the stock showed a breakout towards upside and marching towards higher side.

You will notice that the stock had a tight closing build-up (tight range) just before the breakout zone which signifies that the weak hands have exited the stock at the breakout zone and the stock is due for a potential upside. While the stock went through a tight range, the volume also started rising at the breakout zone which indicated that the buyers of the stock are very strong. The stock formed a bullish candlestick pattern at the breakout zone signalling a potential upside.

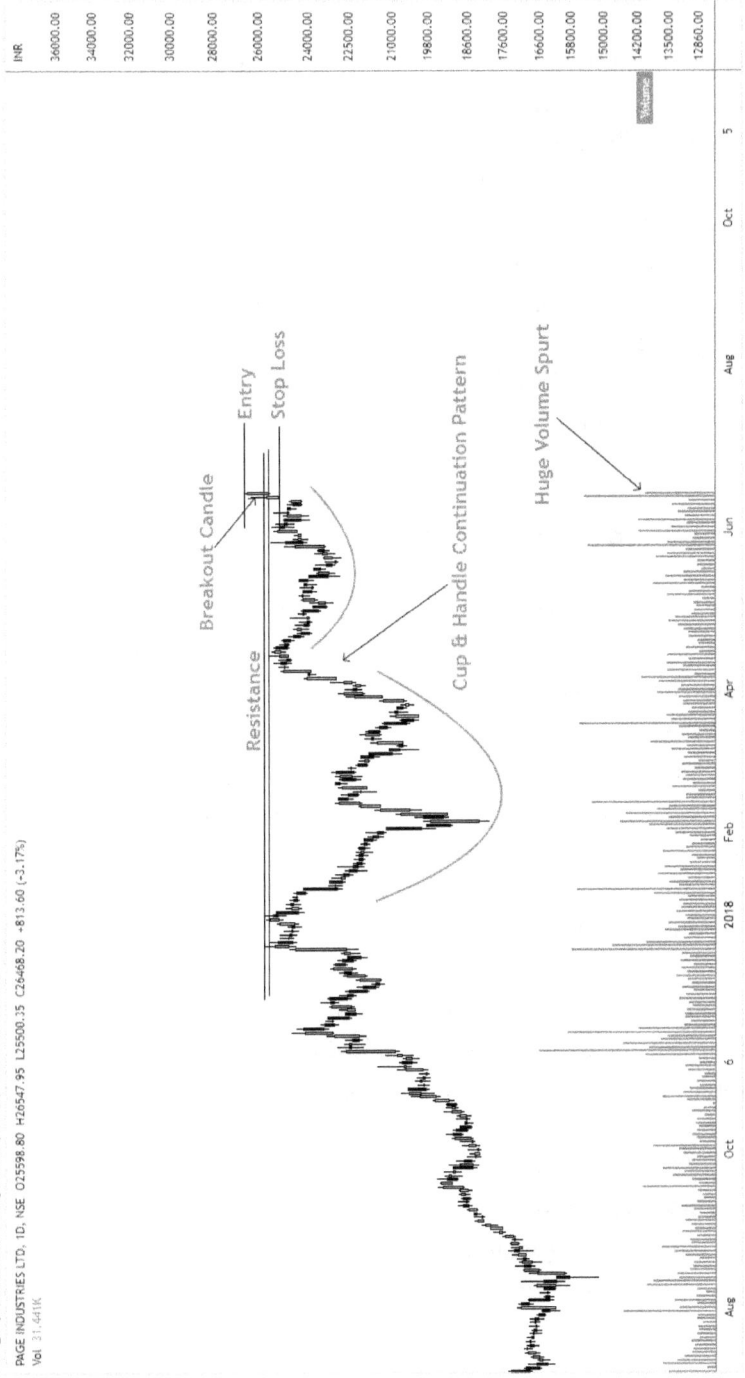

Chart_mojo published on TradingView.com, Jan 21, 2023 17:43 UTC+5:30

PAGE INDUSTRIES LTD, 1D, NSE O25598.80 H26547.95 L25500.35 C26468.20 +813.60 (+3.17%)
Vol 31.441K

Breakout Candle

Entry

Stop Loss

Resistance

Cup & Handle Continuation Pattern

Huge Volume Spurt

Image 7.1: Daily chart of Page Industries Ltd. showing a high breakout candidate.

The buy entry will be taken as and when the break occurs above the breakout candlestick and the stop will be placed at the low of the previous candle of the breakout zone (refer to image 7.1). This is the first chart of the case study. Now let's look at the follow up chart of the breakout candidate.

Image 7.2 shows how the stock performed after the breakout candlestick occurred, breaking through the resistance of cup and handle pattern. The stock has a clear run after the breakout candle and went up substantially. The stock started rising from around Rs 2,600 (from the breakout candle) to all the way up to Rs 3,600 within a span of four to five months.

Breakout soon candidate

They are candidates which have a solid chart structure and the price is trading just below the chart pattern resistance. One should always keep these stocks on radar as the breakout soon candidate is about to show a breakout, indicating a strong momentum for potential upside once the breakout takes place.

The traders who do breakout trading will like the breakout soon candidates, because the stock (security) is on the verge of showing a breakout with strong volume which will benefit the traders most.

One should always be aware of the fact that the structure of the breakout should be towards the upside if trading bullish pattern. If the structure is towards the downside then traders should be trading a bearish pattern.

Chartmojo breakout soon candidates will give the best rewards if you take care of your stop-losses, whenever you trade a breakout soon candidate. Enter the position only if the signal candle (breakout candle) and confirmation candles (candle above the breakout candle) appear above the resistance.

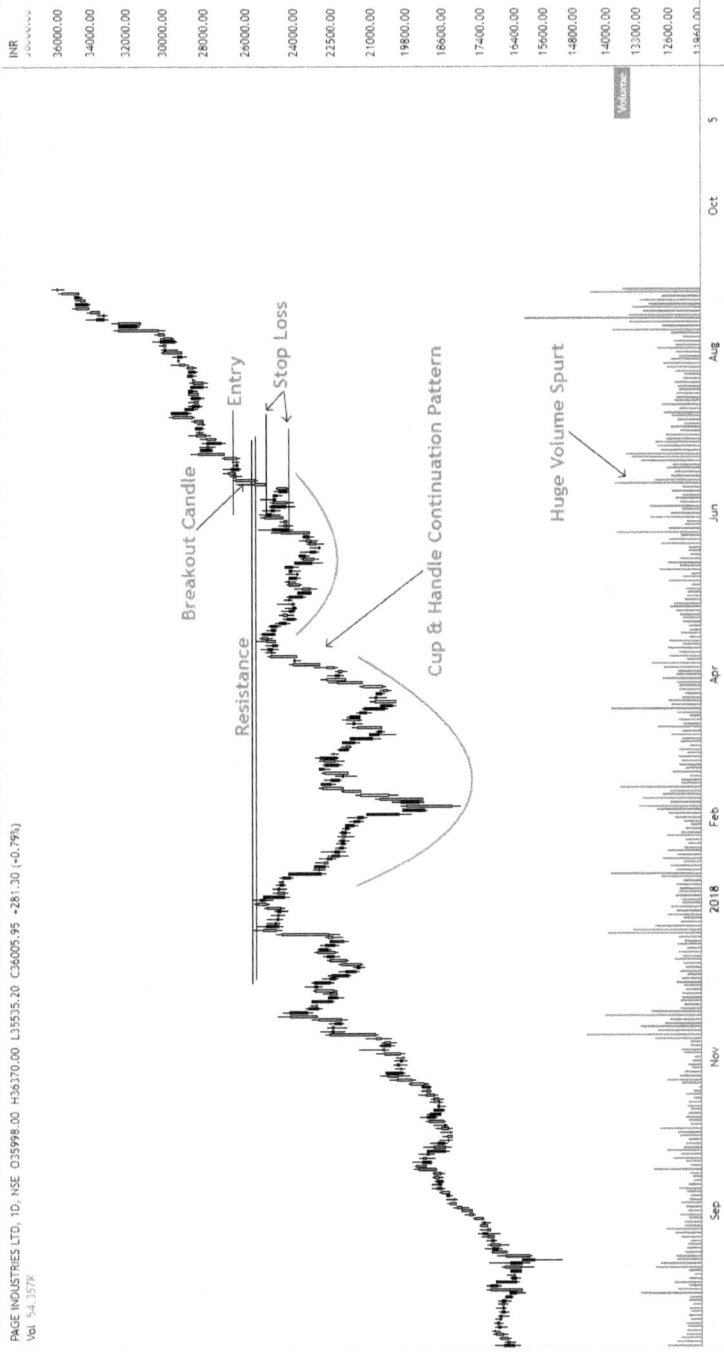

Chart_mojo published on TradingView.com, Jan 21, 2023 17:45 UTC+5:30

PAGE INDUSTRIES LTD, 1D, NSE O35998.00 H36370.00 L35535.20 C36005.95 -281.30 (-0.79%)

Vol 54.357K

Image 7.2: Daily chart of Page Industries Ltd after the breakout.

Case Study: Breakout Soon Candidate.

Image 7.3 shows the daily chart of Atul Ltd. The stock was in a sideways phase and formed a symmetrical triangle pattern. As the stock was forming its symmetrical triangle the price contracted between the upper and lower band (rising support) and reached its peak of the pattern.

The buy entry will be taken at break above the falling resistance (symmetrical triangle) and the stop will be placed at the low of the breakout candle at the breakout zone which we can see in the follow up chart of breakout soon candidate. Image 7.3 is the first chart of the case study. Now let's look at the follow up chart of breakout soon candidate.

Image 7.4 shows how the stock performed after the breakout candle occurred in the form of a strong bullish candlestick at the breakout zone. The stock had a clear run after the bullish breakout candlestick appeared and went up sharply. The stock started rising from around Rs 500 all the way up to over Rs 6,600 within a span of two months.

Breakout retest candidate

These are stocks which have shown a clear breakout from resistance of any chart pattern and the stock price lose momentum after breakout. It removes weak hands and comes back to retest the breakout zone.

The traders who do breakout trading will like the breakout retest candidates, because the stock (security) will give the strong breakout and retest the same breakout zone area which will give the best reward as the stop-loss on the breakout retest candidates will be very less with a huge potential upside.

One should always be aware of the fact that the structure of the breakout retest candidates should be towards upside if

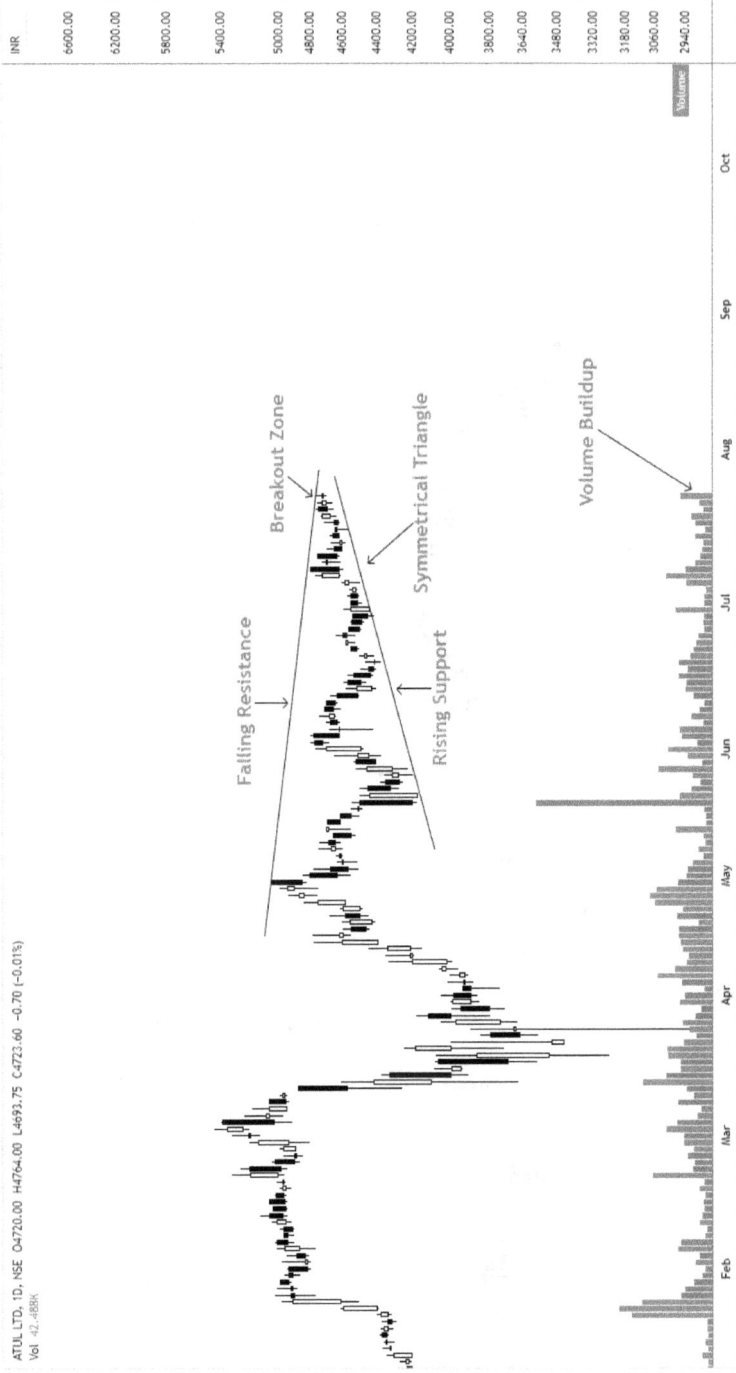

Chart.mojo published on TradingView.com, Jan 21, 2023 16:57 UTC+5:30
ATUL LTD, 1D, NSE O4720.00 H4764.00 L4693.75 C4723.60 −0.70 (−0.01%)
Vol 42.488K

Falling Resistance

Breakout Zone

Symmetrical Triangle

Rising Support

Volume Buildup

Image 7.3: Daily chart of Atul Ltd. showing a breakout soon candidate

ATUL LTD, 1D, NSE O6864.90 H7019.75 L6653.15 C6948.70 +145.85 (+2.14%)

Vol 83.553K

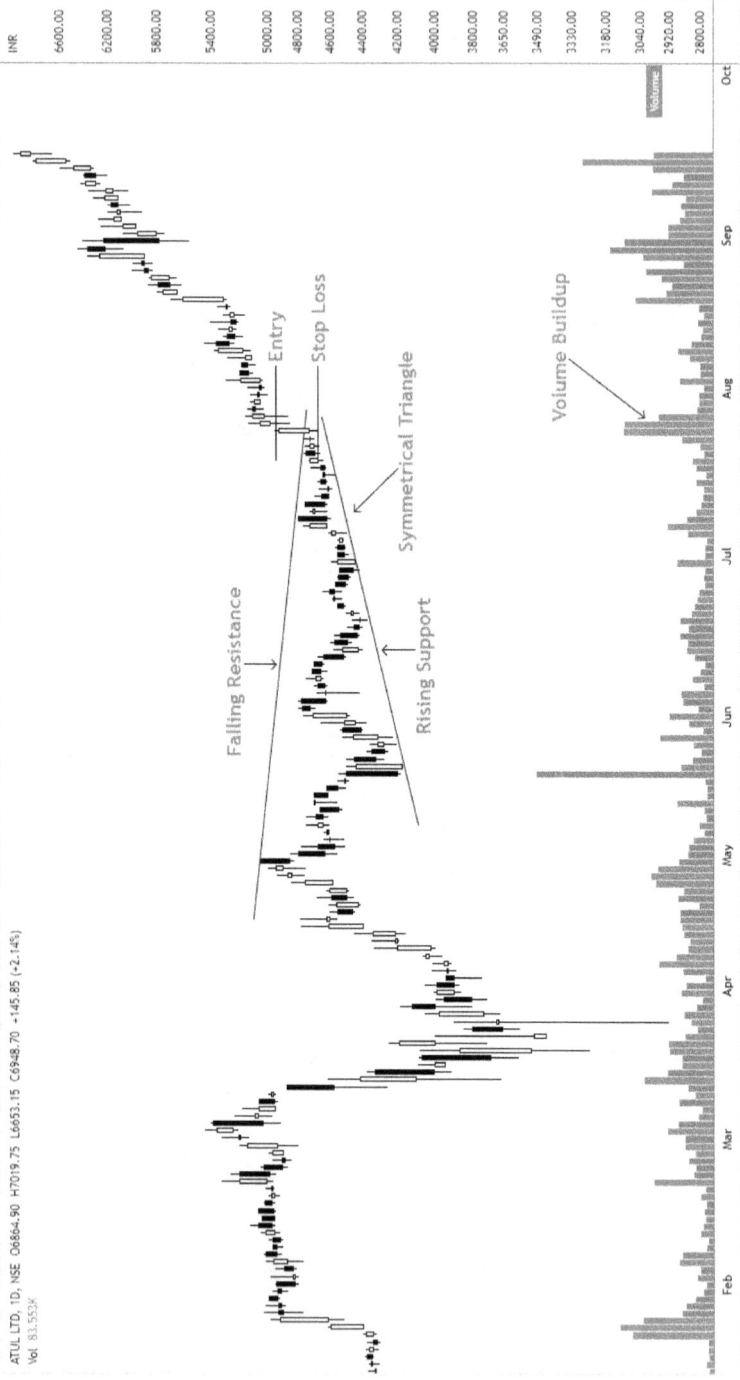

Image 7.4: Daily chart of Atul Ltd. after the appearance of the breakout candle.

trading bullish pattern and if the structure is towards downside then traders should be trading bearish pattern.

Chartmojo breakout retest candidates will give best rewards if you take care of your stop-losses, whenever you trade a breakout retest candidate. Enter the position only if the signal candle (reversal candle) appears the breakout retest area and also the conformation candles (candle above the reversal candle) appear at the resistance.

Case Study: Breakout Retest Candidate.

Image 7.5 is the daily chart of Alkyl Amines Ltd. First the stock was in an uptrend and formed a round basing pattern. Once the basing pattern ended, the stock showed a breakout towards upside and marched towards the higher side.

After a couple of trading sessions of the breakout the stock started coming down and retested the breakout zone. While the stock was retracing down, the volume also kept falling, which indicated sellers fading away. The stock formed a hammer candlestick pattern at retest area and signalled a potential upside.

The buy entry will be taken at a break above the retest candlestick (hammer candlestick) and the stop will be placed at the low of the retest candle at the breakout zone. This is the first chart of the case study. Now let's look at the follow up chart of the retest candidate.

Image 7.6 shows how the stock performed after the reversal candlestick occurred in the form of hammer candlestick at the breakout retest zone. The stock had a clear run after the reversal candlestick appeared and went up drastically. The stock started rising from around Rs 1,550 all the way to over Rs 2,800 within a span of four to five months.

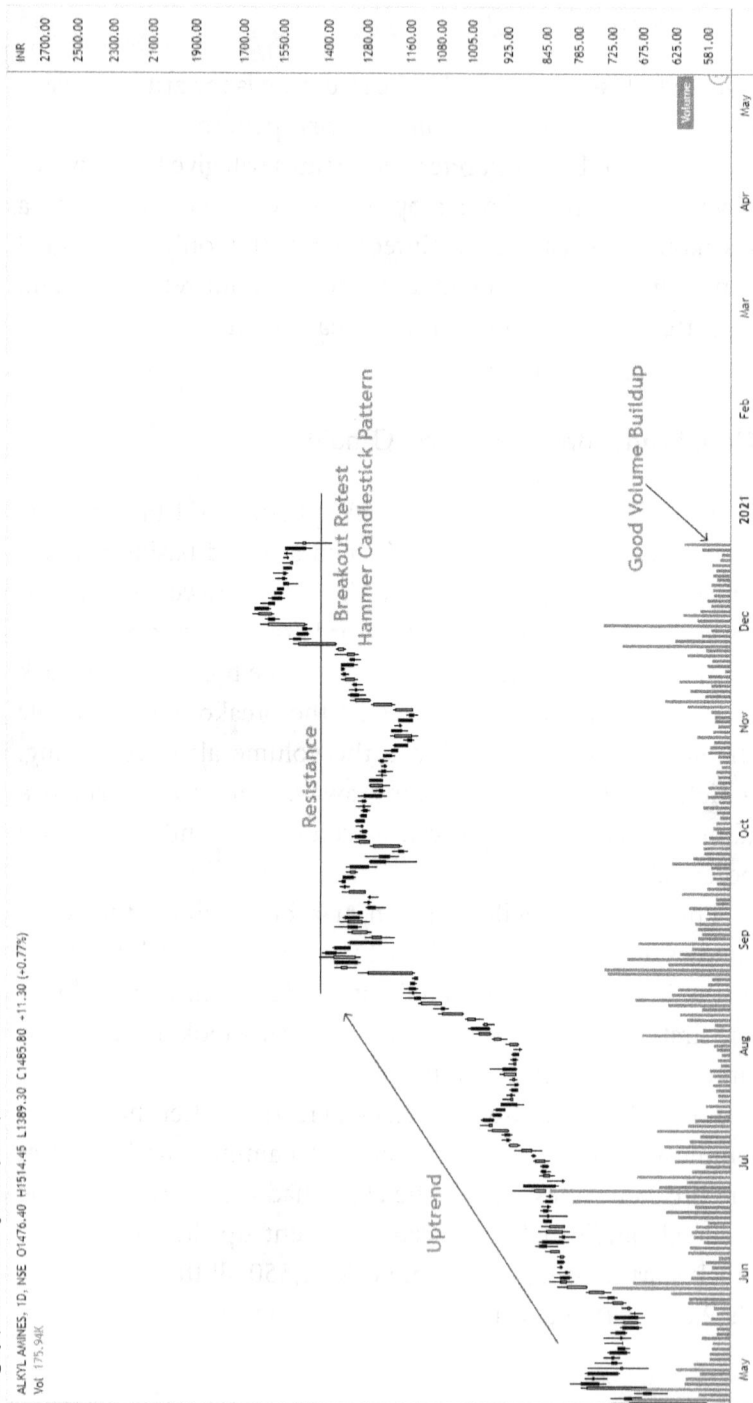

Image 7.5: Daily chart of Alkyl Amines Ltd. showing a high breakout candidate.

ALKYL AMINES, 1D, NSE O2803.80 H3254.35 L2803.80 C3254.35 +542.40 (+20.00%)
Vol 2.073M

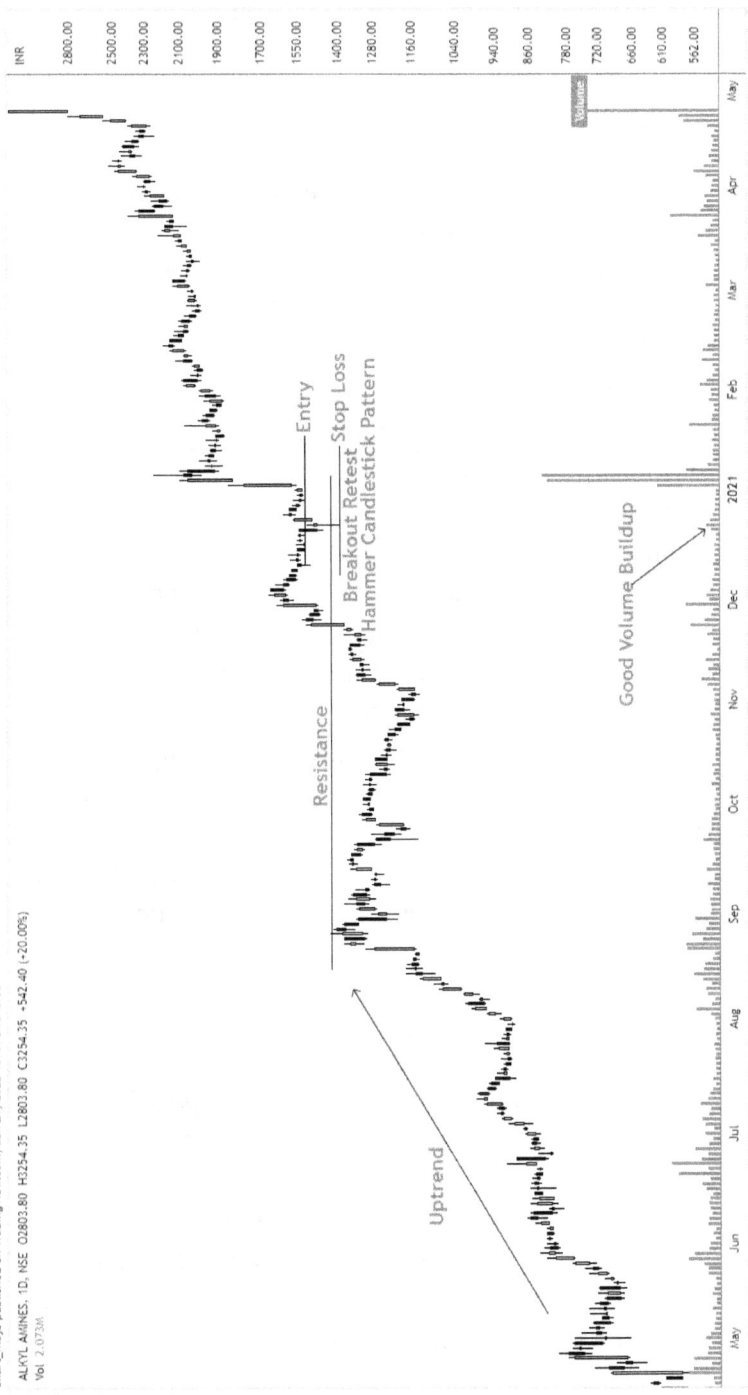

Uptrend

Resistance

Entry

Stop Loss

Breakout Retest

Hammer Candlestick Pattern

Good Volume Buildup

Volume

INR
2800.00
2500.00
2300.00
2100.00
1900.00
1700.00
1550.00
1400.00
1280.00
1160.00
1040.00
940.00
860.00
780.00
720.00
660.00
610.00
562.00

May Jun Jul Aug Sep Oct Nov Dec 2021 Feb Mar Apr May

Image 7.6: Daily chart of Alkyl Amines Ltd. after the reversal candlestick formation.

Squeeze candidates

Squeeze candidates are those which have a solid chart structure with tight range consolidation and the price trades below the chart pattern resistance (overhead resistance). One should always keep these stocks on radar as the squeeze candidate are about to show a breakout and indicate a strong momentum for potential upside once the breakout takes place above the tight high compression squeeze.

The traders who do breakout trading will like the squeeze candidates because the stock (security) is on the verge of a breakout at tight squeeze range with a strong volume. It will benefit the traders most.

One should always be aware of the fact that the structure of the breakout should be towards upside if trading bullish pattern and if the structure is towards downside then traders should be trading a bearish pattern.

Chartmojo squeeze candidates will give best rewards if you take care of your stop-losses whenever you trade a squeeze candidate. Enter the position only if the signal candle (breakout candle) forms and confirmation candles (candle above the breakout candle) appear above the resistance at the squeeze area.

Case Study: Squeeze candidate.

Image 7.7 shows the daily chart of Piramal Enterprise Ltd. The stock was in an uptrend and then it came down and formed a tight squeeze. In the tight squeeze phase, the stock went through minor ups and downs within its upper and lower band of squeeze. At the above-mentioned squeeze area, the stock also tried to break its 50-EMA with volume contraction.

The buy entry will be taken at break above the upper band of squeeze and the stop-loss will be placed at the low of breakout

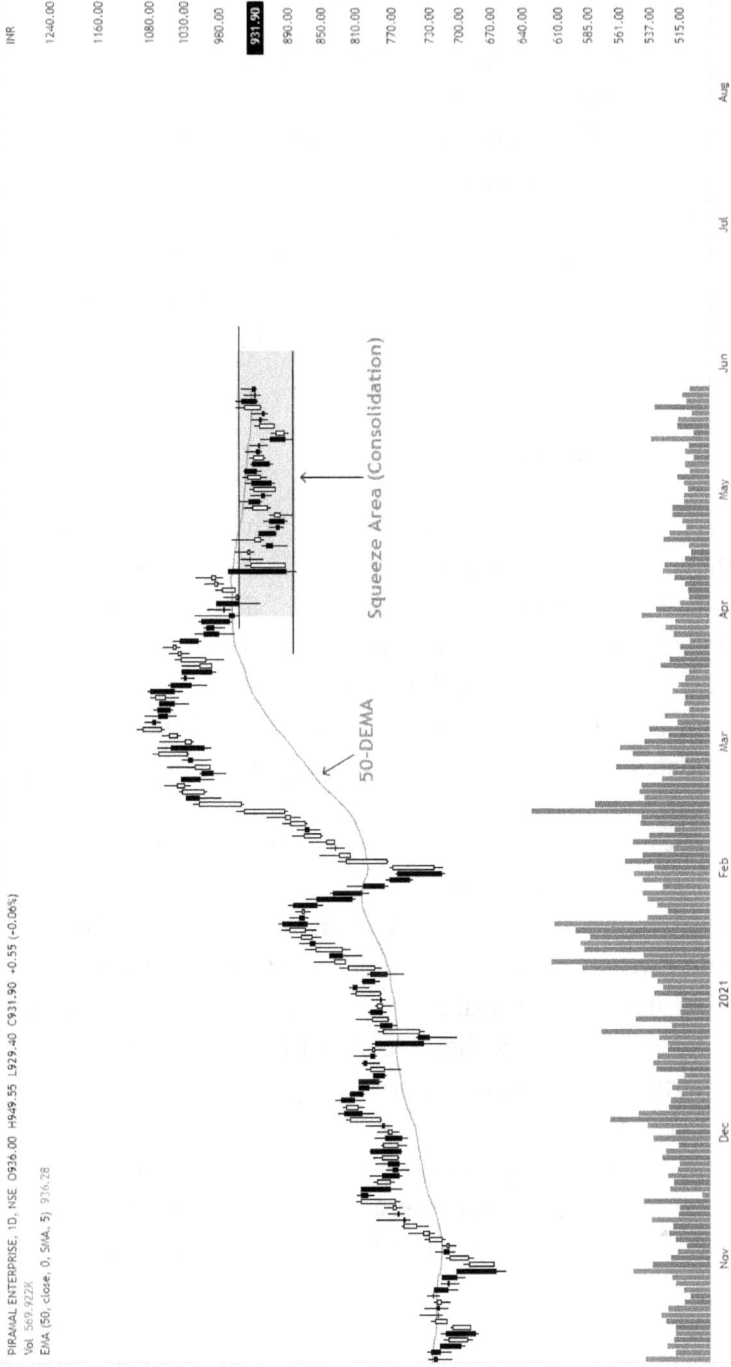

Image 7.7: Daily chart of Piramal Enterprise Ltd. showing a squeeze candidate.

candle from the squeeze area. Now let's look at the follow up chart of squeeze candidate.

Image 7.8 shows how the stock performed after the breakout candlestick occurred, breaking through the resistance of squeeze area and a 50-day exponential moving average. The stock had a clear run after the breakout candle and went up decently. It started rising from Rs 1,000 (from the breakout candle) all the way to over Rs 1,450 within the span of three months.

Reversal candidate

Reversal candidates are those stocks which have been trading at the support area and taking strong support from the demand zone. One will only take the position at the reversal area (demand zone) if any strong bullish candlestick appears and indicates a strong potential upside.

The traders who do reversal trading will like reversal candidates because the stock (security) will show a strong reversal bullish candle at the support zone which gives the best reward as the stop-loss on the reversal candidates will be very less with a huge potential upside.

One should always be aware of the fact that the structure of the reversal candidates should be towards the upside if trading at bullish reversal zone and if the structure is towards downside then traders should be bearish in the reversal zone.

Chartmojo reversal candidates will give best rewards if you take care of your stop-losses, whenever you trade a reversal candidate. Enter the position only if the signal candle (reversal candle) appears and also the confirmation candles (candle above the reversal candle) is bullish in the reversal zone.

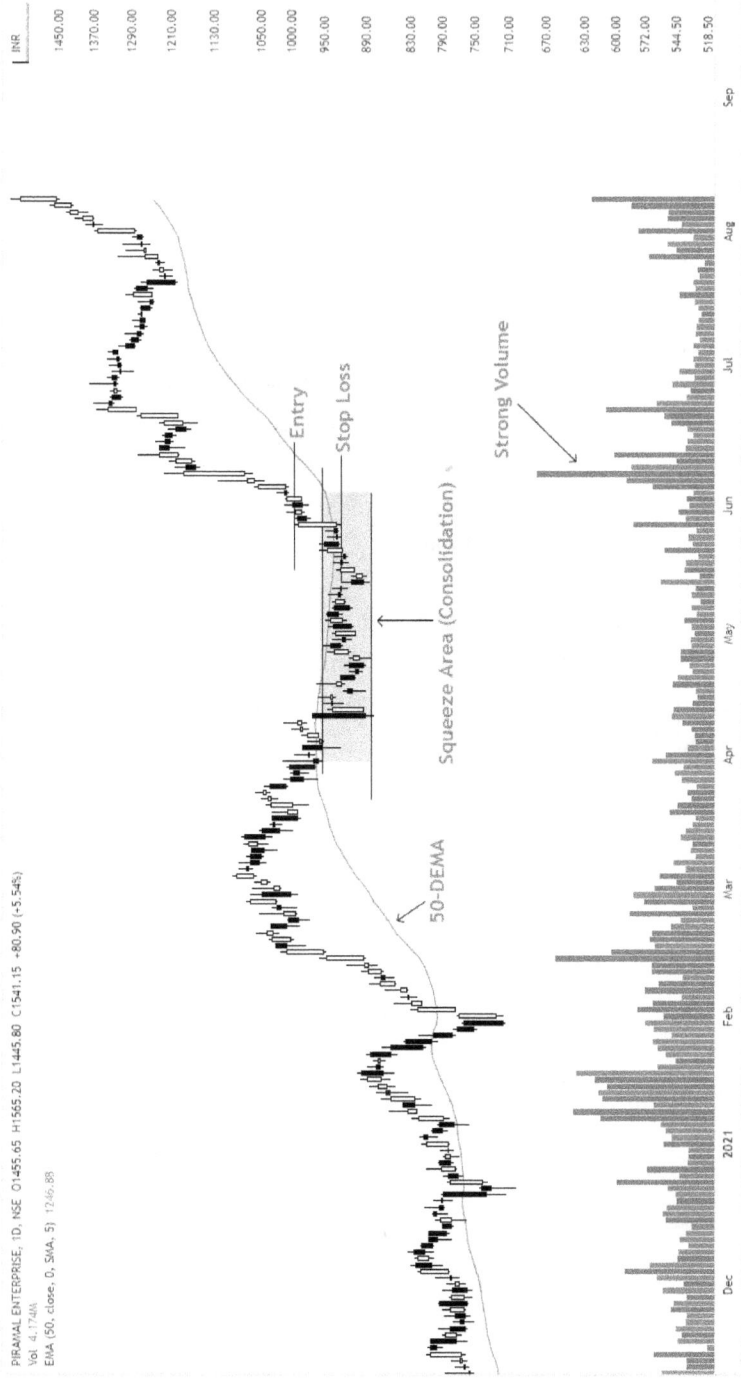

Chartmojos published on TradingView.com, Jan 21, 2023 13:15 UTC+5:30

PIRAMAL ENTERPRISE, 1D, NSE O1455.65 H1565.20 L1445.80 C1541.15 -80.90 (-5.54%)

Vol 4.174M

EMA (50, close, D, SMA, 5) 1246.88

Entry

Stop Loss

Squeeze Area (Consolidation)

Strong Volume

50-DEMA

Image 7.8: Daily chart of Piramal Enterprise Ltd. after the appearance of the breakout candle.

Case Study: Reversal candidate.

Image 7.9 shows the daily chart of SRF Ltd. The stock was in a strong uptrend and then went into a sideways phase. In the consolidation phase the stock tested its demand zone many times and took support. At the above-mentioned support, the stock also had decent volume with a bullish reversal candlestick.

The buy entry is mentioned at the break above signal candle (bullish candlestick) and the stop is placed at the low of tight zone below the bullish reversal candlestick pattern. This chart is the first chart of the case study. Now let's look at the follow up chart of reversal candidate.

Image 7.10 shows how the stock performed after the reversal candlestick formed and started moving up. The stock has a clear run with minor pullbacks midway. The stock started rising from Rs 1,090 all the way to Rs 1,400 within a span of four months.

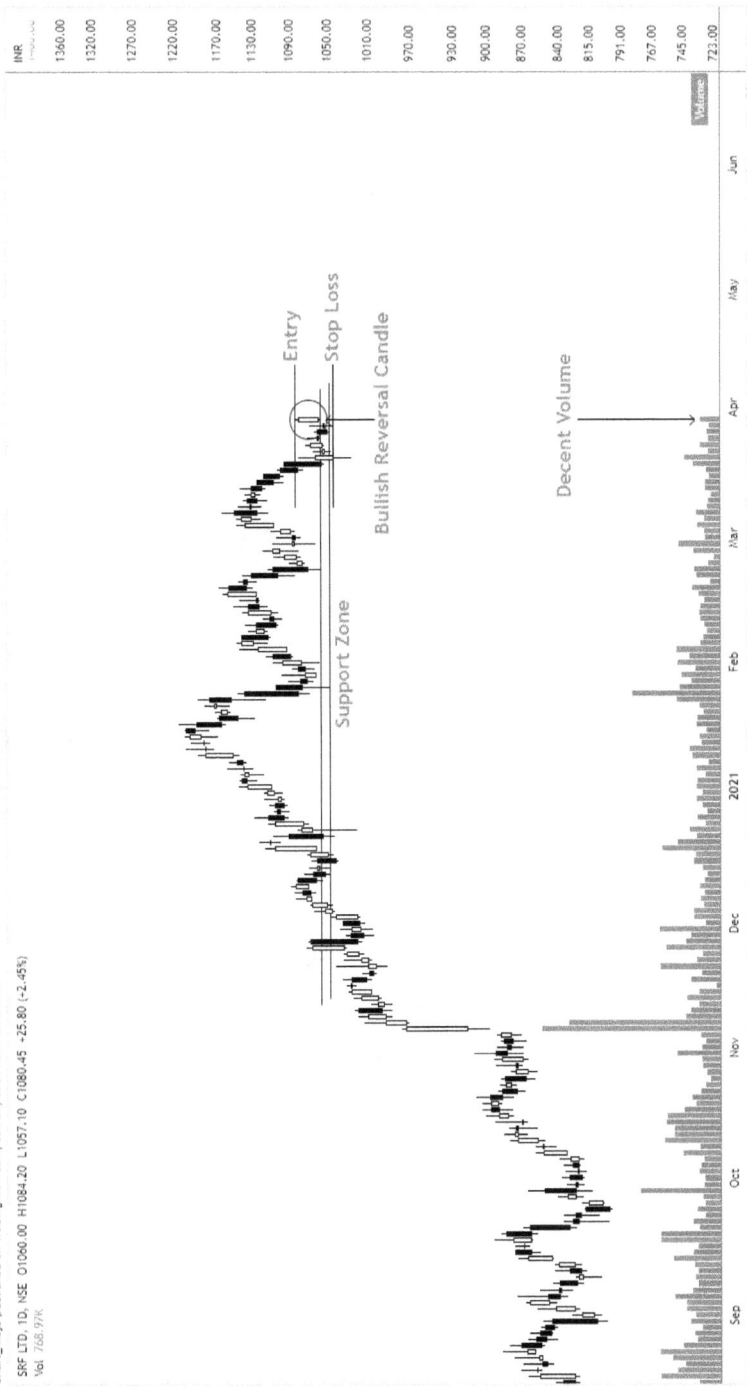

Image 7.9: Daily chart of SRF Ltd. showing a reversal chart pattern.

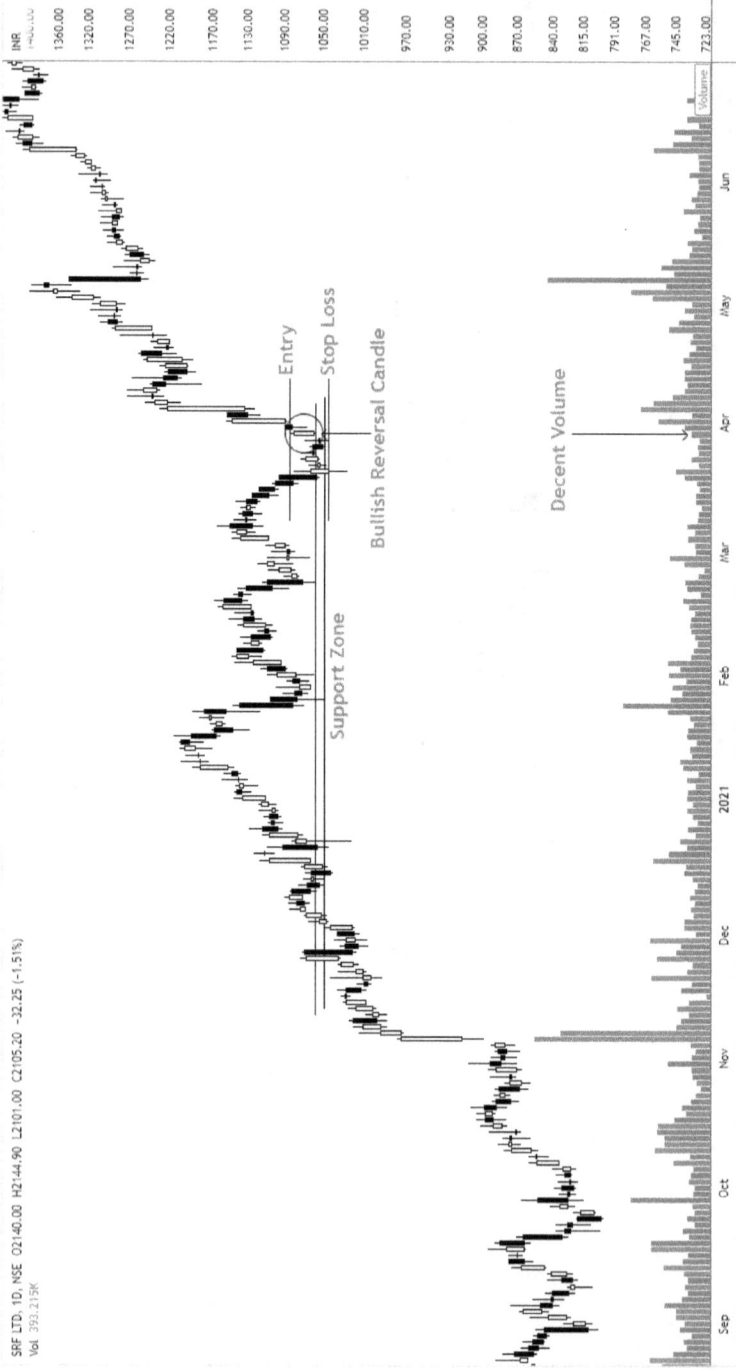

Image 7.10: Daily chart of SRF Ltd. showing after the reversal candlestick formed at the support zone

8

Risk Management and Position Sizing

Risk management must be an integral component of any trading strategy. Learn the fundamentals of risk management and how to implement them into your trading strategy.

You will discover

- Why risk management is crucial to trading, and
- What risk: reward ratios are and how they might benefit your approach

Risk management is one of the most ignored or underestimated areas of trading, while being one of the most important concepts for long-term success on the financial markets. However, why is risk management so crucial, and how can you incorporate it into your own strategies?

Without appropriate risk management, you may be the most gifted trader in the world with a natural eye for trading possibilities and yet burn your account with one wrong decision. Losses are inevitable regardless of one's skill or level of experience. Even the finest traders in the world have incurred losses in their transactions; it is an inevitable aspect of trading. Therefore, risk management is crucial to your trade.

Despite the fact that risk management guidelines are simple to understand—even for novices—it may be difficult to actually apply them when real money is at stake.

Before discussing particular risk management approaches, let's examine the importance of money management to a successful trading plan.

What makes a trading strategy work?

Usually, there are three key parts to a winning strategy:

A trading system with an edge: This requires consistent implementation of a strategy's rules, such as specified entry and exit points or trading with the trend. You might use basic moving averages to spot a new trend early and big volume additional to validate its strength. Your trading technique should be unique to you and used in your transactions.

Keeping your emotions in check: If you've tried out your strategy on both a demo account and a real one, you may have noticed that the results are different. This is because psychology plays a big role when real money is at stake. Emotions like fear, greed, or excitement can make it hard to follow your plan, which could lead to bad things. As a general rule, it's best to let your profits grow and cut your losses short. This can be made easier if you keep your emotions in check and stick to your trading plan.

Money management: It is a key part of your strategy because it tells you how big your position is, how much leverage you use, and where your stop-loss and take profit levels are. Managing your money well is a key part of being successful in trading over the long term. It helps to make the most money and lose as little as possible. It also makes you less likely to take too many risks.

Remember, what Paul Tudor Jones, American billionaire hedge fund manager, conservationist and philanthropist, said;

"Don't focus on making money; focus on protecting what you have."

As mentioned, how well you think about these things will have a big impact on how well you can trade. If you only use two of the three things mentioned here, you might run into a problem that you could have avoided. One important part of trading is to keep going as long as you can.

Managing the Risk

As stated by Bruce Kovner, an American billionaire hedge fund manager,

"I know where I'm getting out before I get in. Whenever I enter a position, I have a predetermined stop. That is the only way I can sleep. The position size on a trade is determined by the stop, and the stop is determined on a technical basis."

Hence, respecting your stop-loss is very important.

As stated before, even the greatest traders incur losses at some time. It is an integral aspect of trade. Limiting your losses to a more manageable level is essential. Thus, you will be able to remain in the market longer, boosting your chances of making more profitable transactions.

One strategy to find the correct balance between reward and risk is to adhere to a 2:1 or even 3:1 reward: risk ratio, in which your targeted gains are always twice your maximum losses. If you adhere to this reward: risk ratio, you only need two winning transactions, even if you incur three losses, for your overall gains to exceed your losses. Although it is not a general rule, it might help you visualise a particular risk management strategy.

Let's examine two traders that both begin with Rs 10,000 and use a 2:1 reward-to-risk ratio, but use vastly different degrees of money management. The first trader uses a very aggressive strategy, risking 60% of their money on each transaction and aiming for a 120% profit. The second trader is far more conservative, risking just 5% of their account money in pursuit of a 10% reward. Let's assume, for the sake of simplicity, that each trader has the same 10 transactions and that every second trade is profitable.

Investor 1	Investor 2
Profit 120%	Profit 10%
Loss 60%	Loss 5%
Every second trade earns a profit	Every second trade earns a profit
10 trades	10 trades

Image 8.1: Case study for risk management of a trading position.

Strategy Effectiveness

	Investor 1					Investor 2		
Period	Capital	Profit + 120%	Loss- 60%		Period	Capital	Profit + 10%	Loss- 5%
0	10,000				0	10000		
1	22,000	12000			1	11000	1000	
2	8800		-13200		2	10450		-550
3	19360	10560			3	11495	1045	
4	7744		-11616		4	10920		-575
5	17037	9293			5	12012	1092	
6	6815		-10222		6	11412		-600
7	14992	8187			7	12553	1141	
8	5997		-8995		8	11925		-628
9	13193	7196			9	13118	1193	
10	5277		-7916		10	12462		-656

Image 8.2: Comparison of strategy effectiveness

These tables show the trading performance of two separate traders with different degrees of risk management.

Despite the fact that both methods had similar success rates, the same beginning capital, and a 2:1 reward-to-risk ratio, the ultimate outcomes are drastically different due to the significantly different money management styles used. The first trader's aggressive strategy resulted in a total loss of 47%, whilst the second trader's overall profit of Rs 12,462 represents about 25%. Therefore, you can see how a little tweak to your risk management strategy might result in improved profits.

Bottom Line

As seen before, risk management may be an important aspect of trading. An expert trader understands how much he or she can risk, but as a novice, you should do all in your power to prevent suffering heavy losses. Losses are a necessary part of trading and cannot be avoided, but it is crucial to understand how to deal with them. Profit management is another component. A skilled trader must strike a balance between the two possible outcomes of a trade: maximising profit while minimising loss.

9

Trading Psychology

Trading psychology is the way a trader thinks about the markets while they are participating in its activities. It can show how much of a profit they make or why they lost a lot of money.

In trading psychology, things like biases and emotions that come from being human are very important. When learning about trading psychology, the main goal is to learn how to avoid the problems that come with having negative psychological traits and to develop more positive ones.

Most of the time, traders who know about the psychology of trading won't act based on bias or emotion. So, they have a better chance of making money on the markets or, at the very least, of losing as little money as possible.

Trading psychology is different for every trader because it depends on how they feel and what they already think. Some of the feelings that have an effect on trading are:

- greed
- fear
- hope
- FOMO (fear of missing out)
- frustration

How to strengthen your trading psychology

The best way to improve your trading psychology is to become aware of your own feelings, preferences, and personality traits. Once you are aware of these things, you can make a trading plan that takes them into account so that they don't have as much of an effect on your decisions.

If you are naturally confident, you may find that your overconfidence and pride make it hard for you to make decisions. For example, instead of taking a small loss on your trading account, you might let losses run in the hopes that the market will turn around. This could cause you to lose more money or even cause your trading account to go bankrupt.

To stop this from happening, you could use stop-loss to limit your losses and decide when to close a trade before you even open the position. By doing this, you have become aware of your own biases and emotions and have decided not to act on them. Instead, you have taken steps to fight them.

How does bias impact trading style?

Biases have an effect on trading because, by definition, a bias is a personal preference for one thing over another that is already set. So, they can make it hard for you to make good decisions on the markets because they can cloud your judgement and make you act based on your gut rather than on technical analysis.

Bias may be classified into five types:

Confirmation bias: It is the tendency to seek out or give more weight to information and analysis that supports your belief systems. It is also possible that you do not seek out or ignore facts which conflict with your beliefs.

Gambler's fallacy: Believing that an asset will continue to climb because it has been rising. Similar to how there is no reason to suppose that a coin should fall with its tail facing up after landing heads-side up many times in a row, there is no reason to believe that it should.

Representative bias: It is the tendency to repeat successful deals made in the past. You may do this without analysing every transaction of this type since it has been profitable in the past. However, even if two deals seem identical, it is essential to evaluate each transaction on its own merits and not based on past performance.

Status quo bias: This bias suggests that you will continue to use old strategies or trades instead of experimenting with new ones; you will maintain the status quo. The risk arises when you ignore evaluating if these outdated strategies are still applicable in the present market.

Negativity bias: This bias makes you more likely to focus on the bad aspects of a deal rather than the positive aspects. This might cause you to reject an entire approach when, in reality, it may have only required minor adjustments to be profitable.

10

Trading Journal

What is a trading journal?

A trading journal is, in its simplest form, a collection of records presented in list form, where each entry represents a trade executed by the trader.

Each trade record contains information on the trade, such as entry and exit timestamps, entry and exit prices, position size, direction, and any other data points that the trader may consider relevant to record.

The records should also include information regarding the trade's result, including whether it was profitable or not, as well as the cash amount and percentage of profit or loss. This information is essential for analysing and quantifying the effects of a successful trade or an error.

In addition to real data and results, a trading notebook may also include personal comments, which may pertain to methods, trends, setups, or simply emotional and mental state observations.

Your trade journal is a record of your whole trading activities. A trading log gives every trader who is serious about making money with a tool for honest self-evaluation.

As someone said, **"Having trading discipline is the beginning; keeping discipline is the progress; staying disciplined is success"**.

So do not forget to stay disciplined with documenting all your trades and record all trading activates.

There are three areas necessary for trading success:

1. Developing and executing an efficient trading plan.
2. Implementing a solid trading strategy into this plan.
3. Examine and enhance your trading performance and techniques.

Simply put, my trading notebook contains the following:

- Date and time
- Name of the stock
- Long/short position
- Position sizing
- Stop-loss
- Points gained and lost
- Screenshot of chart
- Comments

The main goal of my diary is to identify and correct errors. My trading notebook is simple and practical.

Here are some tips for maintaining a useful trading journal.

1. Always begin and stop the journal before and after the trade.
2. Document everything. Don't miss any details. Be honest. If you choose to play Free Fire (game) while in a trade

and forgot to exit the trade, you must write that down and provide an explanation.

3. Pay attention to your feelings. Then, ensure that you record them.

4. Ensure that the journal contains observations on you, your trade, and the financial market.

5. Take a snapshot of intraday charts showing each day's performance and highlight them. Observe and record repeating trends.

6. After a few months, the patterns will begin to emerge in real time.

7. A trading log is a learning tool and an excellent method for training your eye to recognise trade setups.

8. Nothing is too minor to document in your journal. Put it down on paper.

Image 10.1 is the excel template which shows all the information you should record while taking a trade.

You can also alter the format of the trading journal according your style of trading.

Trading Journal								
Date	Security Name	Chart Setup	Long/Short	Position Size	Stop Loss	Points Gained	Point Lost	Comments

Image 10.1: Trading journal format.

Bottom Line

There is no perfect trading diary template. While adding transactions to their own trading diaries, each trader should assess the crucial metrics they require or should avoid using. In light of this, a trade magazine must be modified.

In addition, reviewing your trade log spreadsheet on a daily basis is a useful practice for calculating your present exposure level and any opportunities for extending your trading portfolio.

11

Trailing Stop-Loss

How does a trailing stop work?

A stop-loss order is a type of order that helps you manage risk by letting you choose a point at which your trade should be closed if the price moves against you. The main reason to use a stop-loss is to make sure that your losses are kept to a minimum. Stop-loss orders stay in place until either your position is sold or you cancel the order.

A trailing stop, also called a trailing stop-loss, is a type of market order that sets a stop-loss at a certain percentage below the market price of an asset, rather than at a single value. The stop-loss then moves along with the price of the stock.

What is the purpose of a trailing stop?

With trailing stops, you can lock in your profits and keep your trade open until the price of the asset hits your trailing stop level. Your trailing stop-loss order can be set to a certain number of points or a percentage of the difference between the original price and the current price. When the market price hits your trailing stop, the stop-loss order will be triggered, and your trade will be closed.

A trailing stop can also be better than a regular stop-loss if the market price moves in your favour, but then goes back the other way. This is because your stop-loss will have moved in the same direction as the market price, but not the other way. Like a regular stop-loss, once the price of the instrument hits your trailing stop-loss level, your trade will be closed at the next available price. This keeps you from holding on to a losing trade and risk losing more money.

Graphical example of a trailing stop-loss for long position

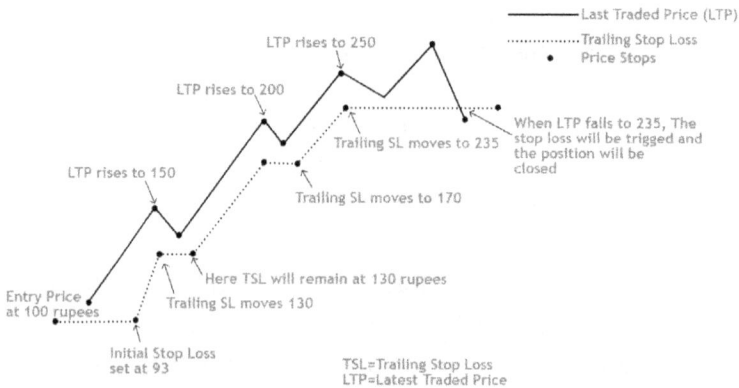

Image 11.1: Trailing stop-loss for long position

Let's take the example of a company which was trading at Rs 100. You bought that company at Rs 100 and with the initial stop-loss of Rs 93.

Thereafter, the stock started inching on the higher side and reached Rs 150 where it took a halt for a while and showed a small pullback. Now our initial stop will change as we use the trailing stop-loss concept which is now pegged at Rs 130.

Once the pullback got over, the stock again started rising up and reached the next peak at Rs 200. You must have noticed that our trailing stop-loss is also inching up higher with price and it has reached the price of Rs 170.

As you can see in this example that after few trading sessions the stock price has reached Rs 250 and showed a little upward movement, then finally came down and hit our trailing stop-loss at Rs 235. This is where we will exit our trading position and close out the long position.

Graphical example of a trailing stop-loss for short position

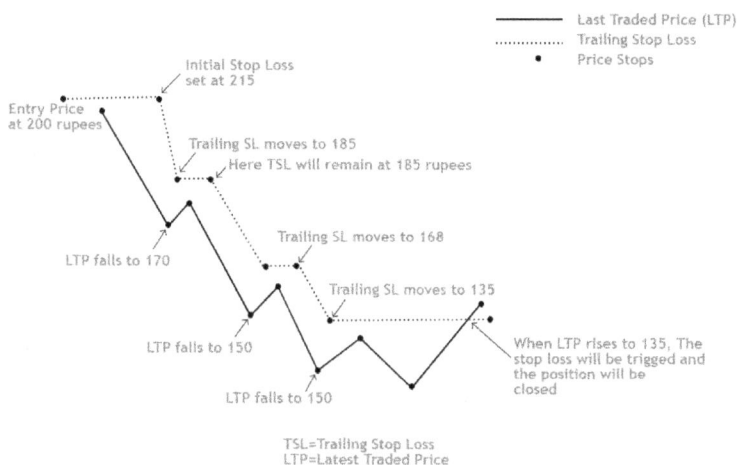

Image 11.2: Trailing stop-loss for short position

Let's take an example of a short position with a trailing stop-loss. For instance, a company was trading at Rs 200 and you took the short position in the company at Rs 200 with the initial stop-loss of Rs 215.

Thereafter, the stock started inching towards the lower side and reached Rs 170 where it took a halt for a while and showed a small upside retracement. Our initial stop will change as we are using a trailing stop-loss concept which is now pegged at Rs 185.

Once the upside retracement gets over, the stock again started rising lower and reached the next trough at Rs 150. Now you must have noticed that our trailing stop-loss is also inching lower with price and it has reached the price of Rs 168.

As you can see in this example, after a few trading sessions the stock price reached Rs 150 and showed a slight downward movement, then finally went up and hit our trailing stop-loss at Rs 135 which is our trailing stop-loss. This is where we will take the exit from our trading position and close out short position.

12

Case Studies

Case Studies of Continuation Patterns

I have written all the case studies of chart patterns to follow and have tried my best to show you different scenarios from taking the trade to exiting the same.

I have shown more than 50 case studies of continuation chart pattern and reversal chart pattern which one can use while breakout trading. Remember, we should only use a chart pattern for breakout trading and not the candlestick patterns which are used for reversal trading.

Real-life examples have been shown with detailed explanation, which will make it easier for you to grasp and understand the same in the best possible manner.

Do remember, I have used 9-EMA as a trailing stop-loss a lot as it lets us ride the respective trend and book maximum gain as opposed to a pattern based target, which you will see in the case studies provided below.

Ascending Triangle

A bullish ascending pattern formed on the daily chart of Ethereum from May 2020 to August 2020 as shown in image 12.1.

Ethereum / U.S. Dollar, 1D, BITSTAMP O245.63 H270.00 L241.76 C264.23 +18.32 (+7.45%)
Vol · ETH 55.327K
Vol · ETH 55.327K

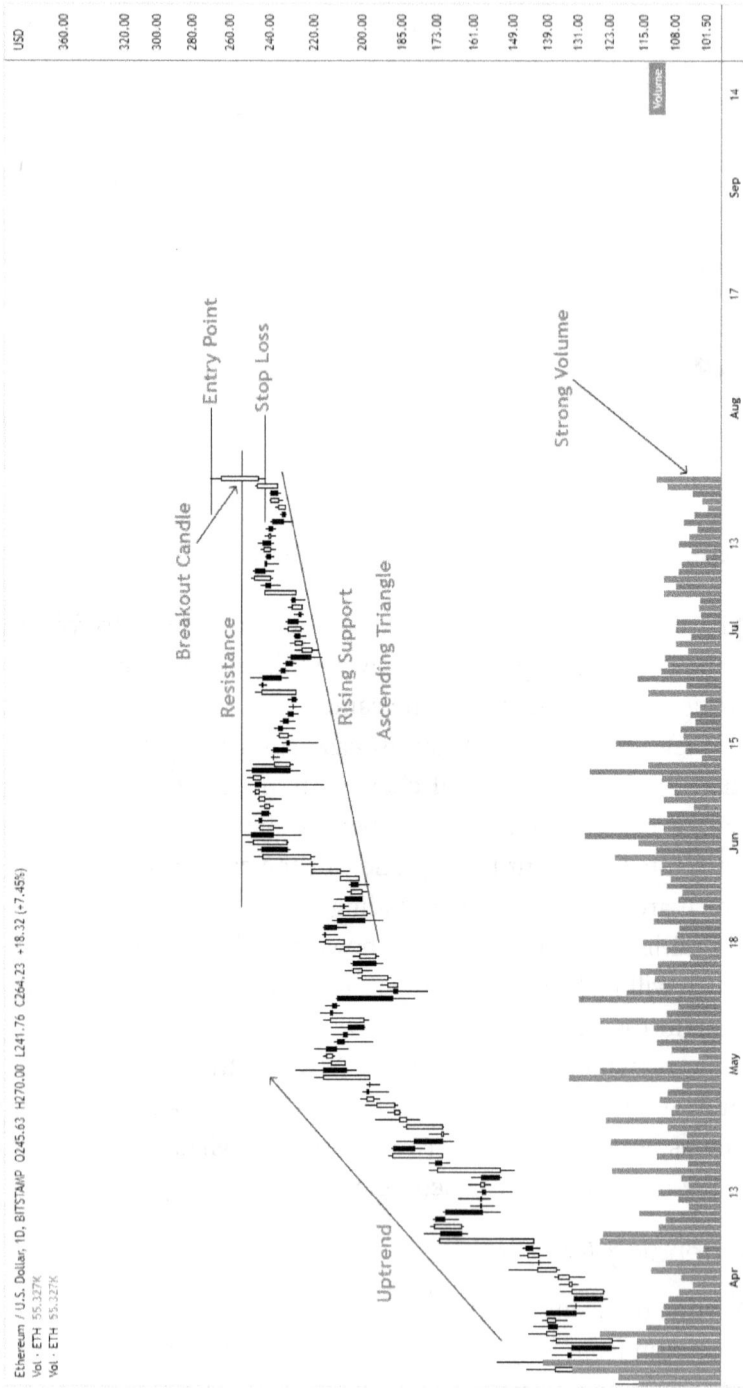

Image 12.1: Daily chart of Ethereum (bullish ascending pattern).

The bullish ascending pattern formed and showed a breakout with a strong bullish candle. The breakout happened with a decent volume spurt which made the breakout more reliable.

Here, the long position is taken above $ 269.38 with a target of around $339 (52 points above the entry area) and the stop is placed around $241.86 (low of the breakout candle which is just below the breakout).

In the chart, you can see how trend continuation takes place after the breakout.

Notice in image 12.2 that the stock rises from levels of $269.38 to $339.48 achieving the target and giving returns of around 26% in period of 10 days.

Instead of booking profit here if a trader would have used the concept of trailing stop-loss, then he could have made some more profit as he would have exited the position when it would have hit trailing stop-loss. We will discuss this in the upcoming chart pattern case studies.

Descending Triangle

A bearish ascending pattern formed on the weekly chart of Future Retail Ltd. from March 2021 to March 2022 as shown in image 12.3.

We can see in the chart that the stock was in a downtrend before the chart formation and it formed a classic downtrend continuation pattern with a decent volume and a strong breakdown candle.

Here, the short position is taken at below Rs 38.35 with no target. We will be using 9-EMA as a trailing stop-loss and once the trailing stop-loss (TSL) is hit, will exit from the position.

Notice that once the breakdown happened, the price went down just one way in a free fall.

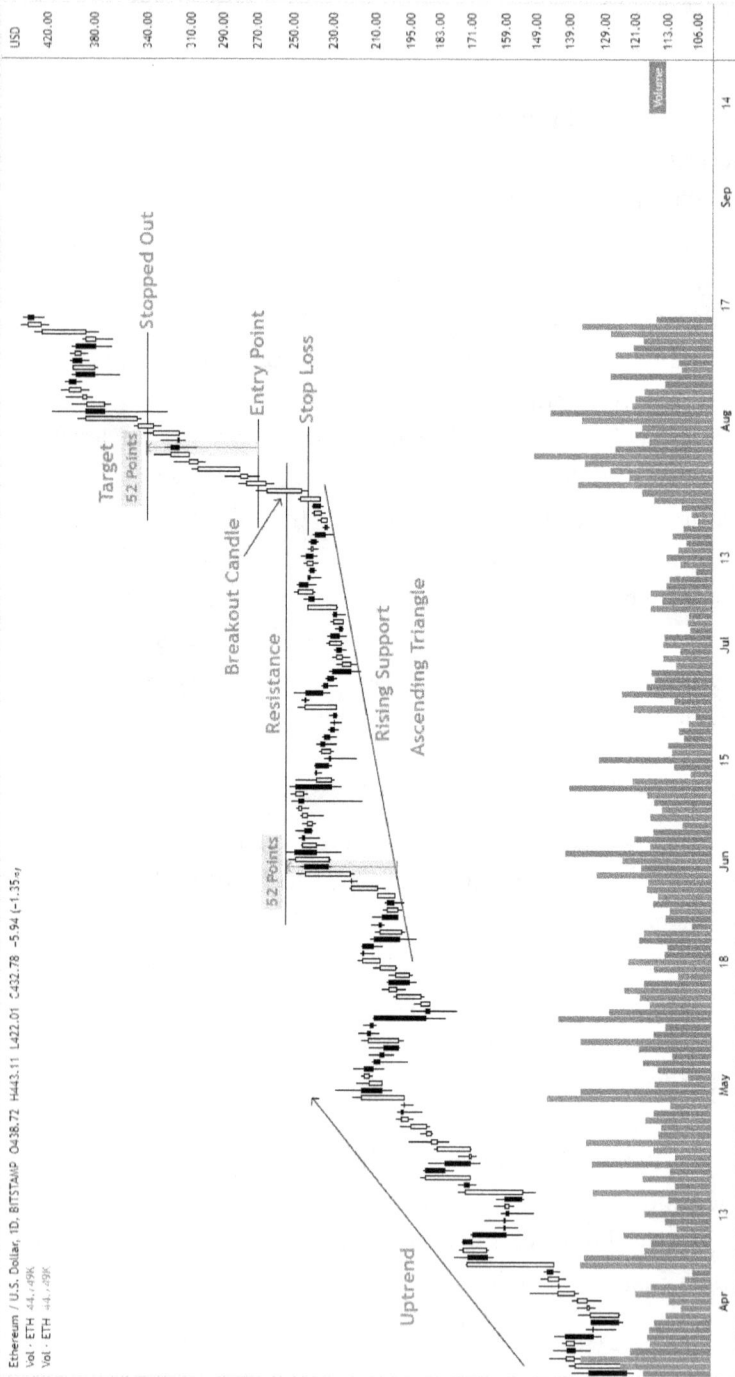

Image 12.2: Trend continuation takes place after the breakout on the Etherum chart.

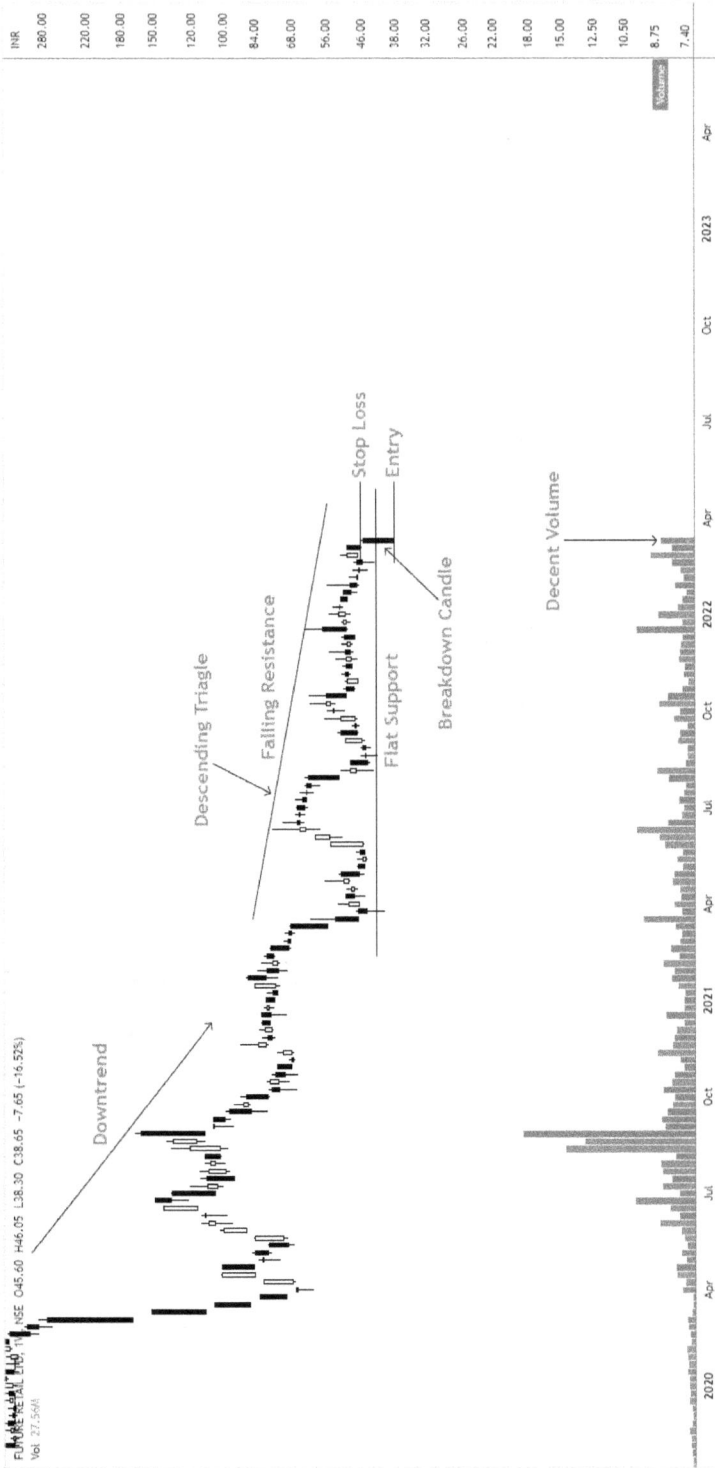

Image 12.3: Weekly chart of Future Retail Ltd. (bearish ascending pattern).

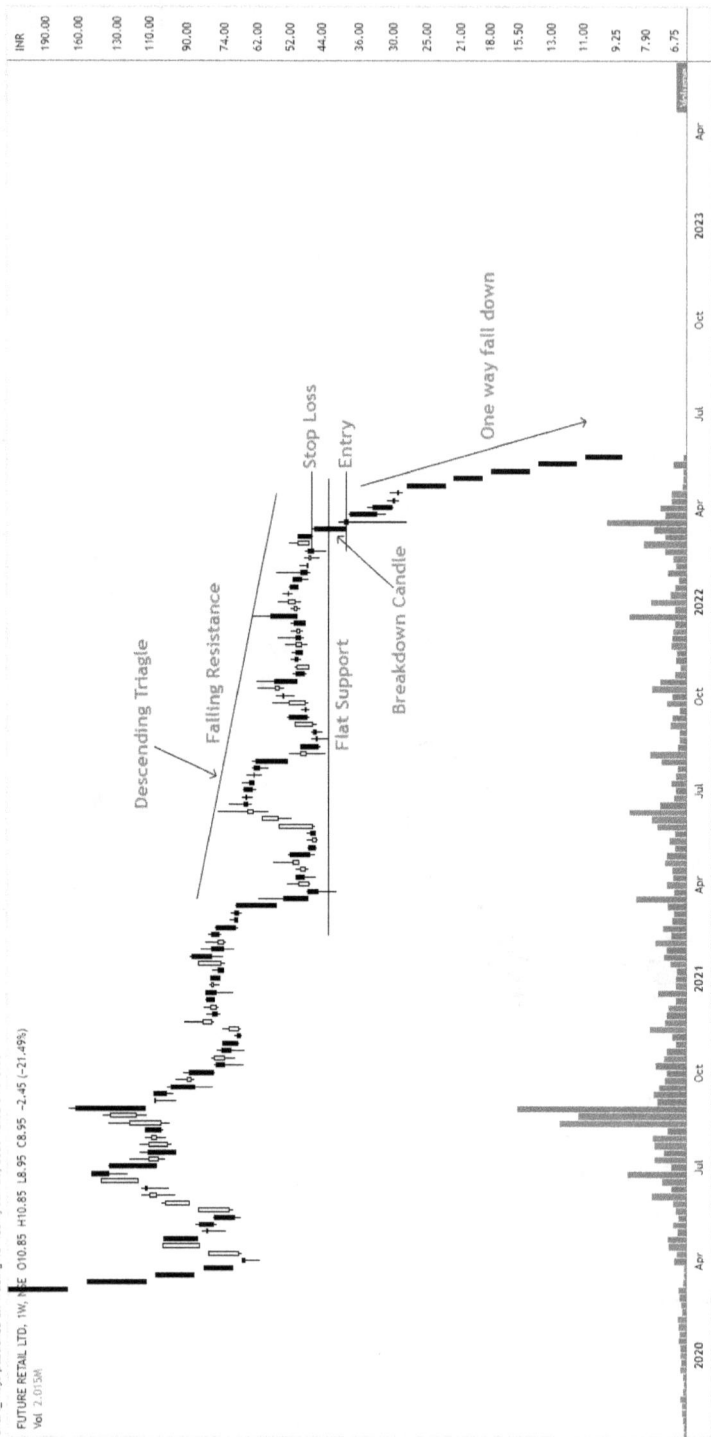

Image 12.4: Daily chart of Future Retail Ltd. showing a descending triangle continuation pattern.

Once again, in image 12.4 you can see how the price action shaped up after the breakdown and gave us a decent downside. The price moved all the way down to Rs 9 and reached from Rs 38 to Rs 9 within very few trading sessions.

Bullish Symmetrical Triangle

A bullish symmetrical triangle pattern formed on the daily chart of Solar Industries India Ltd. from March 2022 to August 2022 as shown in image 12.5.

The stock was in a strong uptrend before the formation of a bullish symmetrical triangle, gave a double bottom breakout and showed a nice upside (if you can notice just before the formation of symmetrical triangle).

The breakout happened with a candle which was very strong (it was in the form of bullish marubozu) and it occurred with a strong volume build-up as well.

Here, the long position is taken above Rs 2,997 with a target of around Rs 3,993 (790 points above the entry area) and the stop is placed around Rs 2,821 (low of the breakout candle).

Image 12.6 is the follow up chart of Solar Industries India Ltd. after the breakout occurred. You can see how trend continuation takes place after the breakout.

Stock rises from a level of Rs 2,997 to Rs 3,993 achieving the target giving returns of around 33% over a period of two months.

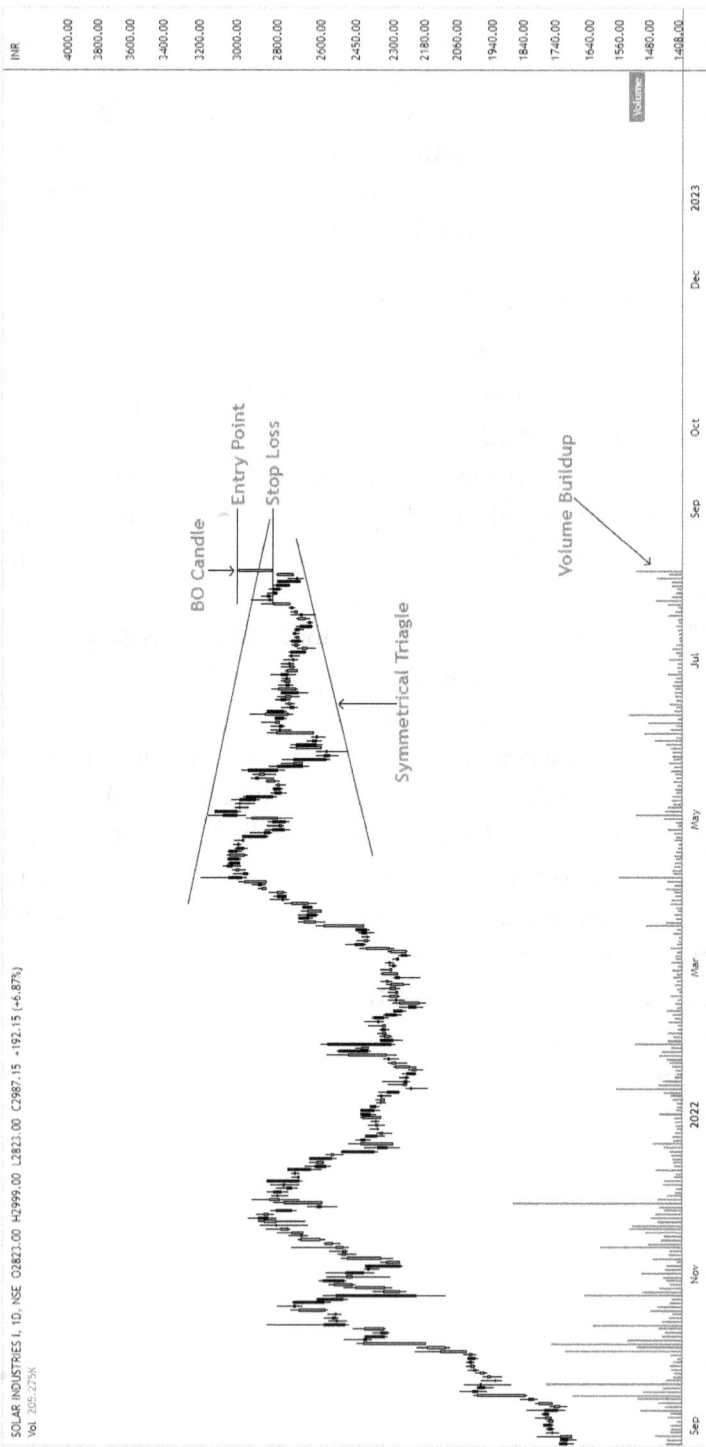

Image 12.5: Daily chart of Solar Industries India Ltd. (bullish symmetrical triangle pattern).

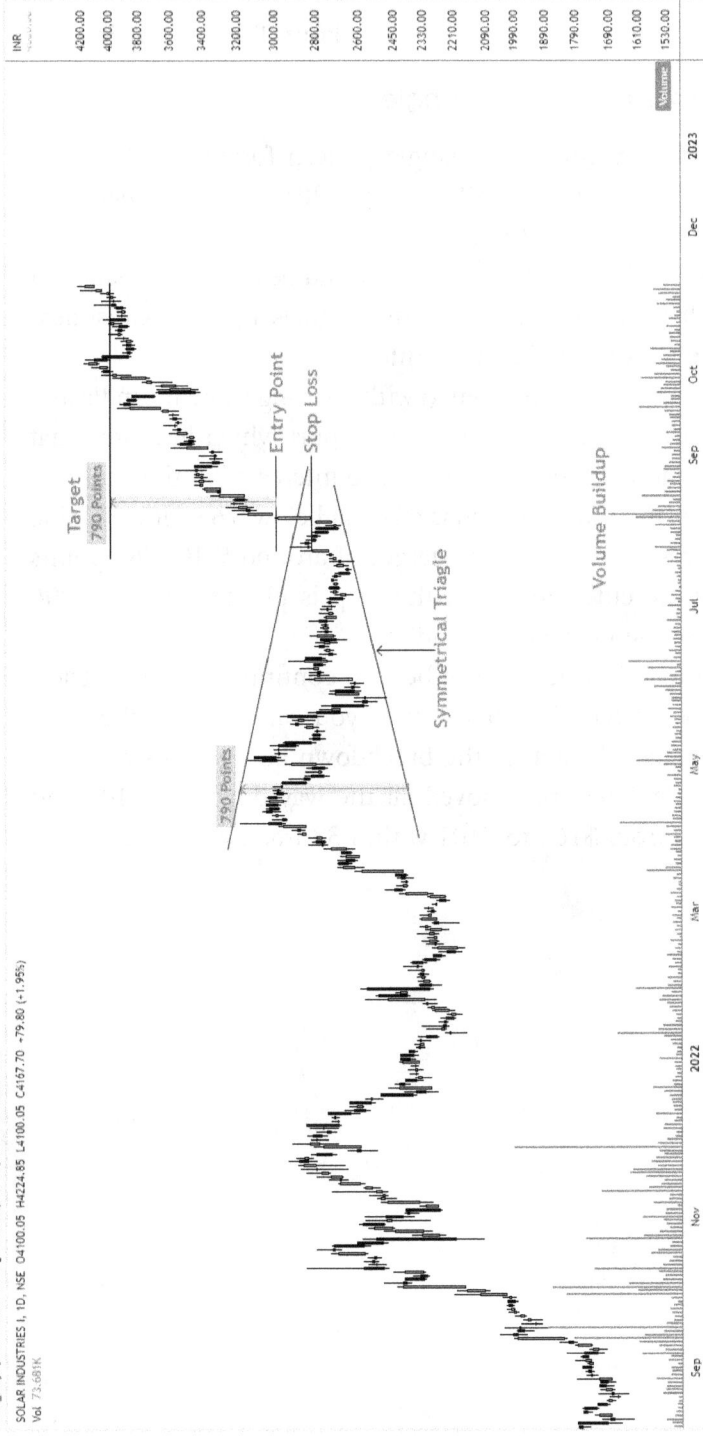

Image 12.6: Daily chart of Solar Industries India Ltd. signifying higher highs and higher lows, price-action formation after the breakout of symmetrical triangle pattern

Bearish Symmetrical Triangle

A bearish symmetrical triangle pattern formed on the daily chart of Ethereum from September 2018 to November 2018 as shown in image 12.7.

The stock was in a strong downtrend before the formation of bearish symmetrical triangle which signals a strong bearishness on the above-mentioned counter.

The breakdown happened with a strong bearish candle and it occurred with a strong volume spurt which indicated that huge market participants were also interested in this counter.

Here, the short position is taken at below $ 65 with a trailing stop-loss which made our target of around $ 101 (64 points below the entry area) and the stop is placed around $ 206 (high of the breakdown candle).

In the follow up chart of bearish continuation symmetrical triangle (image 12.8) once again you can see how the price action shaped up after the breakdown and gave us a decent downside. The price moved all the way down to $ 101 and reached from $165 to $101 within 33 trading sessions.

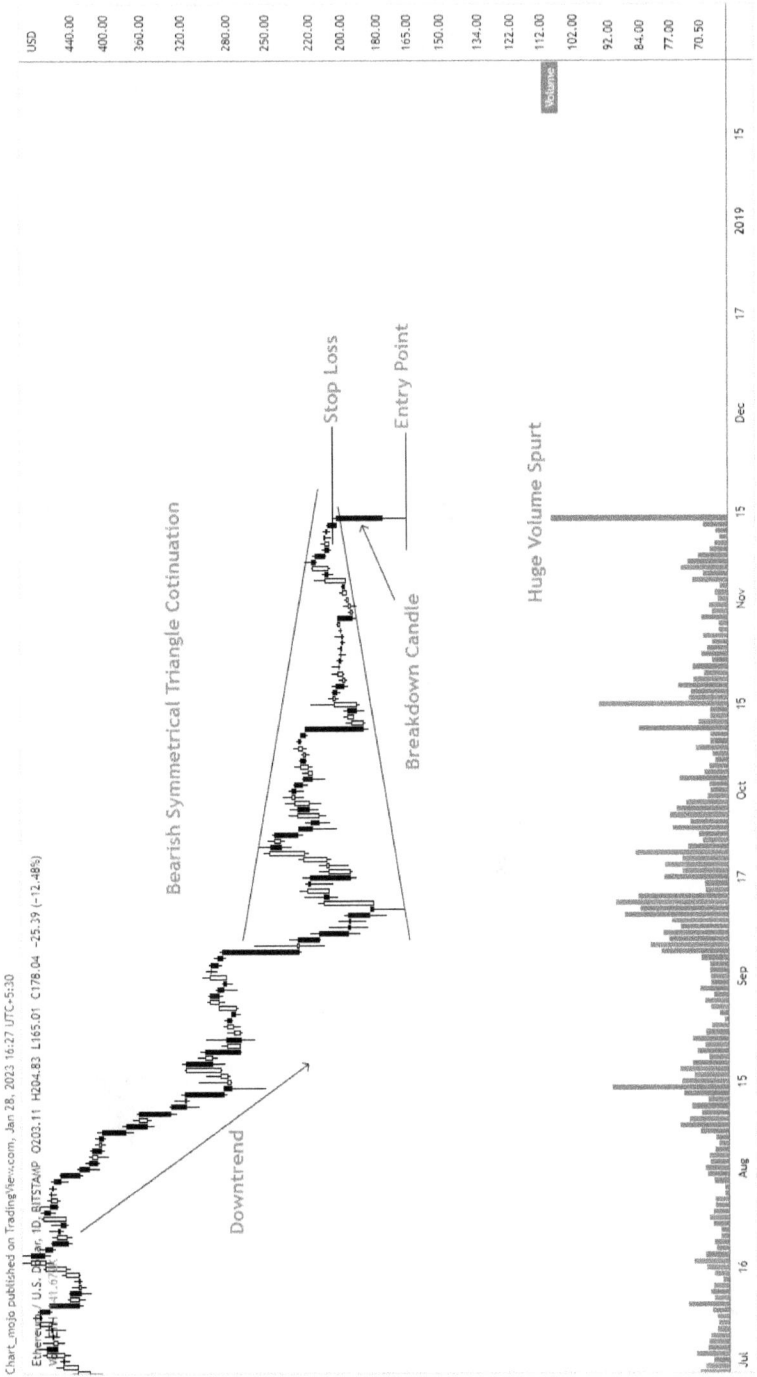

Chart_mojo published on TradingView.com, Jan 28, 2023 16:27 UTC-5:30

Ethereum / U.S. Dollar, 1D, BITSTAMP O203.11 H204.83 L165.01 C178.04 −25.39 (−12.48%)

Downtrend

Bearish Symmetrical Triangle Cotinuation

Stop Loss

Entry Point

Breakdown Candle

Huge Volume Spurt

Volume

Image 12.7: Daily chart of Ethereum (bearish symmetrical triangle pattern).

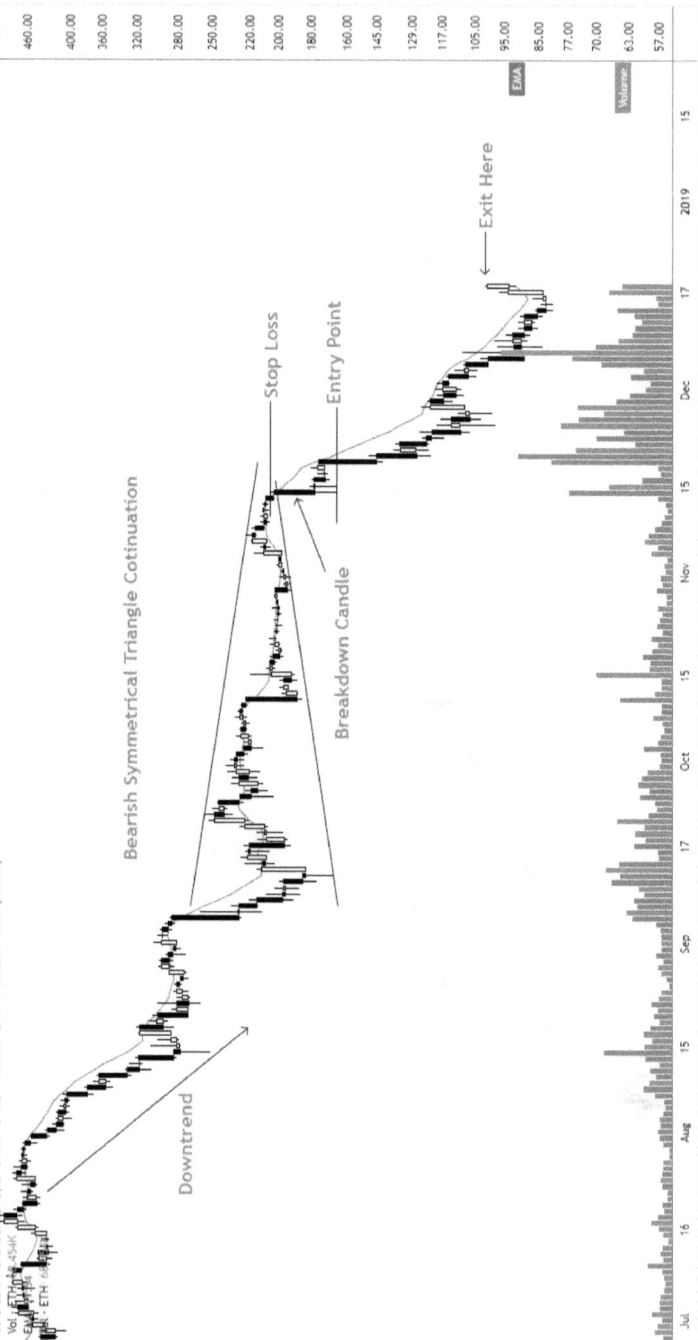

Image 12.8: Daily chart of Etherium/US dollar showing us a clearly visible downside momentum after the breakdown from bearish continuation symmetrical triangle.

Bullish Pennant

A bullish pennant pattern formed on the daily chart of Indian Railway Tourism Corporation Ltd., from September 2022 to October 2022 as shown in image 12.9.

In the chart, the uptrend seems intact with a series of higher highs and higher lows and a clear up trending pole is seen before the bullish pennant occurred.

Notice that the stock pennant breakout occurred with strong breakout candle which was also accompanied by a huge volume build-up.

The long position is taken right above Rs 813 with a target of around Rs 1,193 (380 points above the entry area) and the stop is placed around Rs 762 (low of the wide range breakout candle).

Once the long position was taken, we can see how the stock price drifted towards upside from the breakout zone.

After the breakout candle occurred (image 12.10), the volume accumulation was seen which ultimately indicated that big buyers are also keen to buy this stock.

The stock price drifted from the price of Rs 813 to all the way up to Rs 1,193 in no time (the target was identified using the pole size), as one can see that only one black candle was seen in the entire upward movement from entry to the target price.

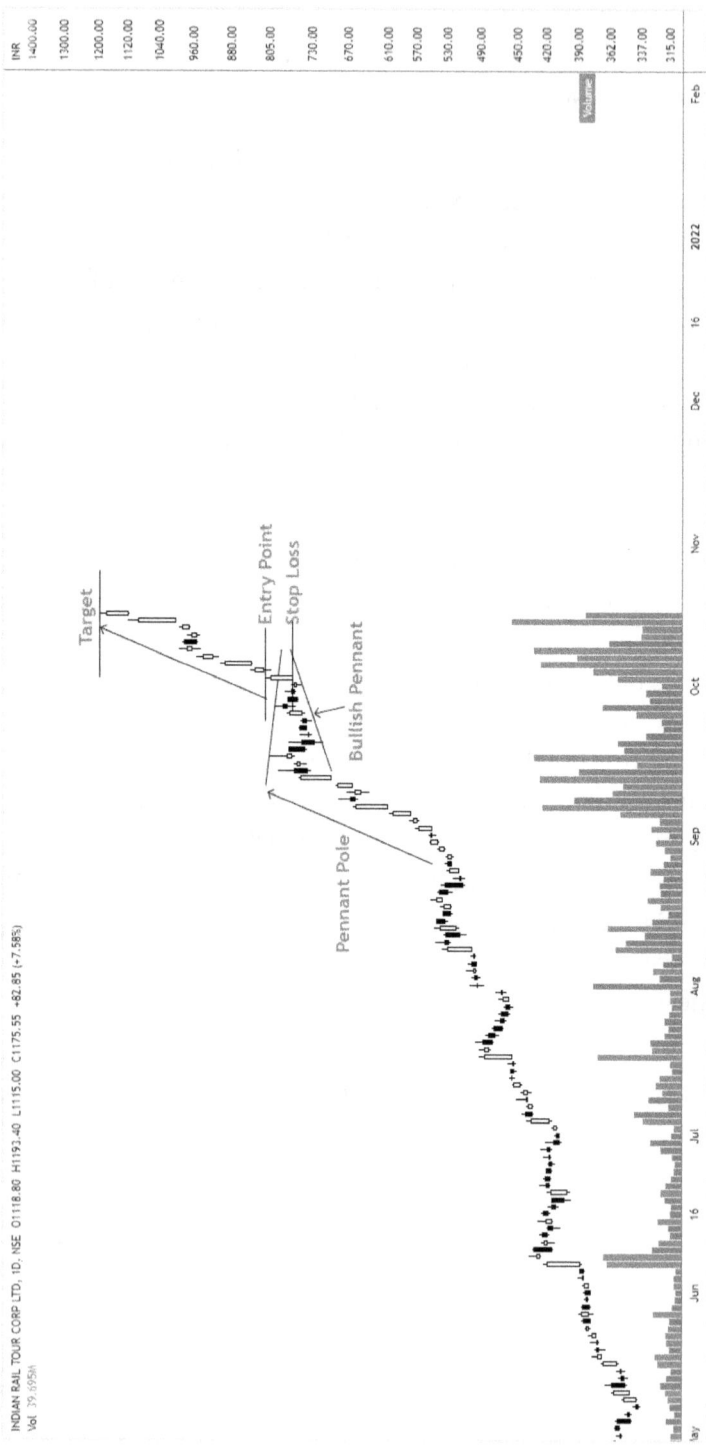

Image 12.9: Daily chart of Railway Tourism Corporation Ltd. (bullish pennant pattern).

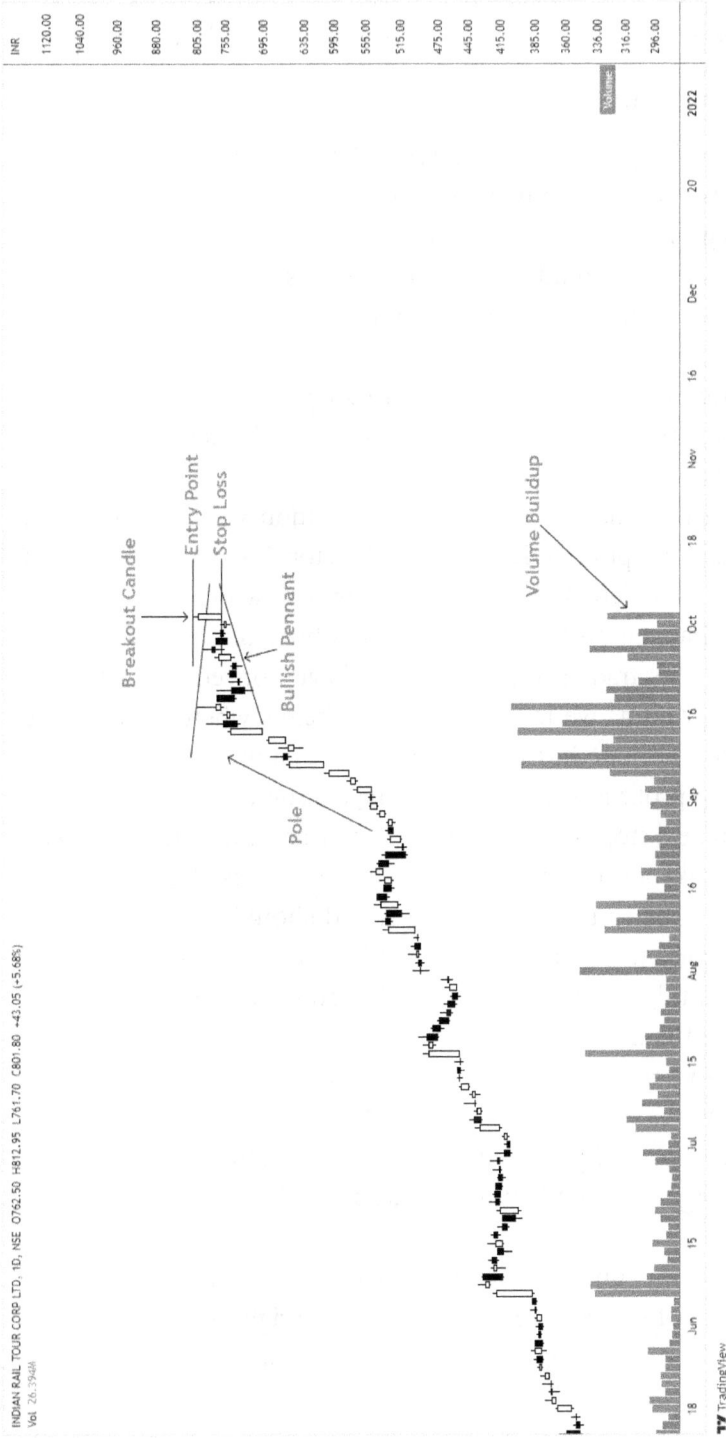

Image 12.10: Daily chart of Indian Railway Tourism Corporation Ltd. showing the bullish pennant pattern.

Bearish Pennant

A bearish pennant pattern formed on the daily chart of Indian Bank from December 2010 to January 2011, as shown in image 12.11.

The downtrend seems intact with strong bearish candles and a clear down trending pole is seen before the bearish pennant occurred.

One can also notice that the stock pennant breakout occurred with strong breakout candle which was also accompanied by increasing volume.

In this chart setup, the short position will be taken right below the price of Rs 239 and the stop-loss will be placed at Rs 250 which is the high of the breakdown candle. The exit will happen on the basis of 9-EMA breakout at Rs 233.

In this trade setup you would have noticed we just made 2% profit as we took the exit just below where we took the entry. So, one has to keep in mind that we are not going to make profit in every trade we make. Sometimes we will have to take a stop-loss hit and, in some trades, we will break even or make a very small gain which was the case here.

Do remember that trading is and should be considered as business wherein you make profit and losses both. Once you build this mindset then only will you be able to make money from the market.

Do respect your stop-loss and take exit without any emotions.

As Peter Lynch, an American investor, mutual fund manager, and philanthropist, said,

"In this business, if you're good, you're right six times out of ten. You're never going to be right nine times out of ten."

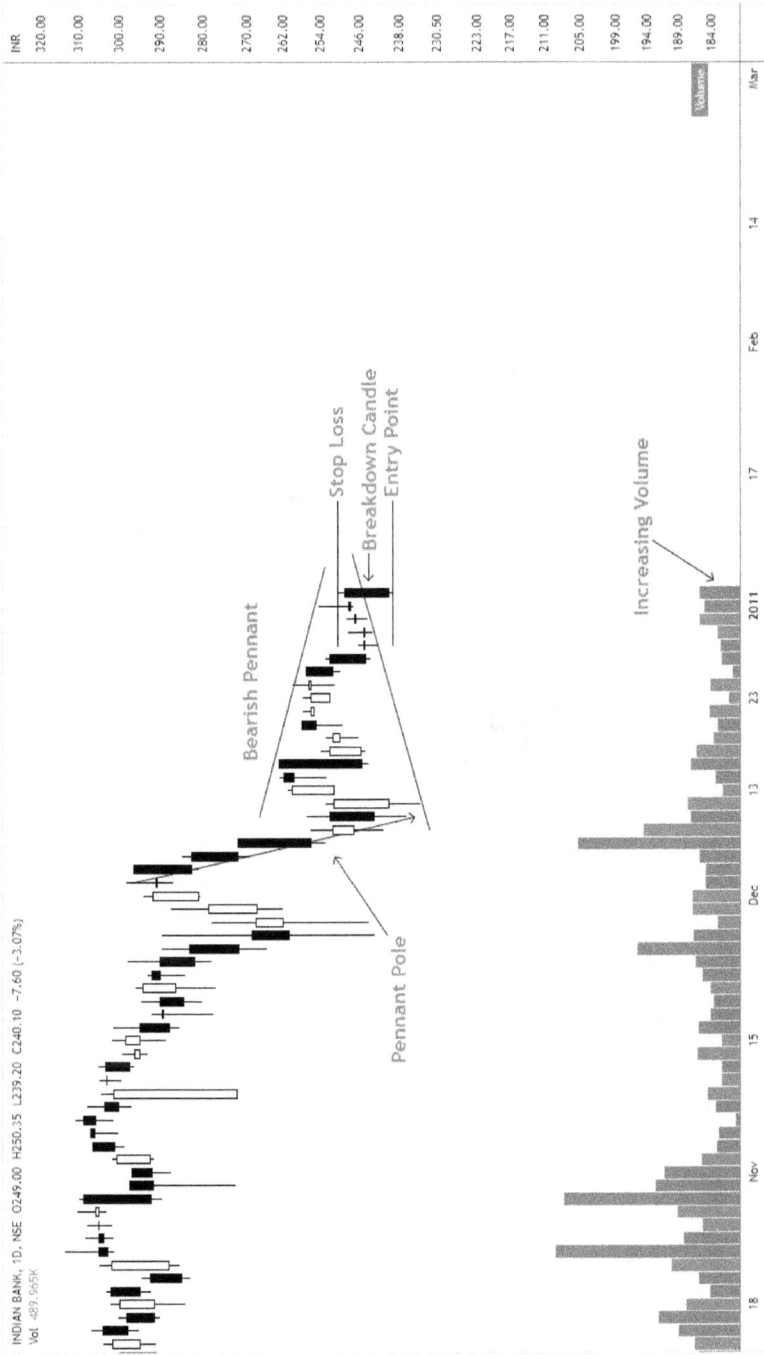

Image 12.11: Daily chart of Indian Bank (bearish pennant pattern).

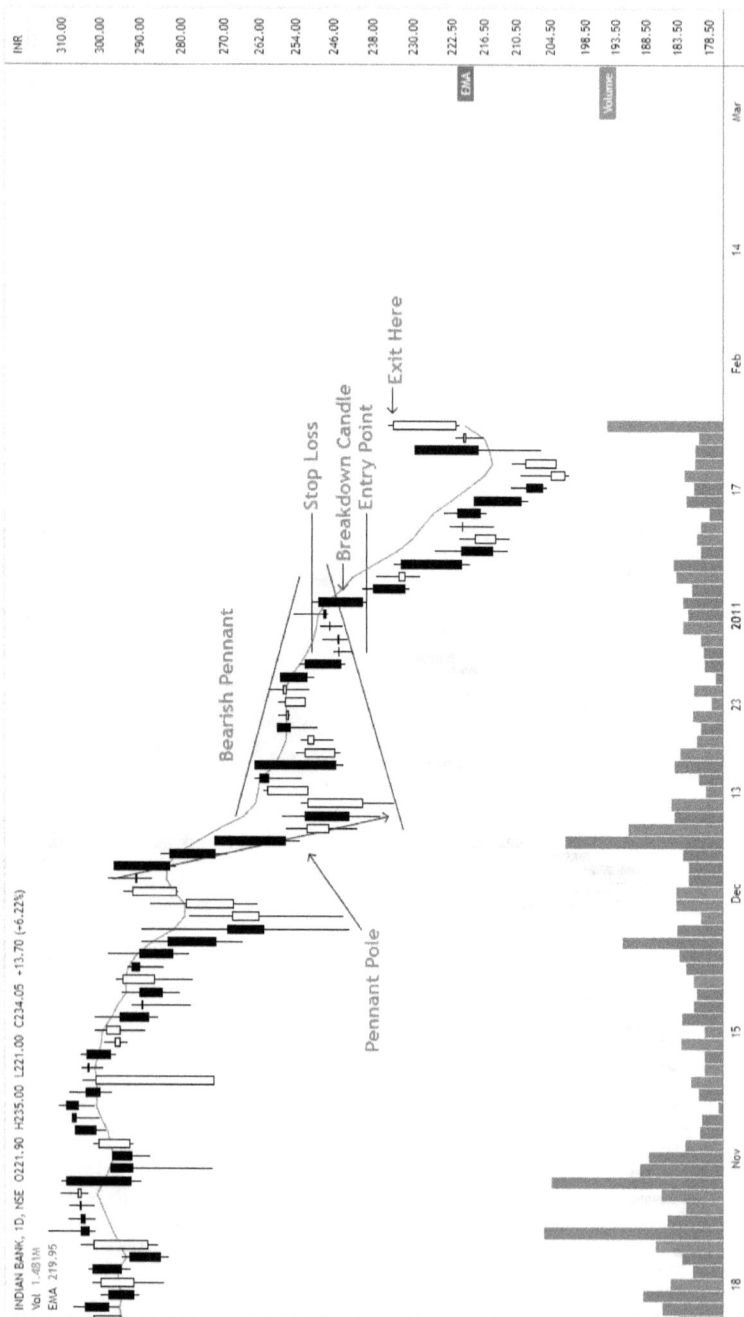

Image 12.12: Daily chart of Indian Bank after breakdown from bearish pennant pattern

Bullish Flag

A bullish flag pattern formed on the daily chart of Aditya Birla Capital, from October 2022 to December 2022 as shown in image 12.13.

One can notice in this chart that the uptrend seems intact with a clear up trending pole which is seen just before the bullish flag occurred.

We can also see that the stock flag pattern breakout occurred with a strong breakout candle which was also accompanied by a nice volume build-up.

Now, the long position is taken right above Rs 130 with a target of around Rs 158 (28 points above the entry area which is exactly the flag pole size) and the stop is placed around Rs 125 (low of the flag pattern breakout candle).

Once the long position was taken, we can see how the stock price drifted towards upside from the breakout zone.

After the breakout candle occurred (image 12.14), the volume accumulation was seen which ultimately indicated that big buyers were also keen to buy this stock.

The stock price drifted from the price of Rs 130 all the way up to Rs 153 in no time (the target was identified using the pole size), as one can see that only one black candle was seen in the form of spinning top in the entire upward movement from entry to the target price.

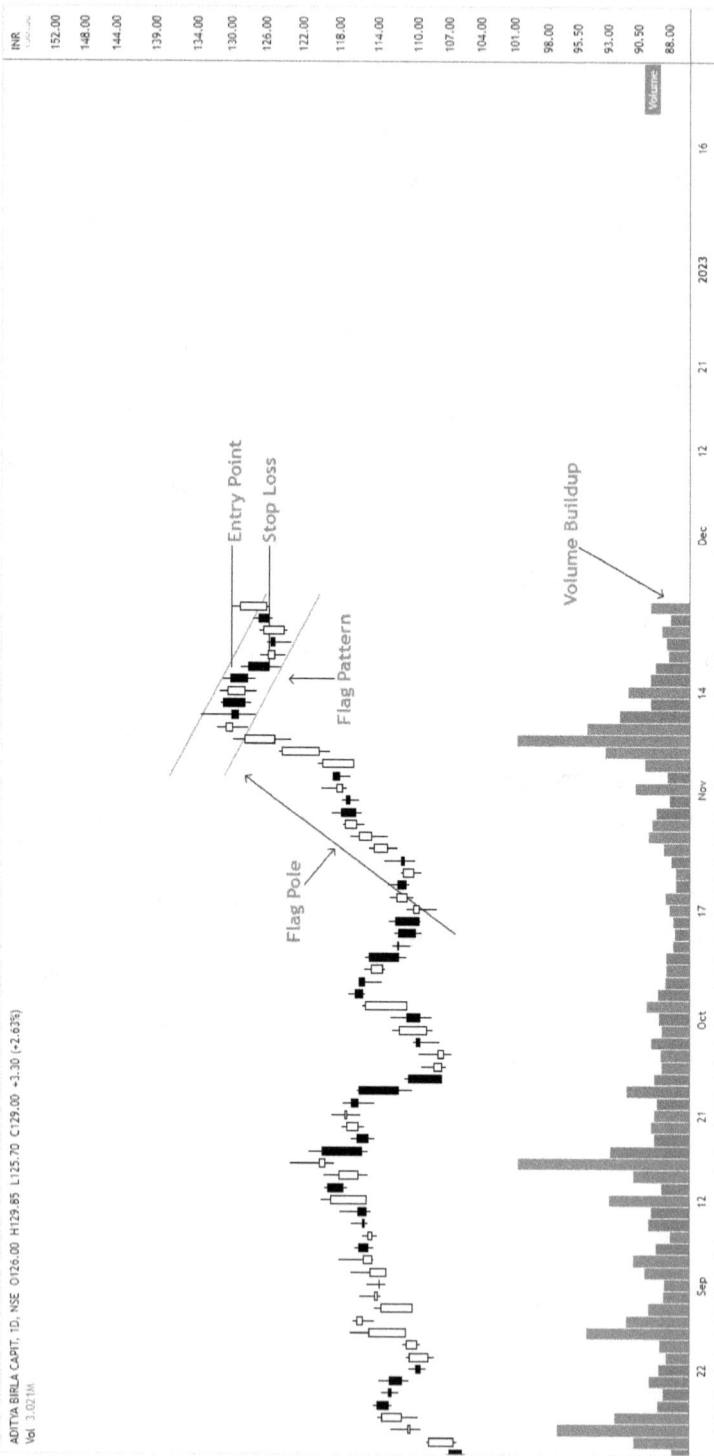

Chart_mojo published on TradingView.com, Jan 25, 2023 13:47 UTC+5:30

ADITYA BIRLA CAPIT, 1D, NSE O126.00 H129.85 L125.70 C129.00 +3.30 (+2.63%)

Vol 3.021M

Entry Point

Stop Loss

Flag Pattern

Flag Pole

Volume Buildup

Volume

Image 12.13: Daily chart of Aditya Birla Capital (bullish flag pattern).

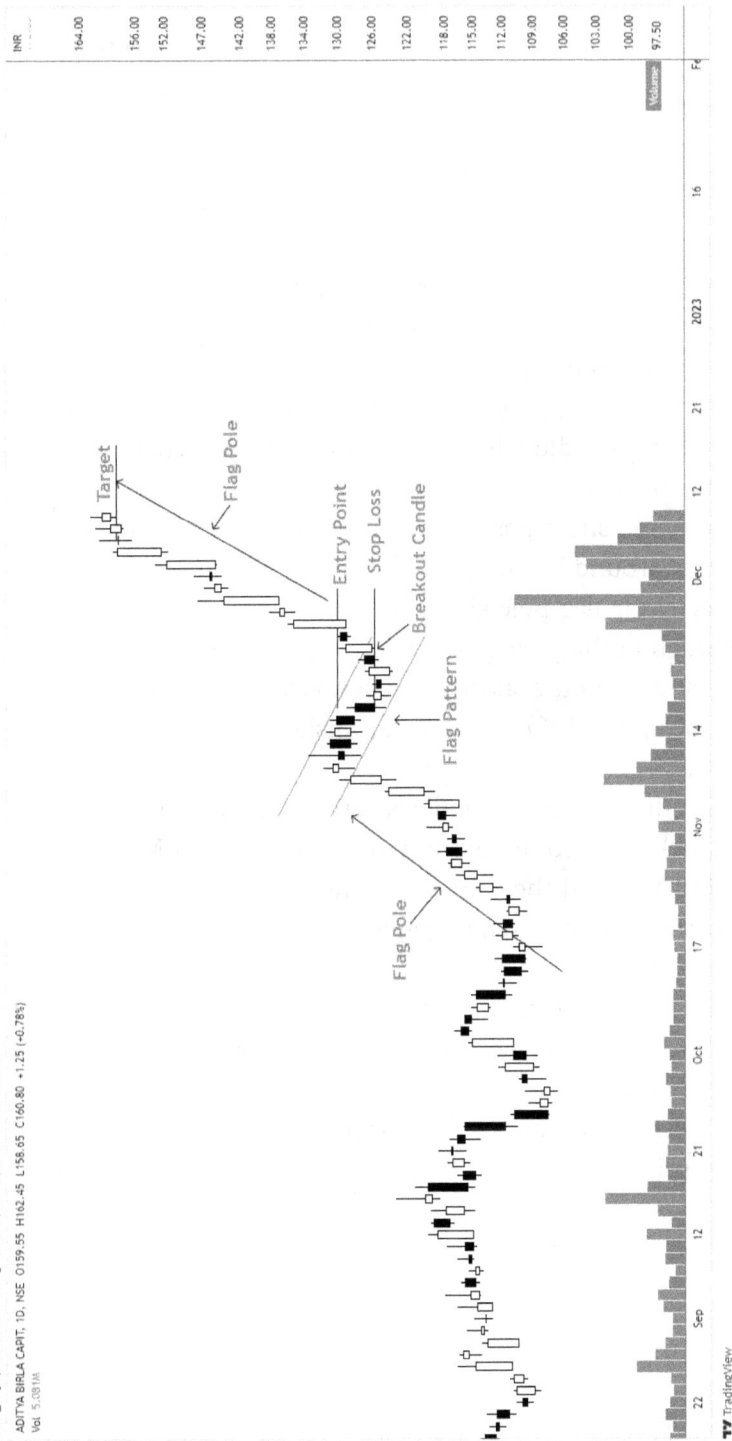

Chart_mojo published on TradingView.com, Jan 25, 2022 13:48 UTC−5:30

ADITYA BIRLA CAPIT, 1D, NSE O159.55 H162.45 L158.65 C160.80 +1.25 (+0.78%)
Vol 5.081M

Image 12.14: Daily chart of Aditya Birla Capital after breakout from the flag pattern.

Bearish Flag

A bearish flag pattern formed on the daily chart of Aditya Birla Fashion from November 2022 to December 2022 as shown in image 12.15.

One can notice in this chart that the downtrend seems intact with a clear down trending pole which is seen just before the bullish flag occurred.

The stock flag pattern breakdown occurred with a strong breakdown candle which was also accompanied by a nice volume build-up.

Now, the short position is taken at below Rs 300 with a target of around Rs 262 (45 points below the entry area which is exactly the flag pole size) and the stop is placed around Rs 318 (high of the previous candle of the breakdown candle).

As and when the short position was taken, we can see how the stock price drifted towards downside from the breakdown zone.

After the breakdown candle occurred, we can also notice that the stock price continued to trade below the 9-EMA. If one would have used the 9-EMA for trailing stop-loss instead of using the pattern-based target, we would have still not gotten the exit from the stock.

The stock price drifted from the price of Rs 300 all the way down to Rs 262 in no time (the target was identified using the pole size), as one can see that only a few bullish candles were seen in the entire downward move from entry to the target price.

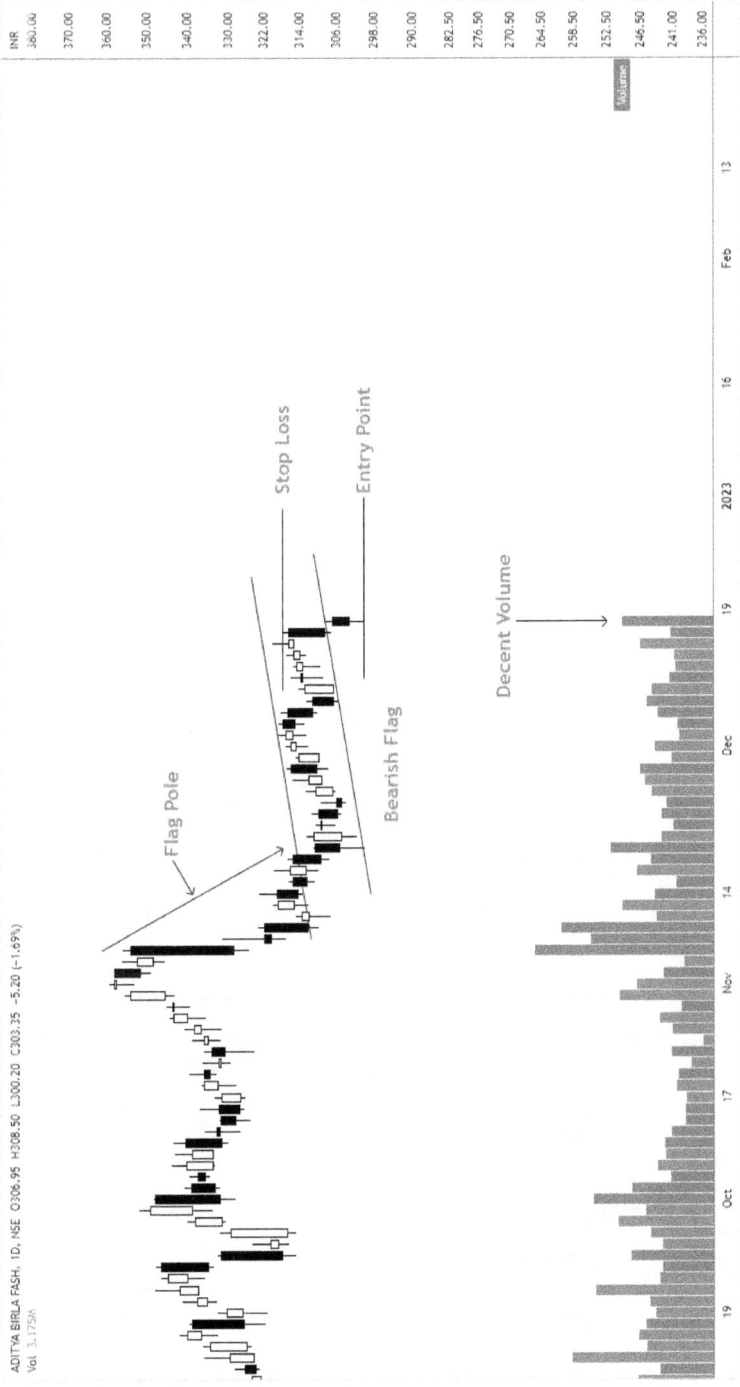

Image 12.15: Daily chart of Aditya Birla Fashion (bearish flag pattern).

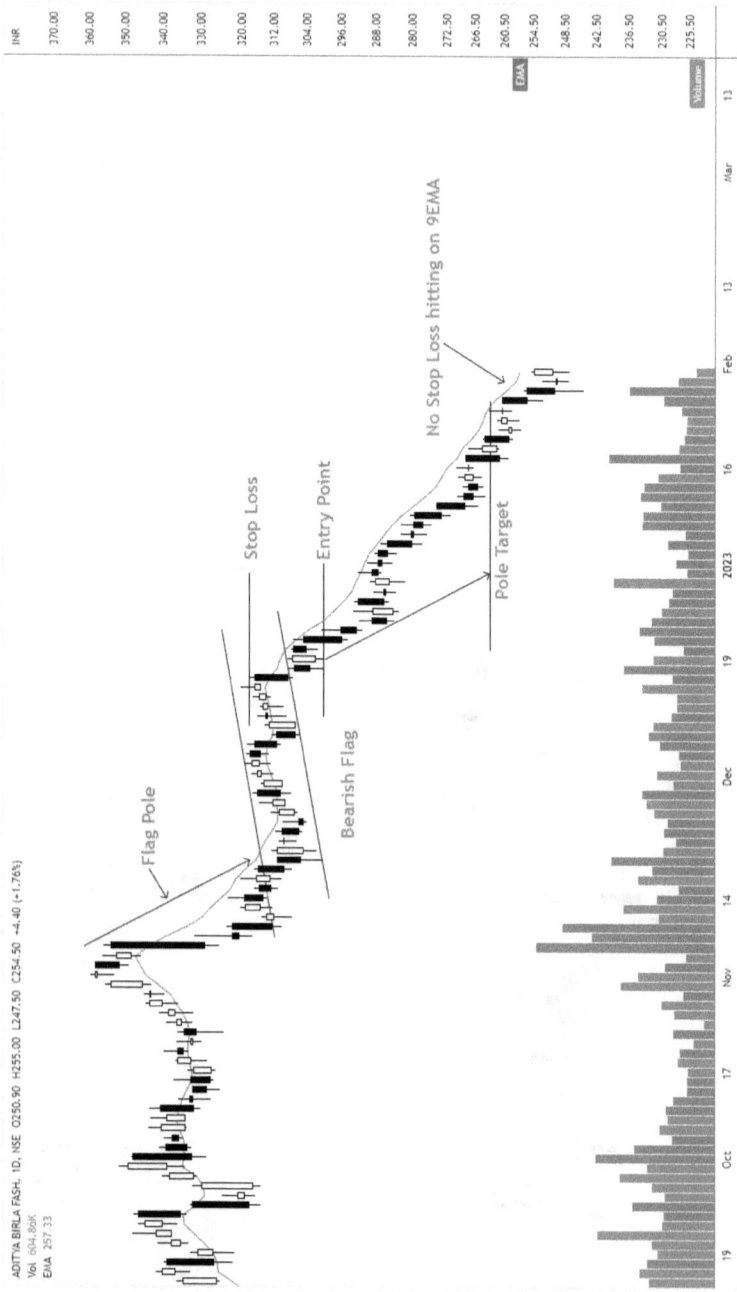

Image 12.16: Daily Chart of Aditya Birla Fashion after breakdown from bearish flag pattern.

Falling Wedge Pattern

A falling wedge pattern formed on the weekly chart of Adani Enterprises from May 2014 to December 2016 as shown in image 12.17.

It is very evident that the uptrend was intact before the pattern got formed—higher high and higher lows can be seen. Finally, price started moving between two falling bands which ultimately formed the falling wedge in an uptrend.

At the time of breakout we can see that it happened with a narrow range candle due to which I had to put the stop-loss at the recent swing low. The volume seen to be completely dry up which is an indication that no more sellers are interested in selling the security.

Here, the long position is taken above Rs 51 with a target of around Rs 123 (72 points above the entry area) and the stop is placed around Rs 41 which is at the recent swing low, just before the breakout candle.

Image 12.18 is the follow up chart of falling wedge continuation pattern. Once the long entry was taken, the price went up swiftly.

Once the breakout happened, the volume also started increasing which was a bullish signal for the stock (image 12.18).

The stock price completed the target within one year and it gave 140% returns wherein the stock price went from Rs 51 to all the way up to Rs 123 in a one-year time span.

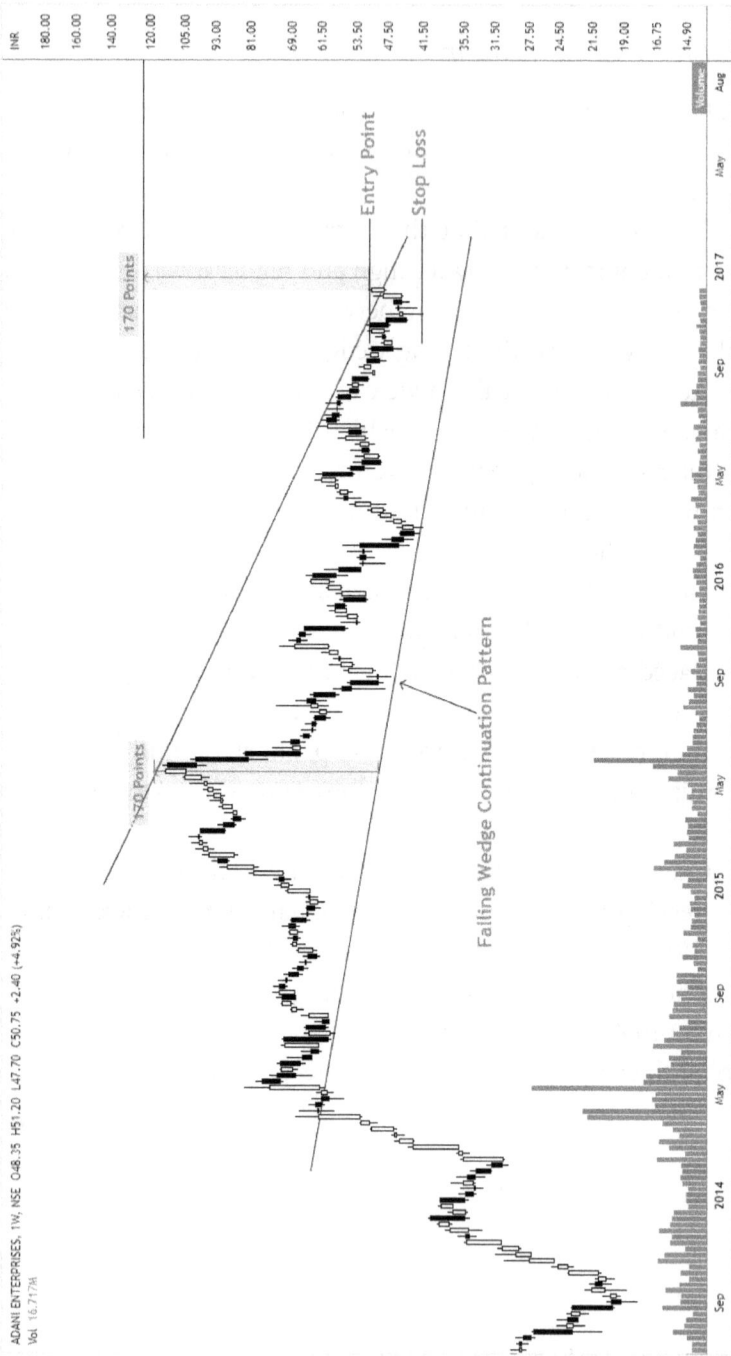

ADANI ENTERPRISES, 1W, NSE O48.35 H51.20 L47.70 C50.75 +2.40 (+4.92%)
Vol 16.717M

170 Points

170 Points

Entry Point

Stop Loss

Falling Wedge Continuation Pattern

Image 12.17: Weekly chart of Adani Enterprises (falling wedge pattern).

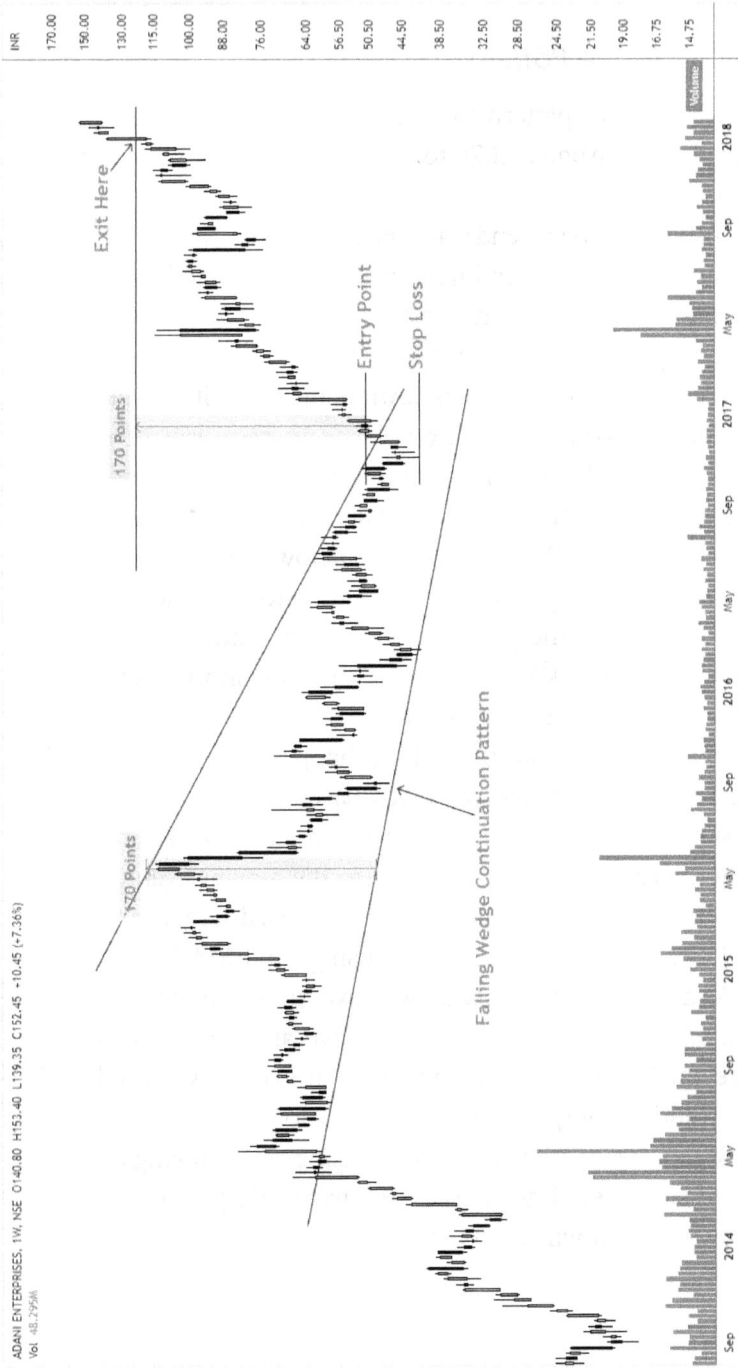

Chart_mojo published on TradingView.com, Feb 27, 2023 12:58 UTC+5:30

ADANI ENTERPRISES, 1W, NSE O140.80 H153.40 L139.35 C152.45 +10.45 (+7.36%)
Vol 48.295M

Image 12.18: Daily chart of Adani Enterprises showing bullish trend continuation pattern

Rising Wedge Pattern

A rising wedge pattern formed on the daily chart of Bank of Baroda from August 2020 to January 2021, as shown in image 12.19.

Notice the downtrend was intact before the pattern formed—lower lows and lower highs can be seen. Finally, the price started moving between two bands which ultimately was the formation of a rising wedge in a downtrend.

We can see that the breakdown happened with a wide range candle and with increasing volume in the form of volume build-up which was an indication of an impending downfall.

Here, the short position is taken below Rs 95.70 with a target of around Rs 262 (45 points below the entry area which is exactly the flag pole size) and the stop is placed around Rs 318 (high of the previous breakdown candle).

Once the breakdown occurred and the short position was taken, the price fell down very drastically. I have mentioned in image 12.20 what would have happened if we would take the pattern-based vis-à-vis EMA based target.

We would have taken exit at the price of Rs 76 using the pattern-based target and Rs 42 using the moving average-based target. However, the moving average-based target is far away and clearly shows the beauty of using the EMA-based target.

As a breakout trader what we have under our control is the risk and not the target. So, when we are wrong, we should take small risk. However, when we are right, we should ride the trend as long as our trailing stop-loss gets hit.

By no means do I recommend using only moving average-based stop-loss. Try and see what works for you and you will know early on what suits you.

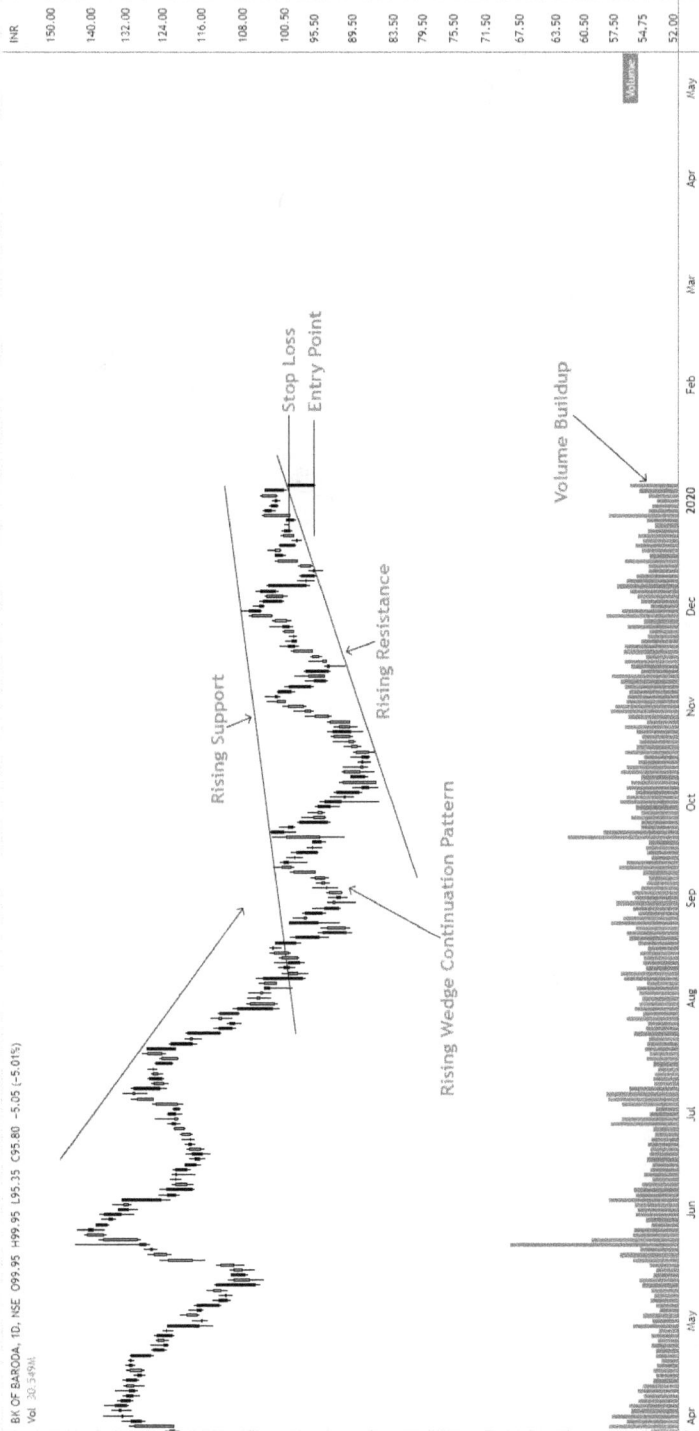

Image 12.19: Daily chart of Bank of Baroda (rising wedge pattern).

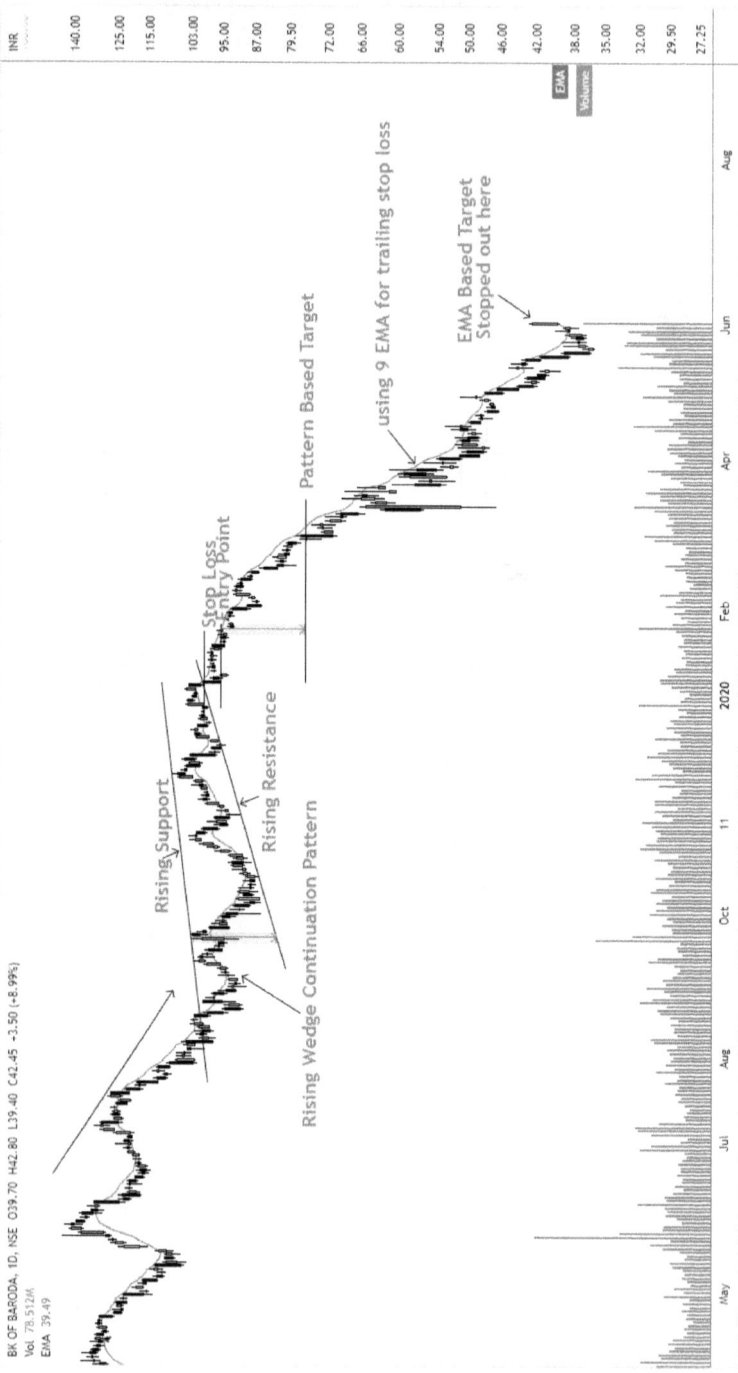

BK OF BARODA, 1D, NSE O39.70 H42.80 L39.40 C42.45 -3.50 (-8.99%)
Vol 78.512M
EMA 39.49

Rising Support

Rising Resistance

Stop Loss
Entry Point

Pattern Based Target

Rising Wedge Continuation Pattern

using 9 EMA for trailing stop loss

EMA Based Target
Stopped out here

INR

140.00
125.00
115.00
103.00
95.00
87.00
79.50
72.00
66.00
60.00
54.00
50.00
46.00
42.00
38.00
35.00
32.00
29.50
27.25

EMA
Volume

Image 12.20: Daily chart of Bank of Baroda showing bearish trend continuation pattern.

Bullish Continuation Cup and Handle

A bullish continuation cup and handle pattern formed on the daily chart of Fertilizers & Chemicals Ltd., from September 2022 to December 2022 as shown in image 12.21.

The cup and handle continuation pattern formed after a short uptrend. During the pattern formation, the volume showed a spike which was a clear indication for a potential upside.

The breakout happened with a wide range breakout candle and a huge volume spurt was seen in the period of pattern breakout. One should also remember that if the breakout candle is very wide, it will increase our stop-loss. In that case, one should not take any position into that particular stock.

Here, the long position is taken above Rs 147 with no target in mind as we use 9-EMA as trailing stop-loss. However, we exited the stock around Rs 332 where our trailing stop-loss got hit. (We got 185 points above the entry area with a whopping 126% returns) and the stop is placed around Rs 127.95 (low of the breakout candle).

Image 12.22 is the follow up chart of Fertilizers & Chemicals Ltd. after the breakout area, the stock price went just one way up after the breakout occurred.

In this trade setup, we got around 127% returns and the price went from Rs 147 to all the way up to Rs 332 within a short period of time.

Notice that after the breakout candle occurred, the volume also started increasing, which made the upside move smoother as it signalled that a lot of buyers are interested in this stock.

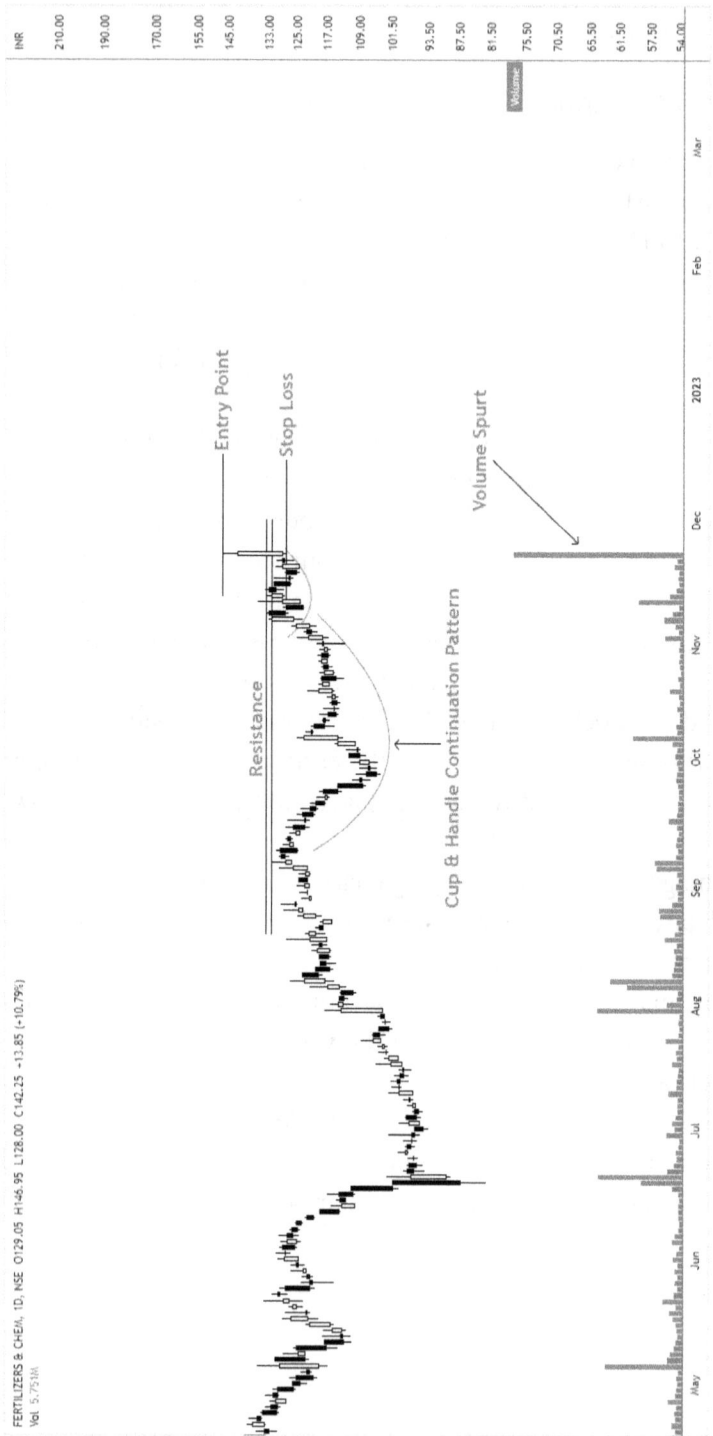

Image 12.21: Daily chart of Fertilizers & Chemicals Ltd. (bullish continuation cup and handle pattern).

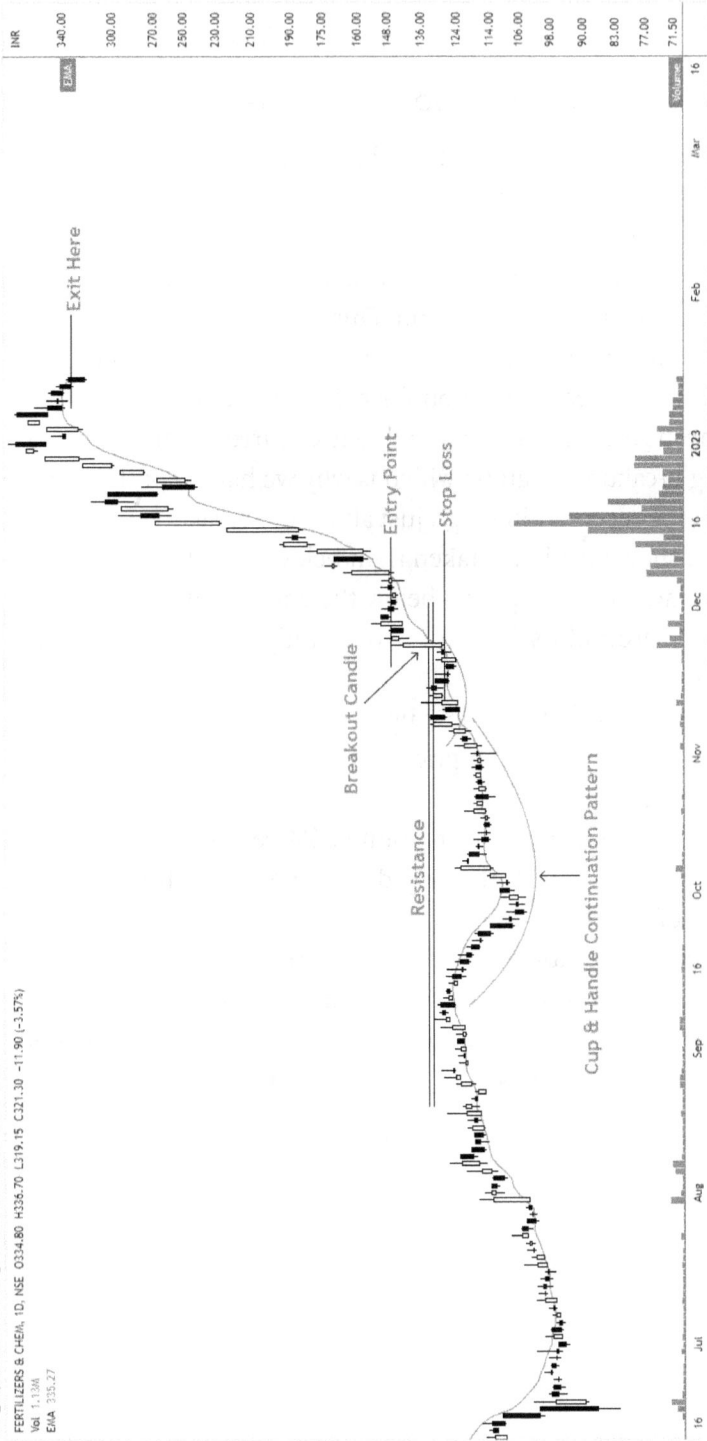

Image 12.22: Daily chart of Fertilizers & Chemicals Ltd. showing bullish cup and handle continuation pattern.

Bearish Continuation Cup and Handle

A bearish continuation cup and handle pattern formed on the daily chart of Nocil Ltd., from February 2020 to July 2020 as shown in image 12.23.

One can notice that cup and handle continuation pattern formed after a short downtrend. During the pattern formation, the volume showed a spike in the form of red volume bars which was a clear indication for a potential downside.

The bearish pattern breakdown occurred with a not so strong breakdown candle which is why we have kept the stop-loss at the recent swing high just above the breakdown candle.

The short position is taken right below Rs 111 with a target of around Rs 84 (27 points below the entry area) and the stop is placed around Rs 122 (at the recent high of the breakdown candle).

Image 12.24 is the follow up chart of Nocil Ltd. After the breakout area, the stock price went just one way down after the breakdown occurred.

In this trade setup we got around 24% returns and the price went from Rs 111 all the way down to Rs 84 within a short period of time.

After the breakout candle occurred, the volume also started increasing in the form of red volume bars which made the downside move smoother as it signalled that a lot of sellers are interested in this stock.

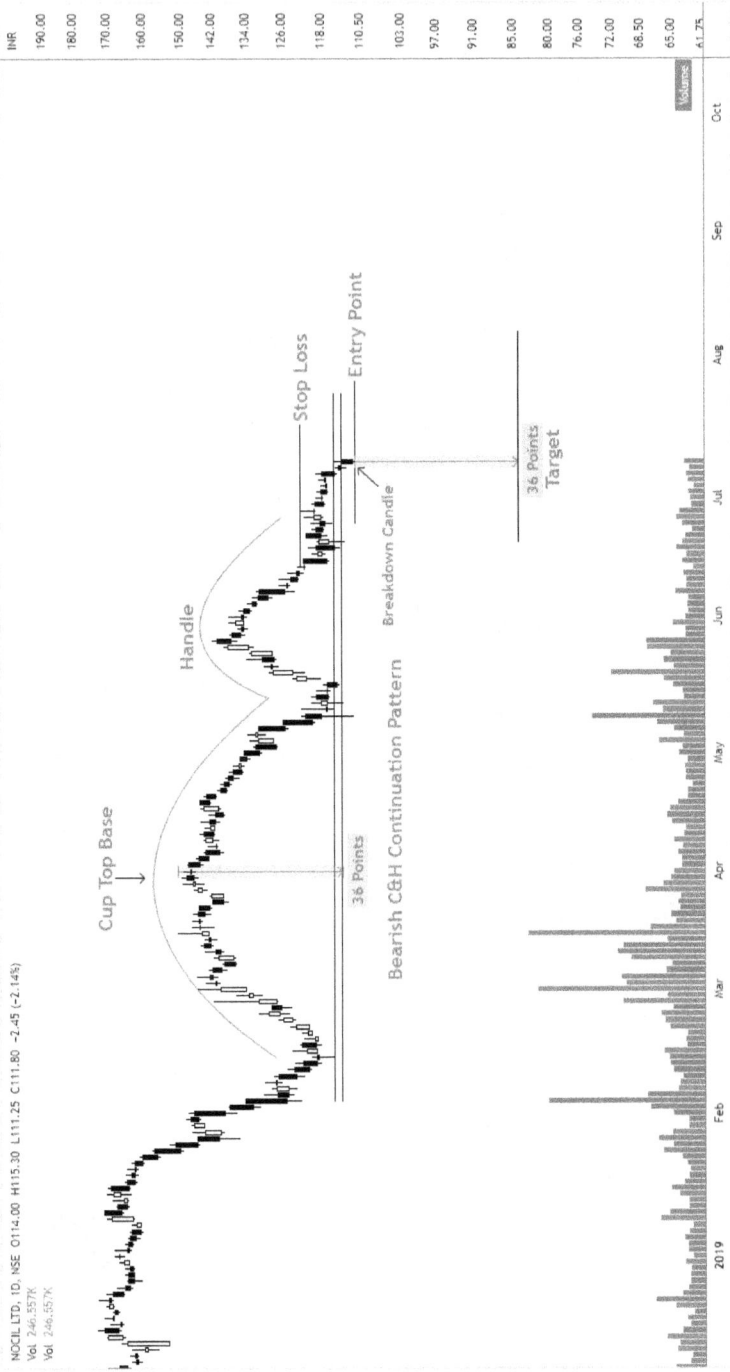

Image 12.23: Daily chart of Nocil Ltd. (bearish continuation cup and handle pattern).

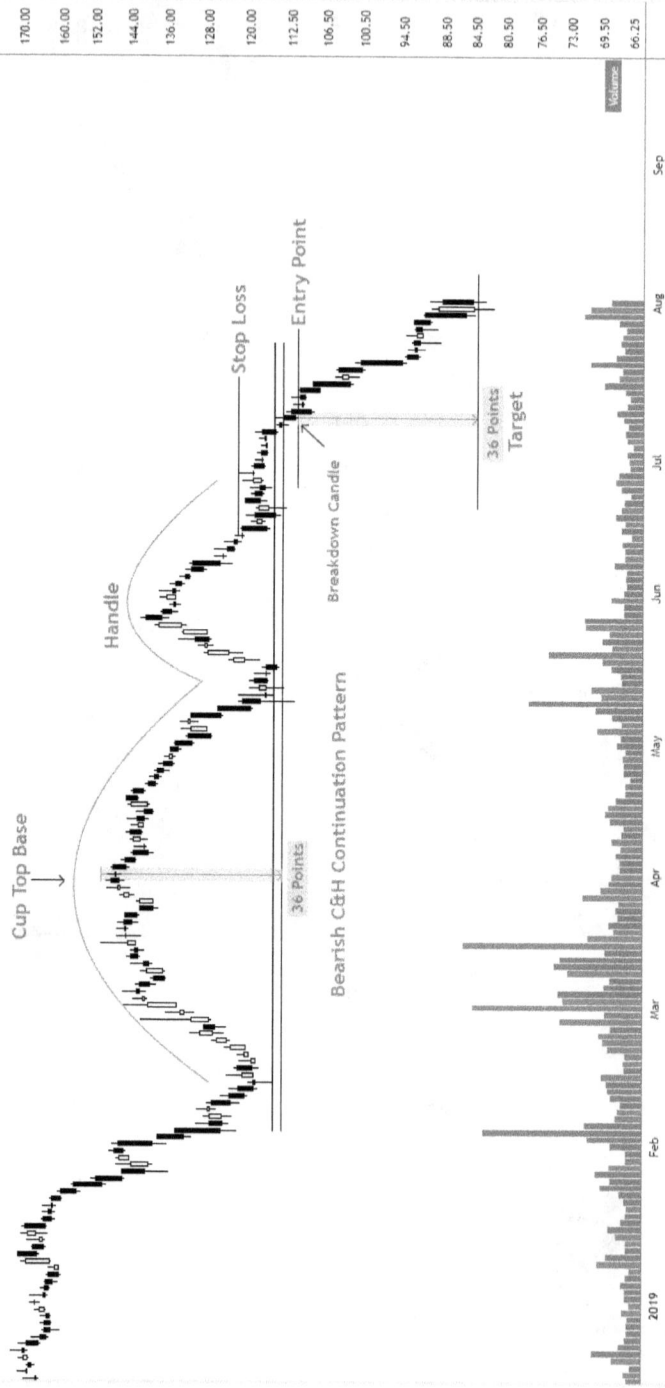

Image 12.24: Daily chart of Nocil Ltd. after breakdown from bearish trend continuation pattern.

Bullish Rectangle

A bullish rectangle continuation pattern formed on the daily chart of Happiest Mind Technology Ltd. from March 2021 to April 2021 as shown in image 12.25.

The uptrend seems intact with a clear up trending price action which is seen over the last couple of months.

The stock rectangle pattern breakout occurred with a wide range candle which was also accompanied by a nice volume spurt.

The long position is taken above Rs 614 with an exit of around Rs 1,352 (738 points above the entry area) and the stop is placed around Rs 543 (low of the breakout candle).

Do remember, in this chart setup I have used 9-EMA as trailing stop-loss and you can clearly notice that it saved us many times from fake moves and showed a decent upside.

Image 12.26 is the follow up chart of Happiest Mind Technology Ltd. After the breakout area, the stock price went just one way upside with many fake moves after the breakout occurred from the rectangle continuation pattern.

In this trade setup, we got around 120% returns and the price went from Rs 614 all the way up to Rs 1,354 within a period of four months.

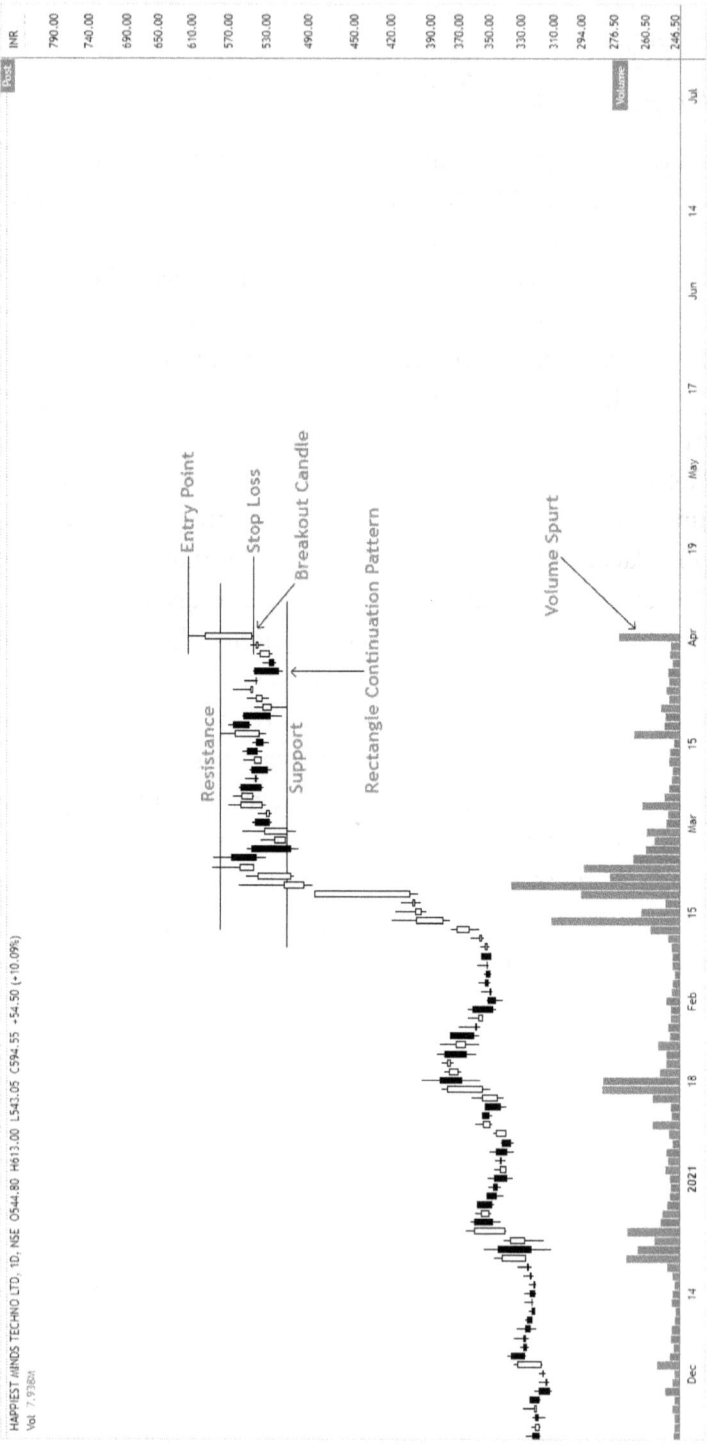

Image 12.25: Daily chart of Happiest Mind Technology Ltd. (bullish rectangle continuation pattern).

HAPPIEST MINDS TECHNO LTD, 1D, NSE O1372.80 H1383.40 L1350.00 C1357.20 −7.30 (−0.53%)
Vol 523.862K
EMA 1370.64

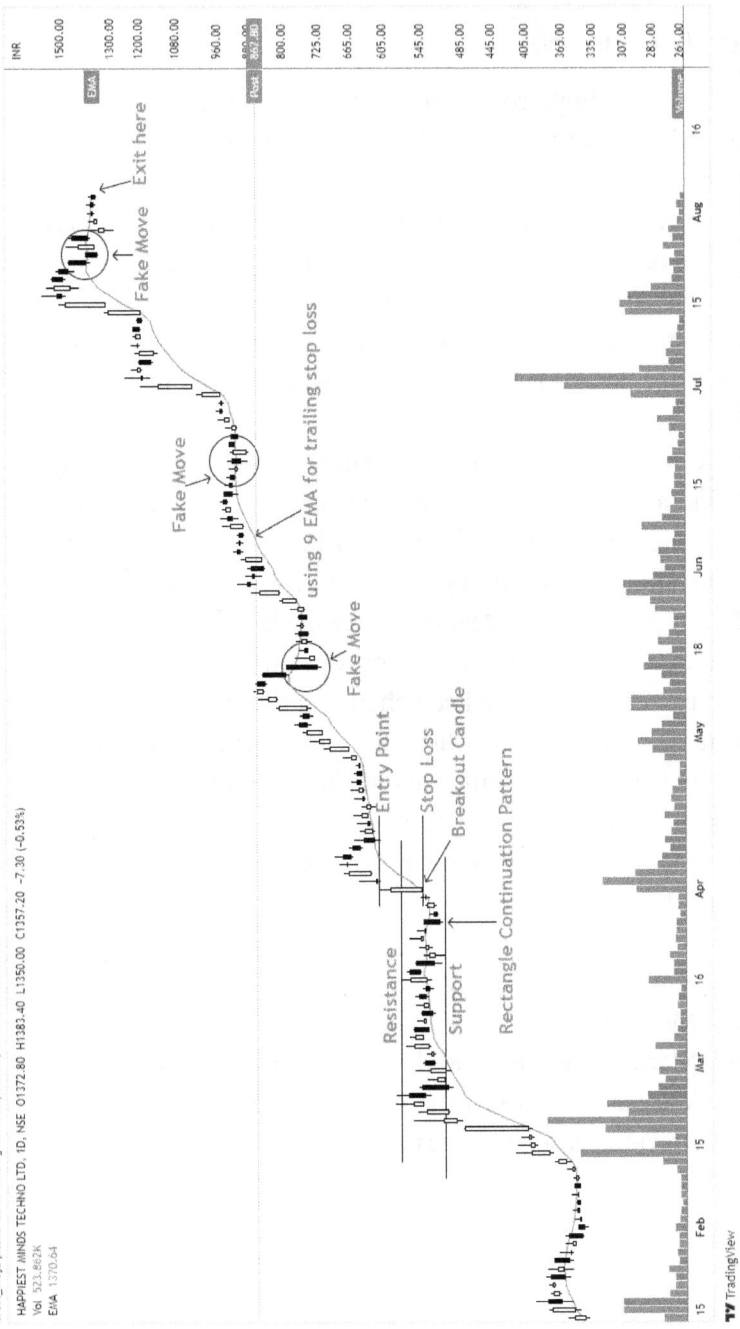

INR

1500.00
1300.00
1200.00
1080.00
960.00
800.00
725.00
665.00
605.00
545.00
485.00
445.00
405.00
365.00
335.00
307.00
283.00
261.00

EMA

Post

Exit here

Fake Move

Fake Move

Fake Move

using 9 EMA for trailing stop loss

Entry Point

Stop Loss

Breakout Candle

Resistance

Support

Rectangle Continuation Pattern

Volume

Feb   15   Mar   15   Apr   16   May   18   Jun   15   Jul   15   Aug   16

TradingView

Image 12.26: Daily chart of Happiest Mind Technology Ltd. after the breakout from the bullish rectangle continuation pattern.

Bearish Rectangle

A bearish rectangle continuation pattern formed on the daily chart of Voltas Ltd. from May 2022 to September 2022, as shown in image 12.27.

One can notice that downtrend seems intact with a clear down trending price action which is seen just before the bearish rectangle continuation occurred.

The stock rectangle pattern breakdown occurred with strong wide range breakdown candle which was also accompanied by a nice volume build-up.

The short position is taken at below Rs 883 with no target in mind as we are using the market structure as trailing stop-loss (which you can see in image 12.27). We will place the stop around Rs 960 (high of the pattern breakdown candle).

In image 12.28, it is clear that once the breakdown occurred it started scaling down with lower tops and lower bottoms.

Do remember that we keep changing the stop-losses to the recent swing top as and when the price keeps drifting down. The breakdown was confirmed at the price of Rs 883 and it came all the way down to Rs 738.

One should also remember that we can keep the targets using three techniques

1. Pattern-based targets
2. Moving average-based targets
3. Market structure-based targets (Shown in image 12.28. We have discussed the other two techniques in some previous case study examples.)

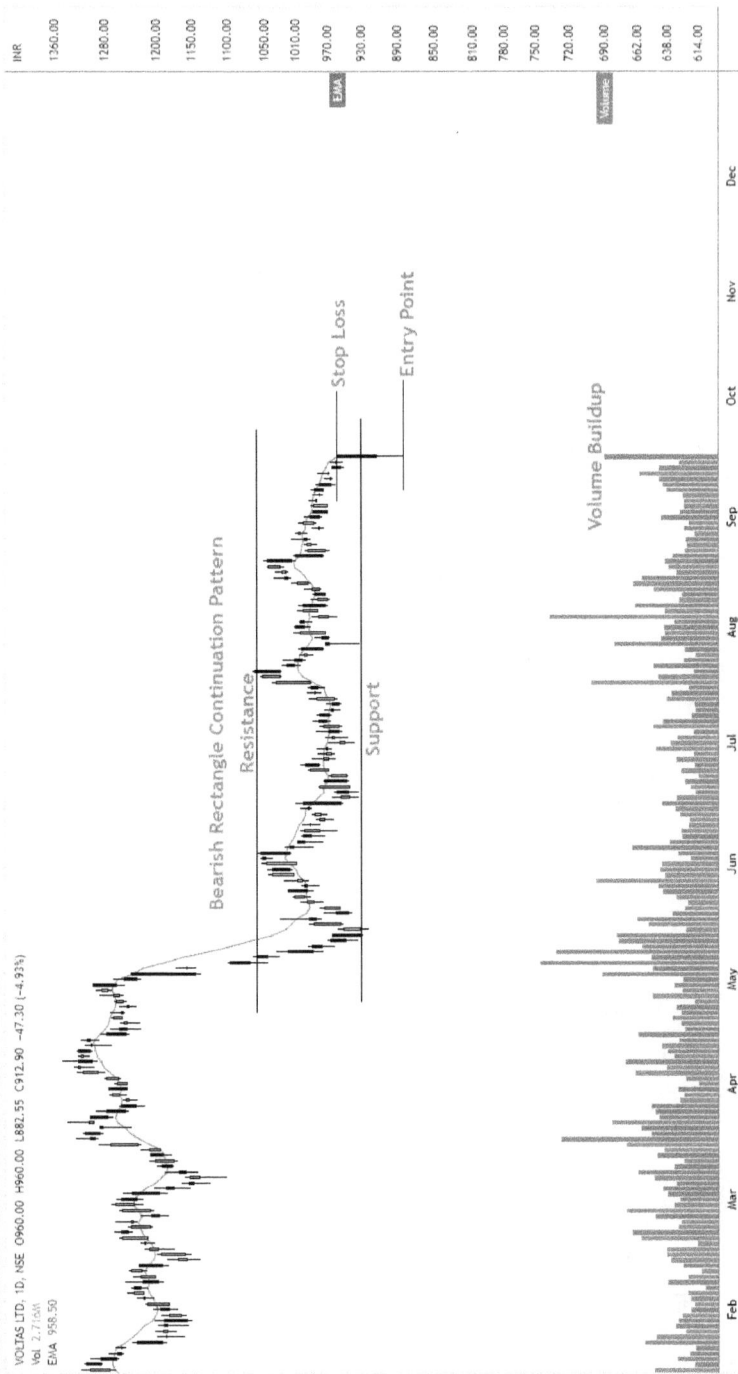

Image 12.27: Daily chart of Voltas Ltd. (bearish rectangle continuation pattern).

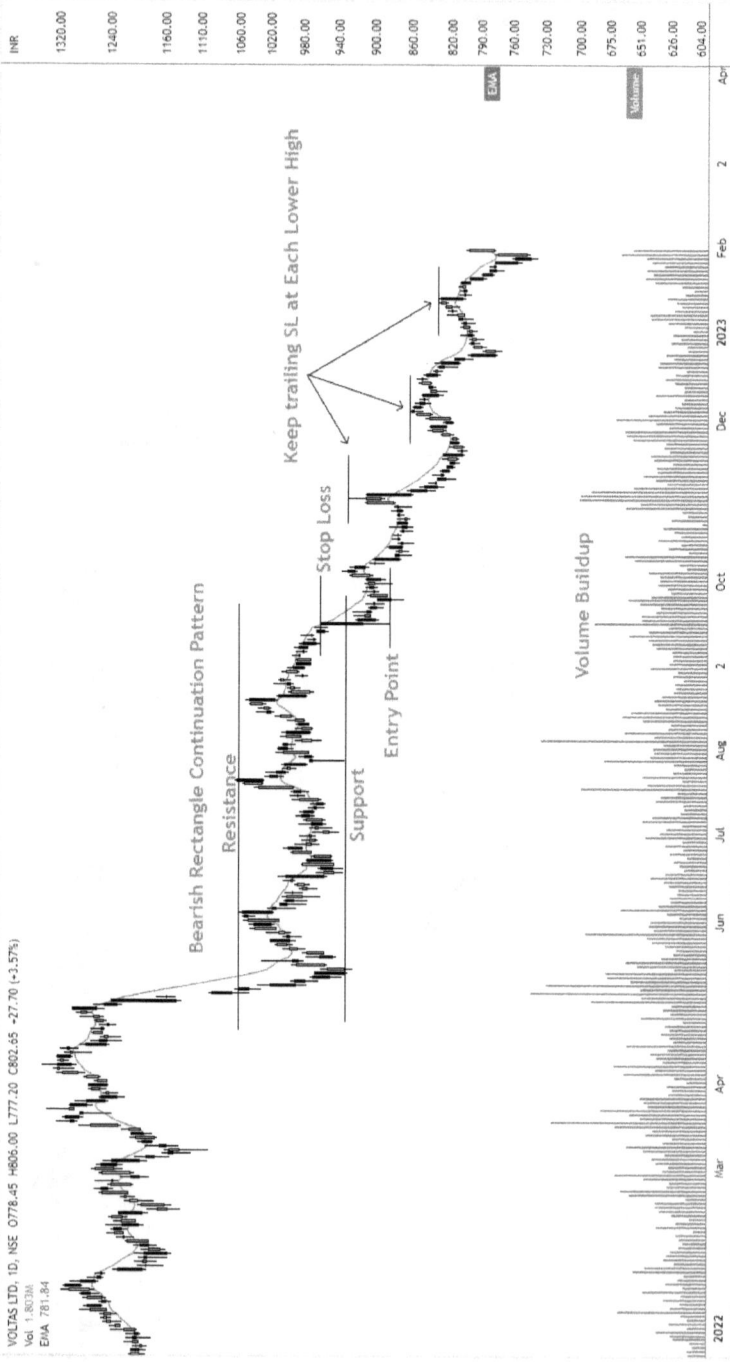

Image 12.28: Daily chart of Voltas Ltd. after breakdown from bearish trend continuation pattern.

Bullish Basing

A bullish basing continuation pattern formed on the daily chart of Punjab National Bank from January 2014 to April 2014, as shown in image 12.29.

The stock was in a strong uptrend before the formation of bullish basing pattern and went through a series of higher highs and higher lows.

The breakout happened with a candle which was not very strong. Due to this we had to keep the stop-loss just at the recent swing low.

Here, the long position is taken just above Rs 133 with a target of around Rs 170 (28 points above the entry area) and the stop is placed around Rs 125 (at the swing low of the breakout candle).

In image 12.30, once the breakout occurred with decent volume, the price action travelled just one way and went on to reaching our target which was at the price of Rs 170.

The price did go through some sideways consolidation while making its way up. However, it went from Rs 133 all the way up to Rs 170 within two months.

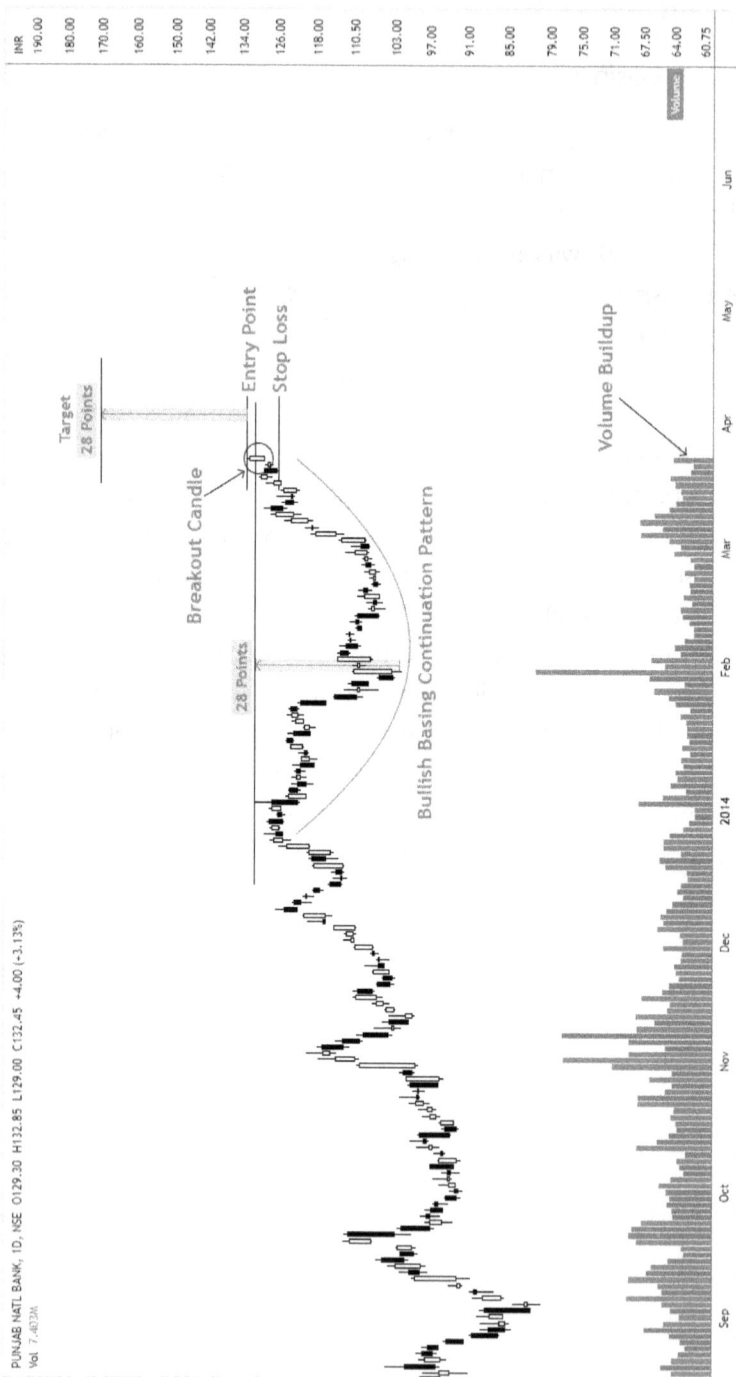

Image 12.29: Daily chart of Punjab National Bank (bullish basing continuation pattern).

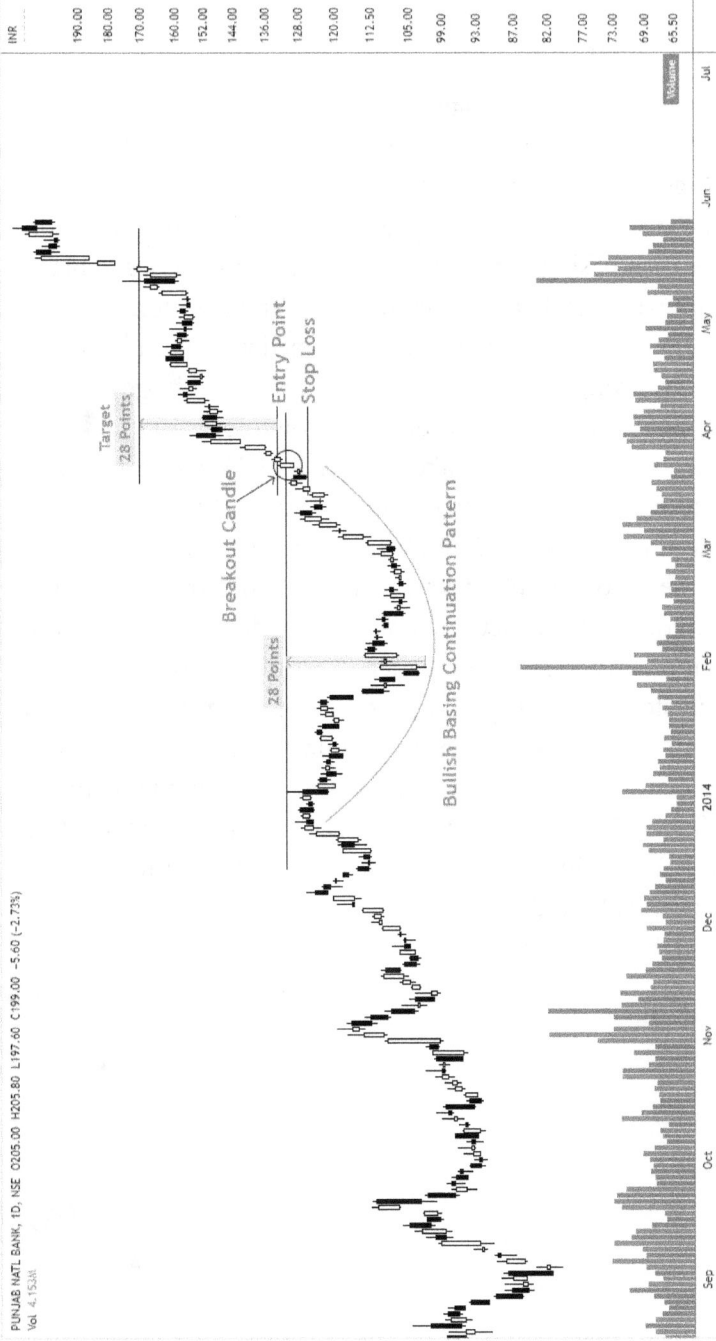

Chart_mojo published on TradingView.com, Jan 26, 2023 13:24 UTC-5:30

PUNJAB NATL BANK, 1D, NSE O205.00 H205.80 L197.60 C199.00 -5.60 (-2.73%)
Vol 4.15*3M

Image 12.30: Daily chart of Punjab National Bank showing breakout from the bullish basing continuation pattern.

Bearish Basing

A bearish basing continuation pattern formed on the daily chart of Indraprastha Gas Ltd. from November 2022 to February 2022, as shown in image 12.31.

The stock was in a strong downtrend before the formation of a bearish basing pattern and going through a series of black candles which indicates bearishness on the counter.

The breakdown of the pattern happened with a candle which was very strong and it was also supported by a huge volume spurt signifying downward pressure going forward.

The short position is taken below Rs 434 with a target of around Rs 384 (61 points below the entry area) and the stop is placed around Rs 455 (high of the breakdown candle).

In the follow up chart (image 12.32), once the breakdown occurred, the price action took its way down and we see a decent downside from the pattern breakdown zone.

The stock price went from Rs 434 all the way down to Rs 384 within a very short period of time. Then if we would use the moving average as trailing stop-loss, we would stand to gain more downside profit as we can see in this chart. The price still continued to come down after the pattern-based target was achieved.

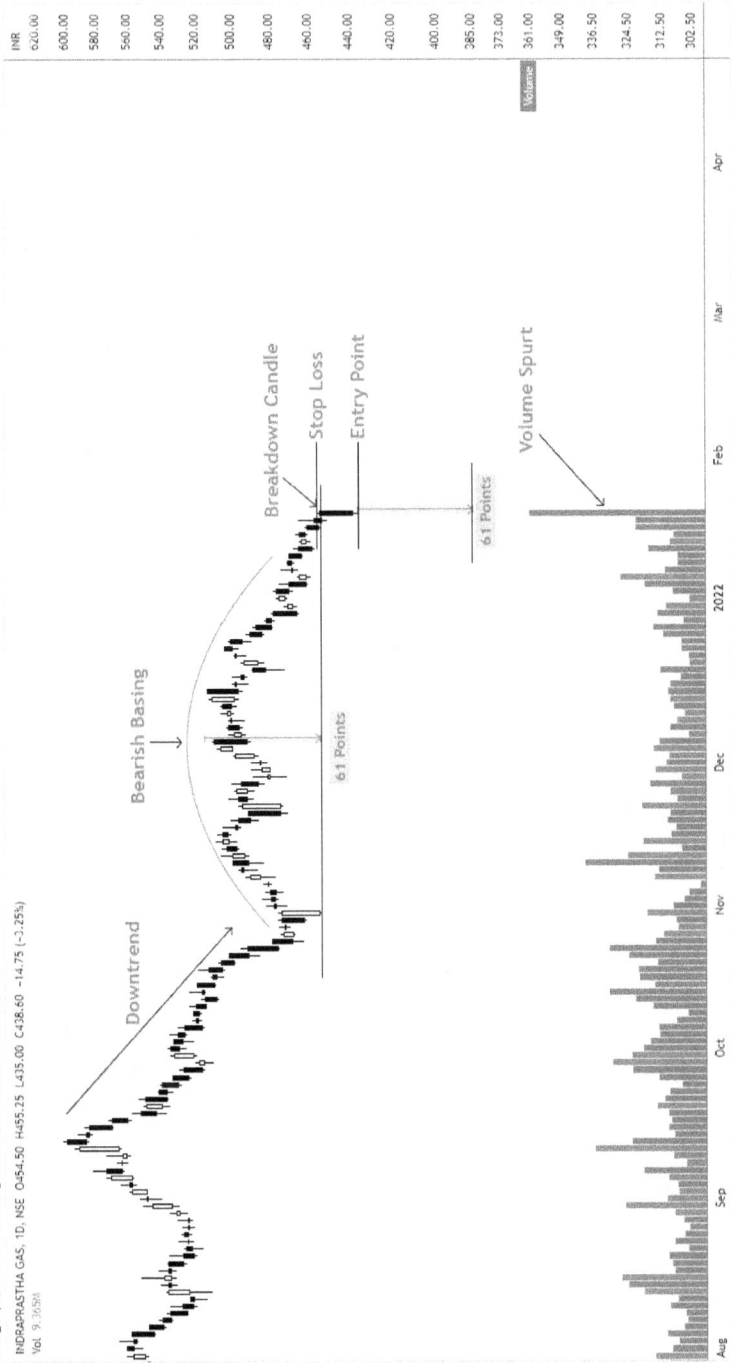

Image 12.31: Daily chart of Indraprastha Gas Ltd. (bearish basing continuation pattern).

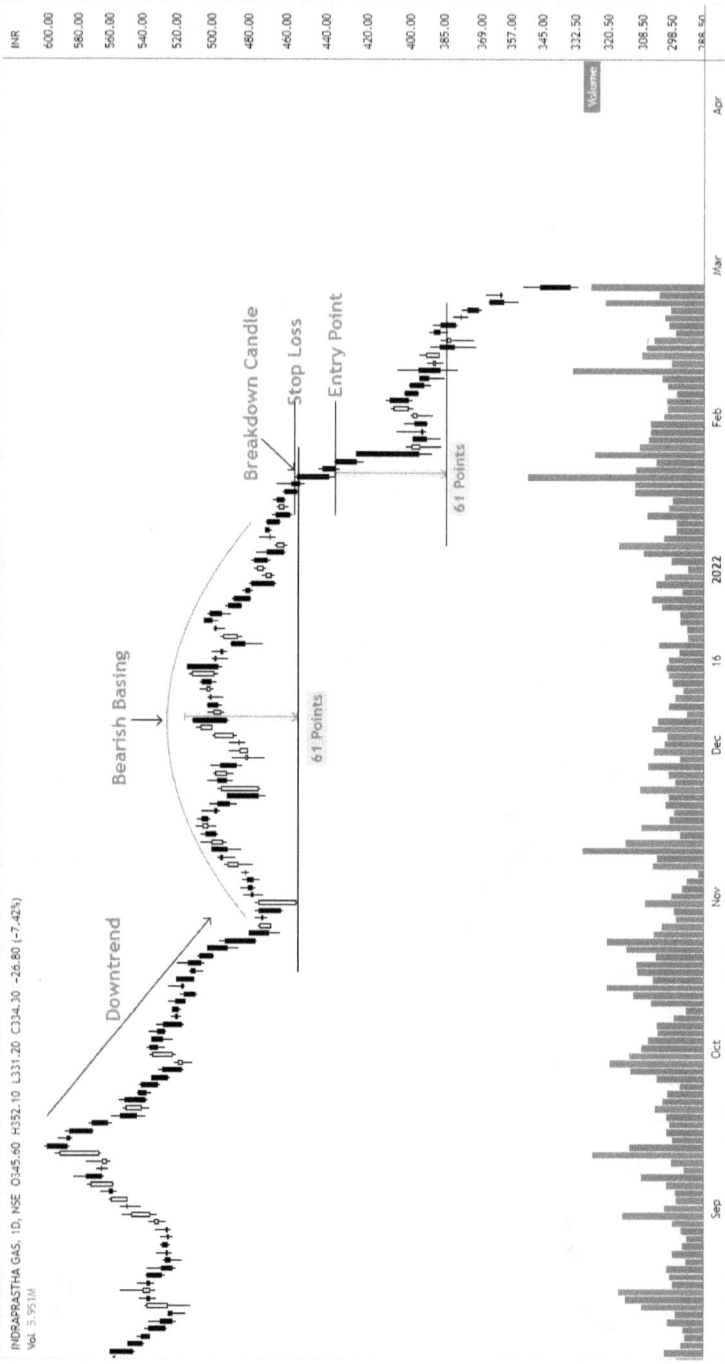

Image 12.32: Daily chart of Indraprastha Gas Ltd. after the breakdown from a bearish trend continuation pattern.

Bullish Head and Shoulder Continuation Pattern

A bullish continuation head and shoulder pattern formed on the daily chart of Voltas Ltd. from December 2014 to March 2015, as shown in image 12.33.

The uptrend is looking clear with a series of higher tops and higher bottoms, with support from buying volume.

The continuation pattern started forming once the left shoulder was formed. Then the head got formed right after the left shoulder. Finally, the right shoulder formed, giving a complete shape to the trend continuation pattern.

The pattern breakout candle occurred with a wide range candle and it had a good support from volume which signifies a healthy breakout towards upside.

Here, the long position is taken a little above Rs 129 with no target in mind as we are using 9-EMA as trailing stop-loss. However, we exited the stock around Rs 157 where our trailing stop-loss got hit. (We got 27 points above the entry area which is 21% returns from the entry point) and the stop is placed around Rs 119.75 (which is the 2X of actual ATR-average true range which is marked on the image. If you notice the standard ATR was Rs 5 so with 2X it became Rs 10 stop-loss).

In image 12.34 it is clear that after the pattern breakout the stock price started moving higher and provided a decent potential upside.

You can also notice that we have used 9-EMA for trailing stop-loss wherein our upside gets locked as and when the price inches towards higher side.

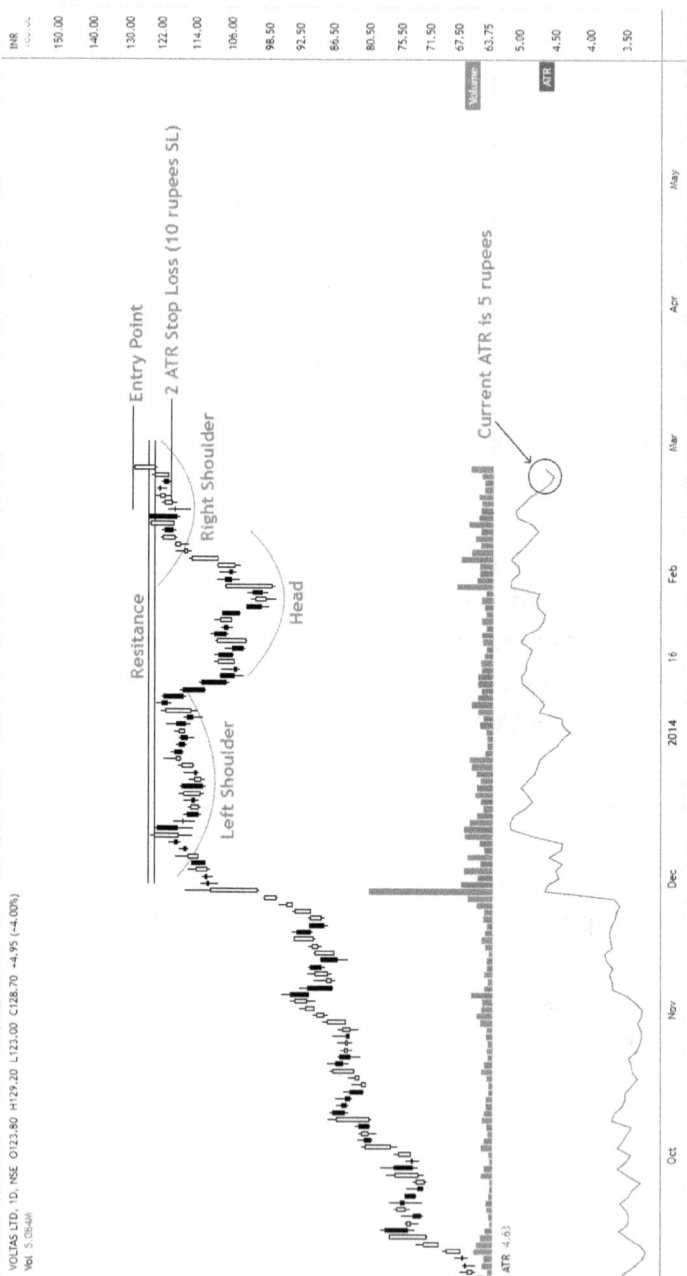

Image 12.33: Daily chart of Voltas Ltd. (bullish continuation head and shoulder pattern).

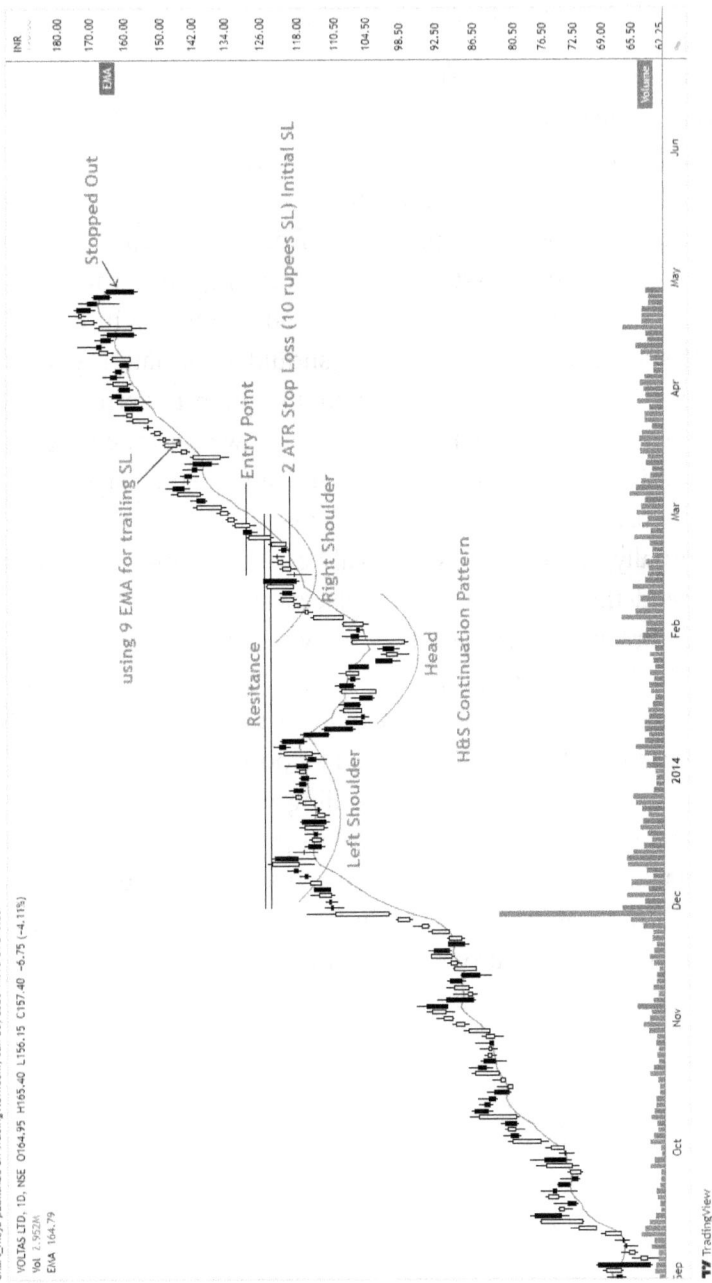

Image 12.34: Daily chart of Voltas Ltd. after breakout from head and shoulder continuation pattern.

Bearish Head and Shoulder Continuation Pattern

A bearish continuation head and shoulder pattern formed on the weekly chart of Dish Network Corporation from January 2010 to March 2015, as shown in image 12.35.

The chart shows a clear downtrend with a series of lower tops and lower bottoms with support from selling volume.

The continuation pattern started forming once the left shoulder was formed and then the head formed right after the left shoulder. Finally, the right shoulder formation gave complete shape to a bearish trend continuation pattern.

The pattern breakdown candle occurred with a wide range candle and it had a good support from volume which signifies a healthy breakdown towards downside.

Eventually, the short position will be taken below the price of $24 and the stop-loss will be placed at $28 which is the high of a breakdown candle. The exit will happen on the basis of 9-EMA breakout at $13.

In image 12.36, once we took the short position the stock price started drifting downward in a smooth down move.

One can also notice that the selling volume also started increasing which supported downward pressure.

In this trade setup, the stock price went down from the price of $24 all the way down to $13 in 21-week trading sessions. We got to book 45% profit at 16% risk.

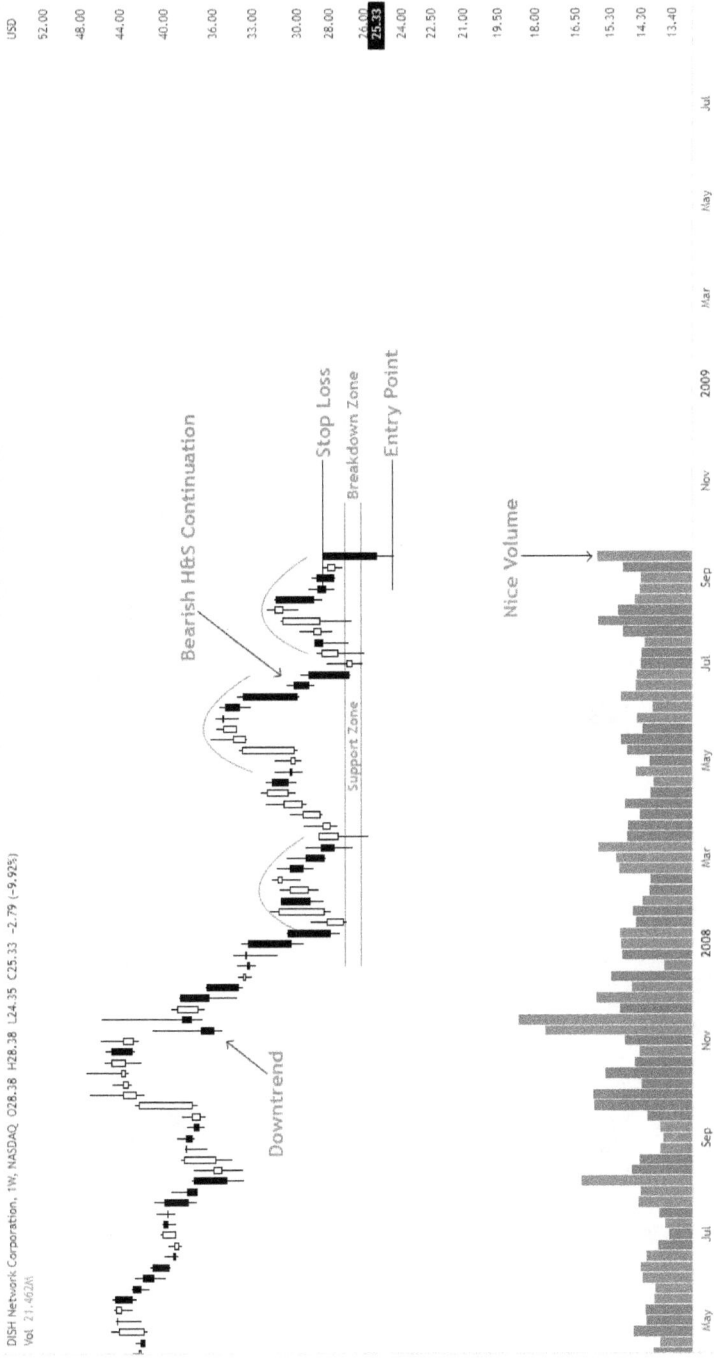

Downtrend

Bearish H&S Continuation

Stop Loss

Breakdown Zone

Entry Point

Support Zone

Nice Volume

Image 12.35: Weekly chart of Dish Network Corporation (bearish continuation head and shoulder pattern).

Image 12.36: Daily chart for Dish Network Corporation after the breakdown from bearish head and shoulder continuation pattern.

Descending Broadening Wedge Continuation Pattern

A bullish descending broadening wedge continuation pattern formed on a daily chart of Ambuja Cement Ltd. from July 2020 to October 2020, as shown in image 12.38.

In this chart, stock was in an uptrend before the pattern got formed in July 2020 and the price started ranging between both a falling band of bullish continuation pattern.

Once the pattern ended, the stock price broke above the pattern breakout zone with a not so great bullish or wide range candle. Hence, we had to put the stop-loss before the breakout candle which looks like a hammer candlestick pattern. If you have doubts regarding the hammer candlestick then you can find more information in my book *Make Money with Price Action Trading*.

The long position is taken above Rs 222 with no target in mind as we are using the 9-EMA as a trailing stop-loss (which you can see in image 12.38). We will place the stop around Rs 214 (At the low of the previous candle of the breakout candle).

Once the breakout trade was done, the price was just trading 9-EMA. At one point, we took the exit because of the exit signal.

Do remember that the exit signal is pointed out in image 12.39. However, the first candle should breakdown below the 9-EMA and right after that the second candle should close below the low of first breakdown candle.

In this trade setup, the price gave us a decent upside and went from the price of Rs 222 all the way up to Rs 255 within two months' time frame.

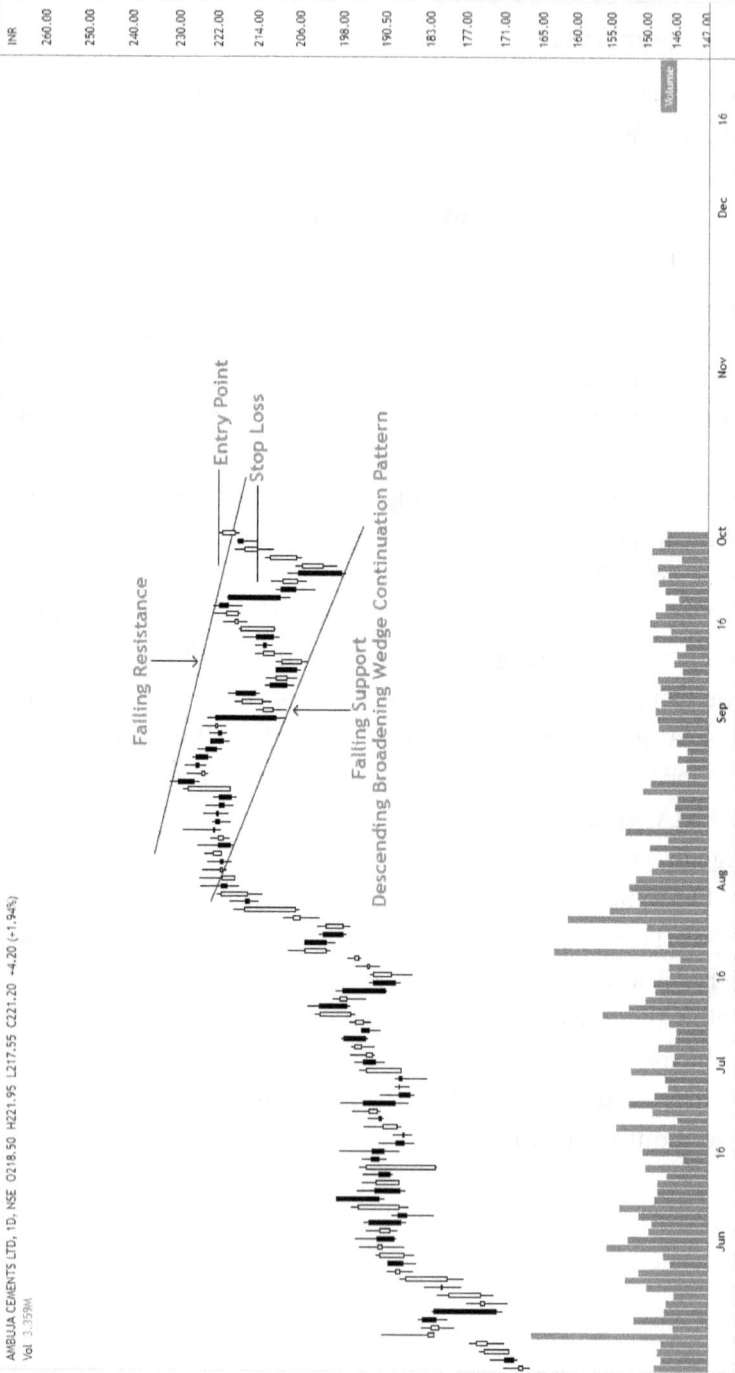

Image 12.38: Daily chart of Ambuja Cement Ltd. (bullish descending broadening wedge continuation pattern).

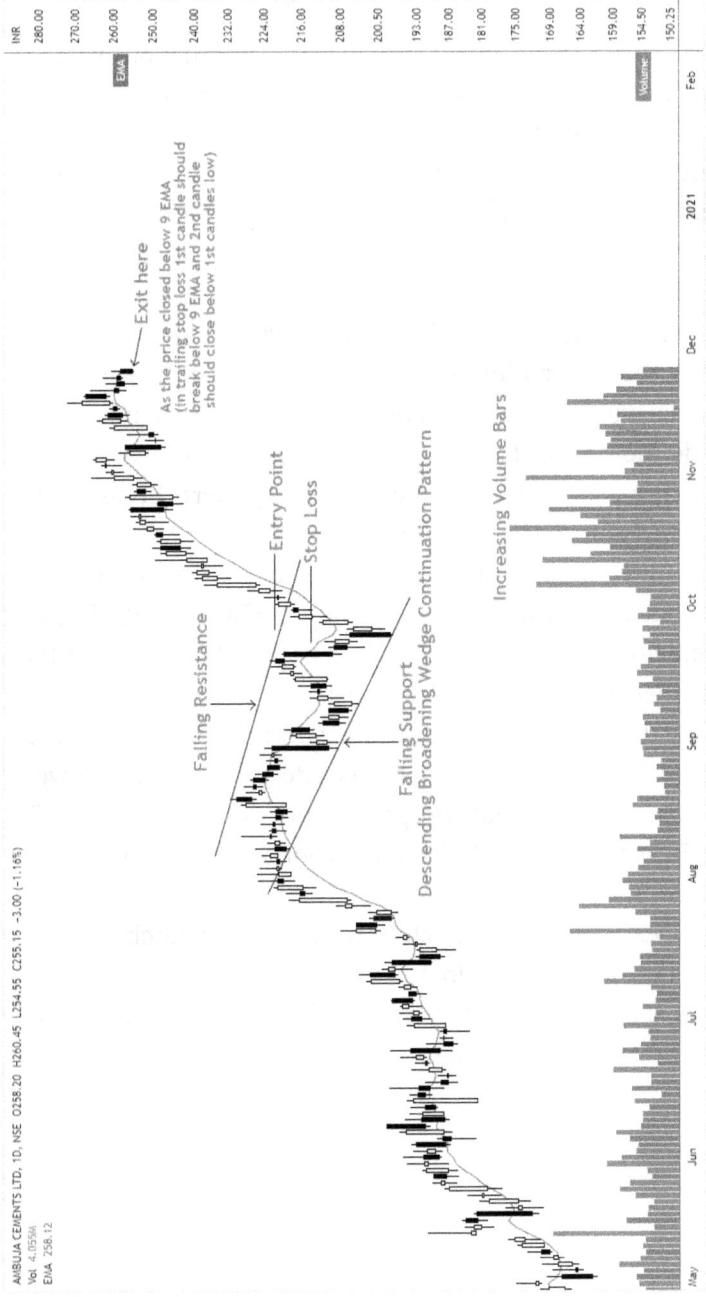

Chart_mojo published on TradingView.com, Feb 28, 2023 12:14 UTC-5:30

AMBUJA CEMENTS LTD, 1D, NSE O258.20 H260.45 L254.55 C255.15 -3.00 (-1.16%)
Vol 4.055M
EMA 258.12

EMA

Exit here

As the price closed below 9 EMA
(in trailing stop loss 1st candle should
break below 9 EMA and 2nd candle
should close below 1st candles low)

Entry Point

Stop Loss

Falling Resistance

Falling Support
Descending Broadening Wedge Continuation Pattern

Increasing Volume Bars

Volume

INR
280.00
270.00
260.00
250.00
240.00
232.00
224.00
216.00
208.00
200.50
193.00
187.00
181.00
175.00
169.00
164.00
159.00
154.50
150.25

May   Jun   Jul   Aug   Sep   Oct   Nov   Dec   2021   Feb

Image 12.39: Daily chart of Ambuja Cements Ltd. showing an uptrend after the breakout from trend continuation pattern.

Ascending Broadening Wedge Continuation Pattern

A bearish ascending broadening wedge continuation pattern formed on the daily chart of Indiabulls Real Estate from March 2022 to April 2022, as shown in image 12.40.

This image shows a clear downtrend with a series of lower tops and lower bottoms and price action signalling downward pressure. In the month of March, the price starts trading between the upper and lower rising band of the pattern and displayed a decent shape of a bearish pattern.

Once the pattern formed, we can see that the breakdown happened with a gap down. This is a strong bearish indication towards the downside with narrow range breakdown candle. Notice the increasing volume with the pattern breakdown suggesting potential downside.

Here, the short position is taken at below Rs 102 with a trailing stop-loss which made our target of around Rs 75 (26 points below the entry area) and the stop is placed around Rs 107 at the gap down resistance level.

Image 12.41 shows that once the short position was taken the price fell drastically and gave us a decent downside move.

We can also see that the price came down from Rs 102 to Rs 75 which is a 25% downfall from the breakdown zone within 46 trading sessions.

It is clearly visible that before we exited the stock, we got a few fake moves wherein the first candle broke above the 9-EMA. However, the second candle occurred and closed above the first candle's high.

Image 12.40: Daily chart of Indiabulls Real Estate (bearish ascending broadening wedge continuation pattern).

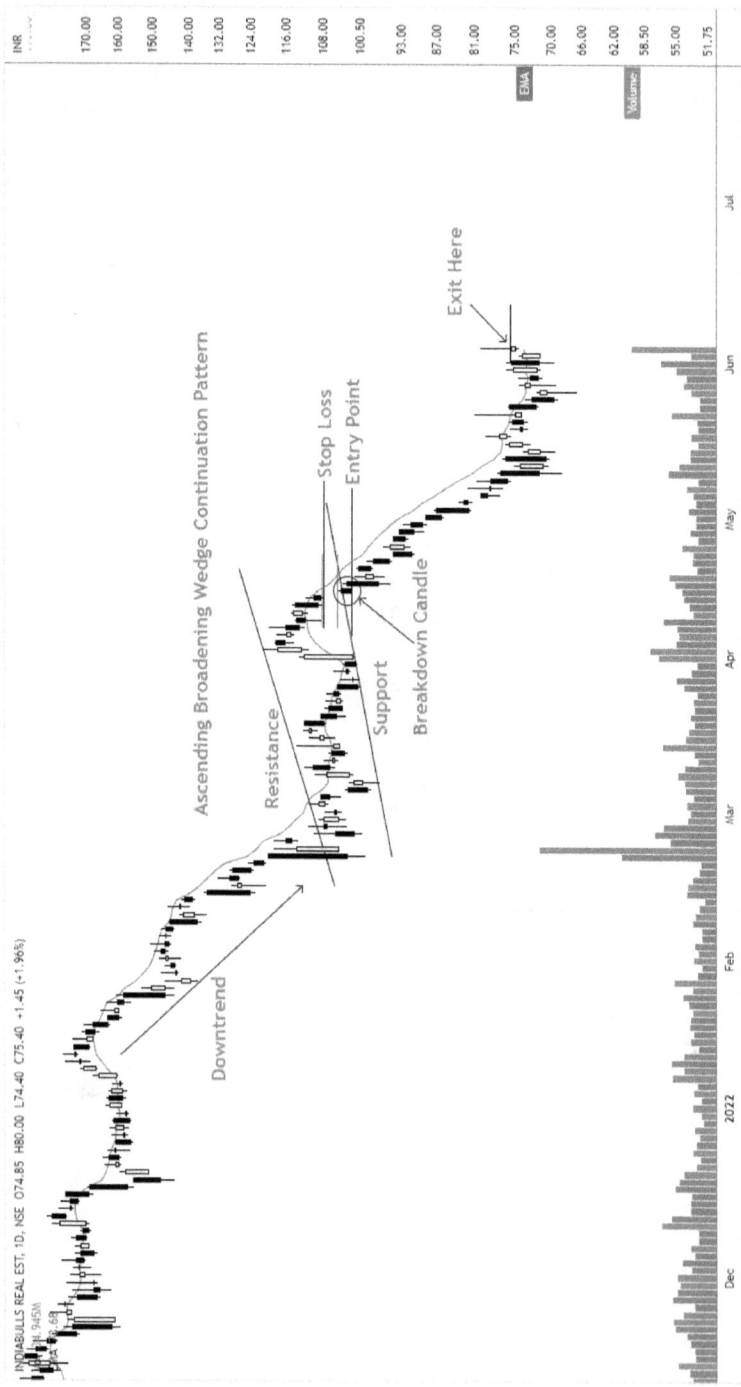

Image 12.41: Daily chart of IndiaBulls Real Estate after the breakdown from bearish trend continuation pattern.

Descending Channel

A bullish descending channel pattern formed on the monthly chart of TVS Motor Company, from July 2010 to October 2013, as shown in image 12.42.

It is very clear that the uptrend is very strong and the bullish candlesticks are taking control over the sellers. The uptrend has unfolded with strong buying volume bars as well.

Once the pattern started forming, the stock price started dancing between the descending channel upper and lower band. Also notice that when the pattern was forming, the volume was also going through ups and downs with price action.

Eventually the pattern breakout occurred with a wide range breakout candle which was supported by volume in a big way.

Now, the long position is taken above Rs 53 with no target in mind as we are using the moving average as trailing stop-loss (which you can see in image 12.43). We will place the stop around Rs 37 (low of the pattern breakout candle).

Image 12.43 is the follow up chart of TVS Motor Company after the breakout area. The stock price went just upside with very less bearish candles after the breakout occurred from the rectangle continuation pattern.

This chart shows that this trade setup gave us around a whopping 318% returns and the price went from 53 all the way up to 223 within a period of 671 trading days.

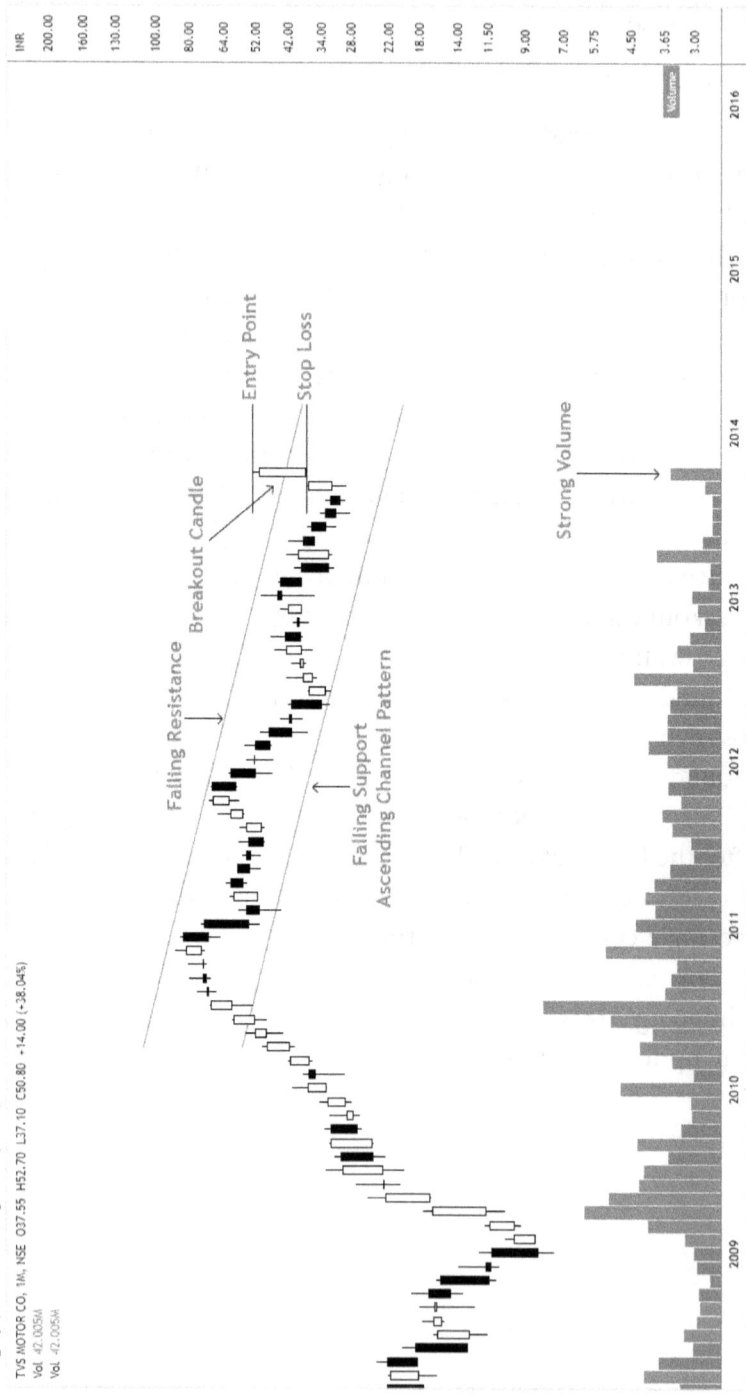

Image 12.42: Monthly chart of TVS Motor Company (bullish descending channel pattern).

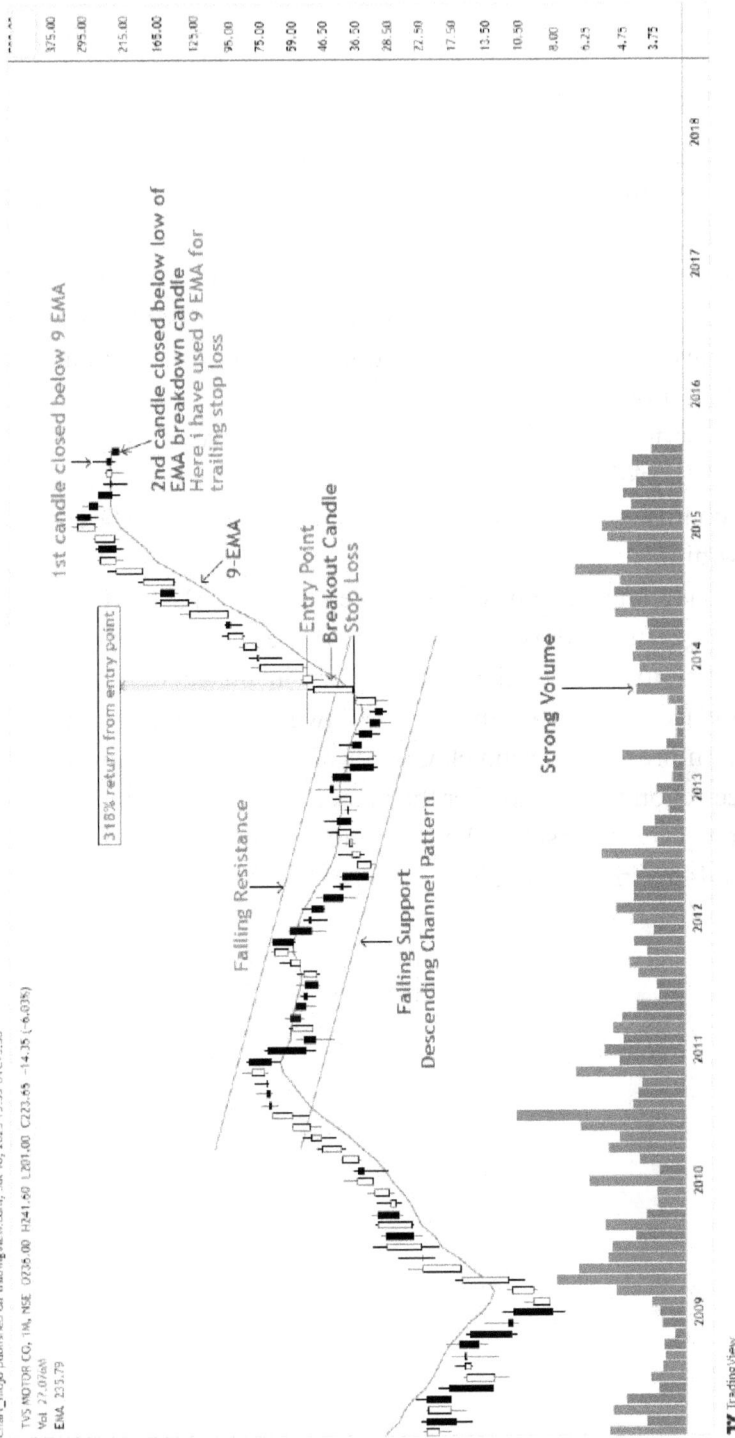

Image 12.43: Monthly chart of TVS Motor Company showing uptrend continuation after the breakout from descending channel pattern.

Ascending Channel

A bearish ascending channel pattern formed on the daily chart of Symphony Ltd. from February 2019 to May 2019 as shown in image 12.44.

In this image, it is very clear that the downtrend is very strong and the bearish candlesticks are taking control over the buyers. The downtrend has unfolded very nicely within a period of one month.

Once the ascending pattern completed, we got to see a strong breakdown candle with increasing volume which cleared the confusion for potential downside and gave a strong bearish view hint.

Finally, the short position is taken at below Rs 1,710 with no target in mind as we will be using the moving average as trailing stop-loss (which you can see in image 12.45). We will place the stop around Rs 1,777 (which is the high of the pattern breakdown candle). Once again, you can see how the price action shaped up after the breakdown occurred and gave us a decent downside. The price moved all the way down to Rs 1,445 within 39 trading sessions.

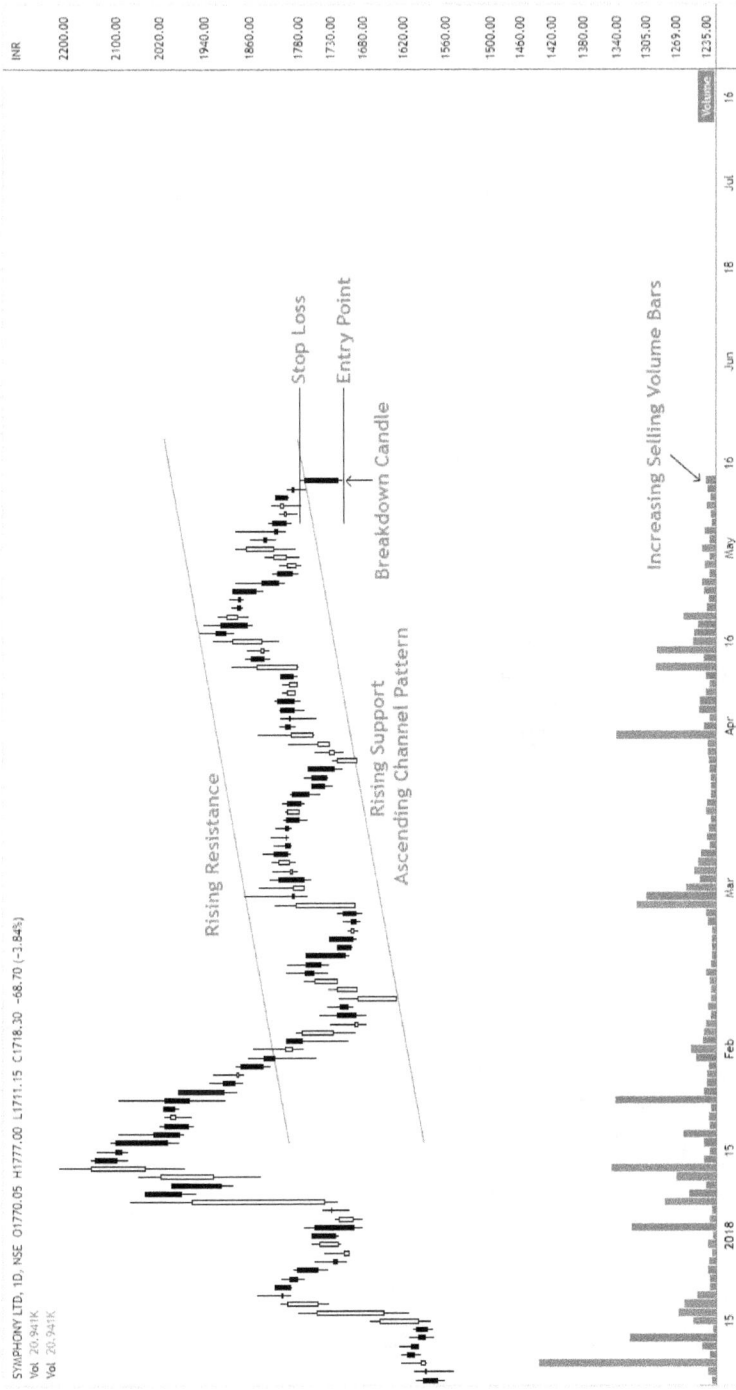

Image 12.44: Daily chart of Symphony Ltd. (bearish ascending channel pattern).

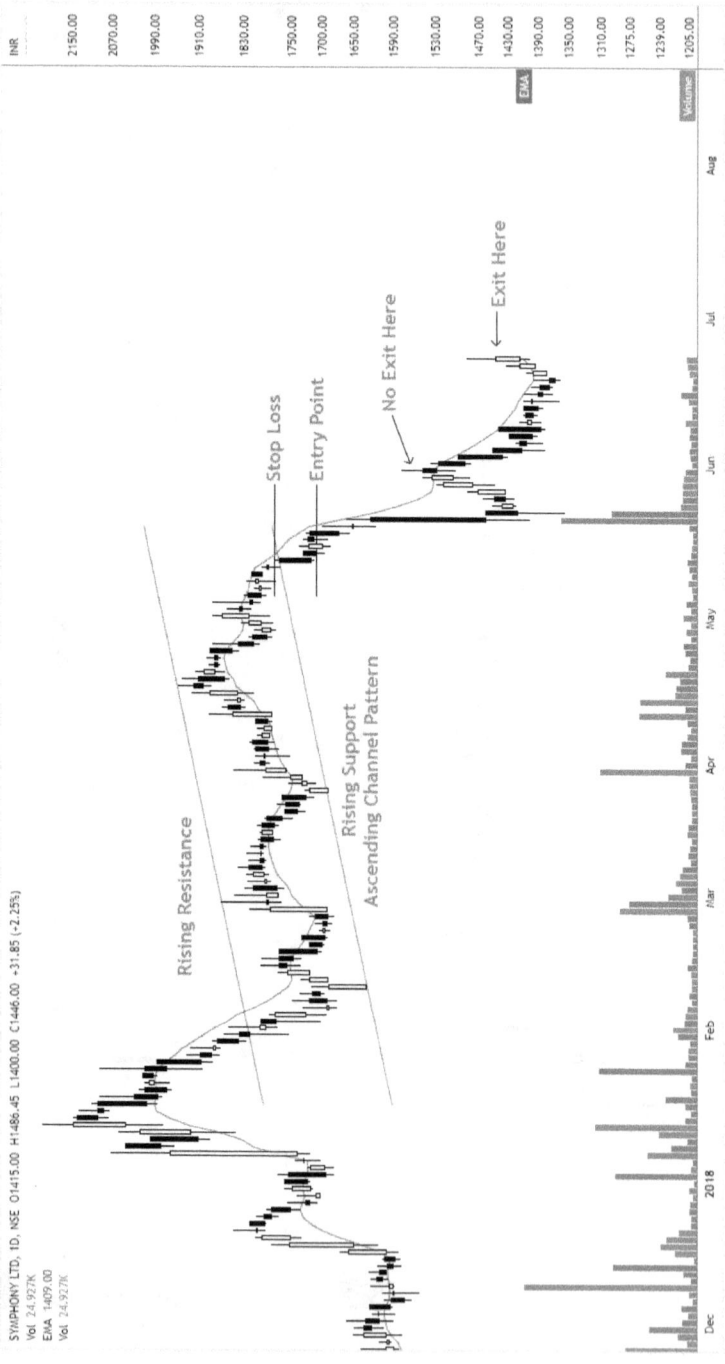

Image 12.45: Daily chart of Symphony Ltd. after the breakdown from ascending channel pattern.

Case Studies of Reversal Patterns

Broadening Bottom

A bullish broadening bottom reversal pattern formed on the daily chart of Conterra Energy Inc, from September 2006 to October 2006 as shown in image 12.46.

In this image we can see that the downtrend continued and eventually the stock went into the secondary phase, where the broadening bottom pattern formed during a short time frame.

It was clear that once the pattern ended, the stock price broke above the resistance of bullish reversal pattern with a breakout candle (narrow range candle). The breakout was also supported by a decent volume build-up signifying the built-in upside momentum into the stock price.

Finally, in this chart setup the long position was taken just above the price of $6.24 and the stop-loss placed at $6, which is the low of the breakout candle. The exit happened on the basis of 9-EMA trailing stop-loss breakdown at $7.74.

In image 12.47 it is clear that once the long position was taken the stock price starting drifting towards the higher side and had a smooth run with just two fake out moves on the way.

It is evident that the price was just trading above our trailing stop-loss and we got stopped at the price of $7.74.

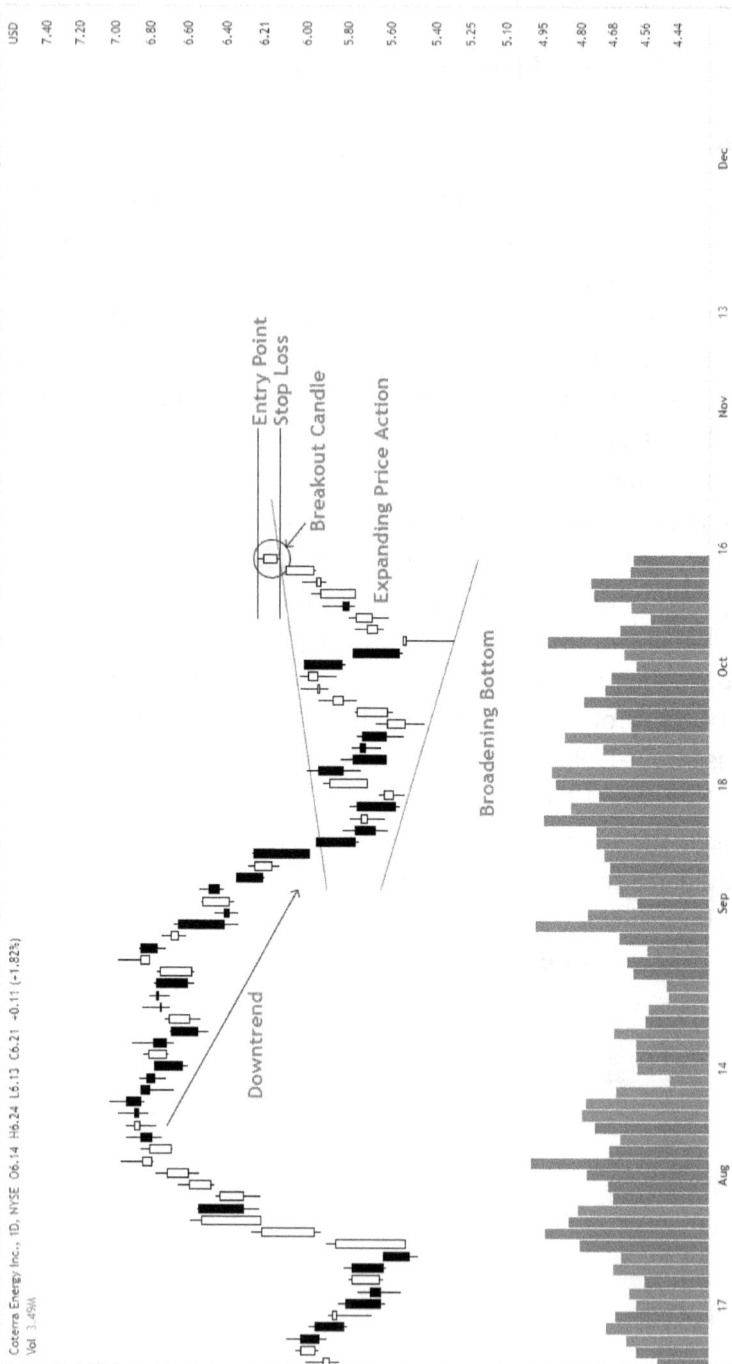

Image 12.46: Daily chart of Conterra Energy Inc, (bullish broadening bottom reversal pattern).

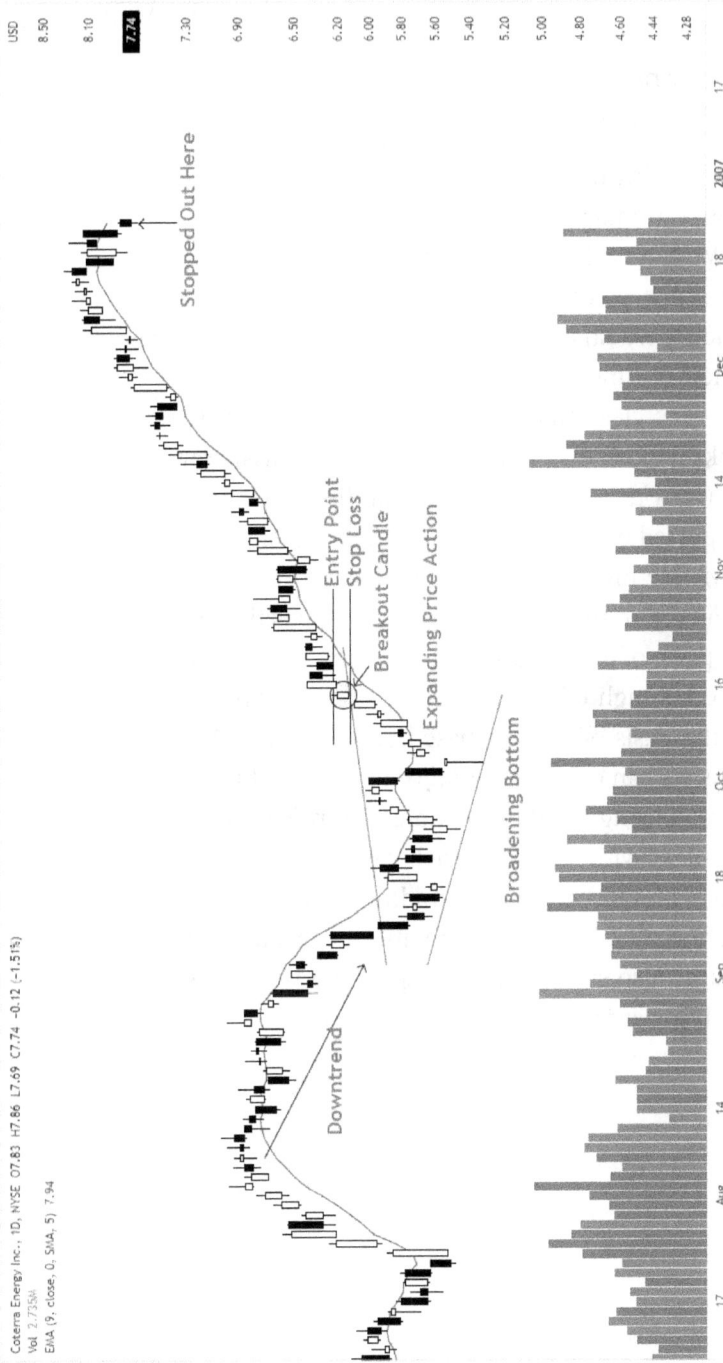

Chartmojos published on TradingView.com, Mar 06, 2022 12:43 UTC+5:30

Coterra Energy Inc., 1D, NYSE O7.83 H7.86 L7.69 C7.74 −0.12 (−1.51%)

Vol 2.775M

EMA (9, close, 0, SMA, 5) 7.94

Stopped Out Here

Entry Point
Stop Loss

Breakout Candle

Expanding Price Action

Broadening Bottom

Downtrend

USD

8.50

8.10

7.74

7.30

6.90

6.50

6.20

6.00

5.80

5.60

5.40

5.20

5.00

4.80

4.60

4.44

4.28

Aug   14   Sep   18   Oct   16   Nov   14   Dec   18   2007   17

17

TradingView

Image 12.47: Daily chart of Conterra Energy Inc. showing uptrend continuation after the breakout from broadening bottom.

Broadening Top

A bearish broadening top reversal pattern formed on the daily chart of Intuit Inc, from August 2008 to October 2008, as shown in image 12.48.

We can notice a small uptrend and at the top of the uptrend the stock price started forming expansionary price action which gave shape to a broadening top pattern over a short period of time.

It was clear that once the pattern ended, the stock price broke below the falling support of bearish reversal pattern with a wide range breakout candle. The breakout was also supported by a decent volume build-up signifying the built-in downside momentum into the stock price.

Finally, in this chart setup, the long position was taken below the price of $27.74 and the stop-loss will be placed at $29.84 which is high of the breakdown candle. The exit will happen on the basis of pattern-based target at $24.81.

As we can clearly see that once the short position was taken with a strong breakout candle, the price started going down smoothly with strong bearish candles. The pattern target was also achieved within four trading sessions.

Do remember when the pattern breakdown happened, the volume also started picking up which is a bearish sign for the stock towards downside (image 12.49).

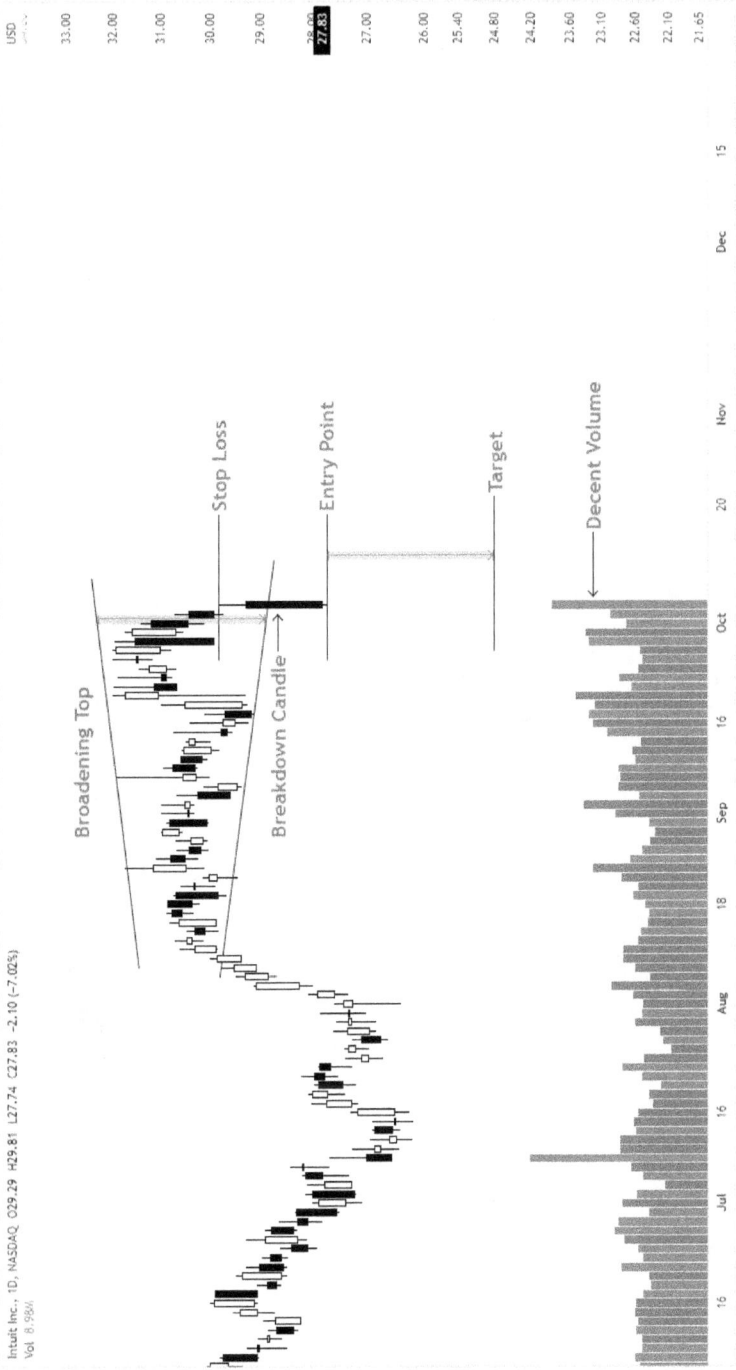

Image 12.48: Daily chart of Intuit Inc, (bearish broadening top reversal pattern).

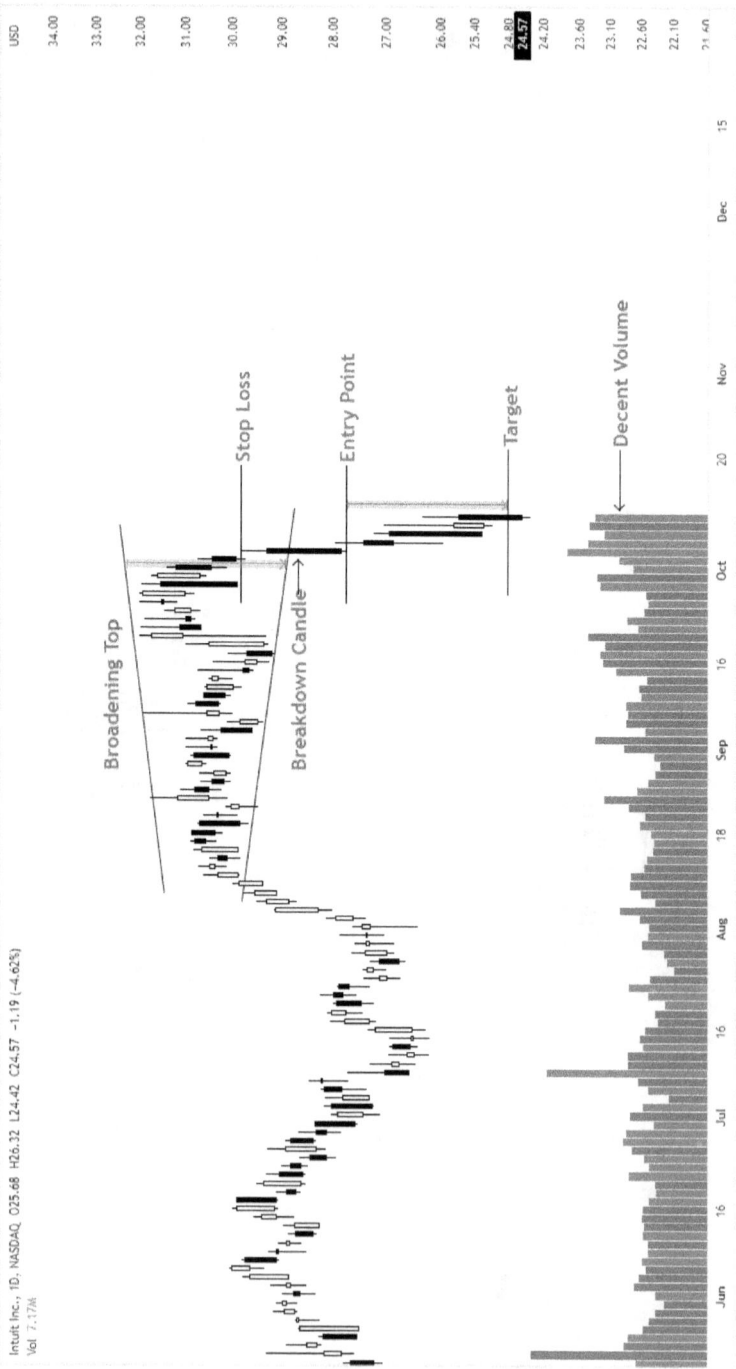

Image 12.49: Daily chart of Intuit Inc. after the breakdown from broadening top pattern.

Right-Angled Descending Broadening Wedge Reversal pattern

A bullish right-angled ascending broadening wedge reversal pattern formed on the weekly chart of Globe Life Inc from March 1997 to September 1997, as shown in image 12.50.

A small downtrend was noticed and finally at the bottom end of the trend the stock price started forming up expansionary price action which gave the shape to bullish right-angled ascending broadening wedge reversal pattern.

It was clear that once the pattern ended, the stock price broke above the horizontal support of bullish reversal pattern with a wide range breakout candle. The breakout was also supported by a decent volume build-up signifying the built-in downside momentum into the stock price.

Finally, in this chart setup, the long position was taken just above the price of $8.61 and the stop-loss placed at $8.32 which is the low of the breakout candle. The exit will happen on the basis of 9-EMA trailing stop-loss breakdown at $10.19.

In image 12.51, it is clear that once the long position was taken, the stock price started drifting towards the higher side and gave a smooth run with not even a single fake out move on the way.

It is clearly visible on the chart that the price was just trading above our trailing stop-loss and we got stopped at the price of $10.19.

Many traders would say that we could have made good money if we would have exited at the right top before the exit signal got triggered.

My answer to those traders is that no one can exit at the top and no one can time the market. This is the cost of using 9-EMA as trailing stop-loss. We will have to put some profit on the table and exit as and when we get stopped out.

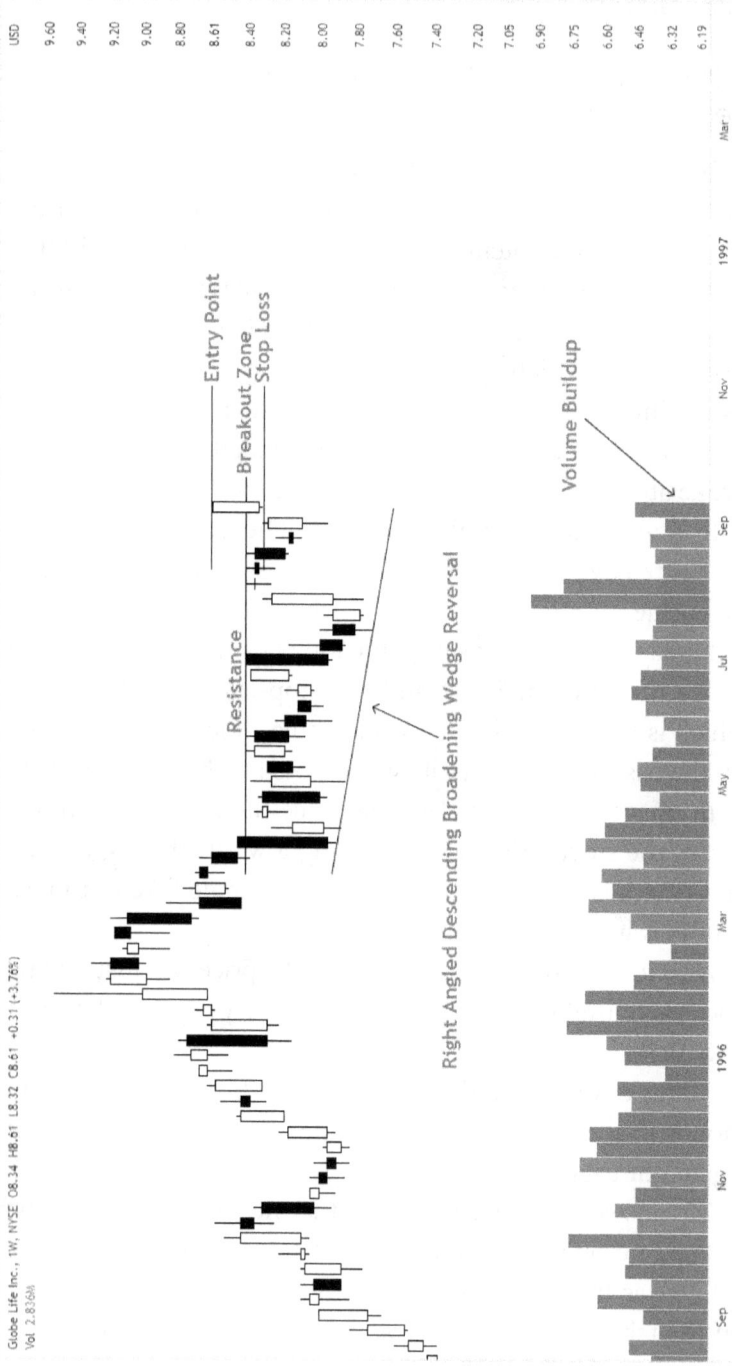

Image 12.50: Weekly chart of Globe Life Inc. (bullish right-angled ascending broadening wedge reversal pattern).

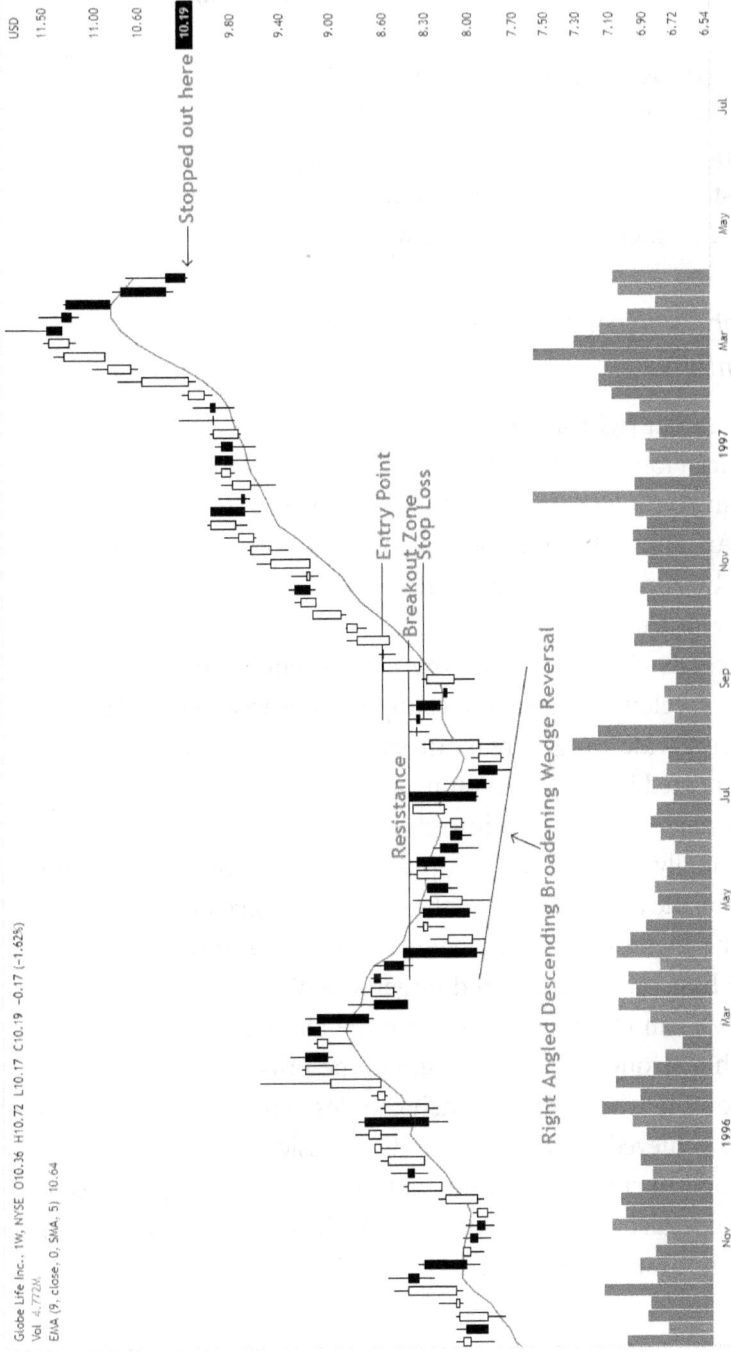

Image 12.51: Weekly chart of Globe Life Inc. after the breakout from bullish trend continuation pattern

Pro Tip: The beauty of using 9-EMA as trailing stop-loss and not using a pattern-based target is that it lets you ride the trend. There would be a situation wherein your stock would go on becoming double and triple and so on, which will reap you a whopping upside.

Right-Angled Ascending Broadening Wedge Reversal pattern

A bearish right-angled ascending broadening wedge reversal pattern formed on the daily chart of MGM Resort International from April 2006 to May 2006, as shown in image 12.52.

An uptrend was noticed before the pattern formation and at the top of the uptrend the stock price started forming a bearish trend reversal pattern.

It was clear that once the pattern ended, the stock price broke below the horizontal support of bearish reversal pattern with a wide range breakout candle. The breakout was also supported by a decent volume build-up signifying the built-in downside momentum into the stock price.

Finally, in this chart setup the short position was taken just below the price of $43 and the stop-loss placed at $44.22 which is the high of the breakdown candle. The exit will happen on the basis of pattern-based target at $40.

We can clearly see that once the short position was taken with a strong breakdown candle, the price starts going down smoothly with strong bearish candles. The pattern target was also achieved within a few trading sessions.

Do remember, when the pattern breakdown happened, the volume also started picking up which is a bearish sign for the stock towards downside.

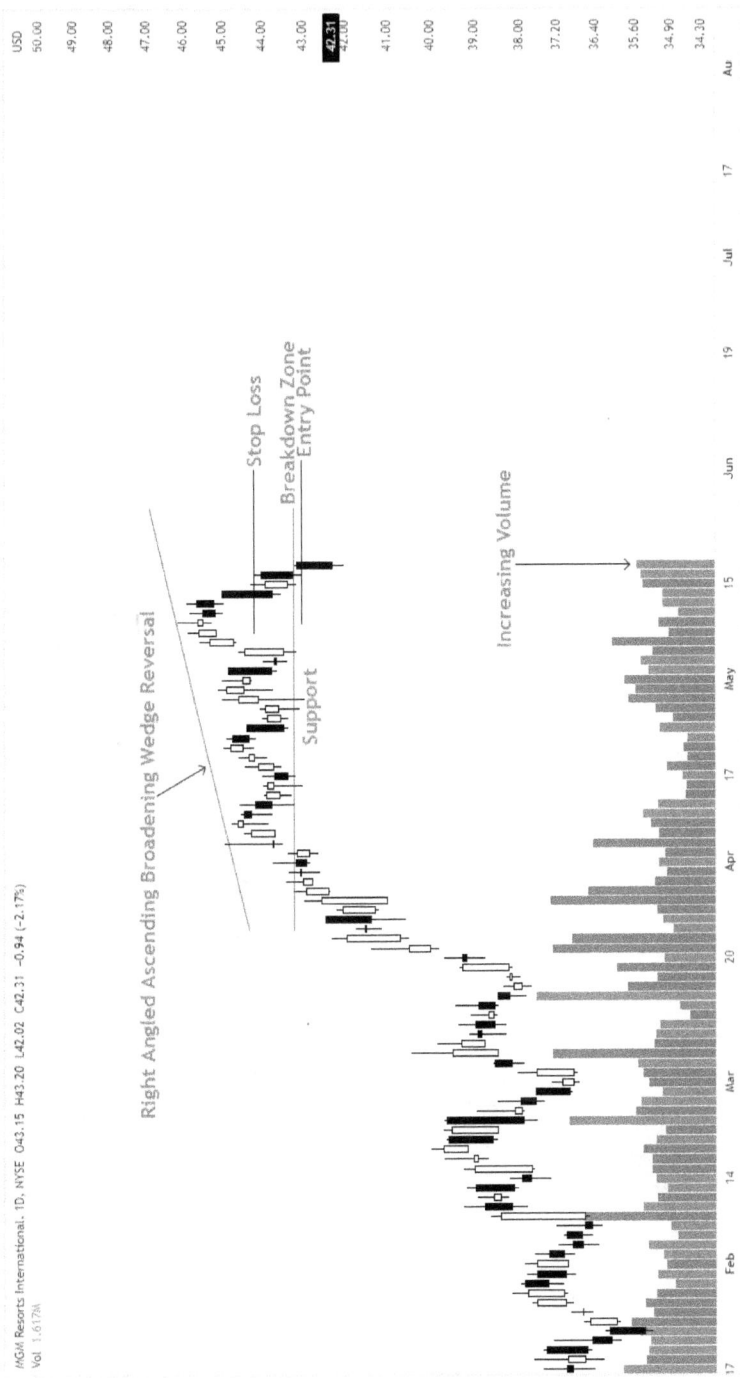

Image 12.52: Daily chart of MGM Resort International (bearish right angled ascending broadening wedge reversal pattern).

MGM Resorts International, 1D, NYSE O38.79 H39.06 L38.15 C38.22 -0.65 (-1.67%)
Vol 1.44BM

Right Angled Ascending Broadening Wedge Reversal

Stop Loss

Entry Point

Support

Target

USD
49.00
48.00
47.00
46.00
45.00
44.00
43.00
42.00
41.00
40.00
39.40
38.80
38.22
37.60
37.00
36.40
35.85

Feb   14   Mar   20   Apr   17   May   15   Jun   19   Jul   17

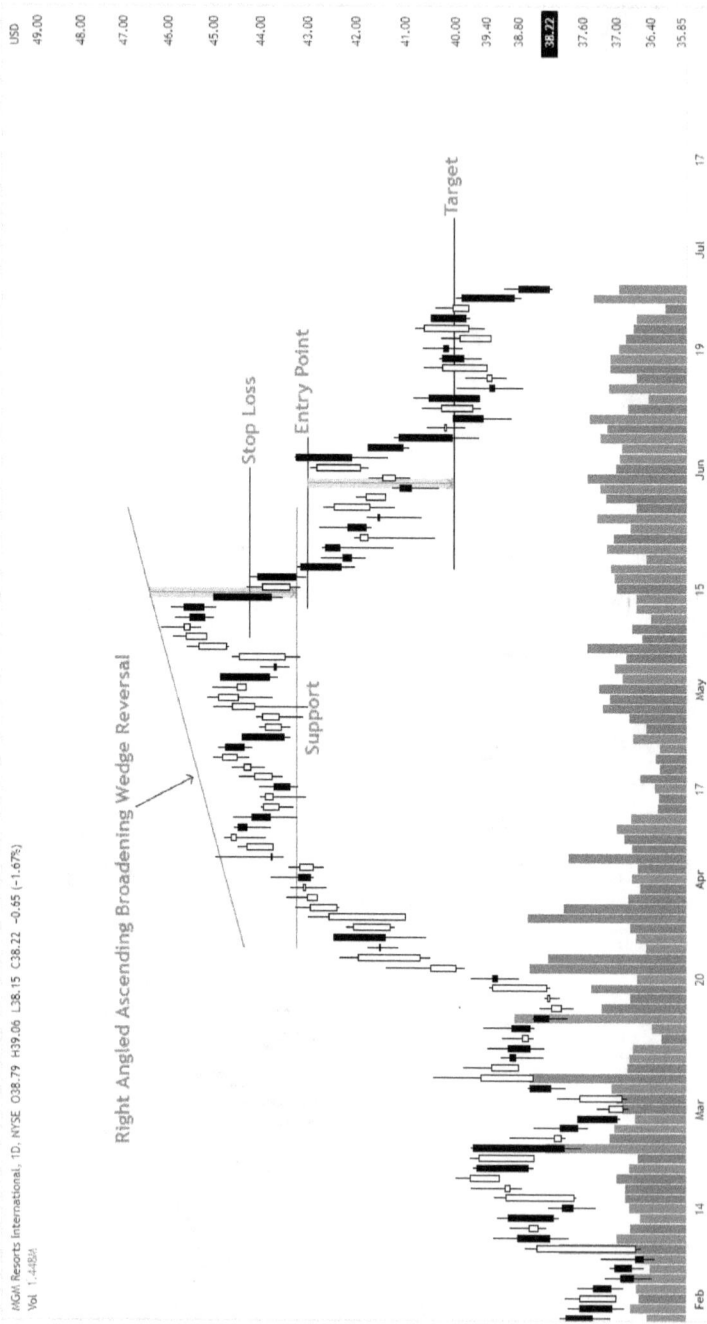

Image 12.53: Daily chart pattern of MGM Resorts International showing a downtrend continuation after breakdown from bearish trend reversal pattern.

Descending Broadening Wedge

A bullish descending broadening wedge reversal pattern formed on the daily chart of Extra Space Storage Inc from May 2022 to July 2022, as shown in image 12.54.

In this image it is very clear that the downtrend is very strong and the bearish candlesticks are taking control over the buyers. The downtrend has also unfolded with strong selling volume bars.

Once the pattern started forming, the stock price started dancing between downward sloping broadening wedge upper and lower band. When the pattern was forming, the volume was also going through ups and down with price action.

Eventually the pattern breakout occurred with a narrow range breakout candle which was supported by a volume pop out.

The long position is taken above $175.41 with no target in mind as we are using the moving average as trailing stop-loss (which you can see in image 12.55). We will place the stop around $171.64 (low of the breakout previous candle).

Once the pattern breakout occurred, the stock price went just one way up, staying above trailing stop-loss for a decent number of days.

In this trade setup we got around 17% returns and the price went from $175.41 to all the way up to $205 within a short period of time.

We can also notice that after the breakout candle occurred, the volume also started increasing which made the upside much smoother as it signalled that a lot of buyers are interested in this stock.

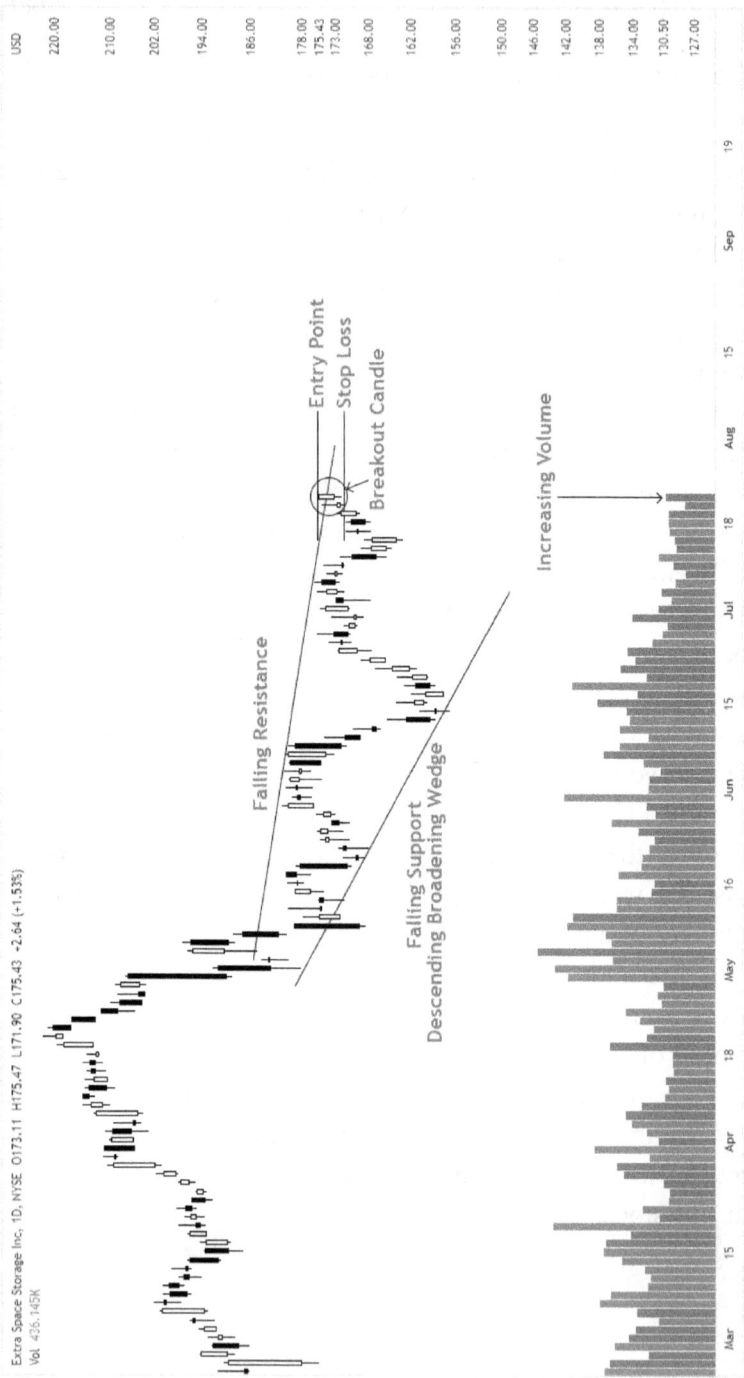

Image 12.54: Daily chart of Extra Space Storage Inc. (bullish descending broadening wedge reversal pattern).

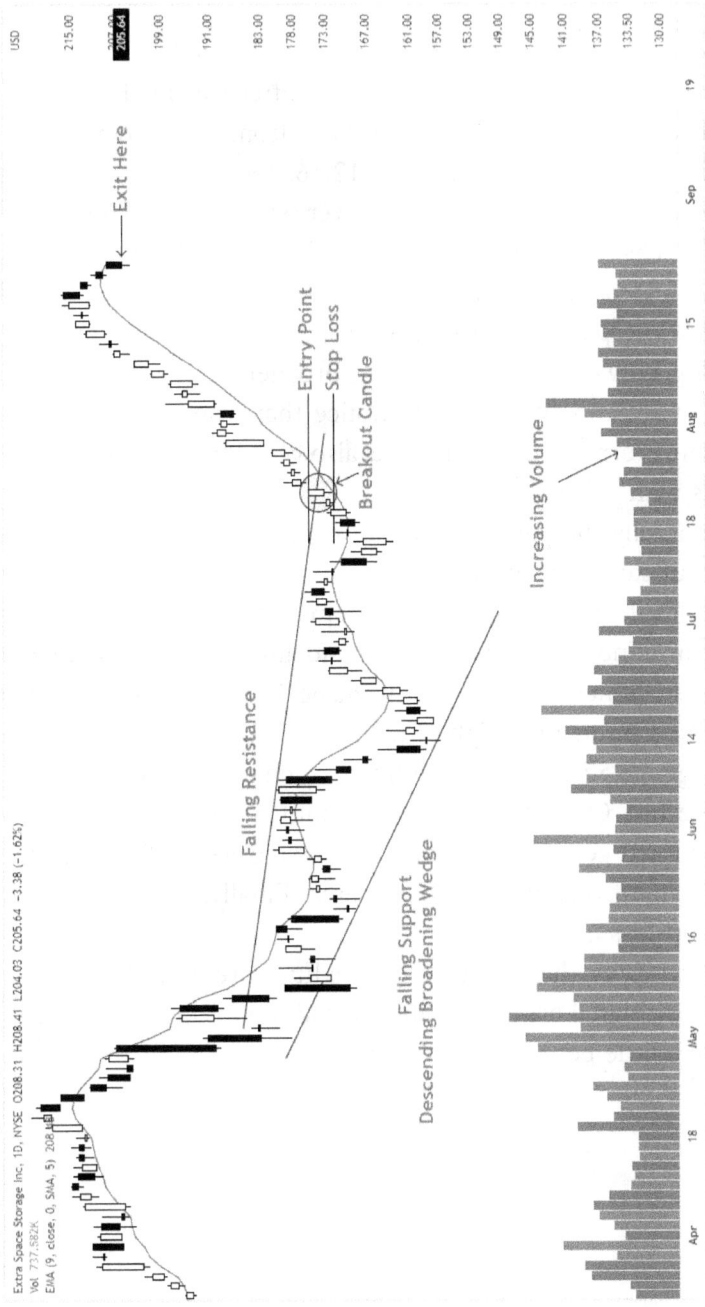

Charrmotjos published on TradingView.com, Mar 06, 2023 14:56 UTC+5:30

Extra Space Storage Inc, 1D, NYSE O208.31 H208.41 L204.03 C205.64 -3.38 (-1.62%)

Vol 737,582K

EMA (9, close; 0, SMA, 5) 208

USD

215.00

205.64

199.00

191.00

183.00

178.00

173.00

167.00

161.00

157.00

153.00

149.00

145.00

141.00

137.00

133.50

130.00

Exit Here

Falling Resistance

Entry Point

Stop Loss

Breakout Candle

Falling Support

Descending Broadening Wedge

Increasing Volume

Image 12.55: Daily chart of Extra Space Storage Inc. showing bullish trend reversal from the breakout zone of descending broadening wedge pattern.

Ascending Broadening Wedge

A bearish ascending wedge reversal pattern formed on the weekly chart of Extra Space Storage Inc. from September 2006 to May 2007, as shown in image 12.56.

It is very clear that the uptrend is very strong and the bullish candlesticks are taking control over the sellers. The uptrend also unfolded with higher highs and higher lows.

Once the pattern started forming, the stock price started dancing between upward sloping broadening wedge upper and lower band. We can also notice that when the pattern was being formed the volume was also going through ups and downs with price action.

Eventually the pattern breakout occurred with wide range breakout candle which was supported by good volume.

Finally, the short position is taken just below $18.11 with no target in mind as we are using the moving average as trailing stop-loss (which you can see in image 12.56). We will place the stop around $19 (high of the breakdown candle).

Image 12.57 shows the follow up chart of Extra Space Storage Inc. Once the pattern breakout occurred, the stock price started going down and it did see a price pullback after a sharp fall from the breakdown area. Finally, it did not hit our stop-loss and came down.

However, we did not get to book a huge profit on this trade as the exit signal came later and we had to cut our position at a price a little below our entry area.

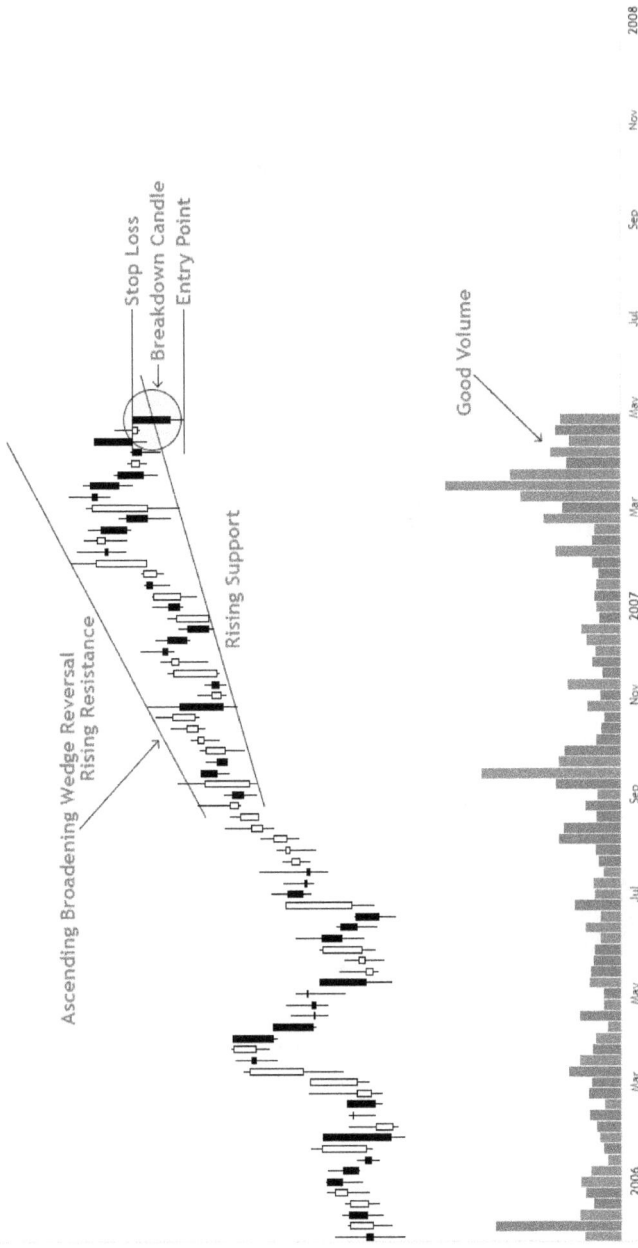

Image 12.56: Weekly chart of Extra Space Storage Inc. (bearish ascending wedge reversal pattern).

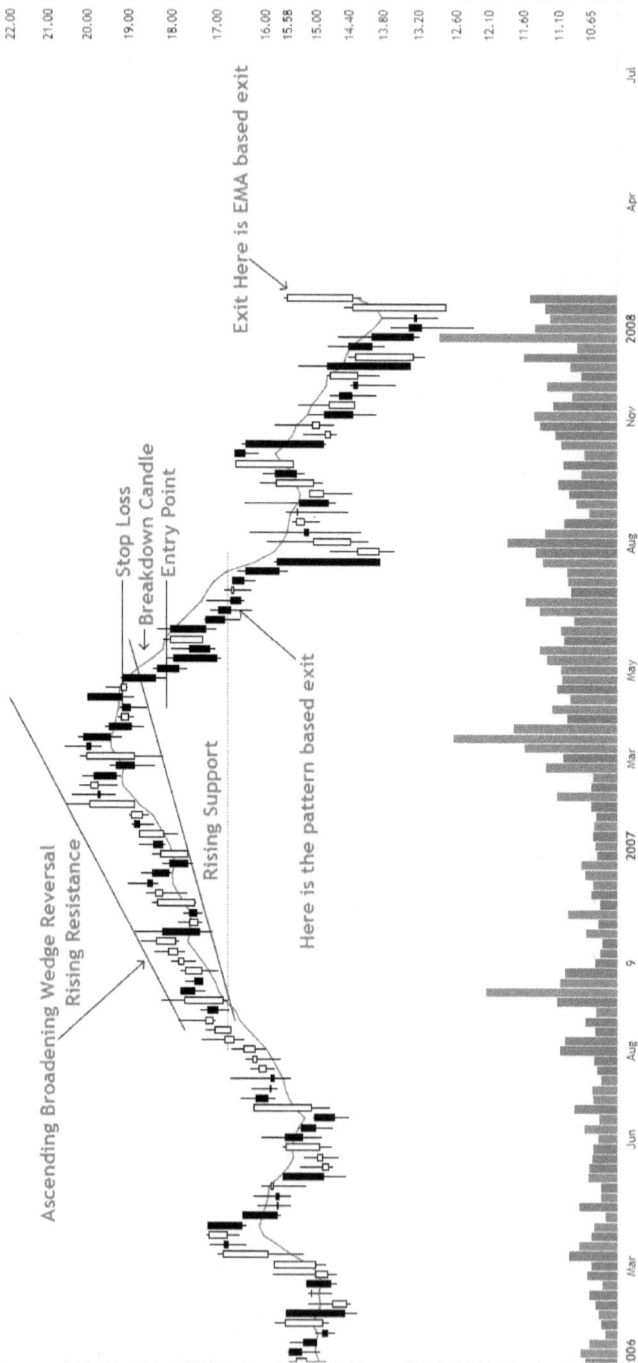

Image 12.57: Weekly chart of Extra Space Storage Inc. after the breakdown from bearish trend reversal pattern.

Bump and Run Reversal Bottom

A bullish bump and run reversal bottom pattern formed on the daily chart of Nagarjuna Construction Company (NCC) Ltd. from April 2013 to February 2014, as shown in image 12.58.

The lead in phase started in April 2013 and then the price came down with lower lows and lower highs. At the bottom of the downtrend, we could see a bump phase followed by a run phase towards upside.

Once the run phase started, the stock price went up and it finally came down to retest the falling trend line and made a W-type pattern. It showed a decent upside breakout with a strong bullish candle which was also supported by a good volume build-up.

Eventually, the long position will be taken a little above the price of Rs 29 and the stop-loss will be placed at Rs 25.75 which is the breakout previous candle low. The exit will happen on the basis of 9-EMA breakout at Rs 72.

In image 12.59, once the long position was taken, the stock price started rising in just one way—in higher highs and higher lows fashion.

The upside was supported with a buying volume which signifies the built-in momentum into the stock price.

The stock price went up from Rs 29 to all the way up to Rs 72, the total upside was a whopping 162% at 11% risk.

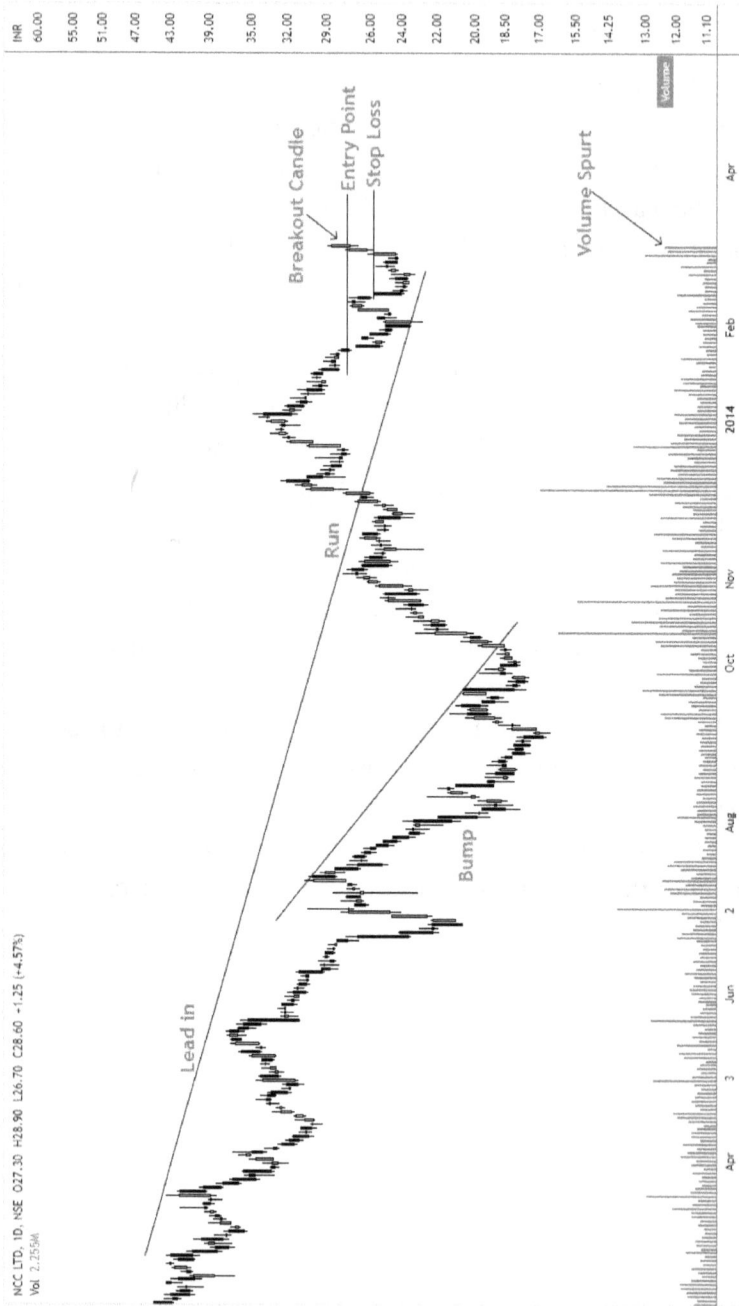

Chart_mojo published on TradingView.com, Mar 08, 2023 12:36 UTC+5:30

NCC LTD, 1D, NSE O27.30 H28.90 L26.70 C28.60 +1.25 (+4.57%)
Vol 2.255M

Image 12.58: Daily chart of NCC Ltd. (bullish bump and run reversal bottom pattern).

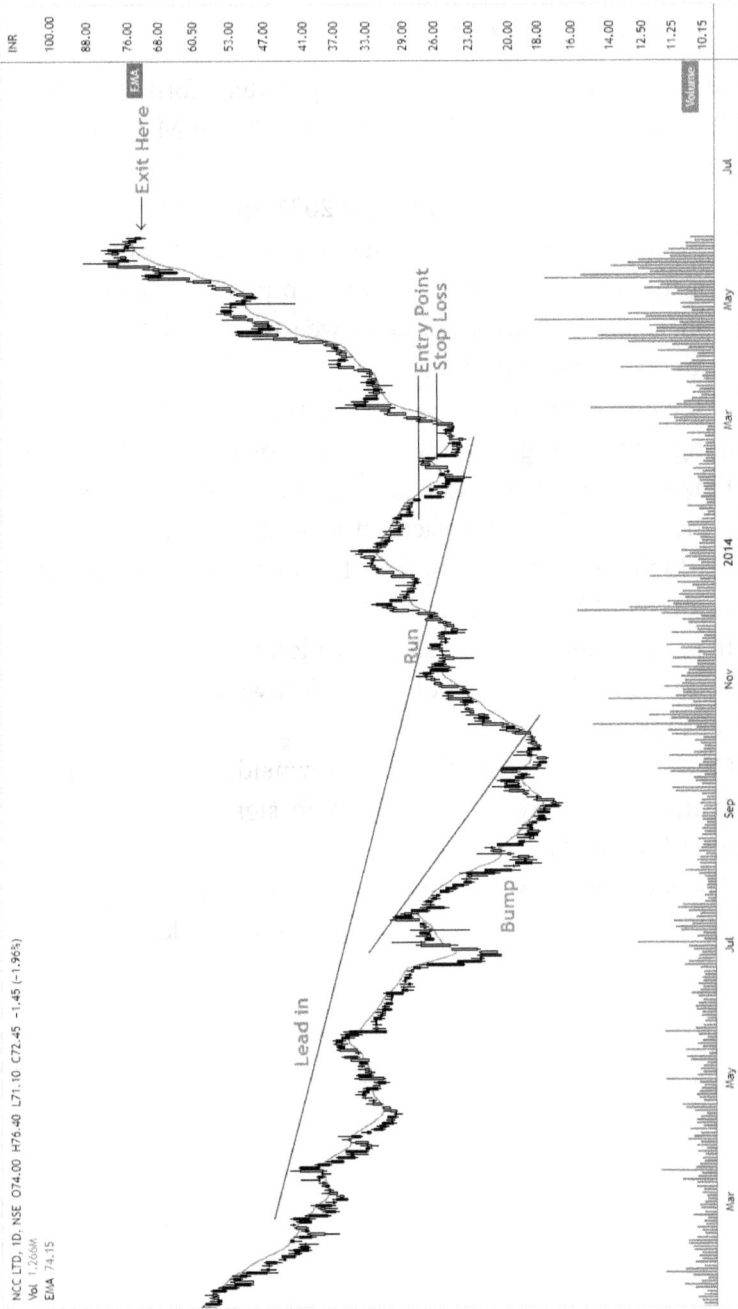

Chart_mojo published on TradingView.com, Mar 08, 2023 12:37 UTC+5:30

NCC LTD, 1D, NSE O74.00 H76.40 L71.10 C72.45 -1.45 (-1.96%)
Vol 1.266M
EMA 74.15

Image 12.59: Daily chart of NCC Ltd. after the breakout from bullish trend reversal pattern.

Bump and Run Reversal Top

A bearish bump and run reversal top pattern formed on the daily chart of Jindal Stainless from July 2021 to May 2022, as shown in image 12.60.

The lead in phase started in July 2021 and then we can see how price went up with higher highs and higher lows. At the top of the uptrend, we can see a bump phase, followed by a run phase towards downside once we saw a breakdown from intermediate rising trend line.

Once the breakdown took place, the stock price started coming down and gave a very smooth downside on 9-EMA.

Finally, the short position will be taken just below Rs 370 and the stop-loss will be placed at Rs 402 which is the recent swing high above the entry price. The exit will happen on the basis of 9-EMA breakout at Rs 225.

In image 12.61, once the short position was taken, the stock price started falling in just one direction with lower lows and lower highs.

One can also notice that the downside was supported with increasing buying volume which signifies the built-in momentum in the stock price.

The stock price went down from Rs 370 all the way up to Rs 225, the total downside was a 39% at 8% risk.

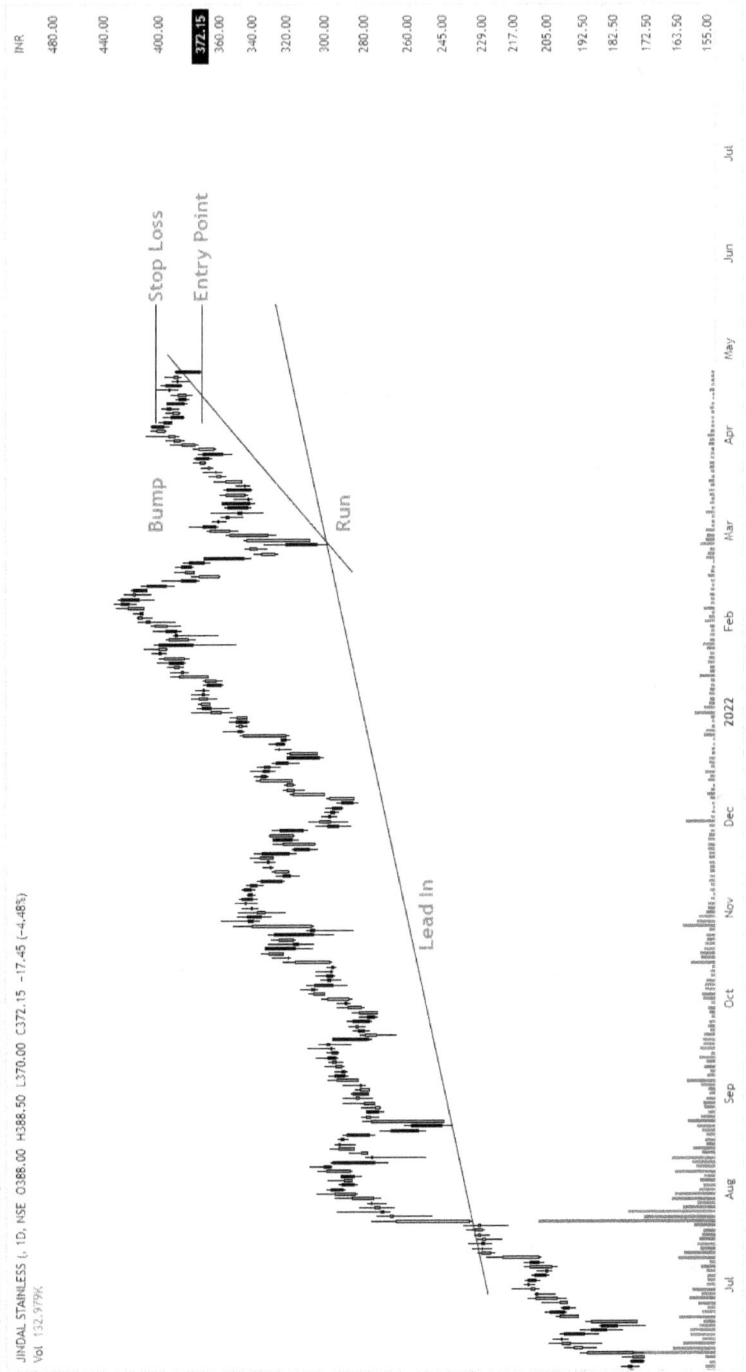

Image 12.60: Daily chart of Jindal Stainless (bearish bump and run reversal top pattern).

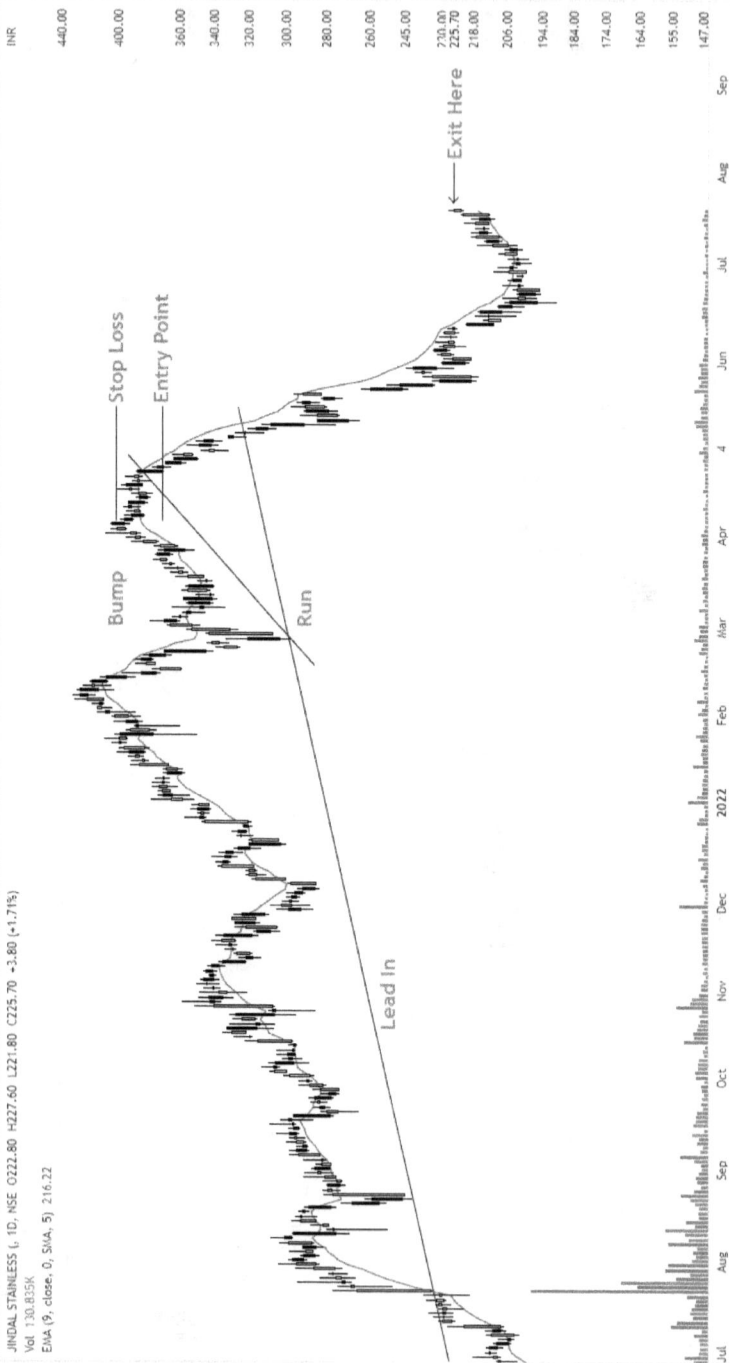

Image 12.61: Daily chart of Jindal Stainless after breakdown from bearish trend reversal pattern.

Cup and Handle Bottom Reversal

A bearish rounding bottom reversal pattern formed on the weekly chart of Ashok Leyland, from June 2013 to April 2014 as shown in image 12.62.

It can be seen that the downtrend was in action and finally the price action took the shape of a cup with handle bottom reversal pattern.

At the time of breakout, we can see that a strong breakout candle occurred. This was accompanied by a huge volume spurt giving us the indication of bullishness towards upside.

Finally, in this chart setup, the long position will be taken just above the price of Rs 24 and the stop-loss will be placed at Rs 18 which is the low of the breakout candle. The exit will happen on the basis of 9-EMA trailing stop-loss breakdown at Rs 65.

Once the long position is taken with a strong breakout candle (image 12.63), the price started marching towards upside with a decent volume spike during the up move.

You can also notice that during the uptrend we used 9-EMA for trailing stop-loss and the stock did give us many fake breakdown moves which have also been pointed out in the chart. However, these fake moves saved us from exiting the stock at a very early stage.

The stock price went up from the price of Rs 24 all the way up to Rs 65, leaving us with the total upside gain of 167% from the entry price.

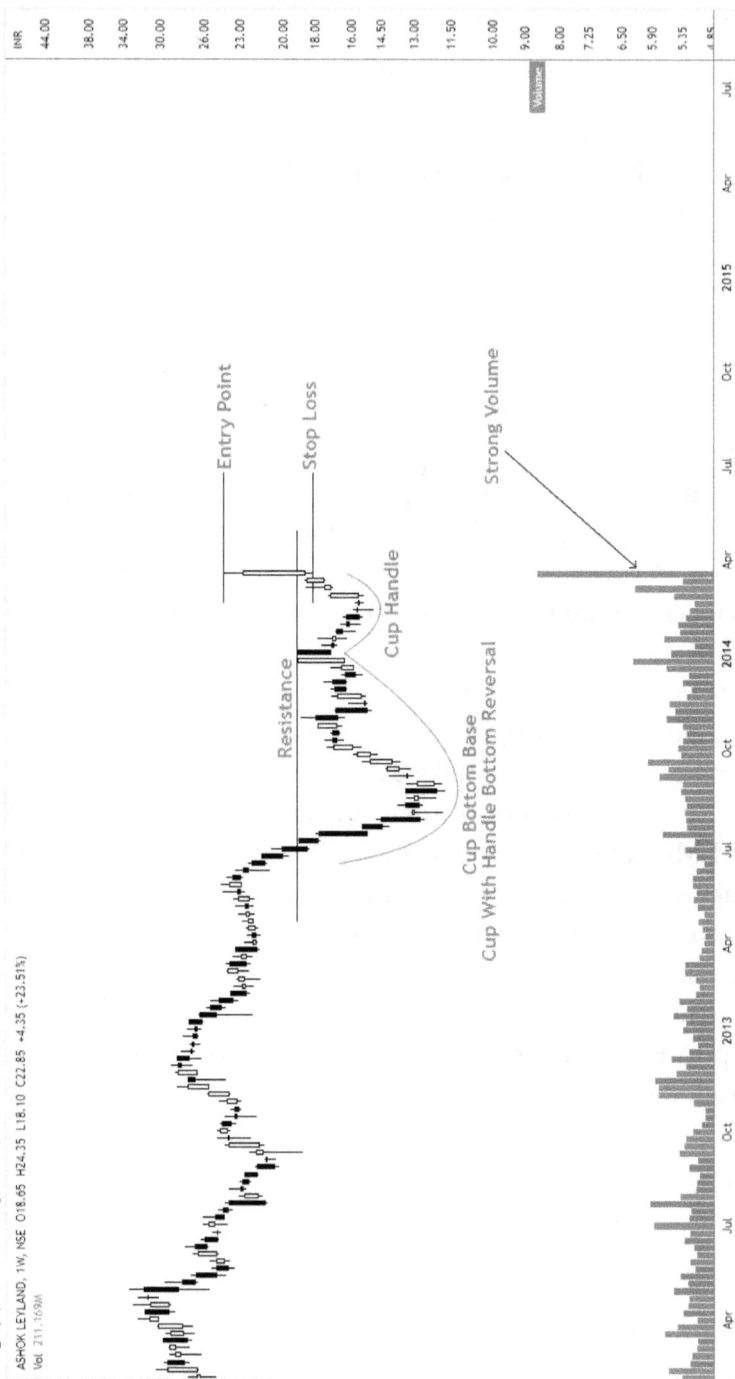

ASHOK LEYLAND, 1W, NSE O18.65 H24.35 L18.10 C22.85 +4.35 (+23.51%)
Vol 211.169M

Image 12.62: Weekly chart of Ashok Leyland (bearish rounding bottom reversal pattern).

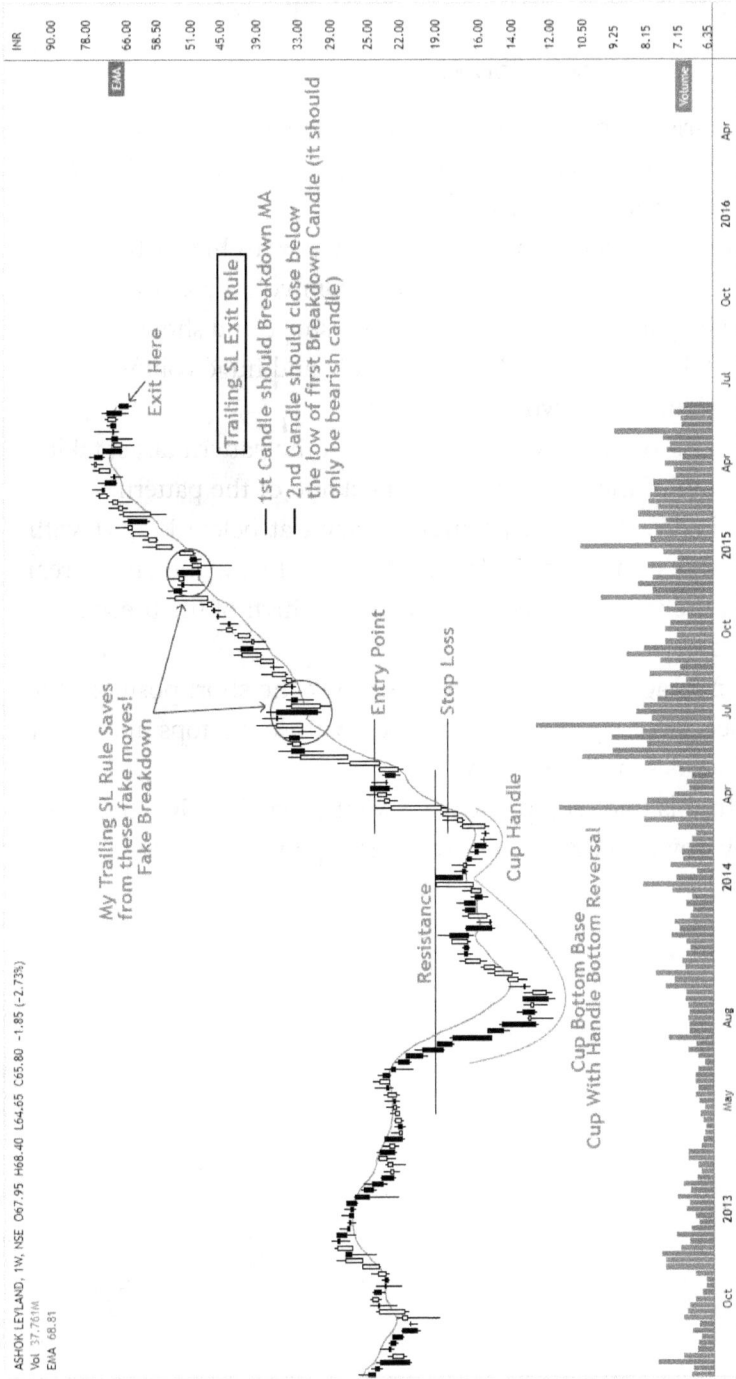

Chart_mojo published on TradingView.com, Feb 02, 2023 12:54 UTC+5:30

ASHOK LEYLAND, 1W, NSE O67.95 H68.40 L64.65 C65.80 -1.85 (-2.73%)
Vol 37.761M
EMA 68.81

Exit Here

My Trailing SL Rule Saves
from these fake moves!
Fake Breakdown

Resistance

Cup Handle

Entry Point

Stop Loss

Cup Bottom Base
Cup With Handle Bottom Reversal

Trailing SL Exit Rule

1st Candle should Breakdown MA

2nd Candle should close below
the low of first Breakdown Candle (it should
only be bearish candle)

Image 12.63: Weekly chart of Ashok Leyland after the breakout from cup and handle reversal pattern.

Cup and Handle Top Reversal

A bearish cup and handle top reversal pattern formed on the daily chart of State Bank of India, from April 2010 to May 2011 as shown in image 12.64.

In this image the uptrend was intact with higher highs and higher lows with a good support from volume as well.

The pattern has taken a textbook shape and shows a strong breakdown with a wide range candle and huge volume build-up, signifying downward pressure.

In this example we have calculated the pattern target taking the top of the cup base to the neckline of the pattern.

Finally, the short position is taken at below Rs 231 with a target of around Rs 162 (104 points below the entry area) and the stop is placed around Rs 266 (high of the breakdown candle).

In image 12.65, as soon as we took the short position, the stock price started coming down with lower tops and lower bottoms sequence.

In this trade setup, the price went down from Rs 231 all the way down to Rs 162 in a very short period of time.

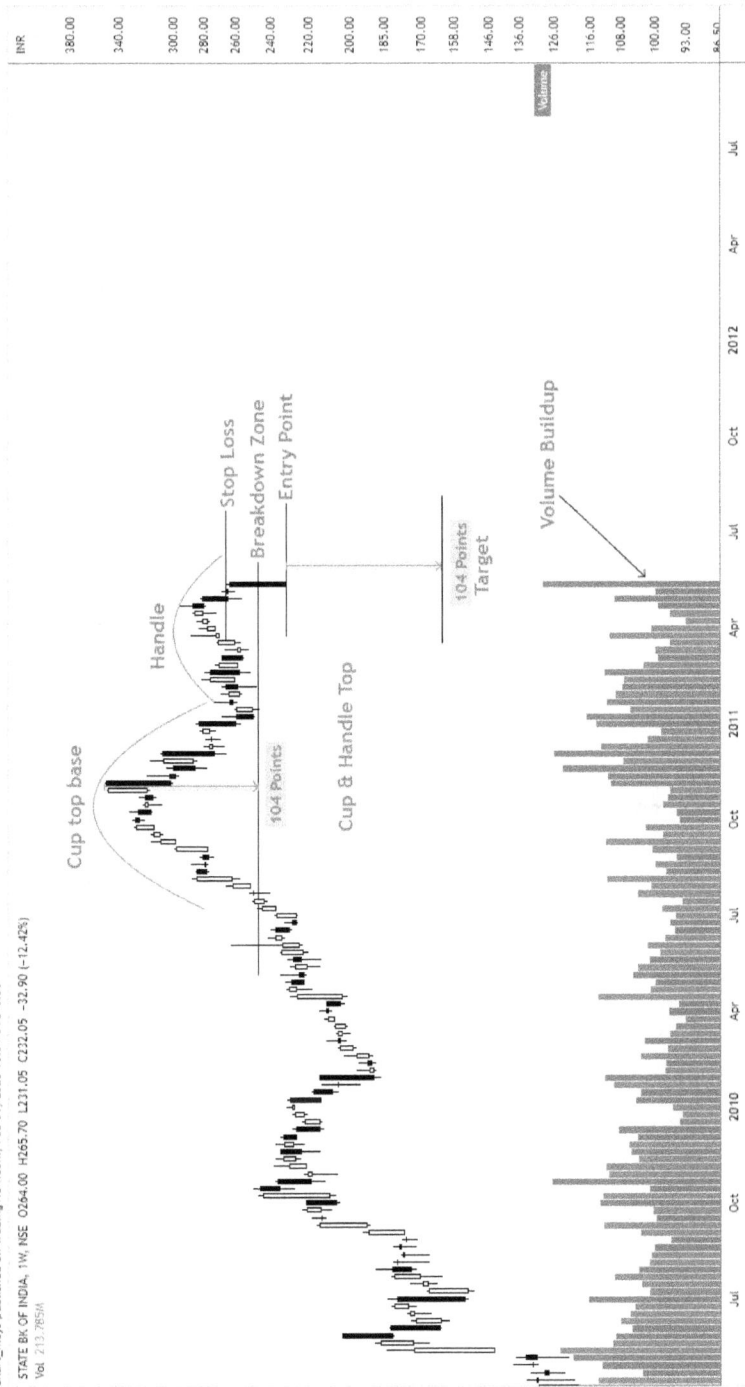

Image 12.64: Daily chart of State Bank of India (bearish cup and handle top reversal pattern).

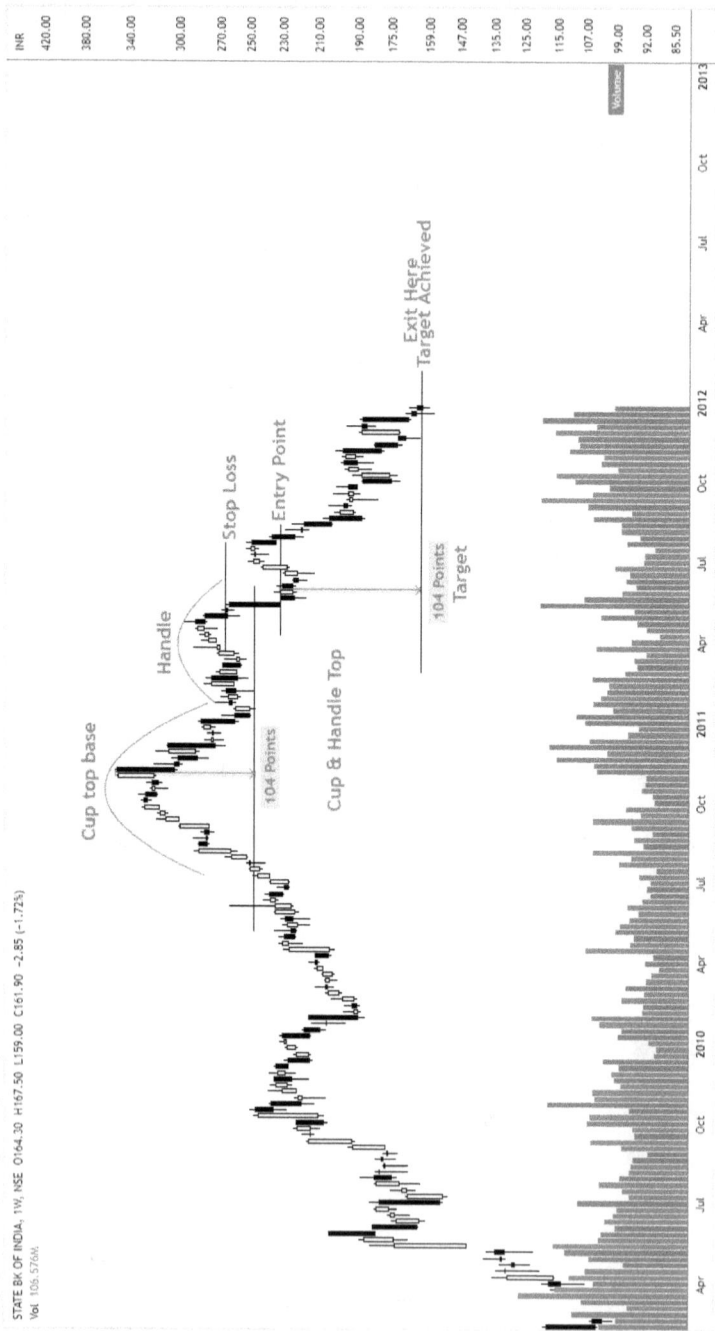

Image 12.65: Weekly chart of State Bank of India showing bearish trend reversal after the breakdown from cup and handle top pattern.

Rounding Bottom Pattern

A bearish rounding bottom reversal pattern formed on the daily chart of ONGC Ltd. from September 2020 to December 2012, as shown in image 12.66.

The downtrend was in action when the price came towards the bottom of the downtrend.

In the month of September, the price started trading in rounding bottom pattern, and very soon it was clearly visible. Right after that, we saw a strong breakout happening from the bottom reversal pattern with a decent volume build-up.

Now, the long position is taken above Rs 80 with a target of around Rs 90 (10 points below the entry area) and the stop is placed around Rs 71.80 (low of the breakout candle).

In image 12.67, it is clearly visible that once the long entry was taken, the price went up drastically and gave us a decent upside. Even when the pattern-based target was achieved, the price kept going up and signalled continued upside bias.

When the price action made its way up, at the same time, the volume also started picking up with huge buying volume bars.

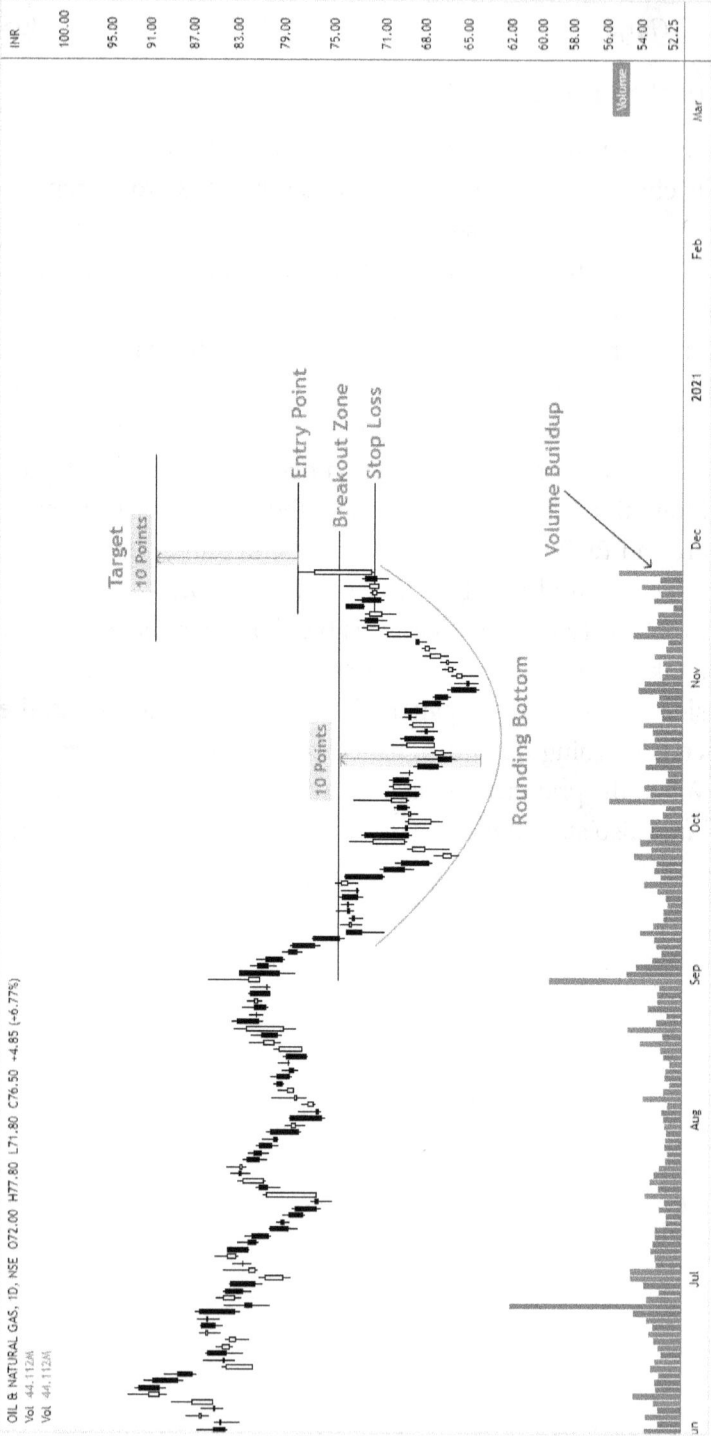

Image 12.66: Daily chart of ONGC Ltd. (bearish rounding bottom reversal pattern).

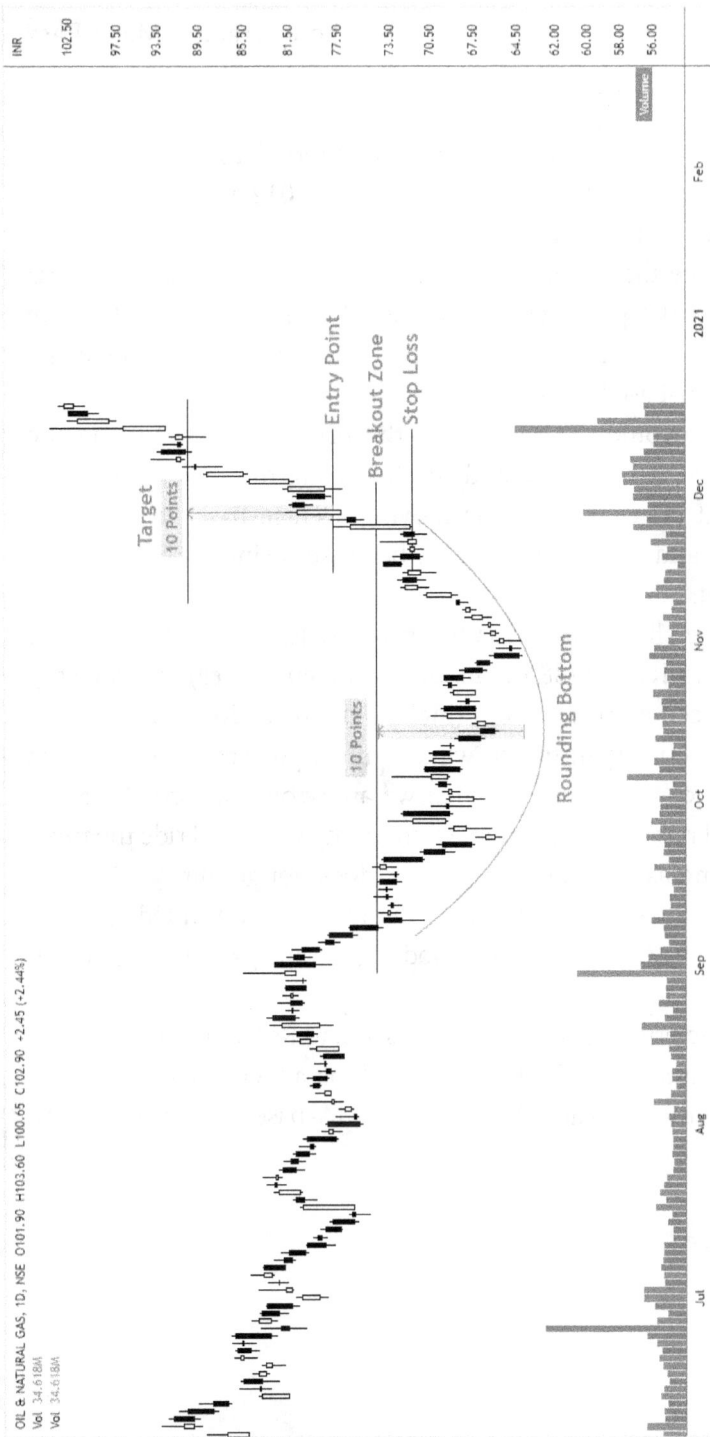

12.67: Daily chart of ONGC Ltd. after breakout from bullish trend reversal pattern.

Rounding Top Pattern

A bearish rounding top reversal pattern formed on the daily chart of BEML Ltd. from February 2012 to April 2012, as shown in image 12.68.

Once the breakdown occurred and the short position was taken, the price fell very drastically. In image 12.69 I have marked what would have happened if we would take the pattern-based target vis-a-vis EMA-based target.

We would have exited at the price of Rs 389 using the pattern-based target and Rs 325 using the moving average-based target. Hence, the moving average-based target is far away and clearly showing the beauty of using the EMA-based target.

The short position is taken below Rs 462 with a target of around Rs 390 (88 points below the entry area) and the stop is placed around Rs 484 (high of the breakdown candle).

As a breakout trader, what is under your control is the risk and not the target, so when we are wrong, we should take a small risk, however when we are right, we should ride the trend as long as our trailing stop-loss does not get hit.

In image 12.69, the price action just continued to trade below 9-EMA for a long period of time and gave us a significant downside.

The price went down from Rs 462 to Rs 390 in four months' time frame. In this entire fall, we look at percentage downside move then we earned 29% on 9-EMA-based trailing stop-loss.

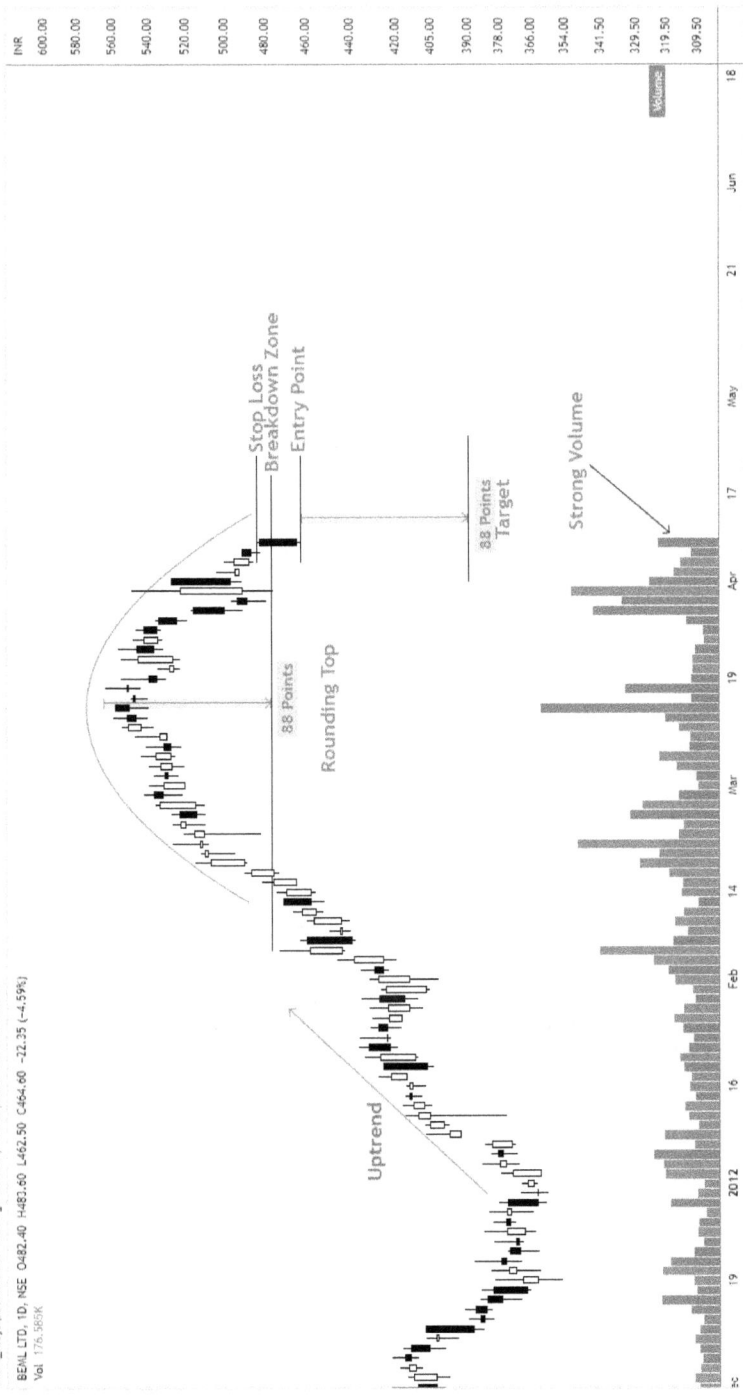

12.68: Daily chart of BEML Ltd. (bearish rounding top reversal pattern).

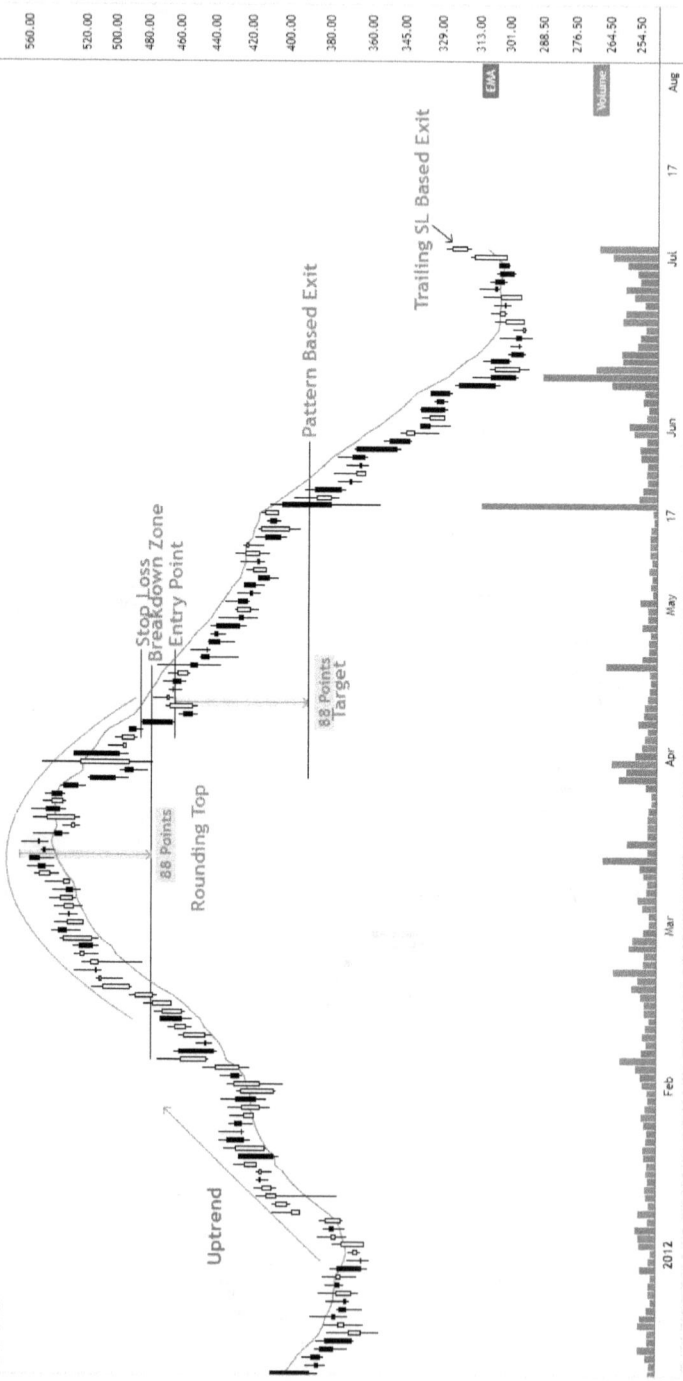

Image 12.69: Daily chart of BEML Ltd. showing downtrend reversal after the breakdown from rounding top pattern.

Head and Shoulder Bottom

A bullish head and shoulder bottom reversal pattern formed on the daily chart of Hindustan Petroleum Ltd. from July 2021 to October 2021, as shown in image 12.70.

On the chart, the stock price came into correction phase and formed the above-mentioned trend reversal pattern.

The breakout of the pattern occurred with a wide range breakout candle supported by decent volume build-up. The pattern is little bit tilted towards upside which also suggests that buyers are impatient to take the price higher.

Finally, the long position is taken above Rs 293 with a target of around Rs 338 (38 points below the entry area) and the stop is placed around Rs 276 (low of the breakdown candle).

Do remember that whenever you keep stop-loss at the breakout candle low or breakout candle high or anywhere else, do keep a little bit buffer of one or two rupees to save yourself from fake moves and sudden spike to that specific candle low price.

In image 12.71, once the long position was taken the price started going up, never looked back and reached our target within a few trading sessions.

Notice that when our target was achieved, the volume also started to tame down which suggests that the trading activity has come down in the stock.

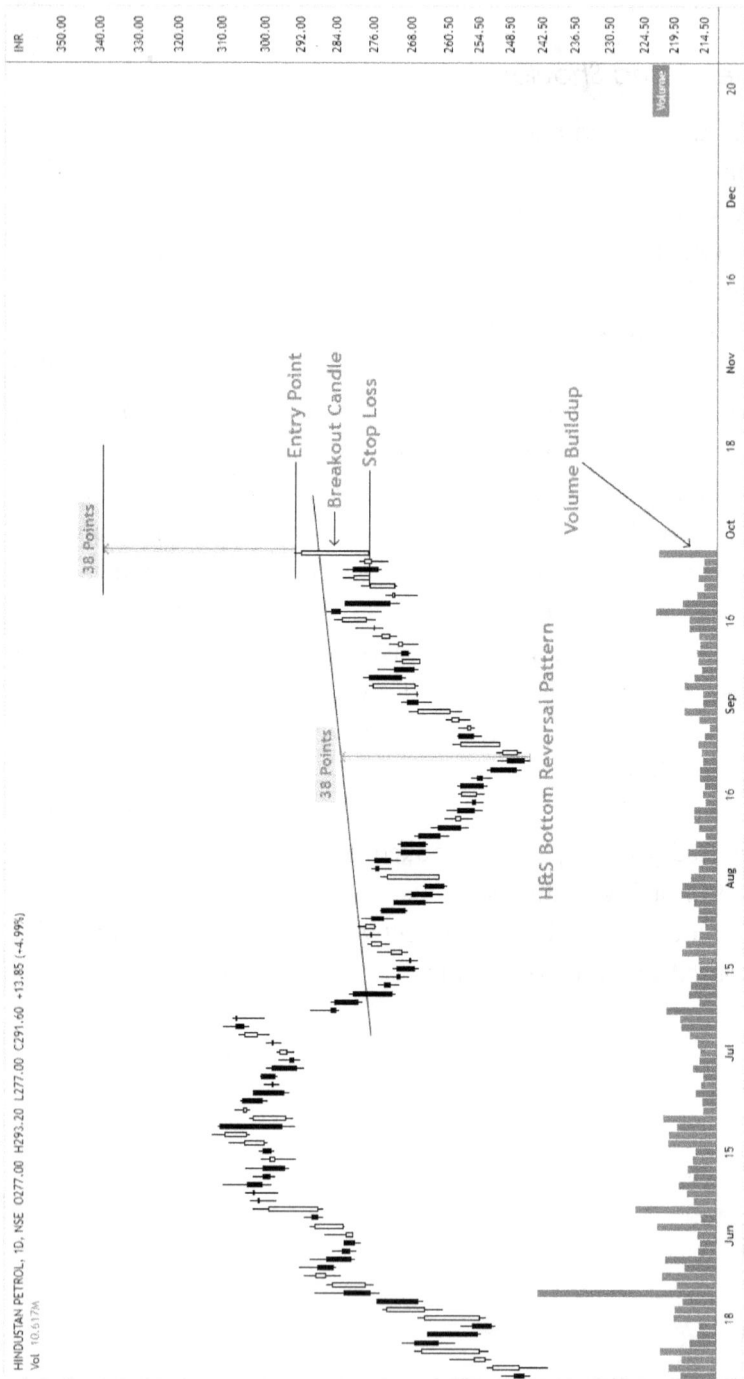

Image 12.70: Daily chart of Hindustan Petroleum Ltd. (bullish head and shoulder bottom reversal pattern).

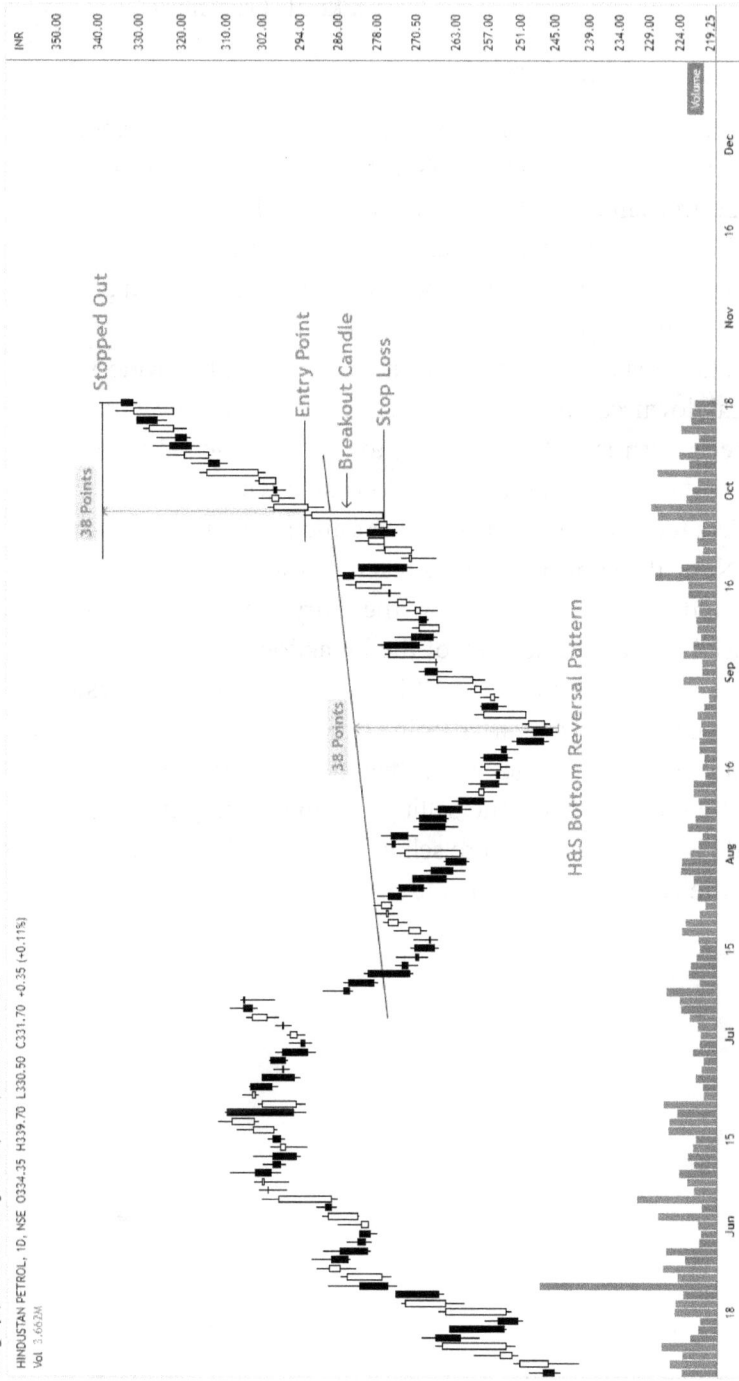

Image 12.71: Daily chart of Hindustan Petroleum Ltd. after the breakout from head and shoulder bottom reversal pattern.

Head and Shoulder Top

A bearish head and shoulder top reversal pattern formed on the daily chart of LTCUSDT (cryptocurrency), from January 2020 to March 2020, as shown in image 12.72.

The stock price was marching towards upside in a Dow theory fashion and gave shape to the above-mentioned bearish trend reversal pattern.

The breakout of the pattern occurred with a wide range breakdown candle supported by a decent volume build-up. The pattern is a little bit tilted towards upside. Then finally, a breakout happens towards downside which suggests that sellers took control over the buyers and pulled the price lower.

Now, the short position is taken below $50 with a target of around $32 (38 points below the entry area) and the stop is placed around $27.6 (low of the breakdown candle).

As we can see in image 12.73 that once the short position was taken the price started going down and never looked back and reached our target within few trading sessions.

We could also see the selling volume making new heights and giving huge support to selling pressure which was a cherry on the cake for the downside bias.

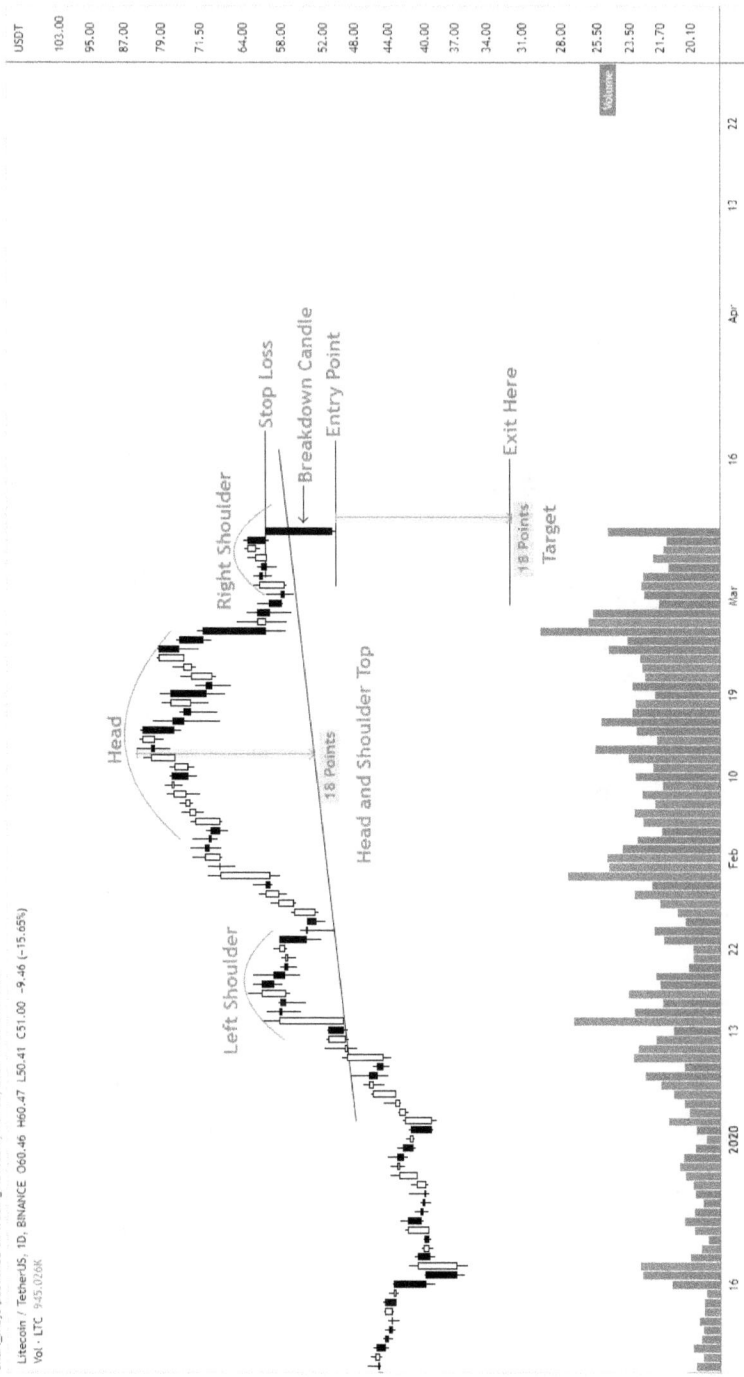

Image 12.72: Daily chart of Litecoin/Tether US (bearish head and shoulder top reversal pattern).

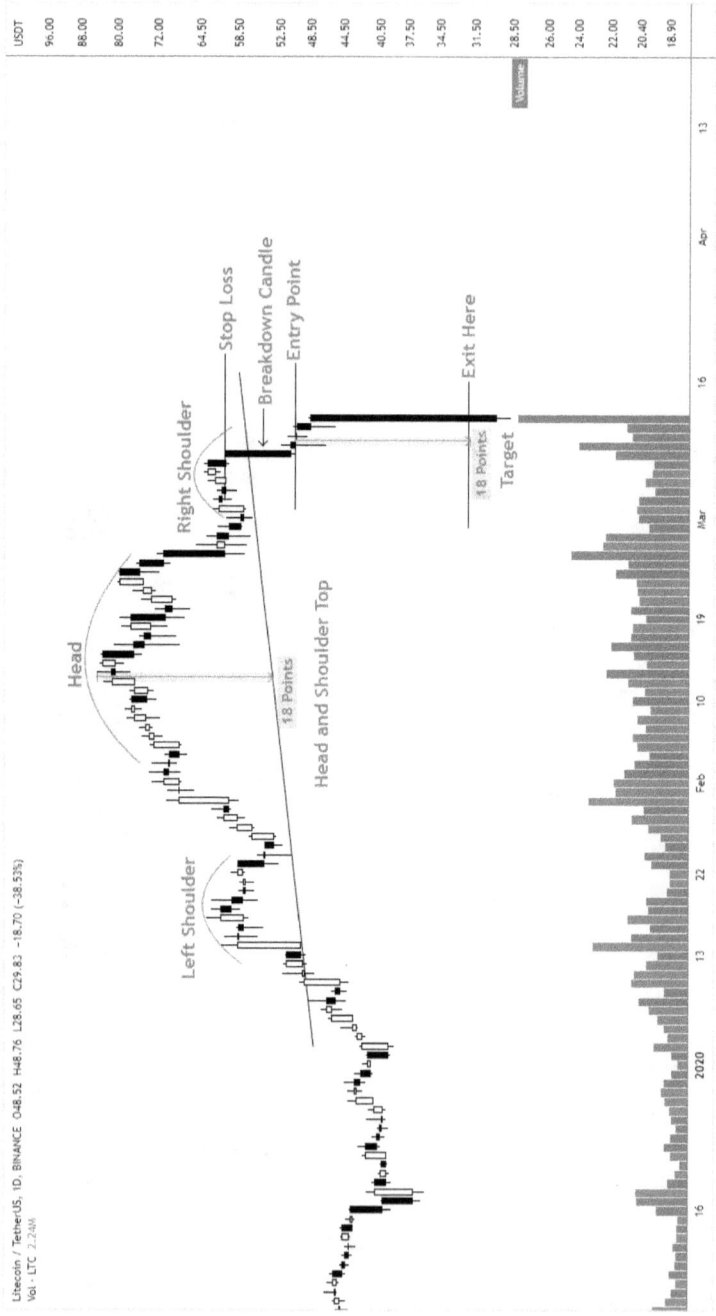

Chart_mojo published on TradingView.com, Mar 02, 2023 14:23 UTC-5:30

Litecoin / Tether US, 1D, BINANCE O48.52 H48.76 L28.65 C29.83 -18.70 (-38.53%)
Vol LTC 2.24M

USDT
96.00
88.00
80.00
72.00
64.50
58.50
52.50
48.50
44.50
40.50
37.50
34.50
31.50
28.50
26.00
24.00
22.00
20.40
18.90

Stop Loss
Breakdown Candle
Entry Point
Right Shoulder
Head
Head and Shoulder Top
18 Points
Left Shoulder
Exit Here
18 Points
Target

Volume

Image 12.73: Daily chart of Litecoin/Tether US showing a bearish trend reversal from the breakdown of head and shoulder top pattern.

Complex Head and Shoulder Bottom Pattern

A bullish complex head and shoulder bottom reversal pattern formed on the daily chart of Jindal Saw Ltd. from November 2008 to May 2009, as shown in image 12.74.

In this chart we can see two left shoulders and one right shoulder which makes the pattern more complex than if we have one left or right shoulder.

Once the right shoulder completely formed, we could see a decent breakout from the falling resistance neckline (breakout zone) on the upper side with a wide range breakout. When the right shoulder was forming, there was a huge volume spurt and accumulation.

After all the above conditions, we take the short position taken above Rs 46, in image 12.75 with a target of around Rs 85 (21 points above the entry area) and the stop is placed around Rs 40 (low of the breakout candle).

Once the long position was taken, the price started coming up in a higher highs and higher lows sequence and saw a drastic rise.

The breakout also happened with a huge volume spurt which made the upside way smoother. Eventually, the price went from Rs 46 all the way up to Rs 85 in the period of one month.

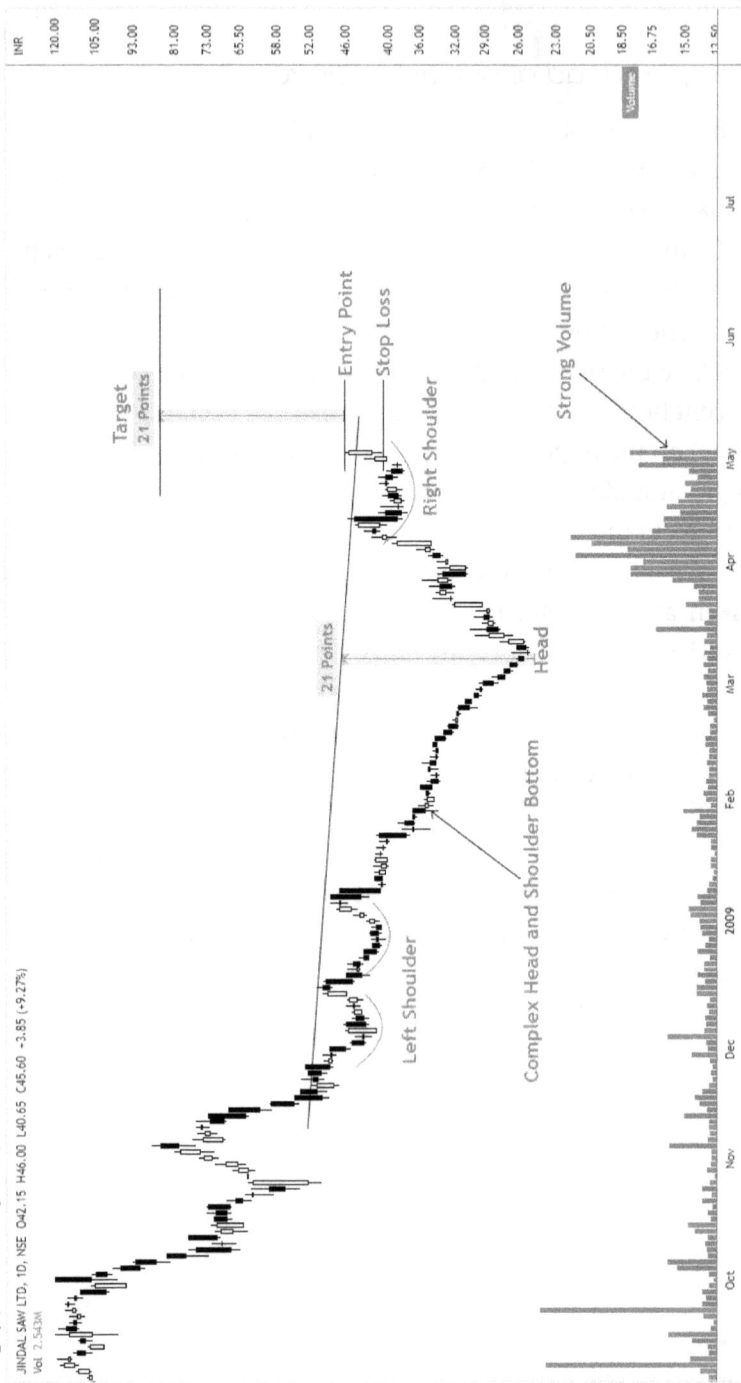

Image 12.74: Daily chart of Jindal Saw Ltd. (bullish complex head and shoulder bottom reversal pattern).

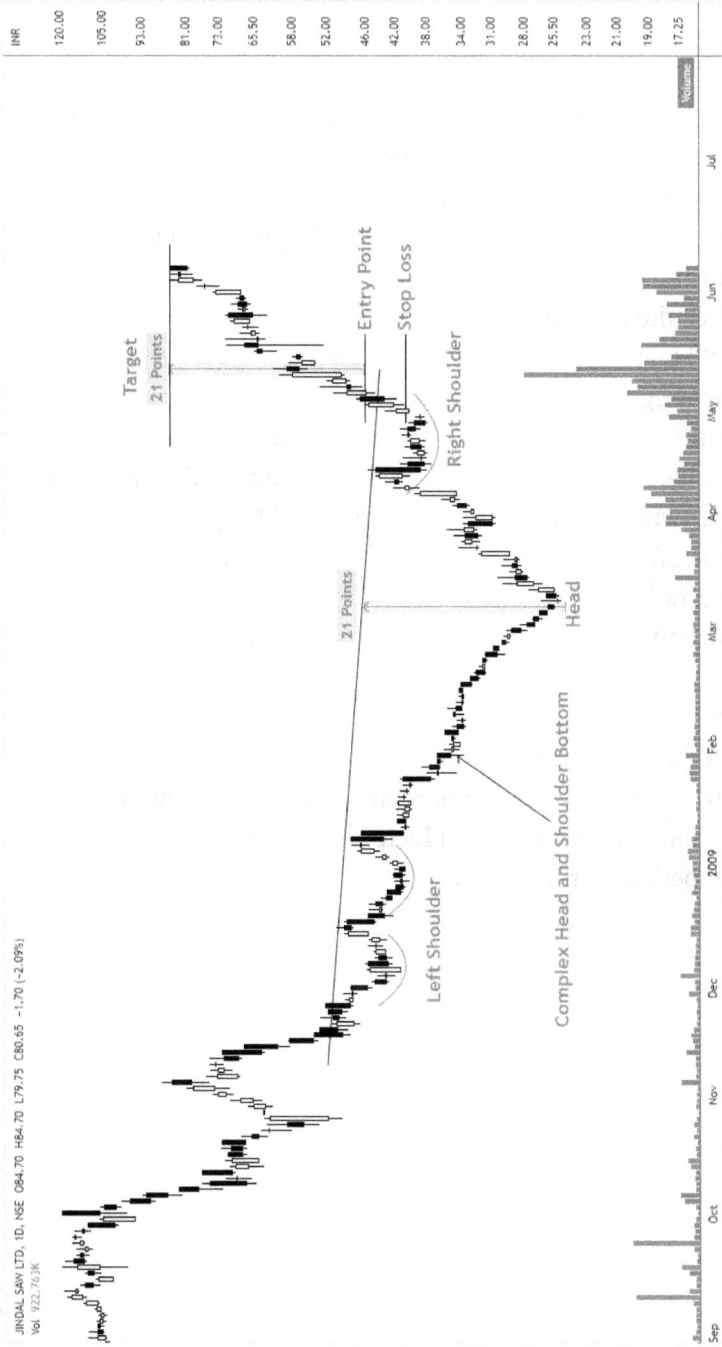

Chart_mojo published on TradingView.com, Feb 02, 2023 10:32 UTC+5:30

JINDAL SAW LTD, 1D, NSE O84.70 H84.70 L79.75 C80.65 −1.70 (−2.09%)
Vol 922.763K

Image 12.75: Daily chart of Jindal Saw Ltd. showing us a bullish trend reversal from the breakout of complex head and shoulder continuation pattern.

Complex Head and Shoulder Top Pattern

A bearish complex head and shoulder top reversal pattern formed on the daily chart of Jindal Saw Ltd. from September 2018 to May 2019 as shown in image 12.76.

We can see many left shoulders and right shoulders which makes the pattern complex.

Once the right shoulder formed completely, we could see a decent breakdown from the chart pattern on the lower side with a wide range breakdown. Also notice, the volume contraction indicates that no more sellers are interested in selling the stock.

Finally, in image 12.77 the short position is taken at below Rs 113 with a target of around Rs 70 (70 points below the entry area) and the stop is placed around Rs 119 (high of the breakdown candle).

Once the short position was taken, the price started coming down in lower lows and lower highs sequence and saw a drastic fall.

The breakdown also happened with a strong volume spurt which made the downside pressure smoother. Eventually, the price came down from Rs 113 to all the way down to Rs 70 in the period of three months.

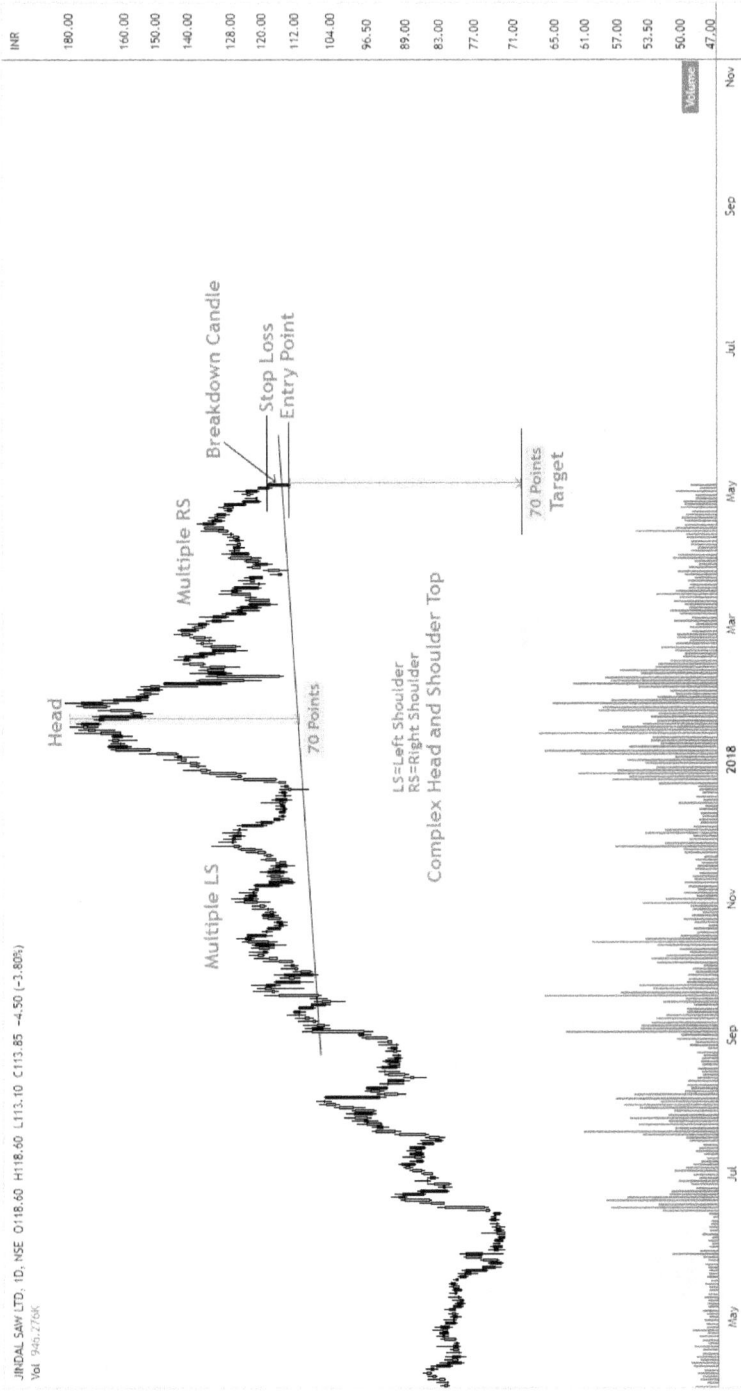

Image 12.76: Daily chart of Jindal Saw Ltd. (bearish complex head and shoulder top reversal pattern).

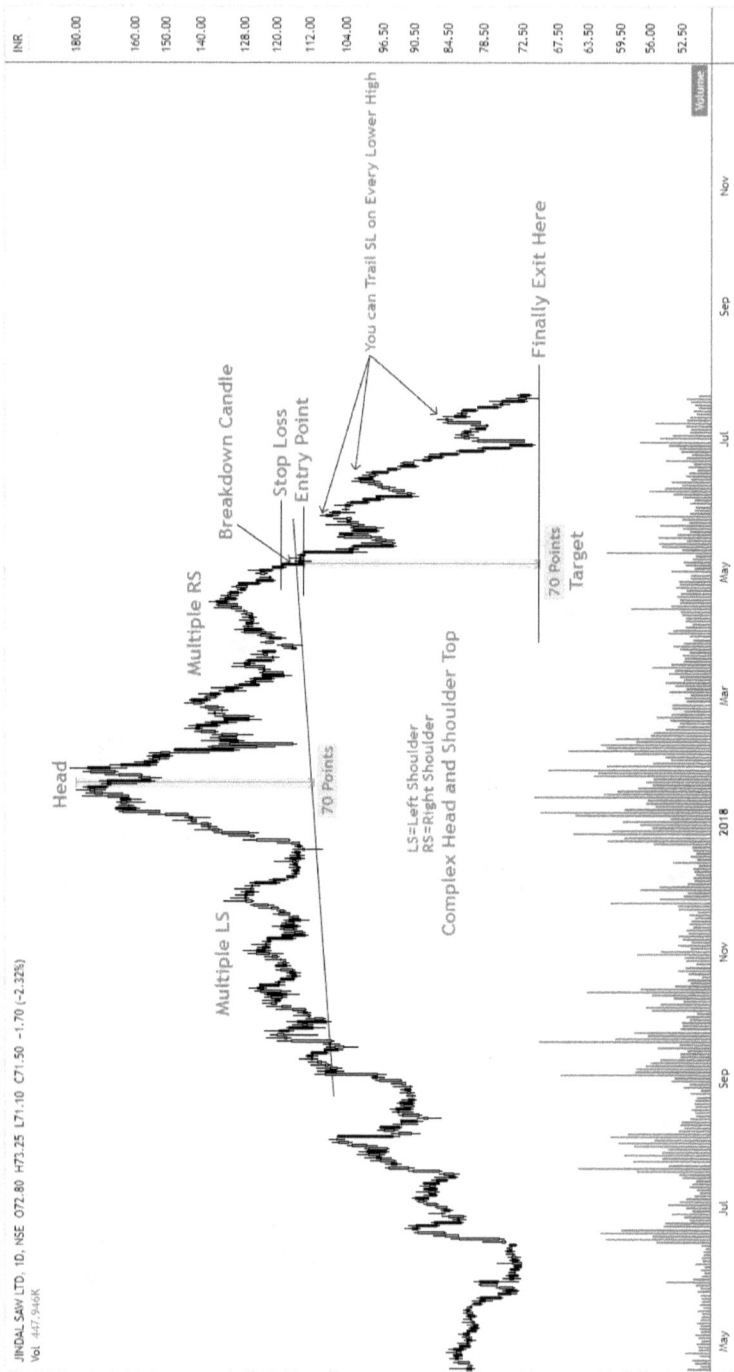

Chart_mojo published on TradingView.com, Feb 02, 2023 10:20 UTC+5:30

JINDAL SAW LTD, 1D, NSE O72.80 H73.25 L71.10 C71.50 -1.70 (-2.32%)
Vol 447.946K

Image 12.77: Daily chart of Jindal Saw Ltd. after the breakdown from bearish trend continuation pattern.

Diamond Bottom

A bearish diamond bottom reversal pattern formed on the daily chart of US Dollar and Japanese Yen (USD/JPY) (currency pair), from December 2020 to February 2021, as shown in image 12.78.

The downtrend is very strong with huge selling pressure and has unfolded with lower lows and lower highs.

Once the pattern started forming, the stock price started dancing between expansion phase and contraction phase. When the pattern was forming, the volume was also going through ups and downs with price action.

In this chart setup, the long position will be taken above the price of $104 and the stop-loss will be placed at $103.56 which is low of the breakout candle. The exit will happen on the basis of 9-EMA breakdown at $109.

Once the long position was taken, we can clearly notice that the price action started going up in the form higher highs and higher lows (image 12.79).

The currency pair price started rising from the price of $104 all the way up to $109 within a few trading sessions. In this trade setup we have used trailing stop-loss for locking upside profit due to which we could ride the trend. Otherwise we would exit very early as the pattern-based target would have been very small.

You can refer to the chapter on chart patterns if you don't know how to identify pattern-based target.

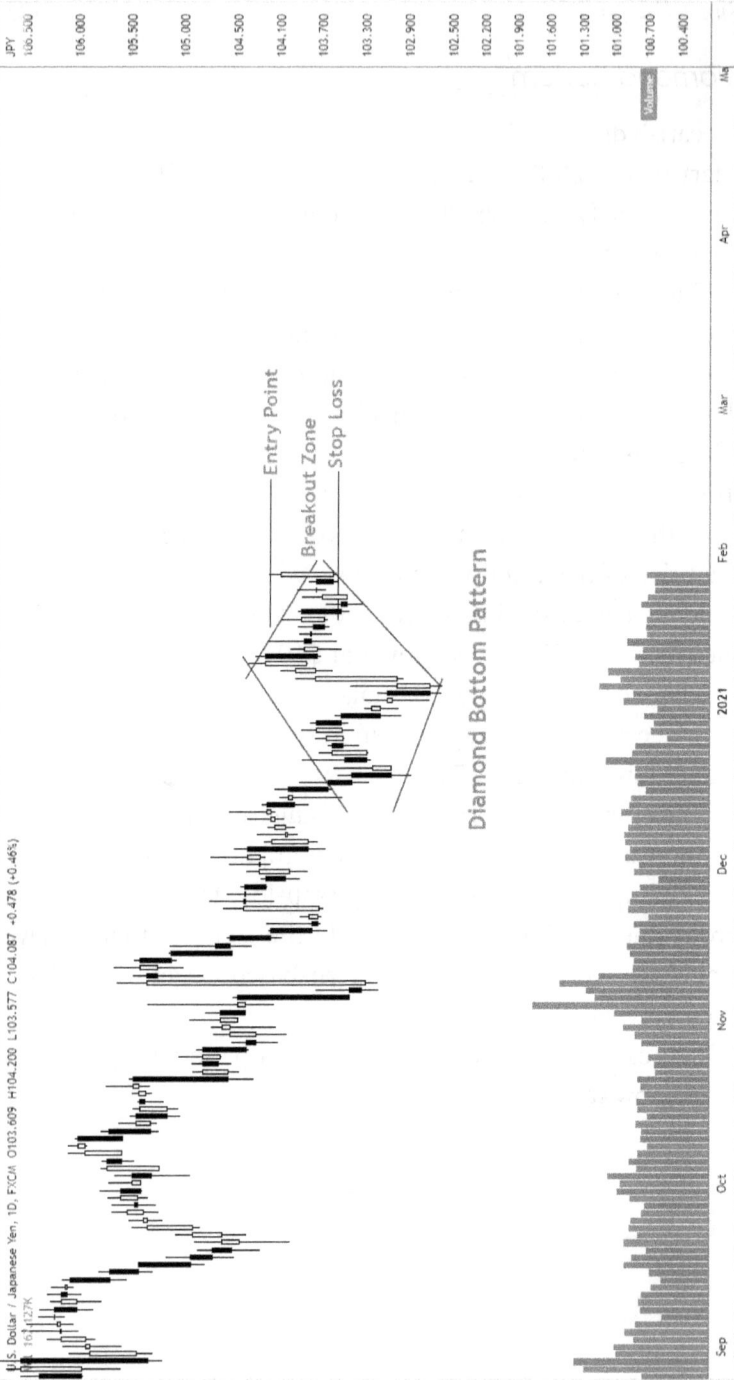

Image 12.78: Daily chart of USD/JPY (bearish diamond bottom reversal pattern formed).

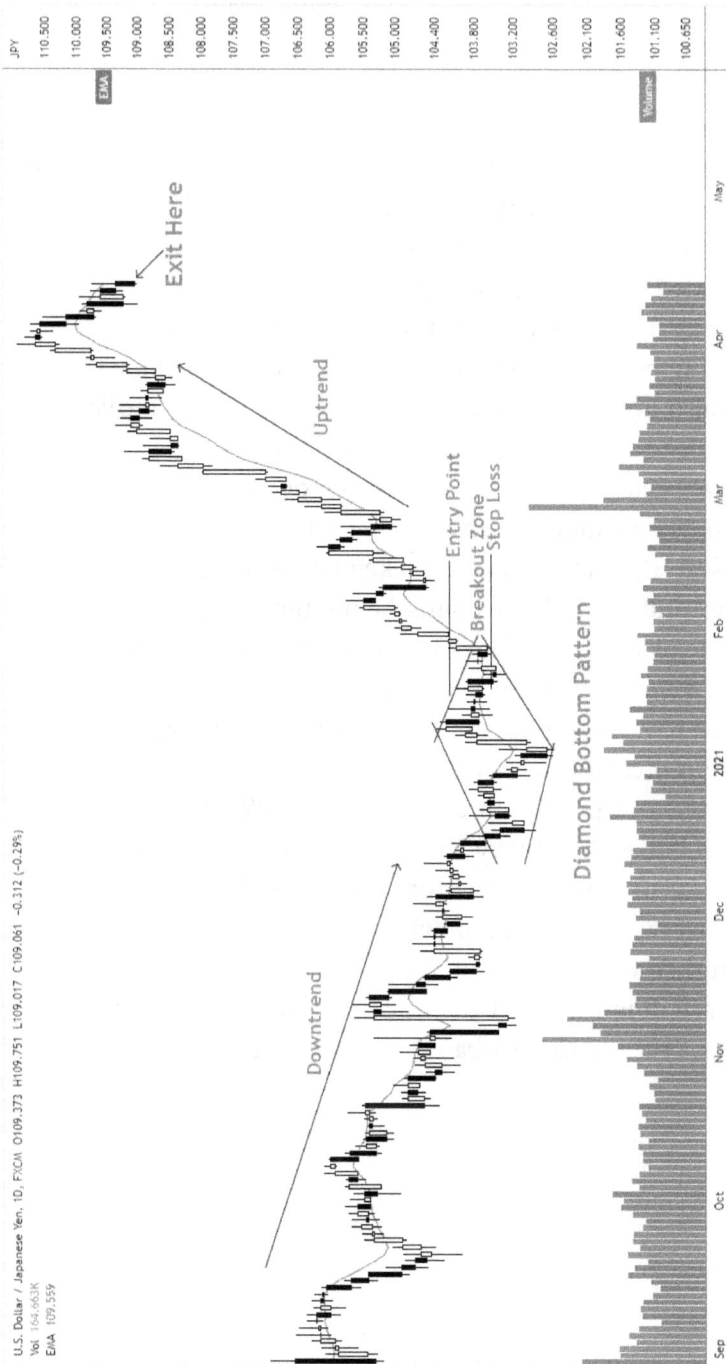

Image 12.79: Daily chart for US dollar/Japanese yen showing bullish trend reversal from diamond bottom pattern.

Diamond Top

A bearish diamond top reversal pattern formed on the daily chart of EID Parry (India) Ltd. from September 2012 to December 2012, as shown in image 12.80.

It is very clear that the uptrend is very strong and has unfolded with strong buying volume bars as well.

Once the pattern started forming, the stock price started dancing between expansion phase and contraction phase. We can also notice that when the pattern was forming the volume was also going through ups and down with price action.

Eventually, the pattern breakdown occurred with a bearish breakdown candle which was supported by volume as well.

Now, the short position is taken below Rs 222 with a target of around Rs 184 (44 points below the entry area) and the stop is placed around Rs 231 (high of the breakdown candle).

In image 12.81, once the breakdown occurred the price action took its way down. We see a decent downside from the pattern breakdown zone.

The stock price went down from Rs 222 all the way down to Rs 184 within a very short period of time. The downside also occurred with a series of bearish candles.

If we would use the moving average as trailing stop-loss then then we would stand to gain more downside profit as we can see in image 12.81 that the price still continued to come down after the pattern-based target was achieved.

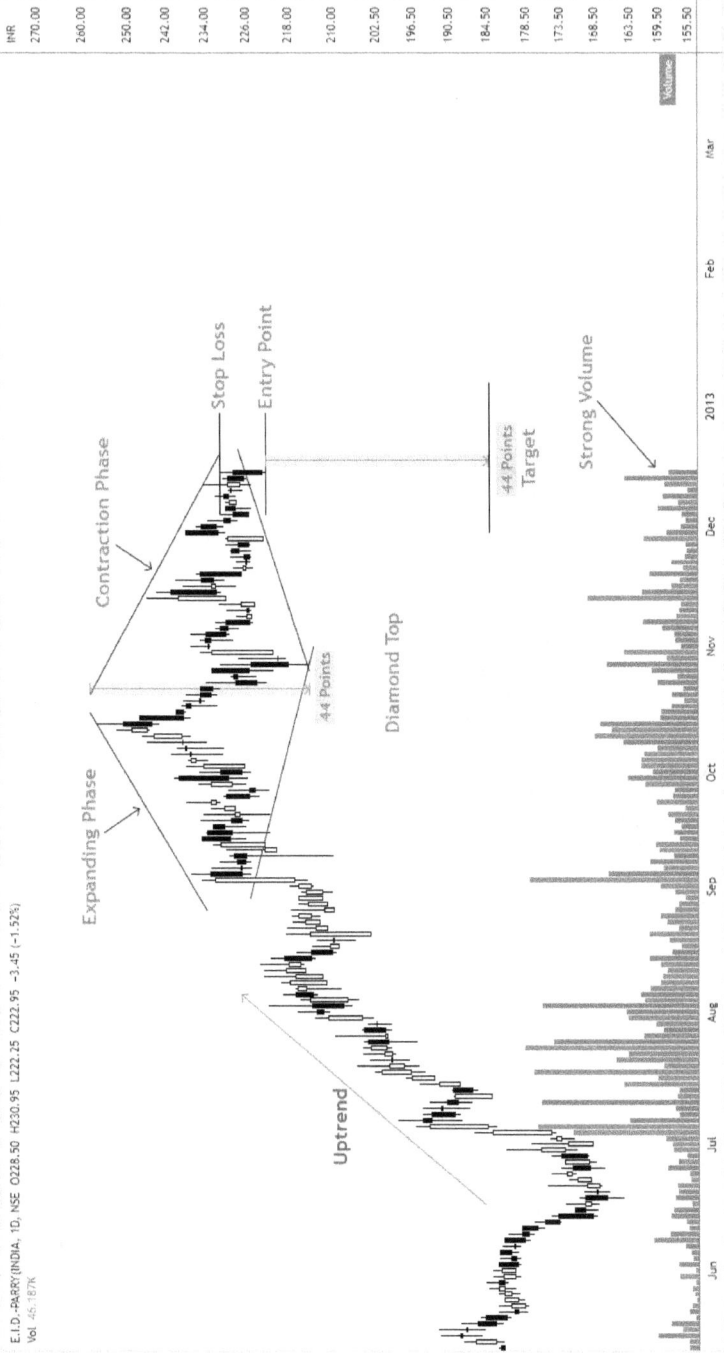

Image 12.80: Daily chart of EID Parry (India) Ltd. (bearish diamond top reversal pattern)

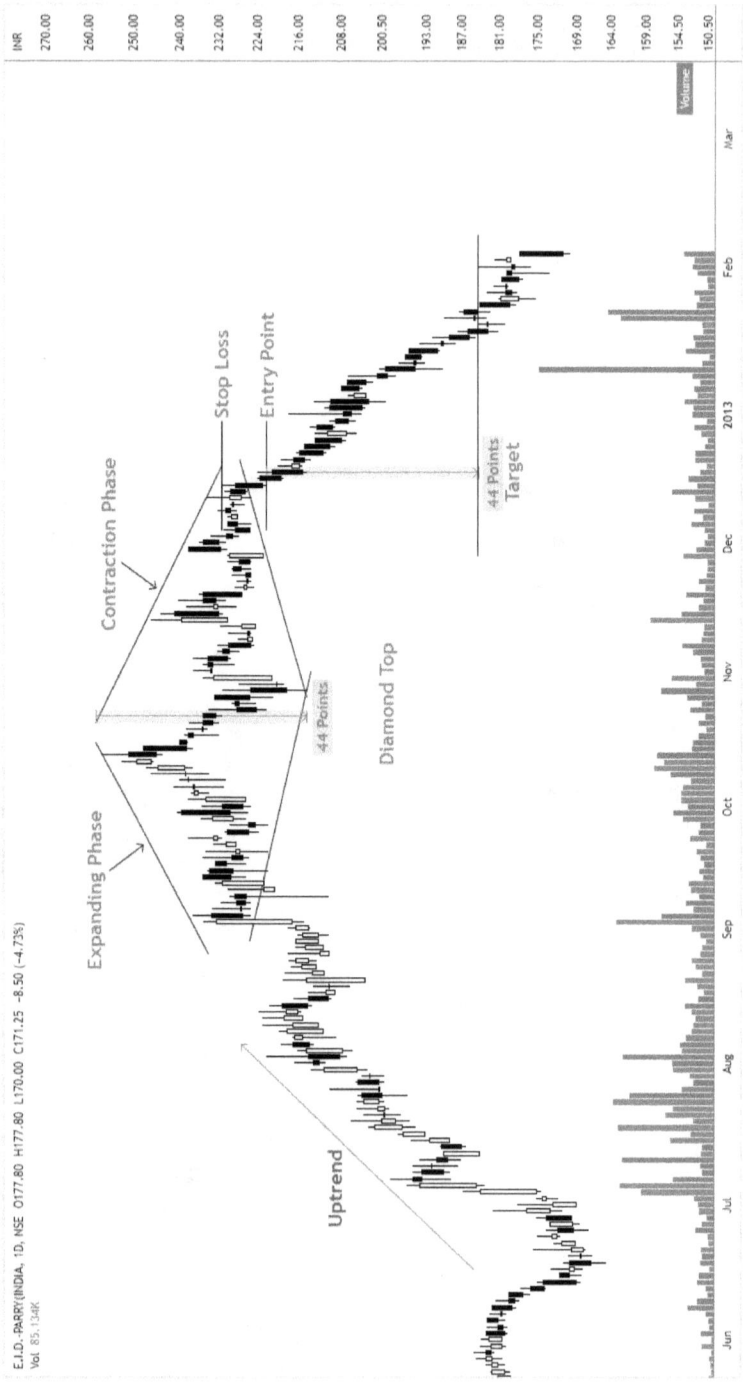

Image 12.81: Daily chart of EID Parry (India) Ltd. after breakdown from diamond top pattern.

Rectangle Bottom Pattern

A bullish reversal rectangle bottom pattern formed on the daily chart of DCM Shriram Ltd. from October 2014 to April 2016 as shown in image 12.82.

The uptrend continued and eventually the stock went into a secondary phase, where the rectangle bottom pattern was formed over a lengthy time frame.

Once the pattern got over, the stock price broke above the resistance of bullish reversal pattern with a wide range breakout candle. The breakout was also supported by a huge volume spurt signifying the built-in upside momentum into the stock price.

In this chart pattern we are calculating the target for it using the base of the pattern till dragging it to the neckline/resistance of the pattern.

Finally, we take the long position above Rs 173 with a target of around Rs 262 (52 points above the entry area) and the stop is placed around Rs 146 (low of the breakout candle).

Once the long position was taken with a strong breakout candle (image 12.83), the price starting going up smoothly with strong bullish candles.

So here, the stock price went up from Rs 173 all the way up to Rs 262 within a few months of trading.

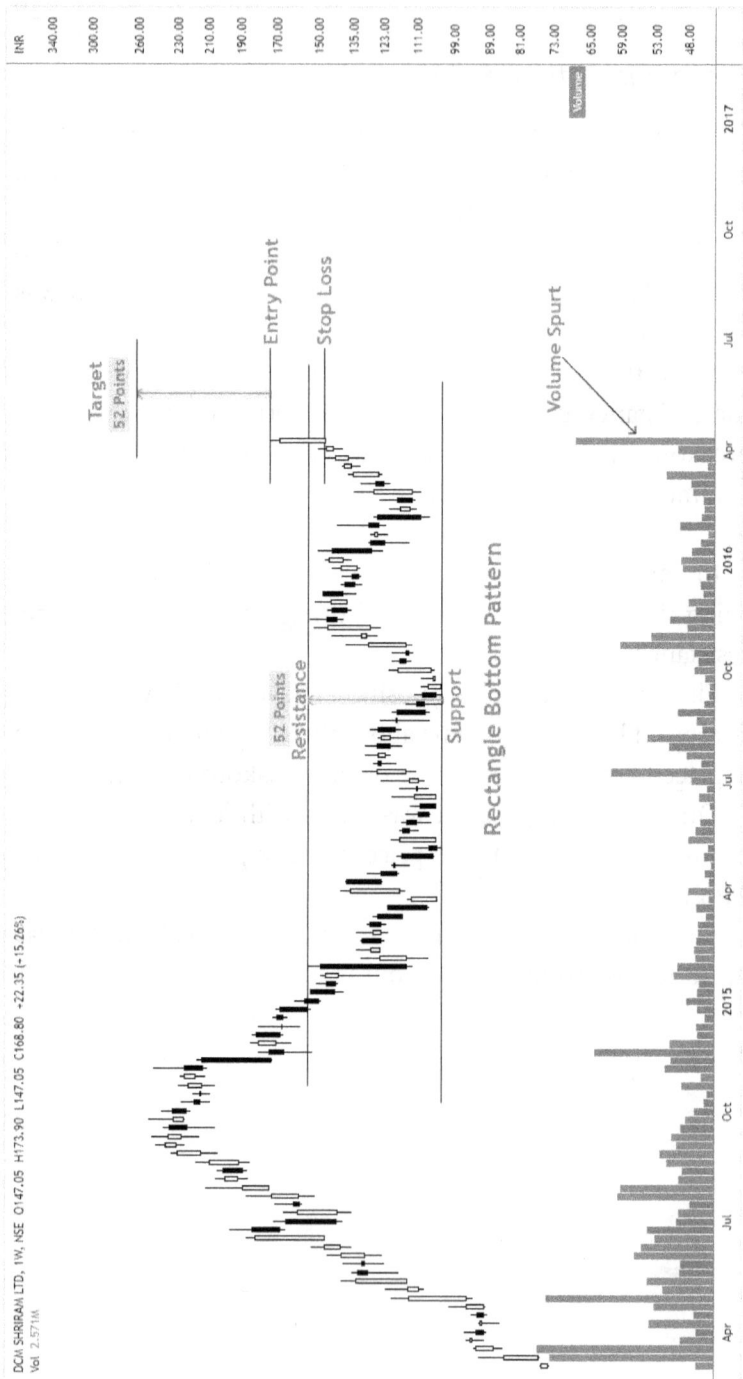

Chart_mojo published on TradingView.com, Feb 06, 2023 12:44 UTC+5:30

DCM SHRIRAM LTD, 1W, NSE O147.05 H173.90 L147.05 C168.80 -22.35 (-15.26%)
Vol 2.571M

Image 12.82: Daily chart of DCM Shriram Ltd. (bullish reversal rectangle bottom pattern).

DCM SHRIRAM LTD, 1W, NSE O262.00 H286.70 L241.65 C256.90 -3.70 (-1.42%)
Vol. 1.66M

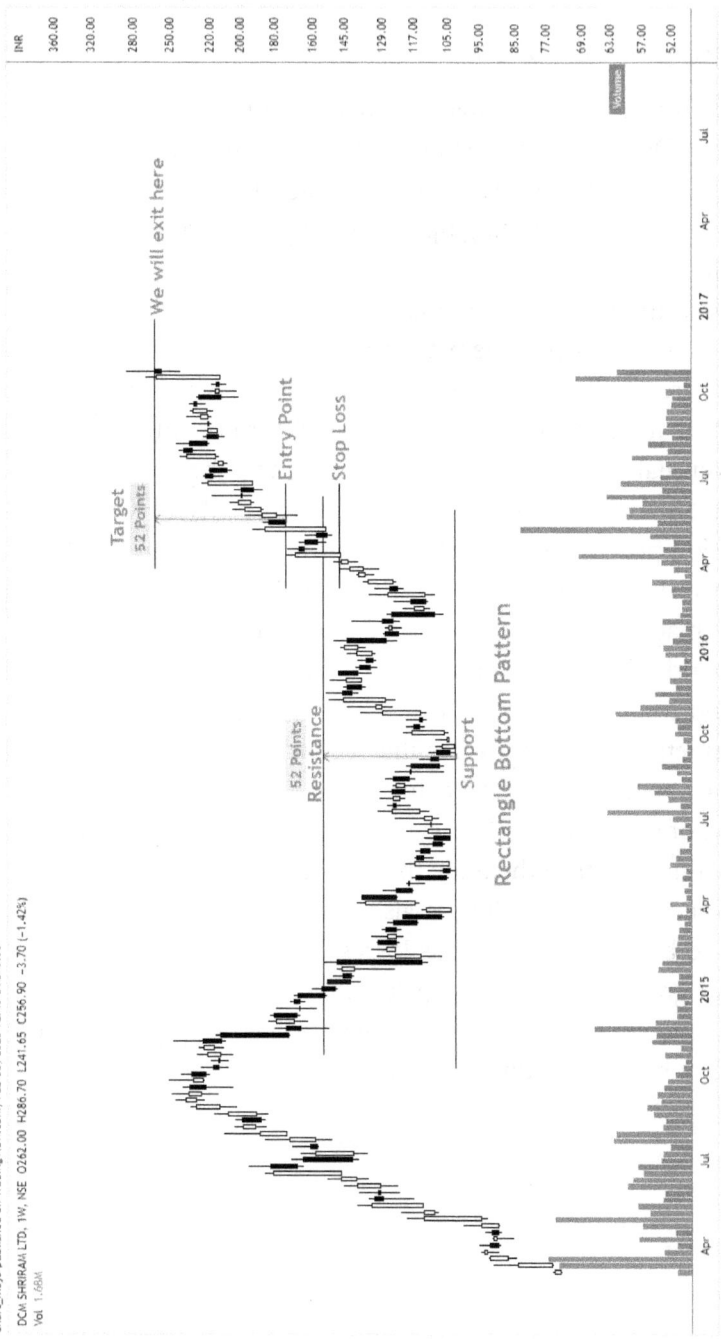

Image 12.83: Weekly chart of DCM Shriram showing a bullish trend reversal once the breakout occurred from rectangle bottom pattern.

Rectangle Top Pattern

A bearish reversal rectangle top pattern formed on the daily chart of Development Credit Bank (DCB) Bank Ltd. from April 2011 to August 2011, as shown in image 12.84.

The price was trending upward strongly before the pattern was formed.

Once the pattern ended, an uncertain candle breakdown occurred. Also, when the pattern was forming up, the volume went through the dip too, forming a U shape, which increases the probability of this pattern being right exponentially.

Eventually, the short position will be taken below the price of Rs 50 and the stop-loss will be placed at Rs 55 which is the high previous candle of breakdown candle. The exit will happen on the basis of 9-EMA breakout at Rs 47.

In image 12.85 you can observe that you got very little gain as the price broke above the trailing stop-loss criteria very early on and we had to take the exit.

Sometimes, situations like this will occur and we won't be able to book a good profit. Just consider this as a part and parcel of your trading journey. If you wish to get bigger profit every time you take the trade then it is never going to happen. Do keep in mind, trading is also a business where you will have to book profit as well as losses.

The greater number of stop-losses you take, the better your experience will be. You will consider trading as a business and not as a money-making machine.

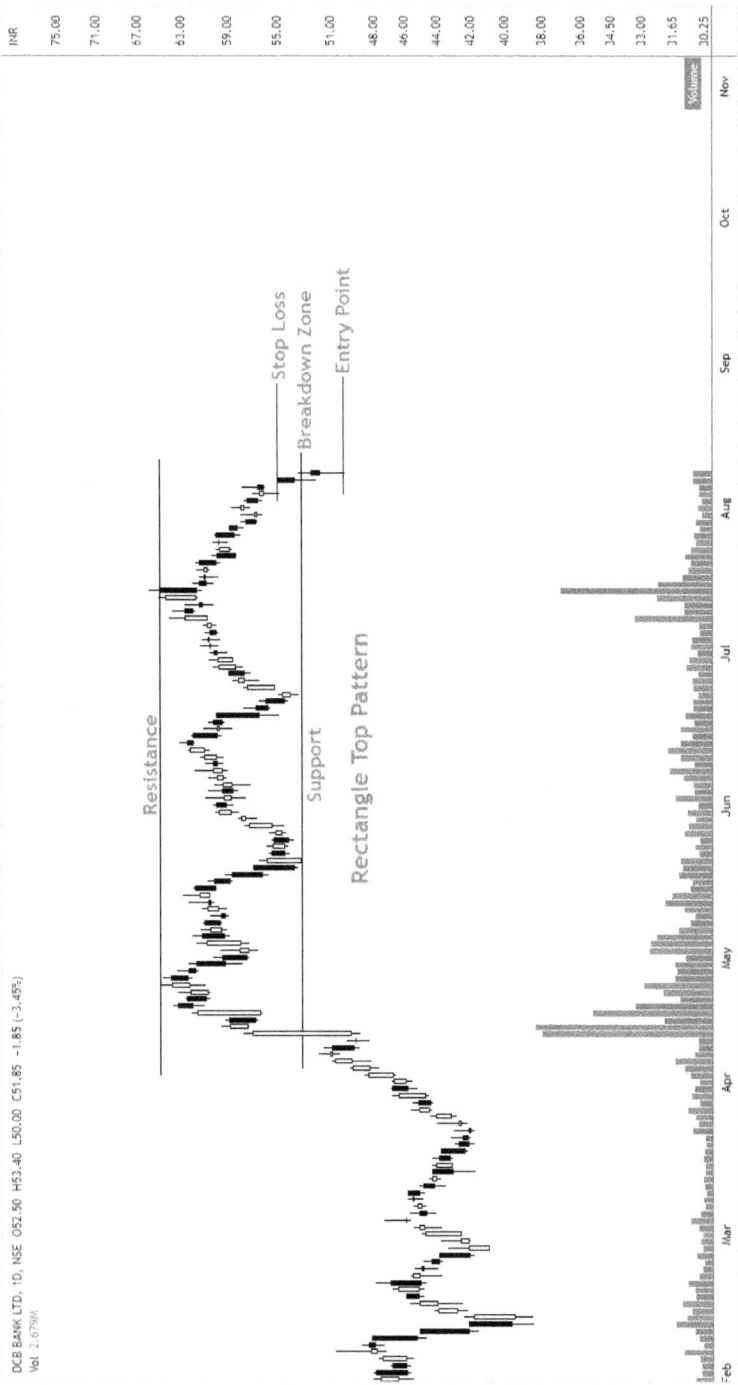

Chart_mojo published on TradingView.com, Feb 06, 2023 15:11 UTC+5:30
DCB BANK LTD, 1D, NSE O52.50 H53.40 L50.00 C51.85 −1.85 (−3.45%)
Vol 2.679M

Resistance

Stop Loss

Breakdown Zone

Entry Point

Support

Rectangle Top Pattern

Volume

Feb   Mar   Apr   May   Jun   Jul   Aug   Sep   Oct   Nov

TradingView

Image 12.84: Daily chart of DCB Bank Ltd. (bearish reversal rectangle top pattern).

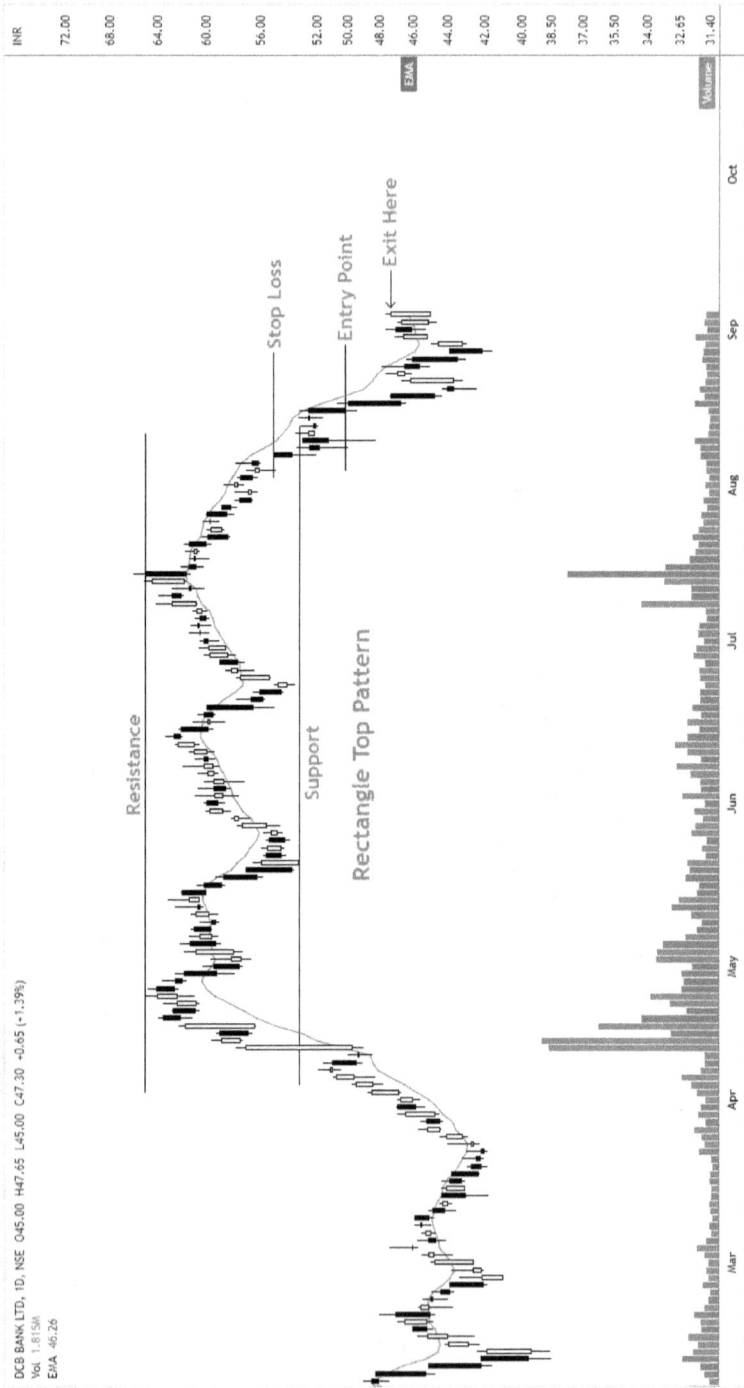

Image 12.85: Daily chart of DCB Bank Ltd. signalling downtrend once the breakdown occurred from rectangle top pattern.

Double Bottom Eve and Adam

A bullish double bottom reversal pattern formed on the daily chart of IndusInd Bank from November 2016 to January 2017, as shown in image 12.86.

It shows a short-lived downtrend with big black bearish candles indicating bearishness and finally the stock price settles down at the lower levels and starts forming double bottom Eve and Adam reversal pattern.

Once the pattern ended, a strong wide range breakout candle occurred at the pattern breakout zone (resistance level) with a huge volume spurt.

Do remember always that Eve will be a U-shape price action and Adam will be a V-shape price action.

In this chart, the long position will be taken above the price of Rs 1,130 and the stop-loss will be placed at Rs 1,104 which is a pattern breakout low as it is the wide range candle. The exit will happen on the basis of 9-EMA breakdown at Rs 1,312.

Once the long position was taken (image 12.87), the stock price started marching towards upside and price action was trading above the trailing stop-loss criteria which is 9-EMA.

The volume action during upside can be seen on the higher side as buying volume bars are bigger than selling volume bars.

The stock price went from Rs 1,130 to Rs 1,312 within two months' time frame. In this trade, we got to see 16% upside at 2.25% risk (stop-loss).

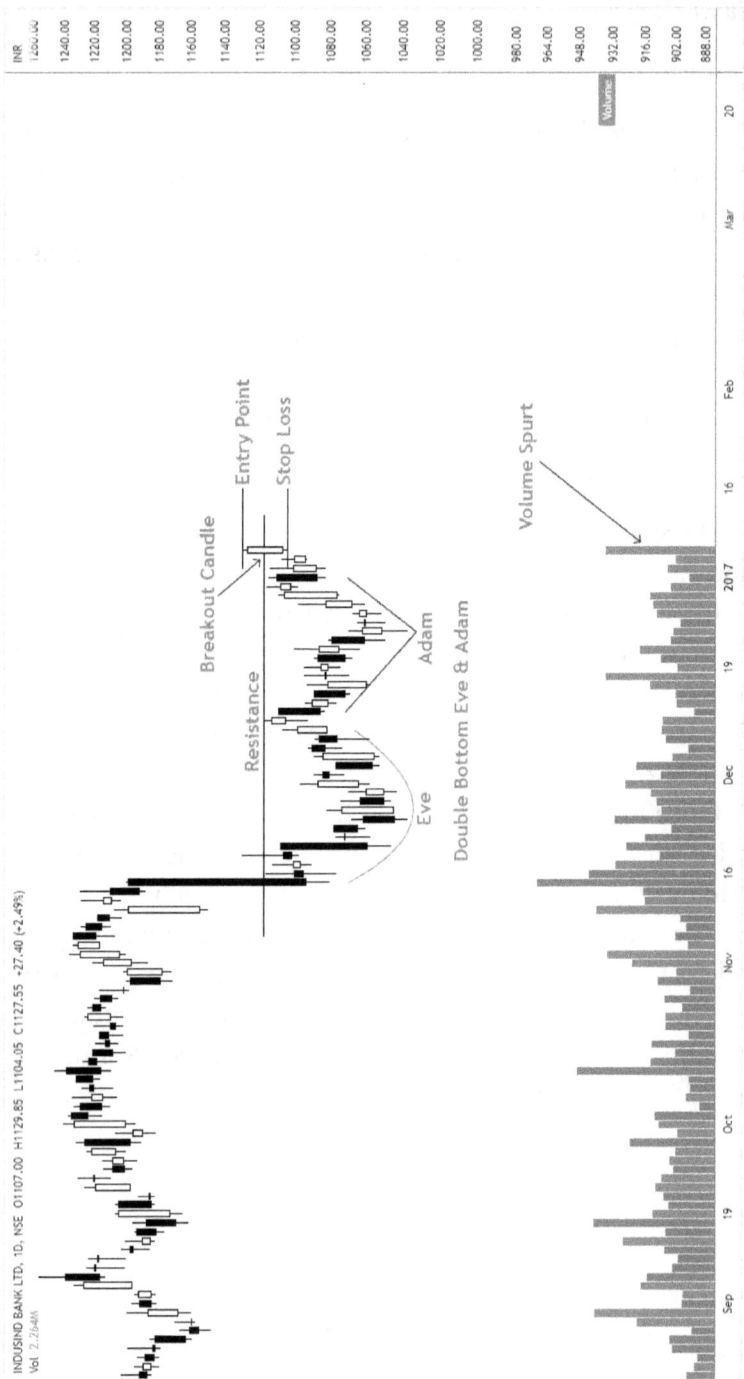

Image 12.86: Daily chart of IndusInd Bank (bullish double bottom reversal pattern).

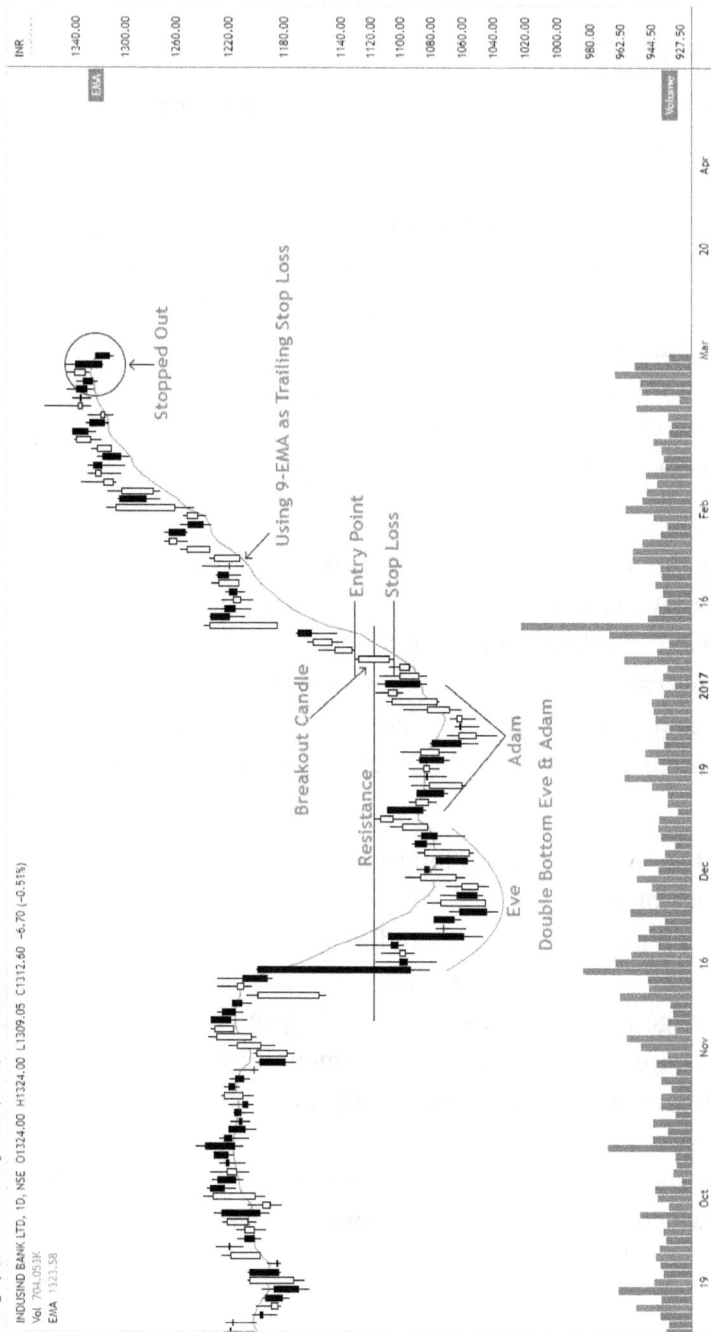

Image 12.87: Daily chart of IndusInd Bank Ltd. signifying strong upside momentum from the breakout of bullish trend reversal pattern.

Double Bottom Adam and Eve

A bullish double bottom Adam and Eve reversal pattern formed on the weekly chart of Tata Motors Ltd. from November 2008 to April 2009, as shown in image 12.88.

It shows a long-lived downtrend with big, black, bearish candles indicating bearishness and finally the stock price settled down at the lower levels. They started forming double bottom Adam and Eve bullish reversal pattern.

Once the pattern got over, we can see a not so strong breakout candle which occurred at the pattern breakout zone (resistance level) with a huge volume spurt.

> **Pro tip**: When breakout is not strong or a wide range breakout candle, we put the stop-loss either at the previous candle low or at the recent swing low. However, in this case, though the breakout is not wide, the candle has a long lower shadow which acts as a rejection level. So, we used this breakout candle low as the stop-loss.

In this chart setup, the long position will be taken above the price of Rs 41 and the stop-loss will be placed at Rs 33 which is a pattern breakout candle low. The exit will happen on the basis of 9-EMA breakdown at Rs 53.

In image 12.89 we can see the upside gain was not so great, so you have to keep in mind that sometimes you get stopped out early on and you do have to take the exit from the stock as the stop-loss is hit.

The entry was taken at Rs 33 and the exit will happen at Rs 53 which gave us around 29% gain in 14 weeks' time frame.

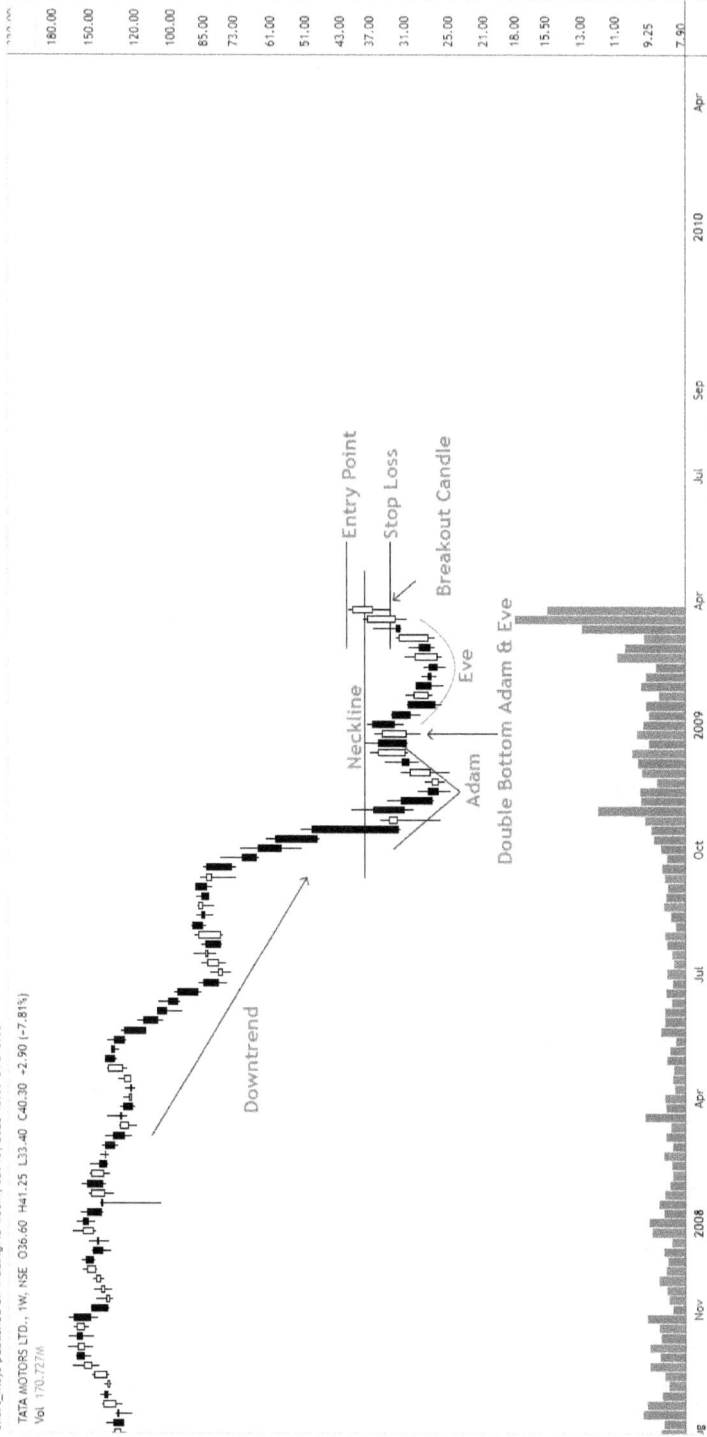

Image 12.88: Weekly chart of Tata Motors Ltd. (bullish double bottom Adam and Eve reversal pattern).

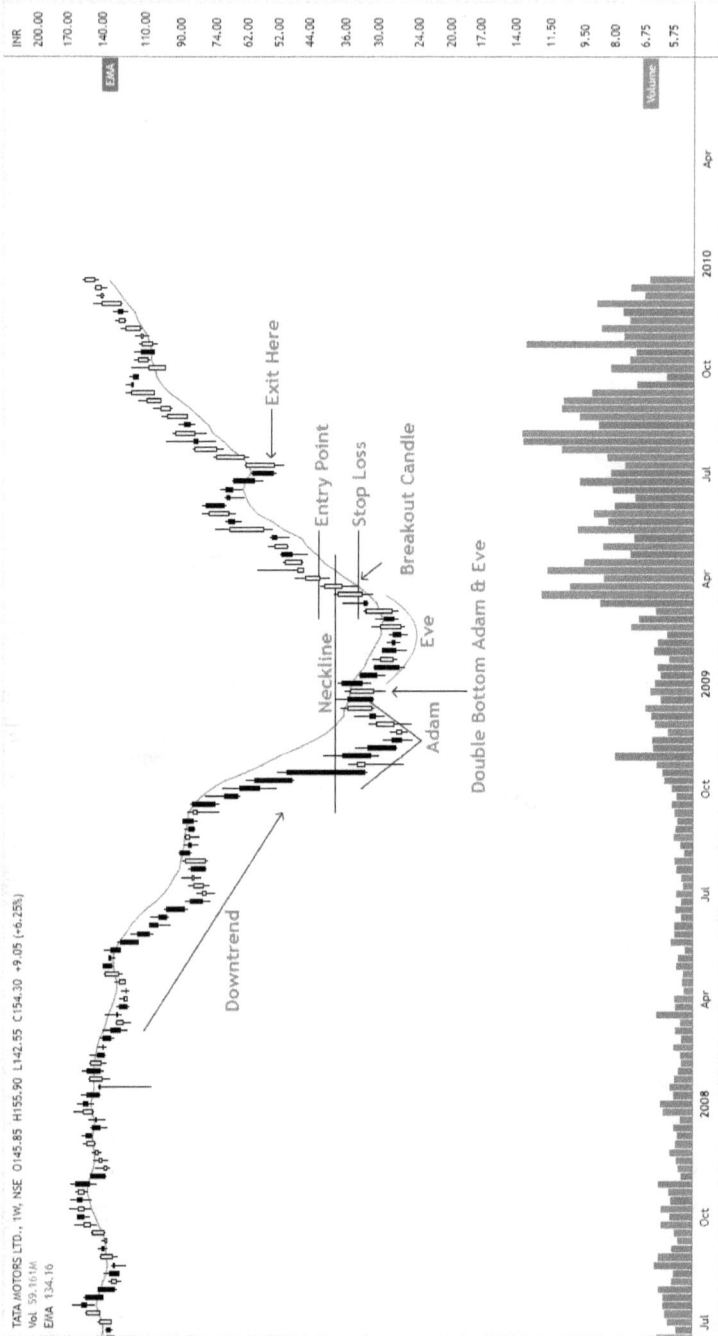

Image 12.89: Weekly chart of Tata Motors Ltd. depicting bullish trend reversal from the breakout zone of double bottom Adam and Eve pattern.

Double Bottom Eve and Eve

A double bottom Eve and Eve bullish reversal pattern formed on the daily chart of REC Ltd. (Rural Electrification Corporation Limited), from February 2016 to July 2016, as shown in image 12.90.

The stock was in a strong downtrend before the formation of a bullish reversal pattern and was going through a series of lower lows and lower highs.

The breakout happened with a candle which was not very strong. We have put the stop-loss just below the low of the breakout candle because if we keep the stop-loss at the previous candle low then our risk increases drastically.

In this chart setup, the long position will be taken above the price of Rs 71 and the stop-loss will be placed at Rs 67 which is a pattern breakout candle low. The exit will happen on the basis of 9-EMA breakdown at Rs 91.

Once the long position was taken (image 12.91), the stock price started marching towards upside and price action was trading above the trailing stop-loss criteria which is 9-EMA. It did show one false breakdown before the actual exit on 9-EMA.

The volume action during the upside can be seen on the higher side as buying volume bars are bigger than selling volume bars. Eventually the volume started taming down as we got closer to the exit price.

The stock price went from Rs 71 to Rs 91 within five months' time frame. In this trade, we got to book 27% upside at 6% risk (stop-loss).

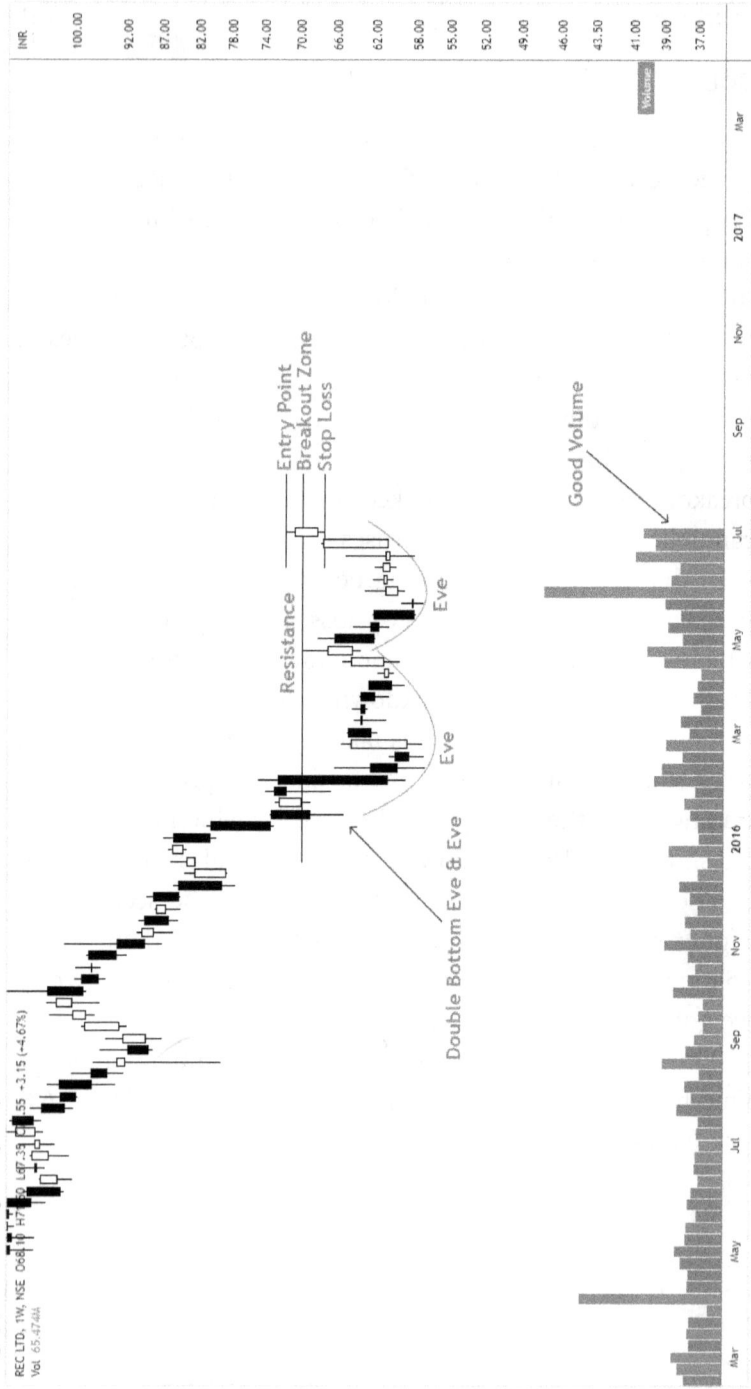

Image 12.90: Daily chart of REC Ltd. (bullish double bottom Eve and Eve bullish reversal pattern).

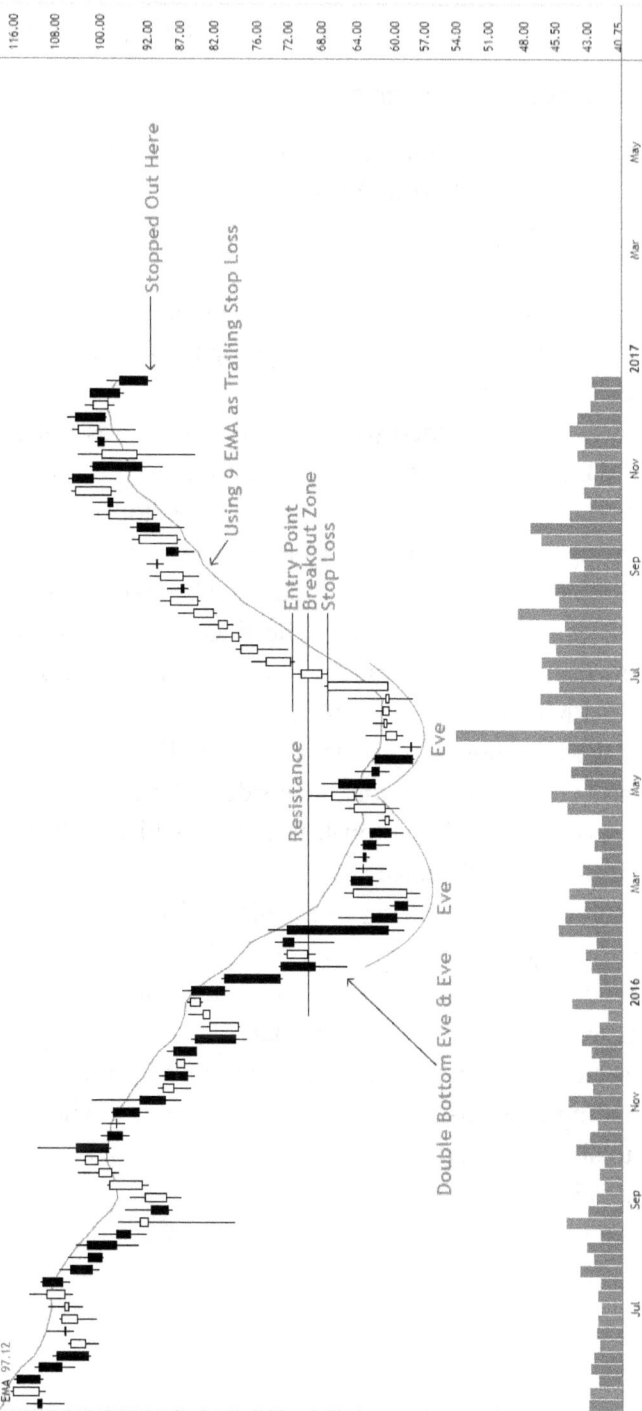

Image 12.91: Weekly chart of REC Ltd. showing a bullish trend reversal from the breakout zone of double bottom Eve and Eve pattern.

Double Bottom Adam and Adam

A bullish double bottom Adam and Adam reversal pattern formed on the daily chart of AVAXUSDT (a crypto currency) from November 2016 to January 2017, as shown in image 12.92.

The stock was in a strong downtrend before the formation of a bullish reversal pattern and was going through a series of lower lows and lower highs.

The breakout happened with a candle which was not very strong. We have put the stop-loss just below the low of a breakout candle. But if you want to keep the stop-loss at the recent swing low then that is a good place as well.

In this chart setup the long position will be taken above the price of $15 and the stop-loss will be placed at $13.35 which is the low of the breakout candle. The exit will happen on the basis of 9-EMA breakdown at $39.

Once the long position was taken (image 12.93), the stock price started marching towards the upside and price action was trading above the trailing stop-loss criteria which is 9-EMA and gave us a smooth upside.

The volume action during the upside price action can be seen on the higher side as buying volume bars are bigger than selling volume bars. Eventually, the volume started taming down as we got closer to the exit price.

The security price went from $15 up to $39 within a period of 30 trading sessions. In this trade we booked a whopping 160% upside at 11.50% risk (stop-loss) as you can see in image 12.93.

AVAX / TetherUS, 1D, BINANCE O13.83 H15.08 L13.39 C14.77 -0.94 (-6.77%)
Vol · AVAX: 2.10RM

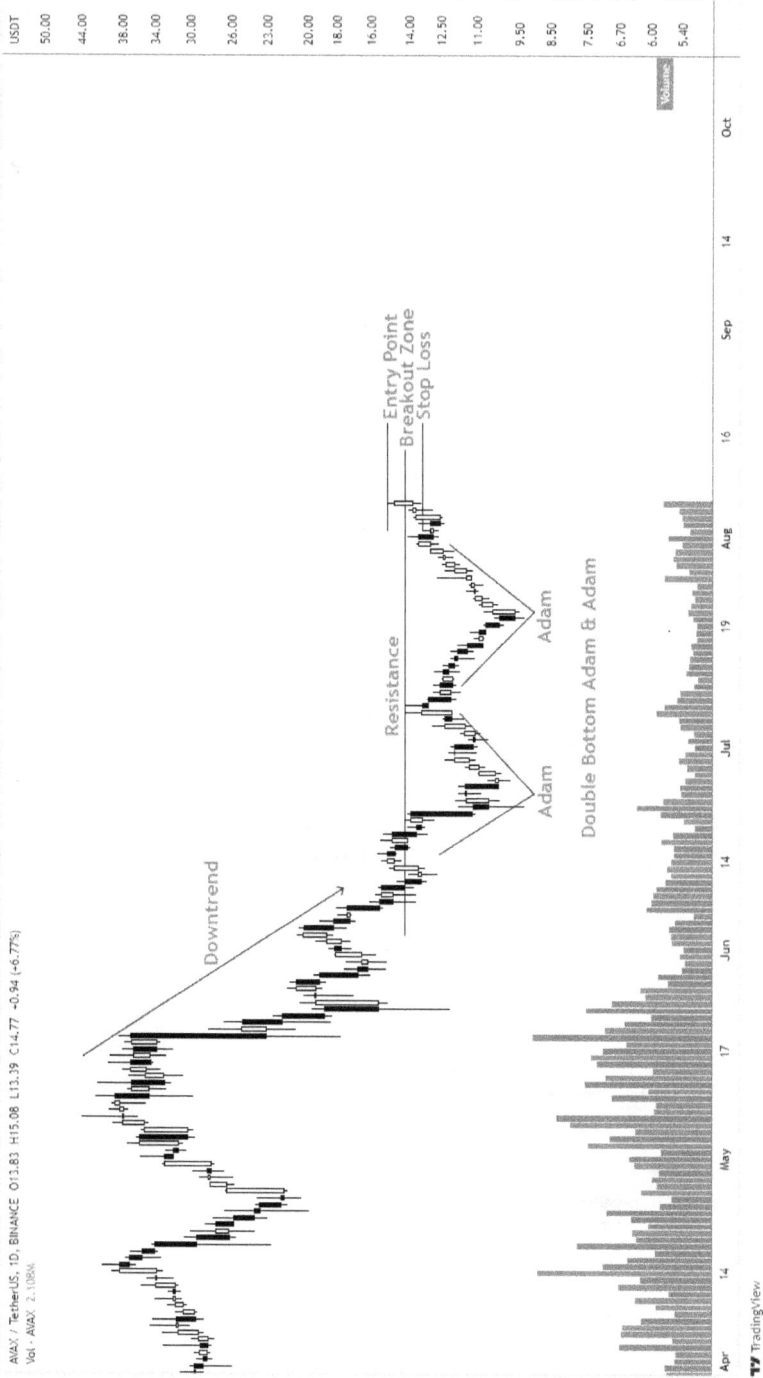

Image 12.92: Daily chart of AVAX/Tether US (bullish double bottom Adam and Adam reversal pattern).

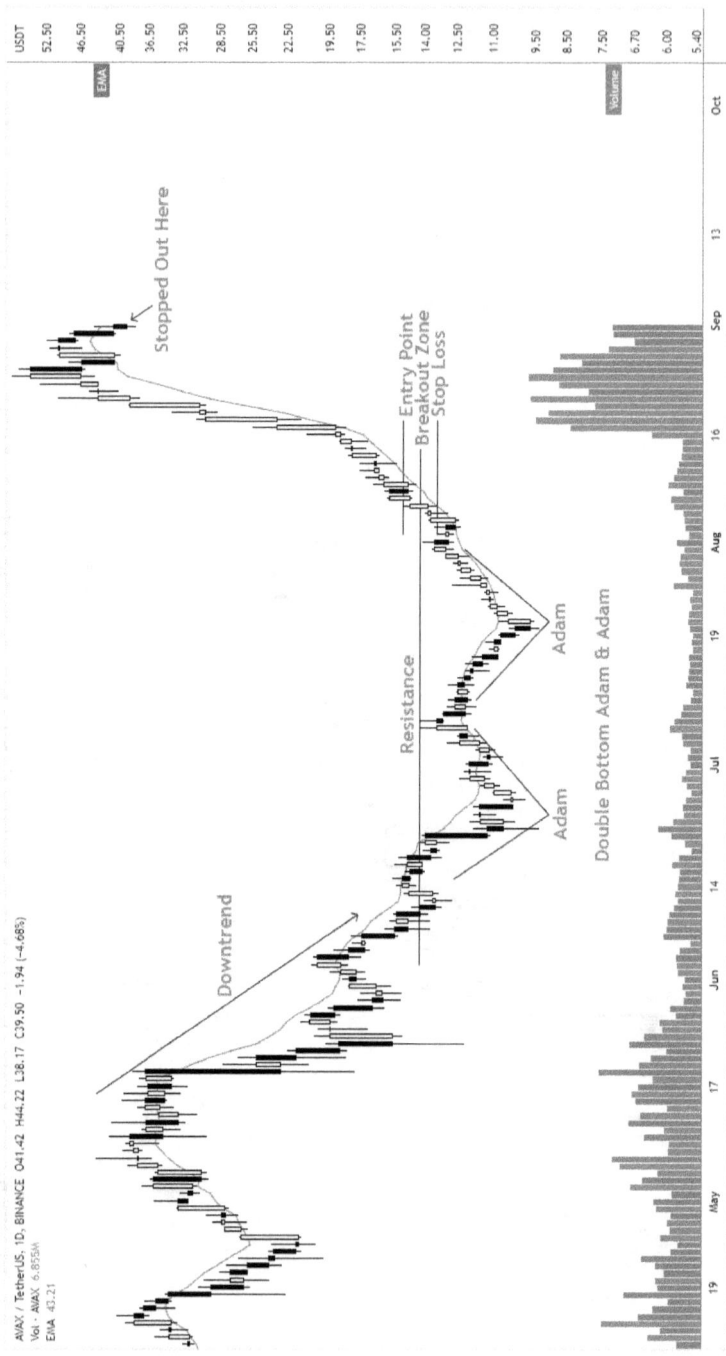

Image 12.93: Daily chart for AVAX/Tether US signalling a strong upside momentum from the breakout zone of bullish trend reversal pattern.

Double Top Eve and Adam

A bearish double top Eve and Adam reversal pattern formed on the daily chart of Sterlite Technologies Ltd. from March 2022 to April 2022, as shown in image 12.94.

A short-lived uptrend with white (bullish) candles indicate bullishness. Finally, the stock price settles down at the upper levels and starts forming a double top Eve and Adam reversal pattern.

Once the pattern ended, we can see a strong wide range breakout candle occurred at the pattern breakout zone (support level) with a huge volume build-up.

In image 12.95, the short position was taken below Rs 189 with a target of around Rs 155 (42 points below the entry area) and the stop is placed around Rs 207 (high of the breakdown candle).

Once the short position was taken, the price action started drifting towards downside with not even one bullish candle indicating strong the downward pressure.

The stock price went down from Rs 189 all the way down to Rs 155 within a few trading sessions. We got to book the downside target of 17% at 9% risk.

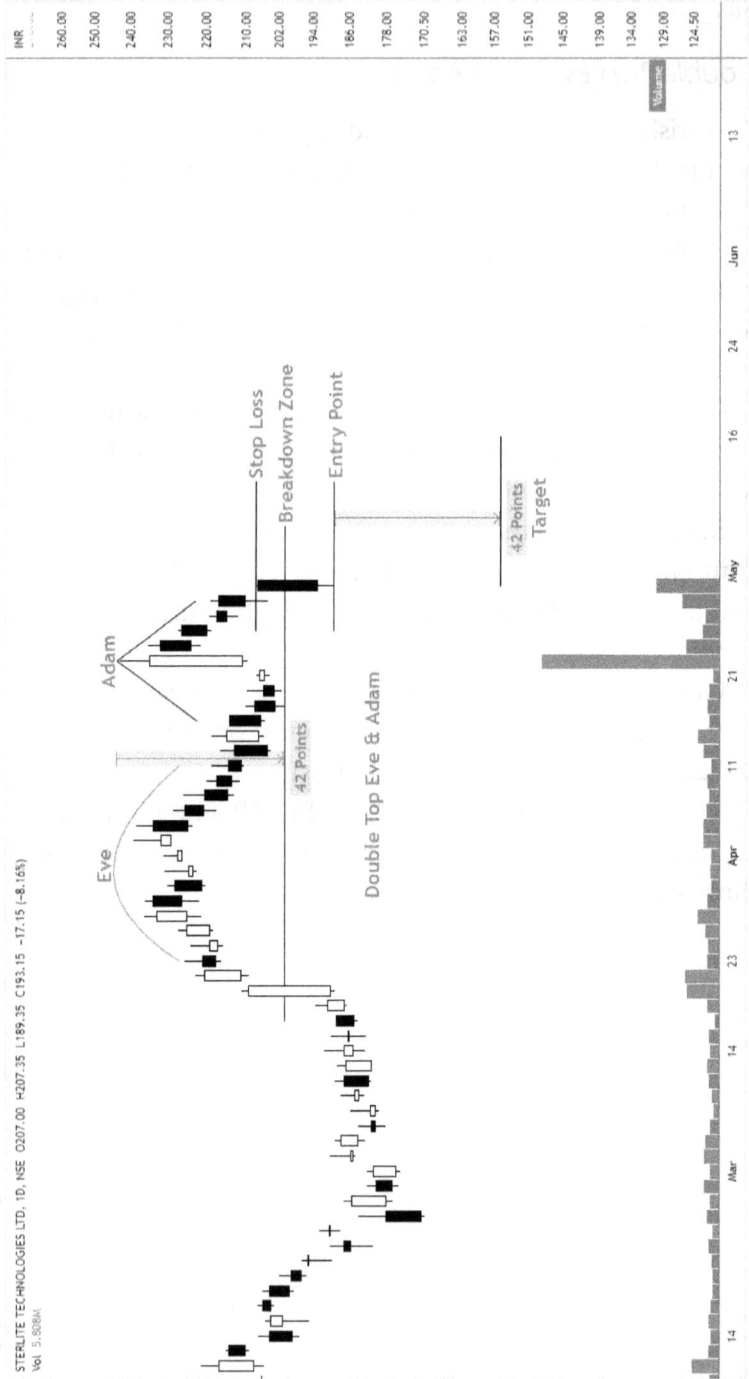

Image 12.94: Daily chart of Sterlite Technologies Ltd. (bearish double top Eve and Adam reversal pattern)

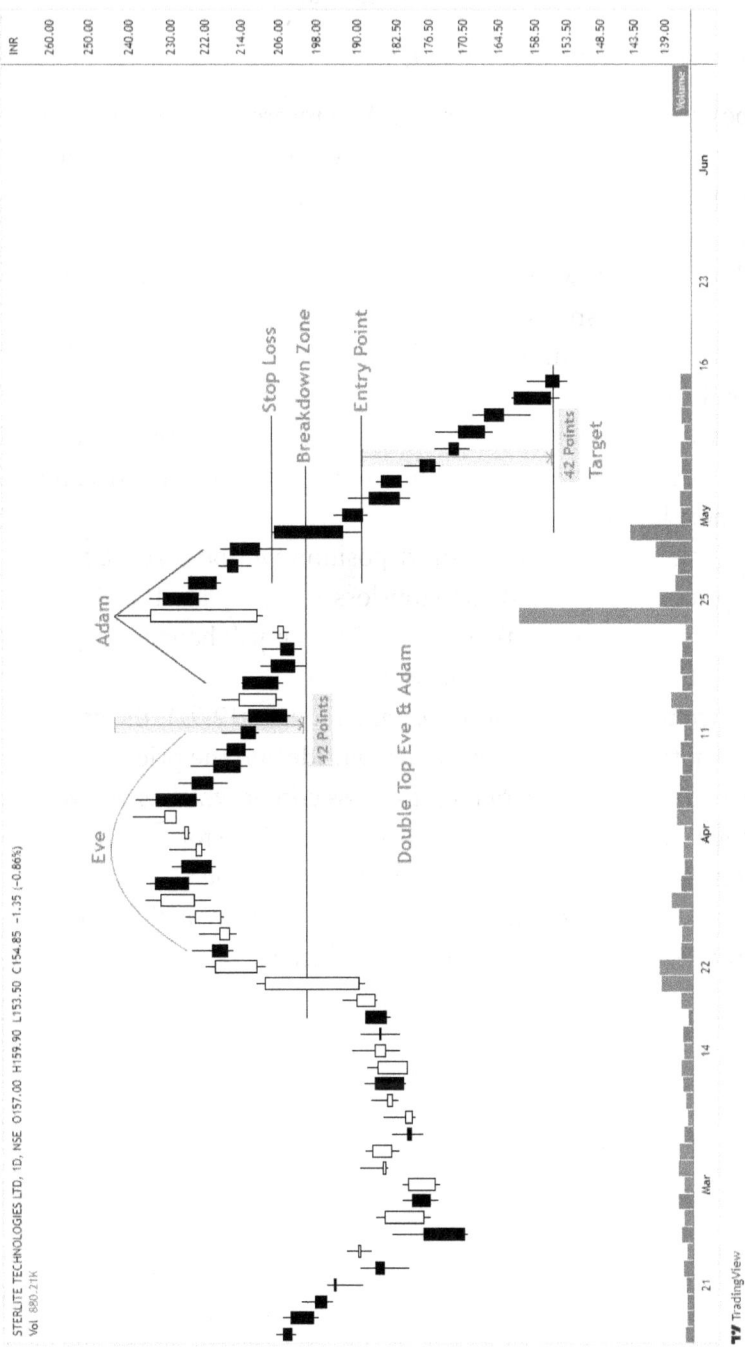

Image 12.95: Daily chart of Sterlite Technologies Ltd. showing a strong bearishness after the breakdown from double top Eve and Adam pattern.

Double Top Adam and Eve

A bearish double top Adam and Eve reversal pattern formed on the daily chart of Infrastructure Development Finance Company (IDFC) Ltd. from October 2017 to November 2017, as shown in image 12.96.

This chart shows a long-term uptrend with big white candles indicating bullishness. Finally the stock price settles down at the upper levels and starts forming double top Adam and Eve bearish reversal pattern.

Once the pattern ended, we can see a decent wide range breakdown candle occurred at the pattern breakdown zone (support level).

In this chart setup the short position will be taken below the price of Rs 63 and the stop-loss will be placed at Rs 66 which is a pattern breakout high. The exit will happen on the basis of 9-EMA breakout at Rs 57.

Once the short position was taken (image 12.97), the stock price started marching towards downside and the price action was trading below the trailing stop-loss criteria which is 9-EMA despite the two fake moves above the trailing stop.

The stock price went down from Rs 63 all the way to Rs 57 within a short time frame. As and when the price action broke above 9-EMA, our exit criteria got satisfied.

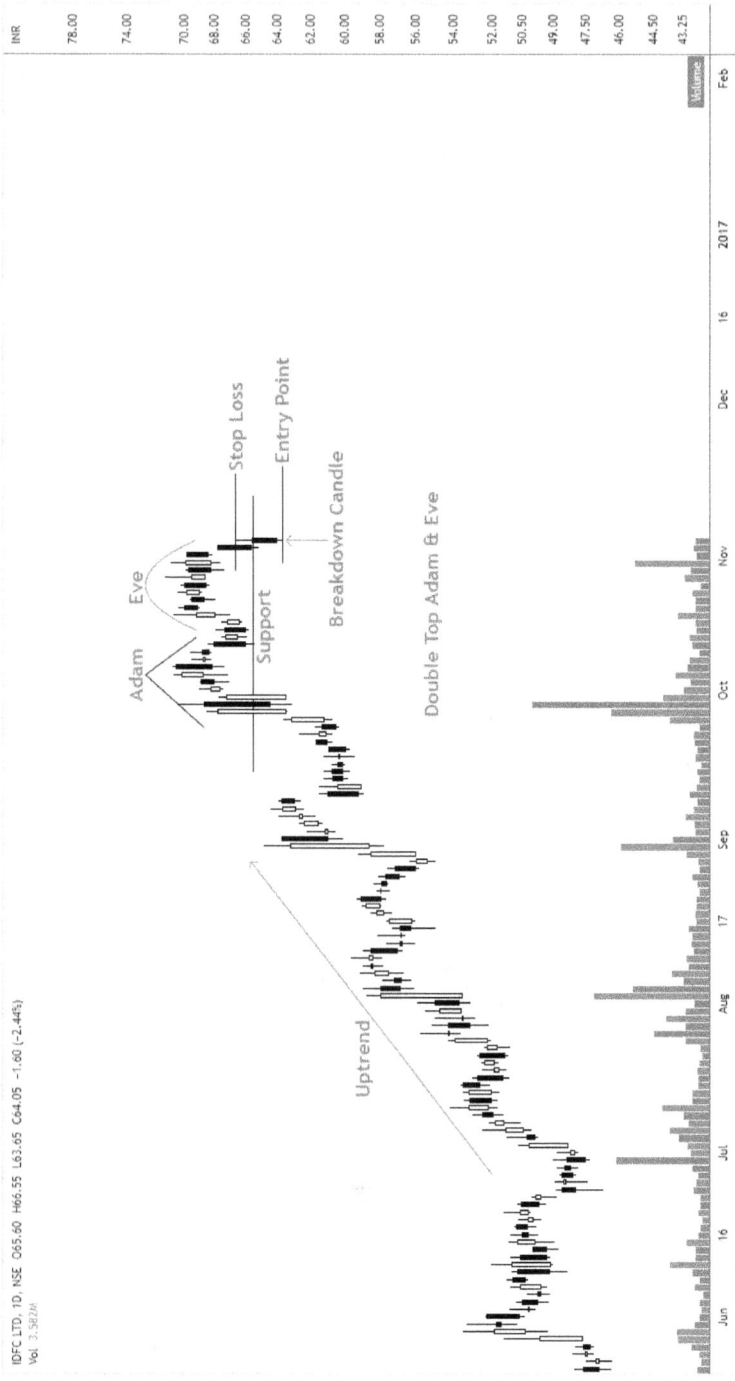

Image 12.96: Daily chart of IDFC Ltd. (bearish double top Adam and Eve reversal pattern)

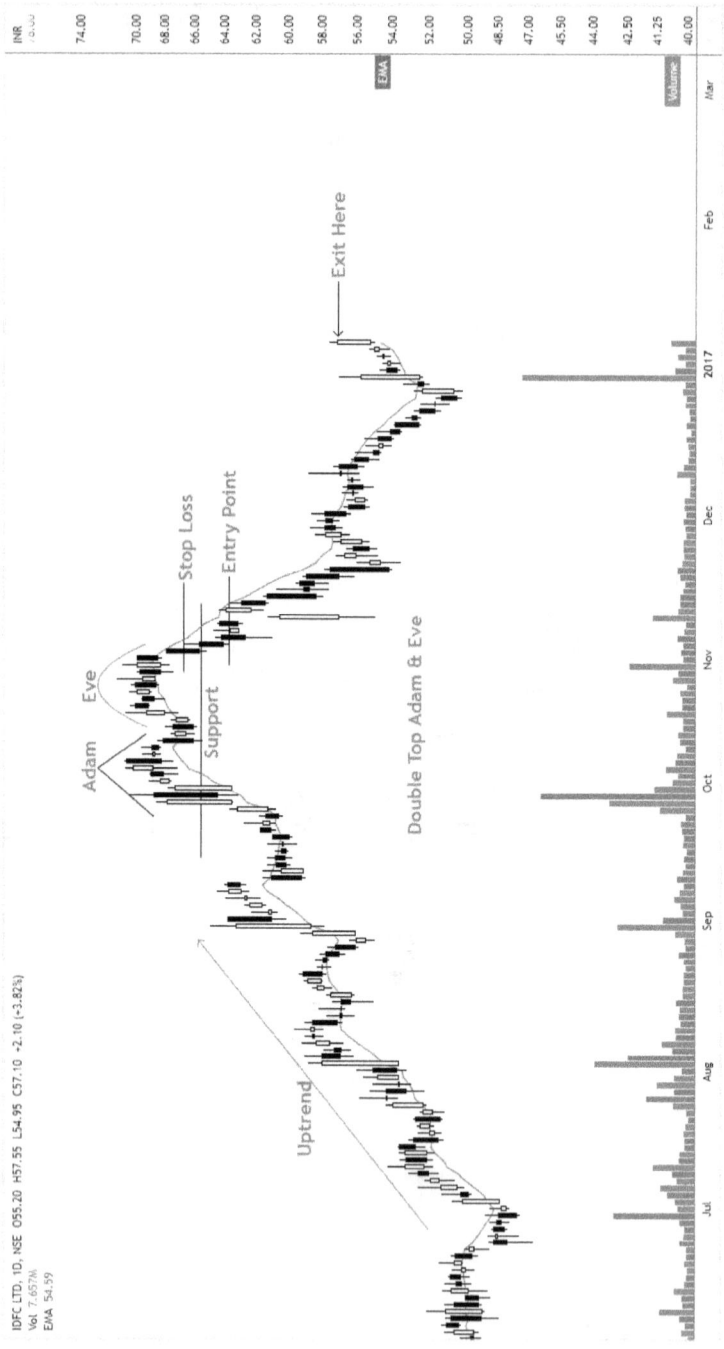

Chart_mojo published on TradingView.com, Feb 02, 2023 10:48 UTC+5:30

IDFC LTD, 1D, NSE O55.20 H57.55 L54.95 C57.10 -2.10 (-3.82%)
Vol 7.657M
EMA 54.59

Image 12.97: Daily chart of IDFC Ltd. signalling a bearishness after the breakdown from double top Adam and Eve pattern.

Double Top Adam and Adam

A bearish double top Adam and Adam reversal pattern formed on the daily chart of Vardhman Textiles Ltd. from December 2021 to April 2022, as shown in image 12.98.

The stock was in a strong downtrend before the formation of a bearish reversal pattern. It went through a nice uptrend with a supportive buying volume. Eventually, the price settled down at the top of the uptrend and formed the bearish reversal pattern.

The breakdown happened with a candle which was very strong and we put the stop-loss just above the high of the breakdown candle.

In this chart setup, the short position will be taken at below the price of Rs 447 and the stop-loss will be placed at Rs 508, which is high of the breakdown candle. The exit will happen on the basis of 9-EMA breakdown at Rs 350.

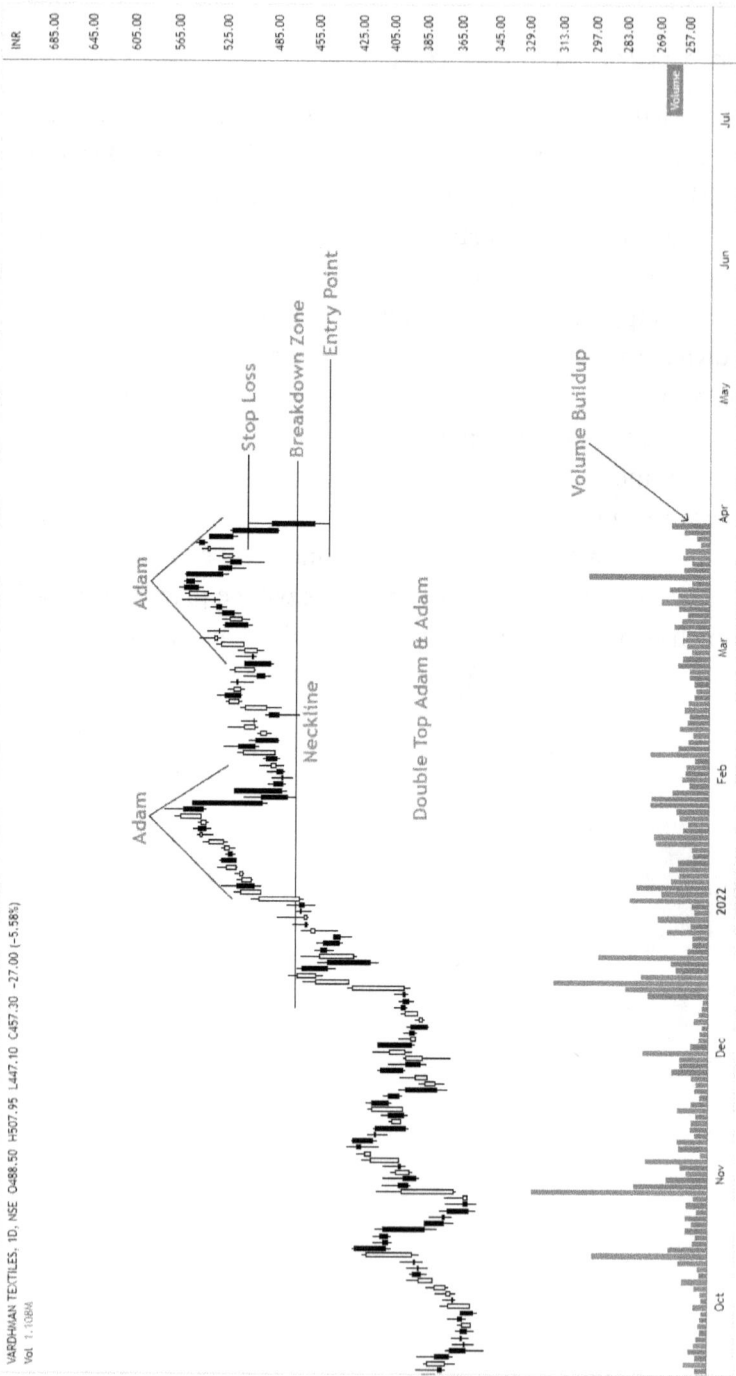

Image 12.98: Daily chart of Vardhman Textiles Ltd. (bearish double top Adam and Adam reversal pattern)

Double Top Eve and Eve

A bearish double top Eve and Eve reversal pattern formed on the daily chart of RBL Bank Ltd. from May 2021 to July 2021 as shown in image 12.99.

As we can see, the stock was in a strong uptrend before the formation of a double top Eve and Eve reversal pattern.

Finally, the breakdown happened with a wide range breakdown candle which was very strong and it was also accompanied by a decent volume build-up which signifies bearishness on the stock.

In this chart setup, the short position will be taken below the price of Rs 198 and the stop-loss will be placed at Rs 205 which is a pattern breakout candle high. The exit will happen on the basis of 9-EMA breakdown at Rs 171.

Once the short position was taken (image 12.100), the stock price came down smoothly and did not even touch the trailing stop-loss once in the entire downfall.

The security price went from Rs 198 all the way down to Rs 171 within a period three months. However, one thing is very clear that downside happened with clean downside price action.

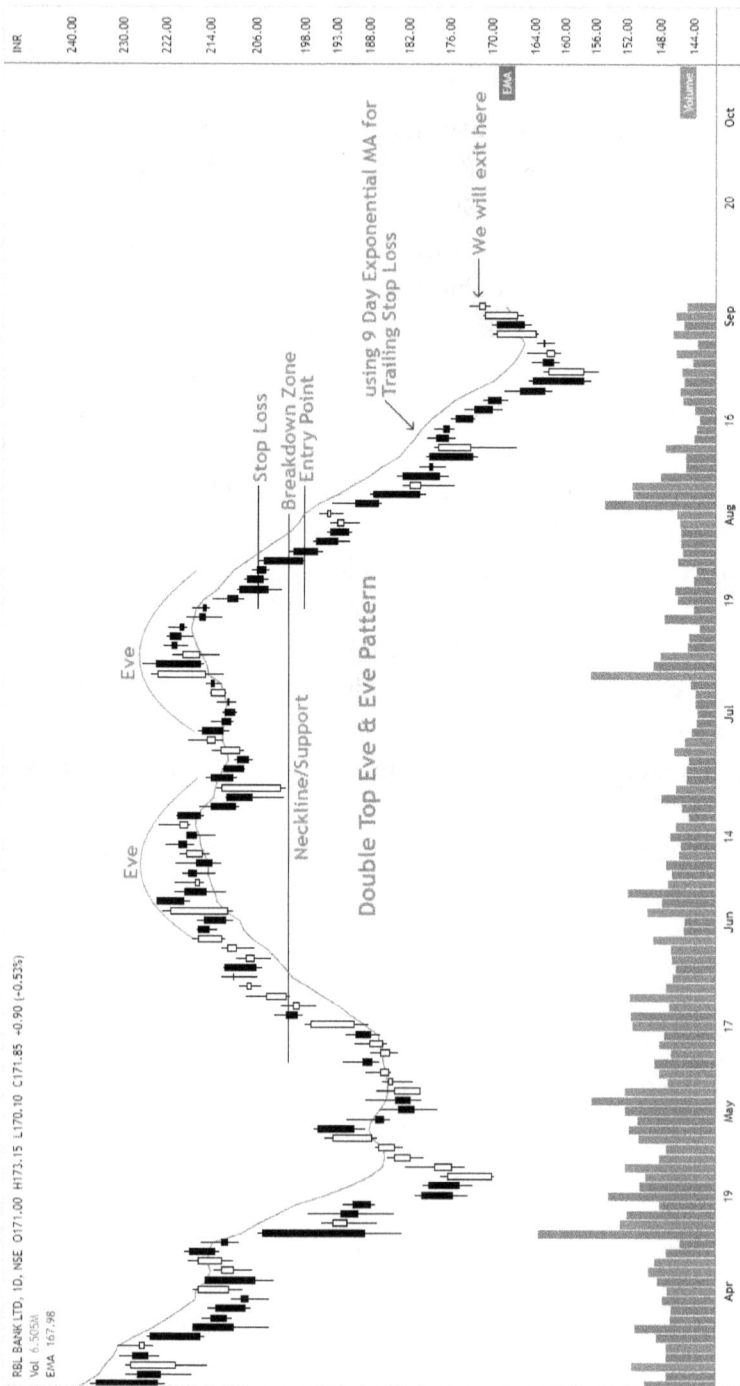

Image 12.99: Daily chart of RBL Bank Ltd. (bearish double top Eve and Eve reversal pattern)

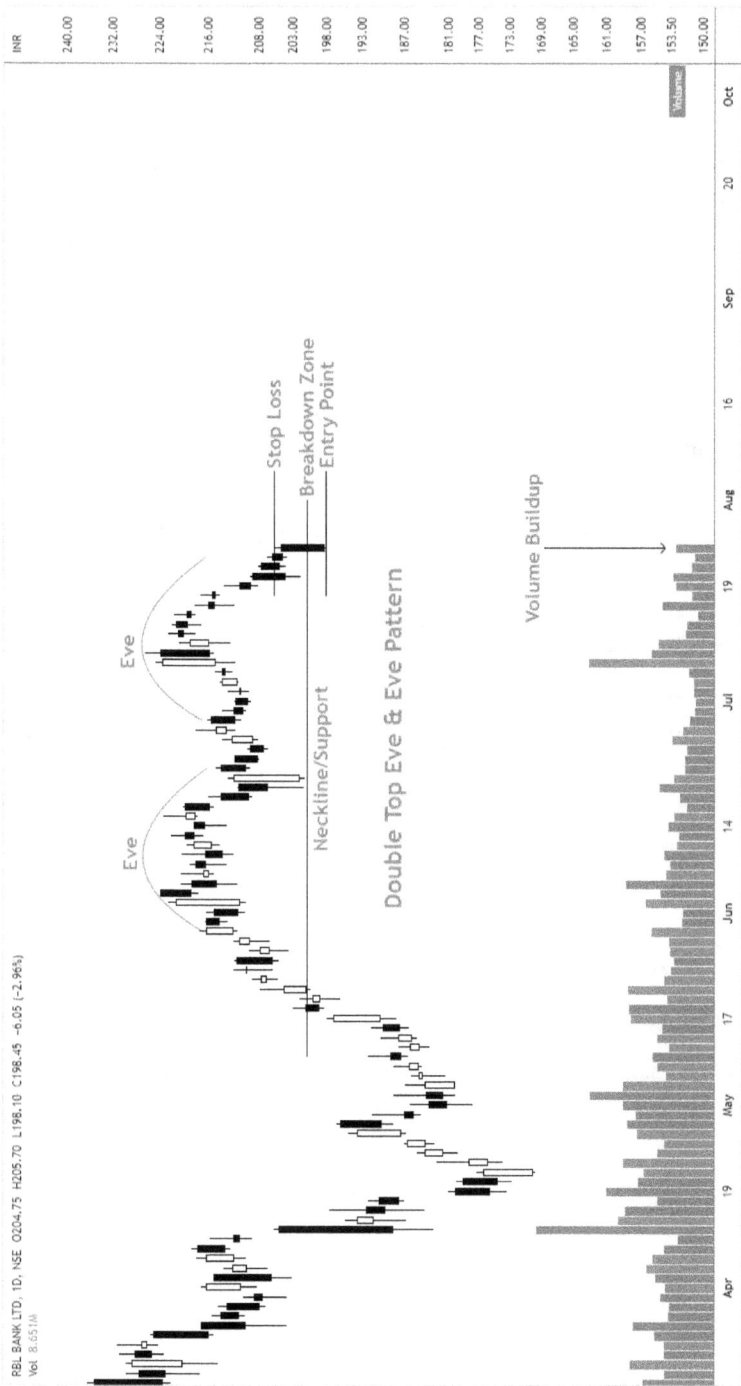

Image 12.100: Daily chart of RBL Bank Ltd showing us a downtrend reversal from double top Eve and Eve pattern.

Double Top Adam and Adam

A bearish double top Adam and Adam reversal pattern formed on the daily chart of Vardhman Textiles Ltd. from December 2021 to April 2022, as shown in image 12.101.

Once the short position was taken, the stock price started marching downside and the price action traded below the trailing stop-loss criteria which is 9 EMA and showed a smooth downside move.

The volume action during the downside price action can be seen on the higher side as selling volume bars are bigger than buying volume bars. Eventually, the volume started taming down as we got closer to the exit price (which is mentioned with 'stopped out here').

The security price went from Rs 447 up to Rs 350 within a period of 34 active trading sessions (51 Days). In this trade we got to book 21% downside.

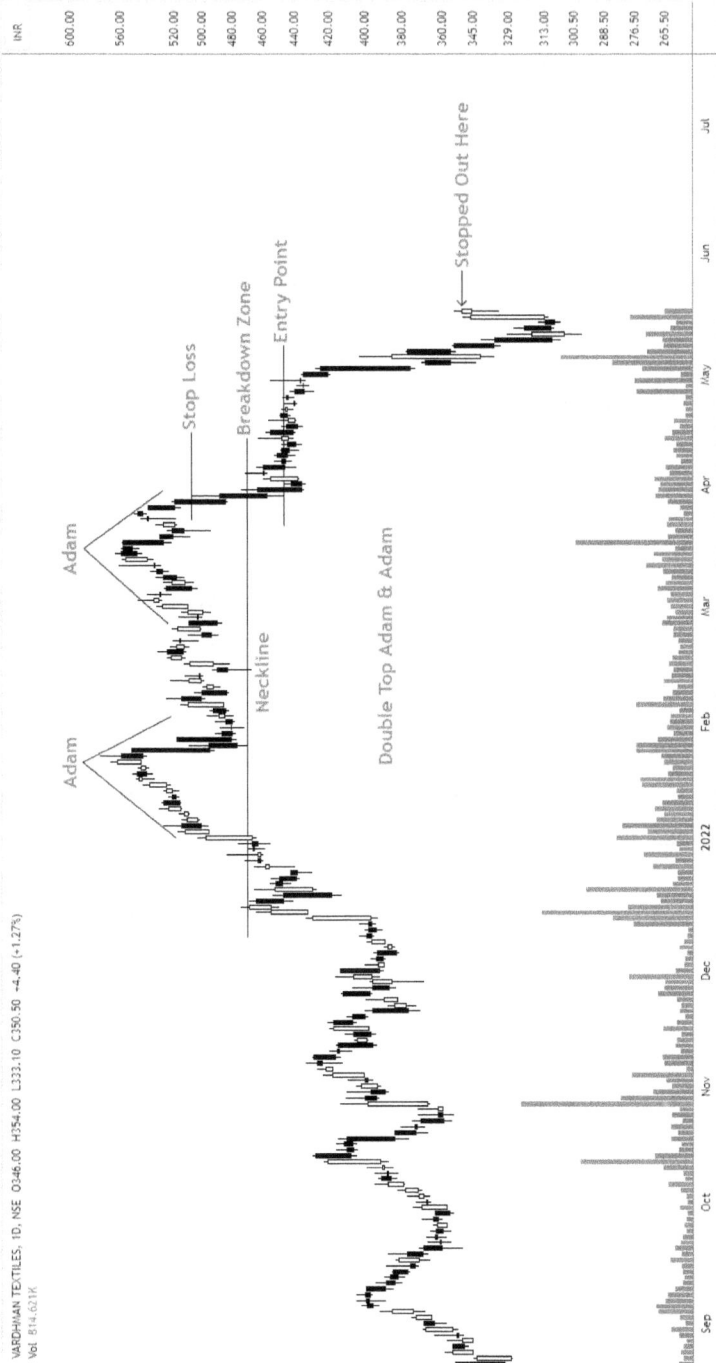

Image 12.101: Daily chart of Vardhman Textiles Ltd. (bearish double top Adam and Adam reversal pattern)

Triple Bottom Pattern

A bullish triple top reversal pattern formed on the daily chart of Tata Motors Ltd. from May 2001 to November 2001, as shown in image 12.102.

The price was trending downward strongly with just a one-way lower bottom and lower top fashion.

Once the pattern ended, we can see a strong wide range breakout occurred with a decent volume build-up. One is also able to see that when the pattern was forming, the volume also took a dip and formed a U shape. This increases the probability of this pattern being right exponentially.

Finally, we take the long position above Rs 17 with a target of around Rs 25 (8 points above the entry area) and the stop is placed around Rs 15 (low of the breakout candle).

Clearly, once the short position was taken with a strong breakout candle, the price started going up smoothly with strong bullish candles.

So here (image 12.103), the stock price went up from Rs 17 all the way down to Rs 25 within a few months of trading sessions.

Do remember when the pattern breakout happened the volume also started picking up—a bullish sign for the stock

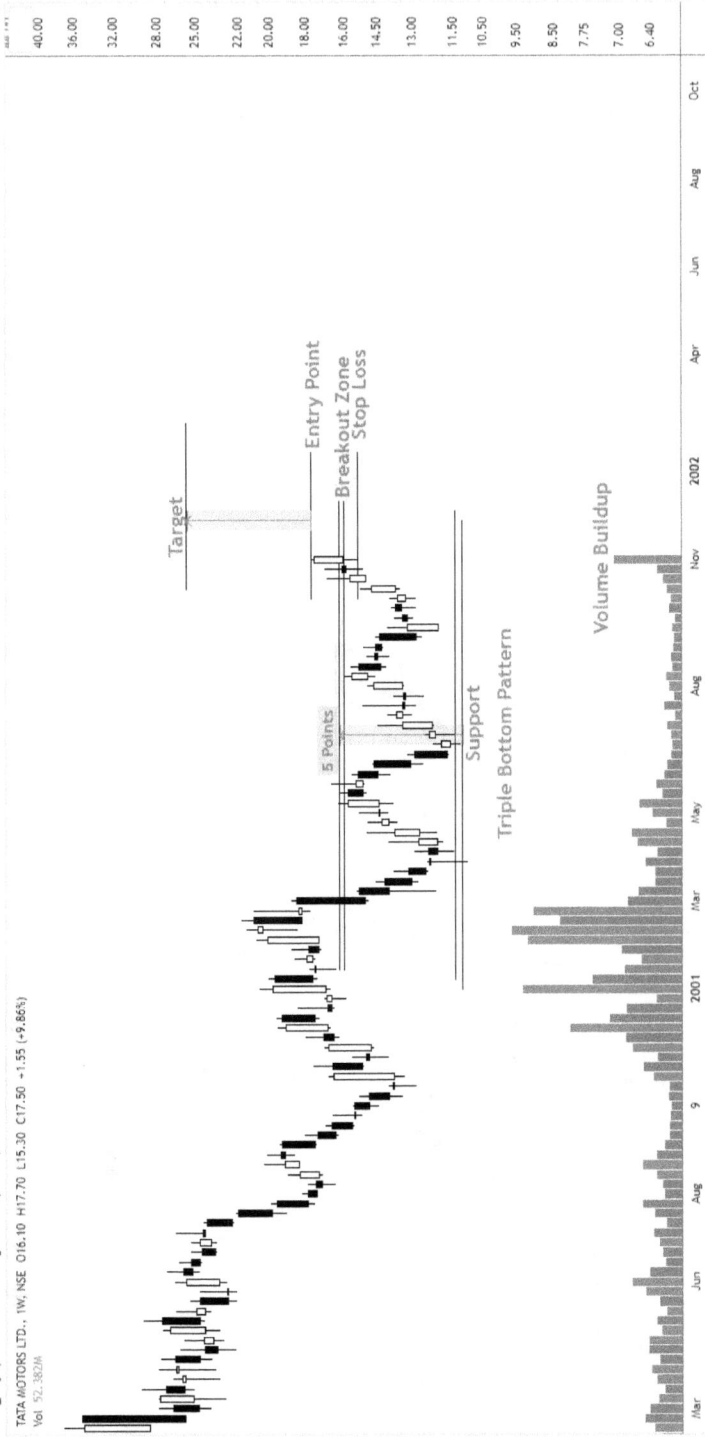

Chart_mojo published on TradingView.com, Jul 10, 2023 12:20 UTC-5:30

TATA MOTORS LTD., 1W, NSE O16.10 H17.70 L15.30 C17.50 -1.55 (+9.86%)

Vol 92.382M

Image 12.102: Daily chart of Tata Motors Ltd. (bullish triple top reversal pattern)

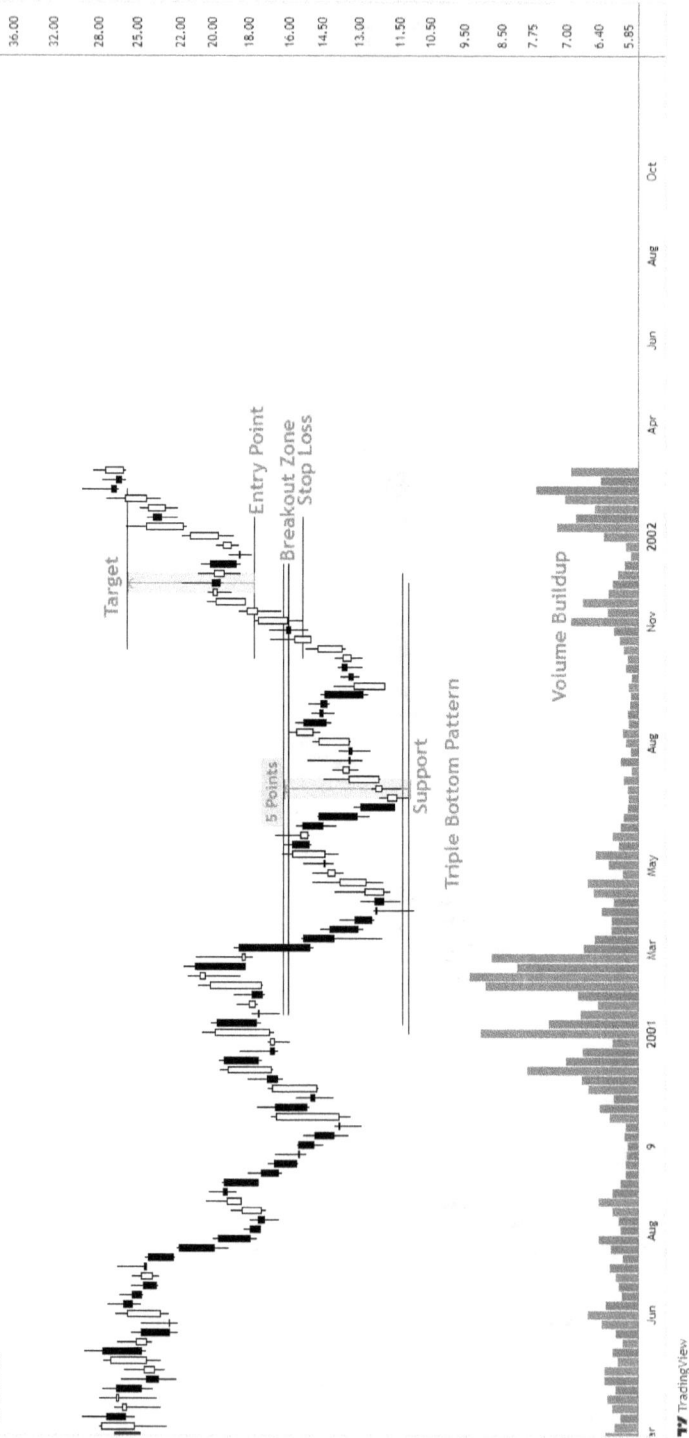

Image 12.103: Weekly chart of Tata Motors Ltd. giving us a strong bullish trend reversal once the breakout occurred from triple bottom pattern.

towards upside.

Triple Top Pattern

A bearish triple top reversal pattern formed on the daily chart of BEML Ltd. (formerly Bharat Earth Movers Ltd.), from July 2010 to January 2011, as shown in image 12.104.

The price was trending up strongly with just one-way wide range bullish candle. In the month of July 2010, the pattern started shaping up and it was a lengthy pattern.

Once the pattern ended after a long period, we can see a strong breakdown occurred with volume contraction. The volume dry up signifies scarcity of selling pressure.

Finally, the short position will be taken at below the price of Rs 699 and the stop-loss will be placed at Rs 769 which is a pattern breakout candle high. The exit will happen on the basis of 9-EMA breakdown at Rs 434.

Once the short position was taken with a strong breakdown candle (image 12.105), the price started coming down smoothly with strong bearish candles.

So, the stock price went down from Rs 769 all the way down to Rs 434 within 10 months' time frame. In this entire downfall we got to book 37% gain at 10% risk which was nothing but the stop-loss.

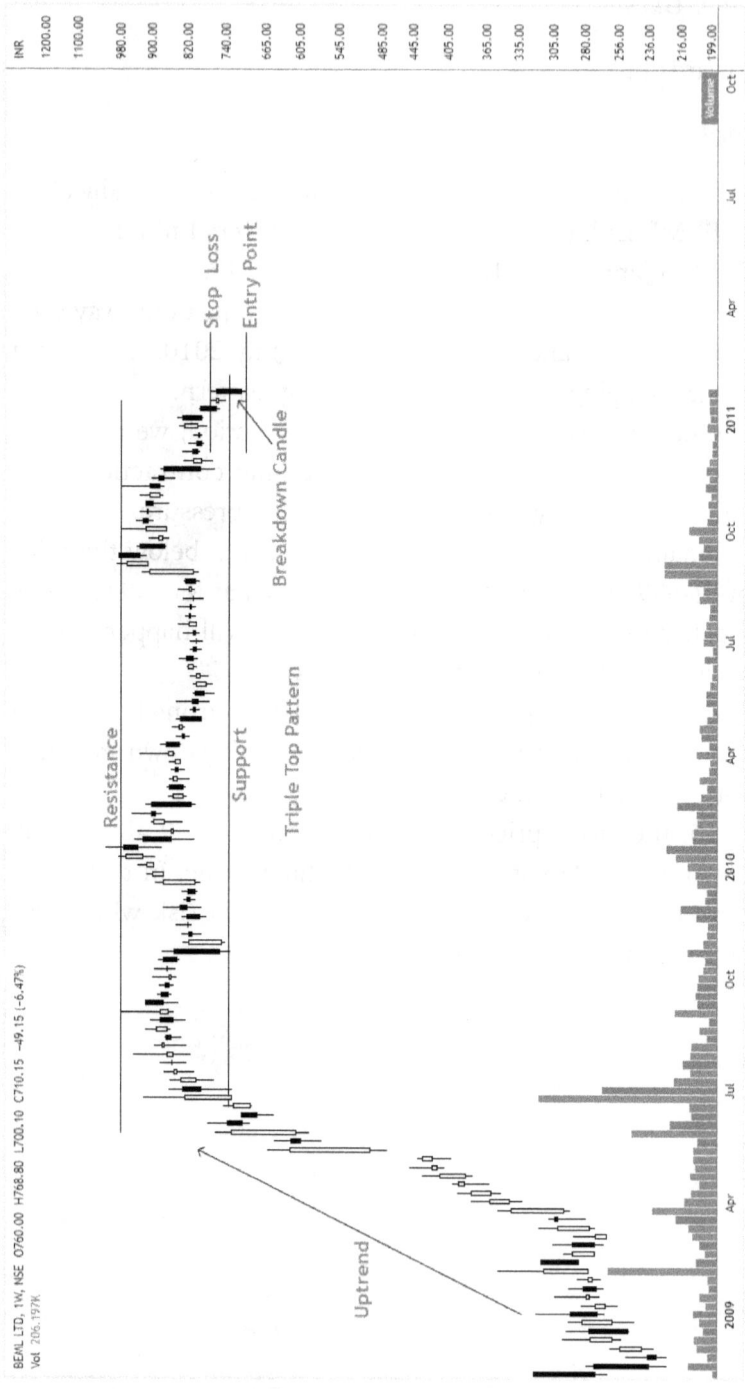

Image 12.104: Daily chart of BEML Ltd. (bearish triple top reversal pattern)

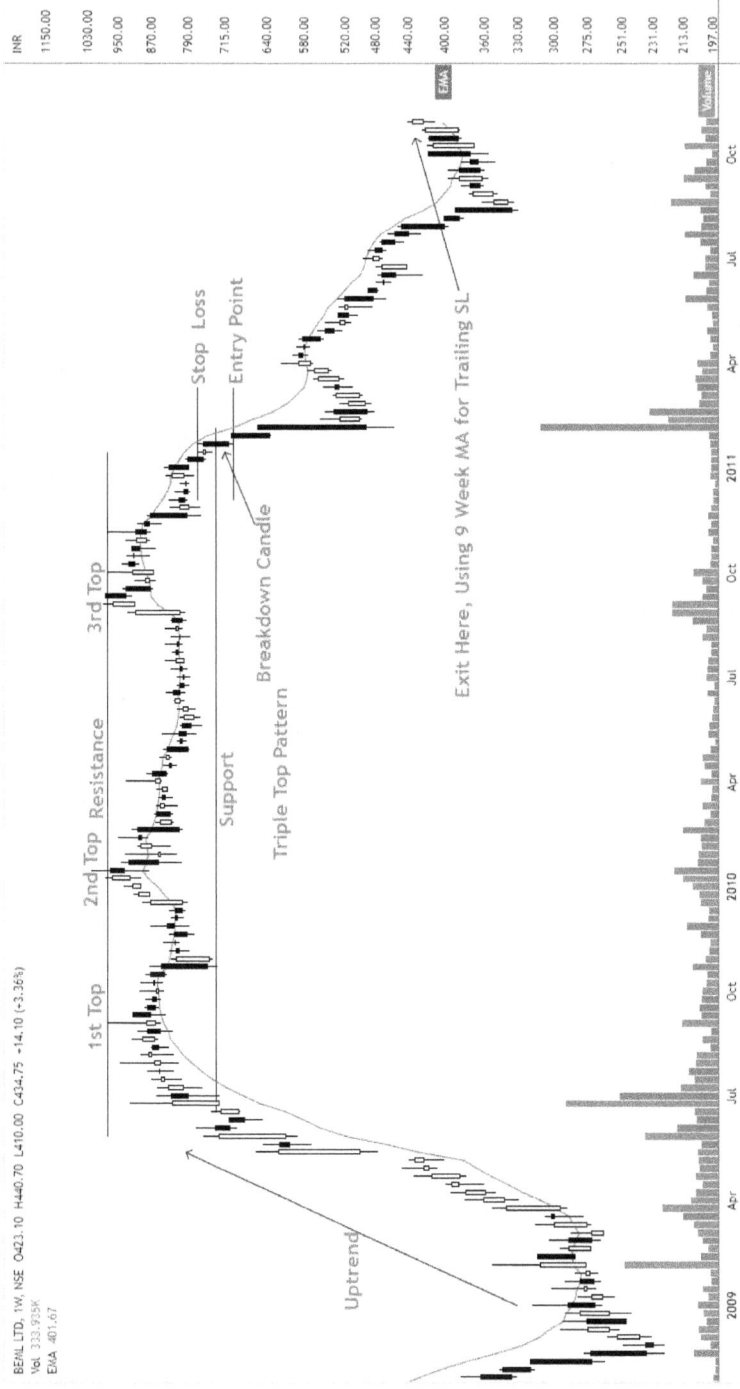

Chart_mojo published on TradingView.com, Feb 01, 2023 14:24 UTC+5:30

BEML LTD, 1W, NSE O423.10 H440.70 L410.00 C434.75 -14.10 (-3.36%)
Vol 333,935K
EMA 401.67

Image 12.105: Weekly chart of BEML Ltd. signifying a strong bearishness from the breakdown zone of triple top pattern.

Island Bottom Reversal

A bearish island bottom reversal pattern formed on the daily chart of Price Pipe Fittings Ltd. from May 2021 to August 2021, as shown in image 12.106.

The downtrend continued and eventually the stock showed a gap down in March 2021 and gap up in August 2021. It provided the shape for this bullish reversal pattern.

Once the pattern got over and it showed the gap up, it was clear that finally the price would start drifting towards the upside. We saw a gap up with a huge bullish candle supported by a nice buying volume pop up bar signifying the built-in upside momentum into the stock price.

Eventually, the long position will be taken above the price of Rs 142 and the stop-loss will be placed at Rs 122 which is the gap up support zone. The exit will happen on the basis of 9-EMA breakout at Rs 220.

Once we took the long position (image 12.107), the stock price started inching higher in a higher highs and higher lows sequence. The upside was supported by huge buying volume bars—a clear signal from the market that big market participants are also interested in this counter.

There was not even a single breakdown on 9-EMA and the upside was very smooth. The stock price went from Rs 142 all the way up to Rs 220 within a period of two months' time frame.

In this trade setup, we got around a whopping 55% upside profit against 14% risk on the trade.

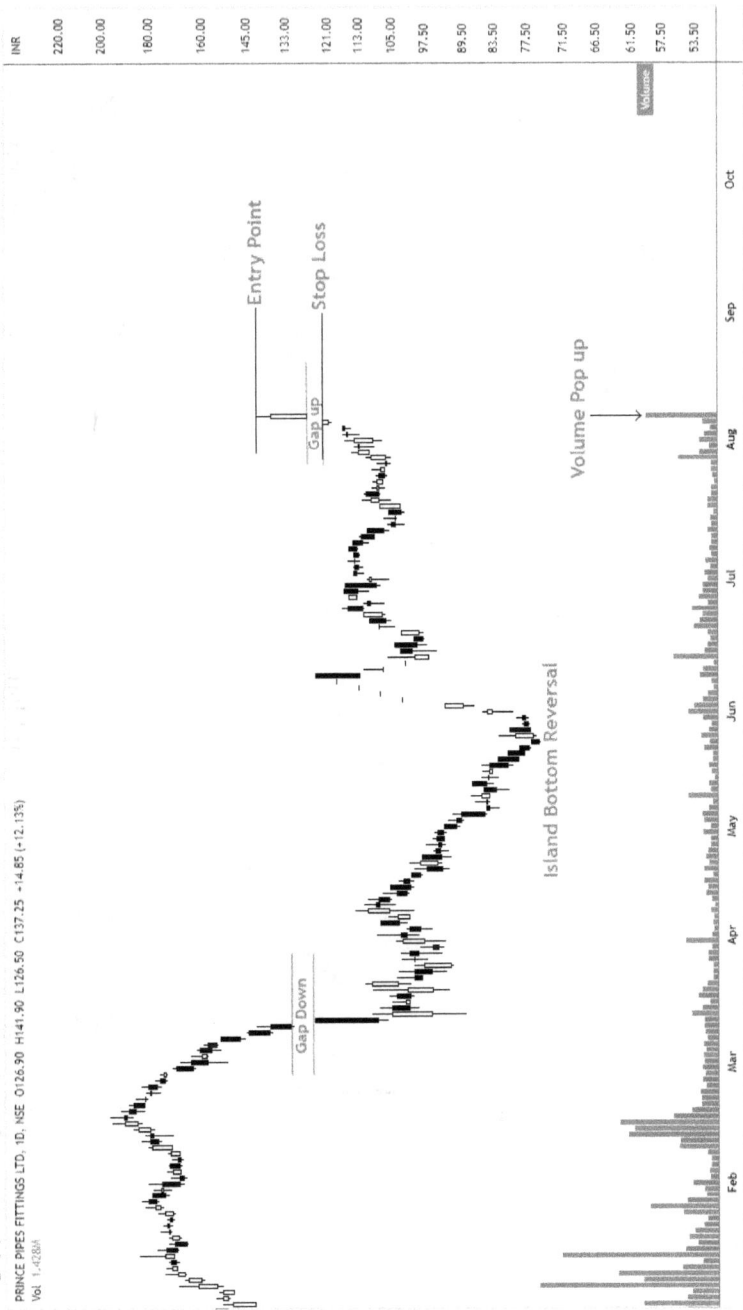

Image 12.106: Daily chart of Price Pipe Fittings Ltd. (bearish island bottom reversal pattern)

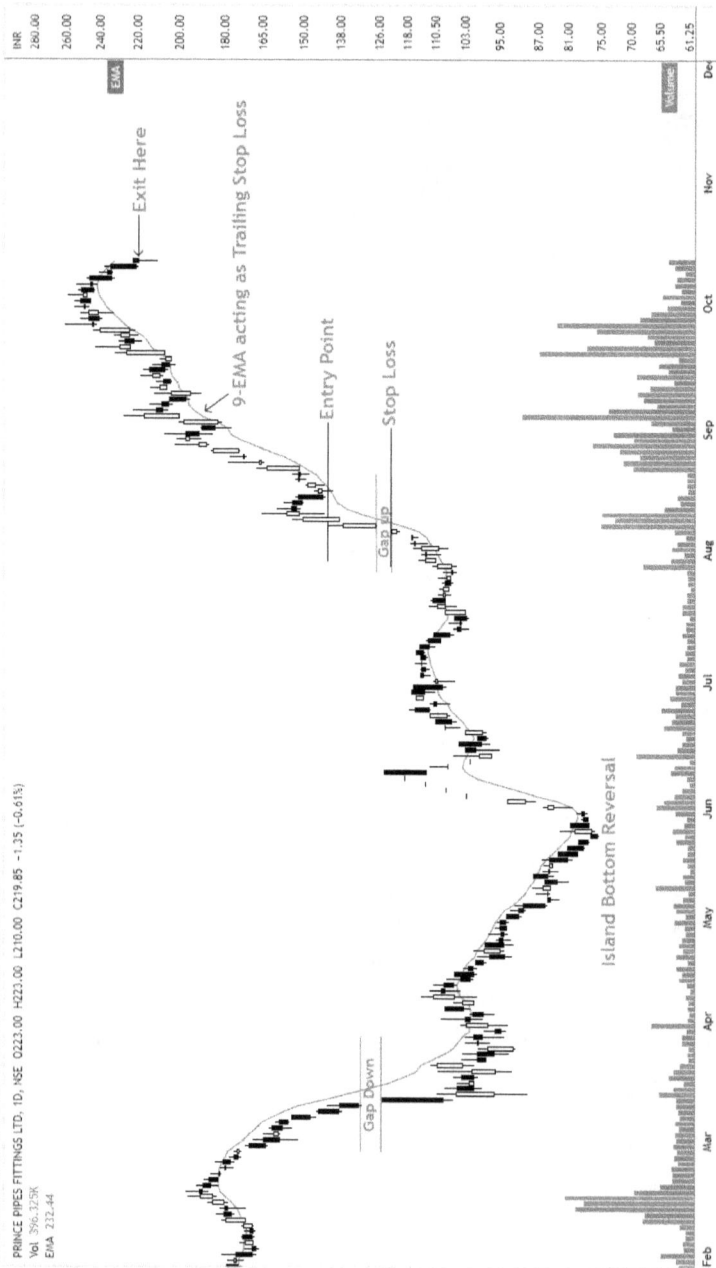

Image 12.107: Daily chart of Prince Pipes and Fittings Ltd. giving a strong upside from the entry point of a bullish trend reversal pattern.

Island Top Reversal

A bearish island top reversal pattern formed on the daily chart of HDFC Bank Ltd. from May 2019 to July 2019, as shown in image 12.108.

The uptrend prevailed and eventually the stock showed a gap up in May 2019 and a gap down in July 2019 which gave shape to this bearish reversal pattern.

Once the pattern ended and it showed a gap down, it was clear that the price will start drifting towards the downside. After a gap down, we saw a huge bearish candle with a good selling volume pop up bar. This signifies the built-in downside momentum into the stock price.

Eventually, the short position will be taken below the price of Rs 1,141 and the stop-loss will be placed at Rs 1,175 which is the gap down resistance zone. The exit will happen on the basis of 9-EMA breakout at Rs 1,141.

In this trade setup (image 12.109), we did not even make 1% profit as we took the exit exactly where we took entry. So one has to keep in mind that we are not going to make profit with every trade. Sometimes we will have to take a stop-loss hit, and in some trades we will break even, which was the same as this case.

Do remember that trading is and should be considered as a business wherein you make profit and losses both. Once you build your mindset like that you will be able to make money from the market.

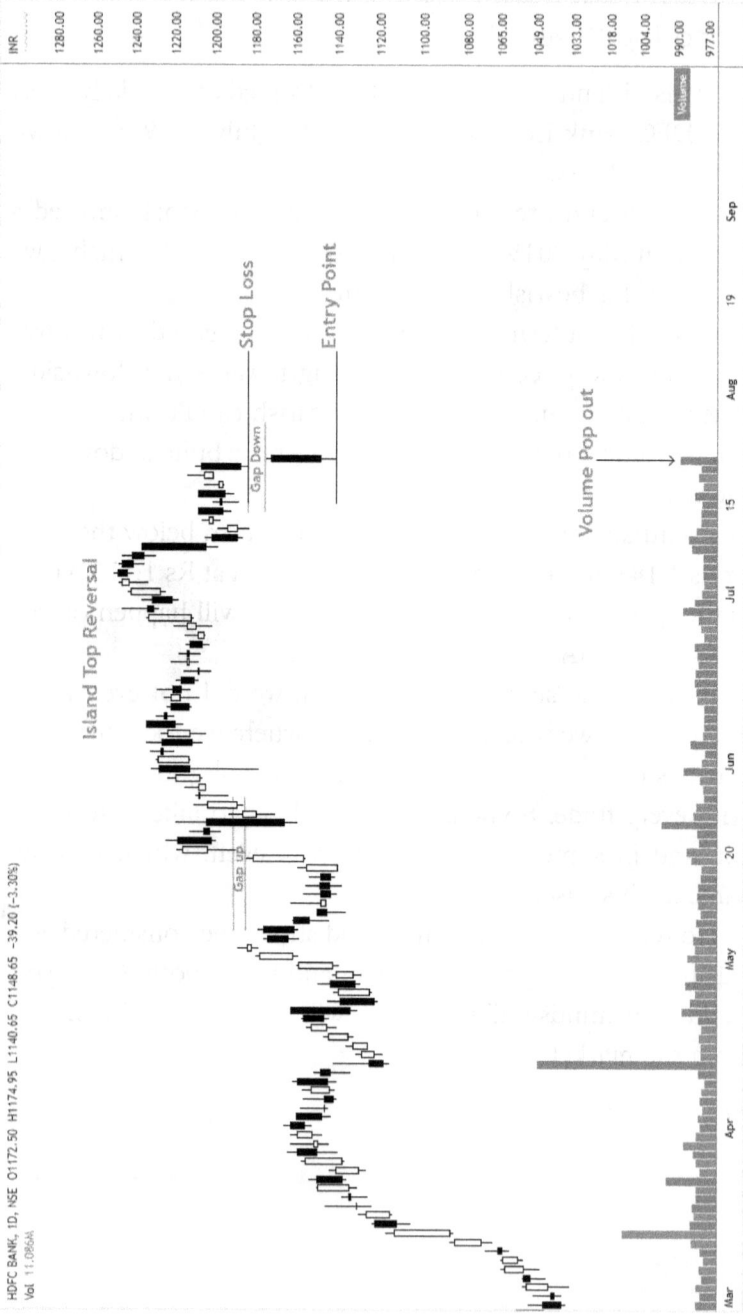

Image 12.108: Daily chart of HDFC Bank Ltd. (bearish island top reversal pattern)

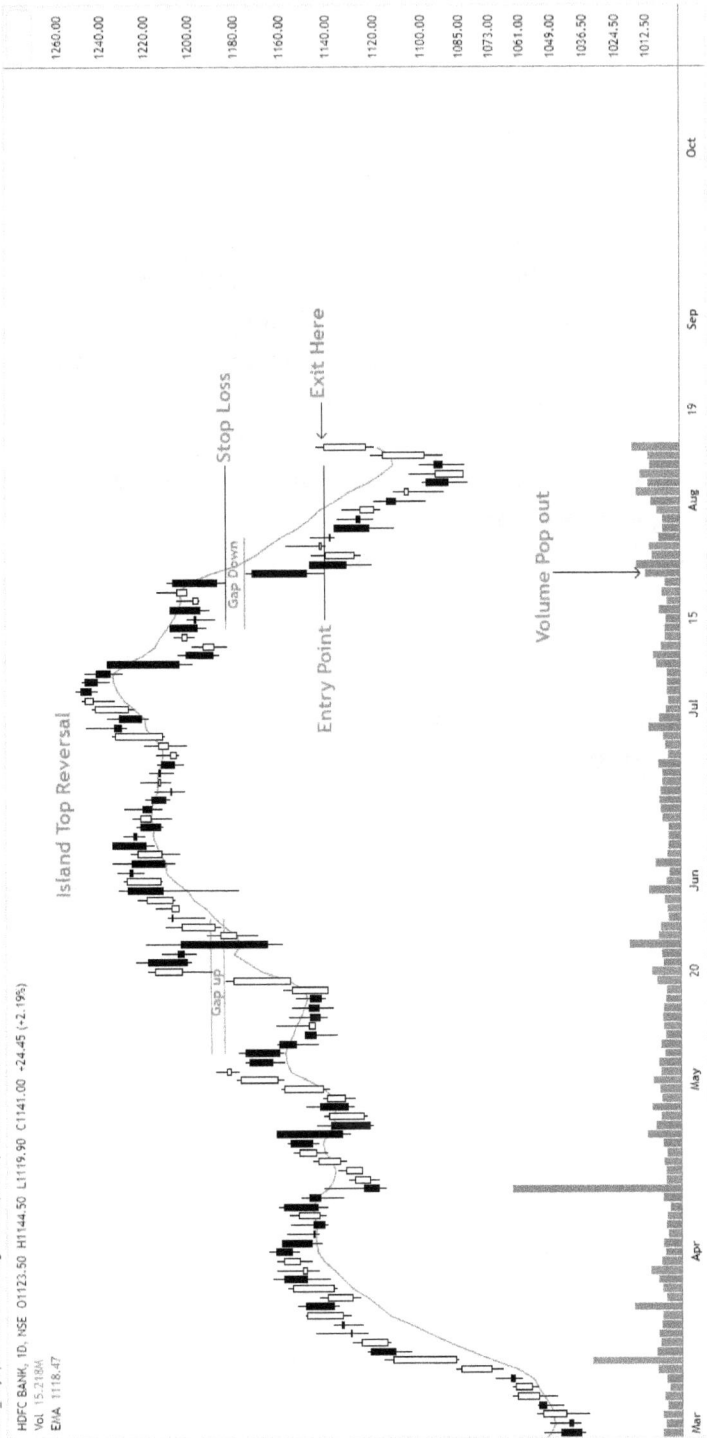

Chart_mojo published on TradingView.com. Jul 10, 2023 12:30 UTC+5:30

HDFC BANK, 1D, NSE O1123.50 H1144.50 L1119.90 C1141.00 -24.45 (-2.19%)
Vol 15.218M
EMA 1118.47

Island Top Reversal

Gap up

Gap Down

Stop Loss

Exit Here

Entry Point

Volume Pop out

Image 12.109: Daily chart of HDFC Bank Ltd. showing us a downside pressure from the gapdown zone of bearish trend reversal pattern.

Descending Broadening Wedge Reversal

A bullish descending broadening wedge reversal pattern formed on the daily chart of Discover Financial Services from July 2017 to September 2017, as shown in image 12.110.

As we can see, the stock was in a downtrend before the formation of bearish ascending broadening wedge pattern. In the month of July 2017, the pattern started taking shape.

Once the pattern ended, the breakout of the pattern happened with a candle which was very strong. It was also supported by a decent volume build-up, signifying upward pressure going forward.

Eventually, the long position will be taken (image 12.111) above the price of $59.52 and the stop-loss will be placed at $58.50 which is the low of the breakout candle. The exit will happen on the basis of 9-EMA breakout at $63.73.

Once the long position was taken, the stock price started marching towards the upside and price action was trading above the trailing stop-loss criteria which is 9 EMA and showed a smooth upside.

The volume action during the upside price action can be seen on the higher side as buying volume bars are bigger than selling volume bars. Eventually, the volume started taming down as we got closer to the exit price and finally got stopped out at $63.73.

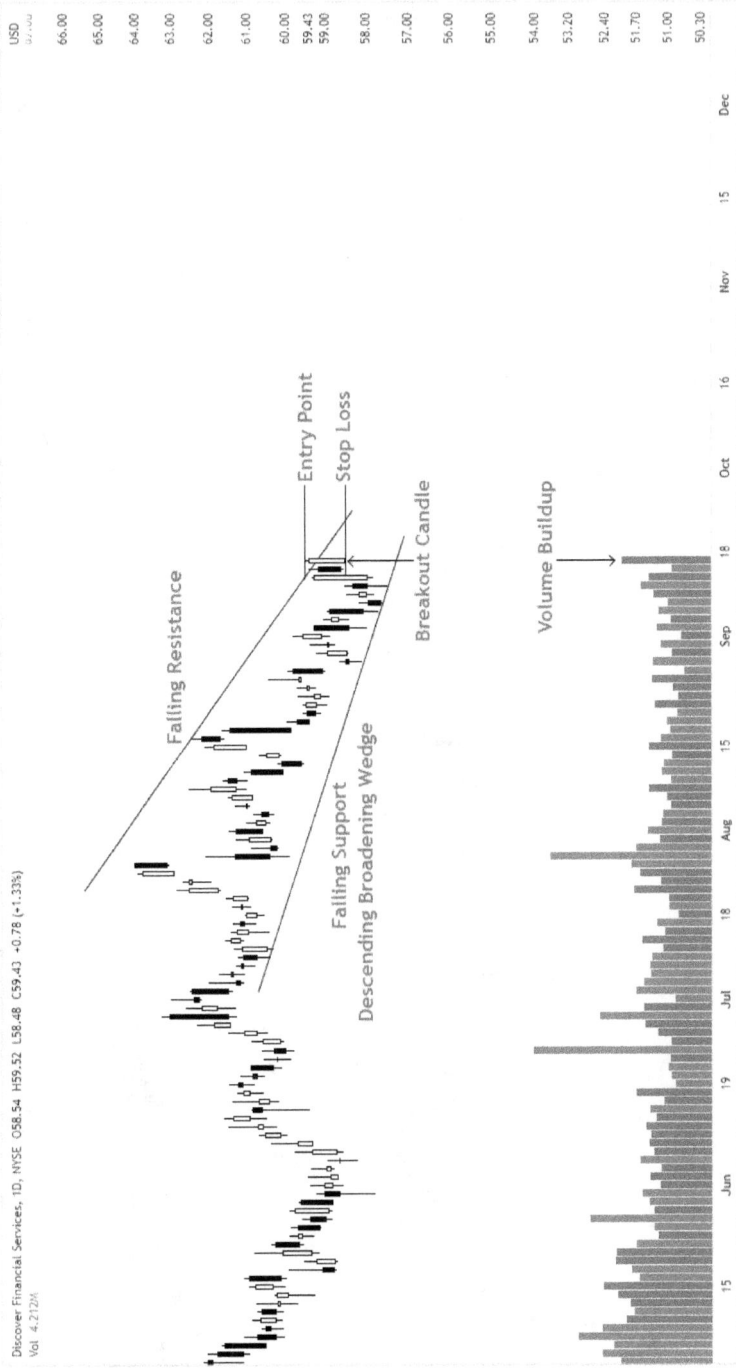

Image 12.110: Daily chart of Discover Financial Services (bullish descending broadening wedge reversal pattern)

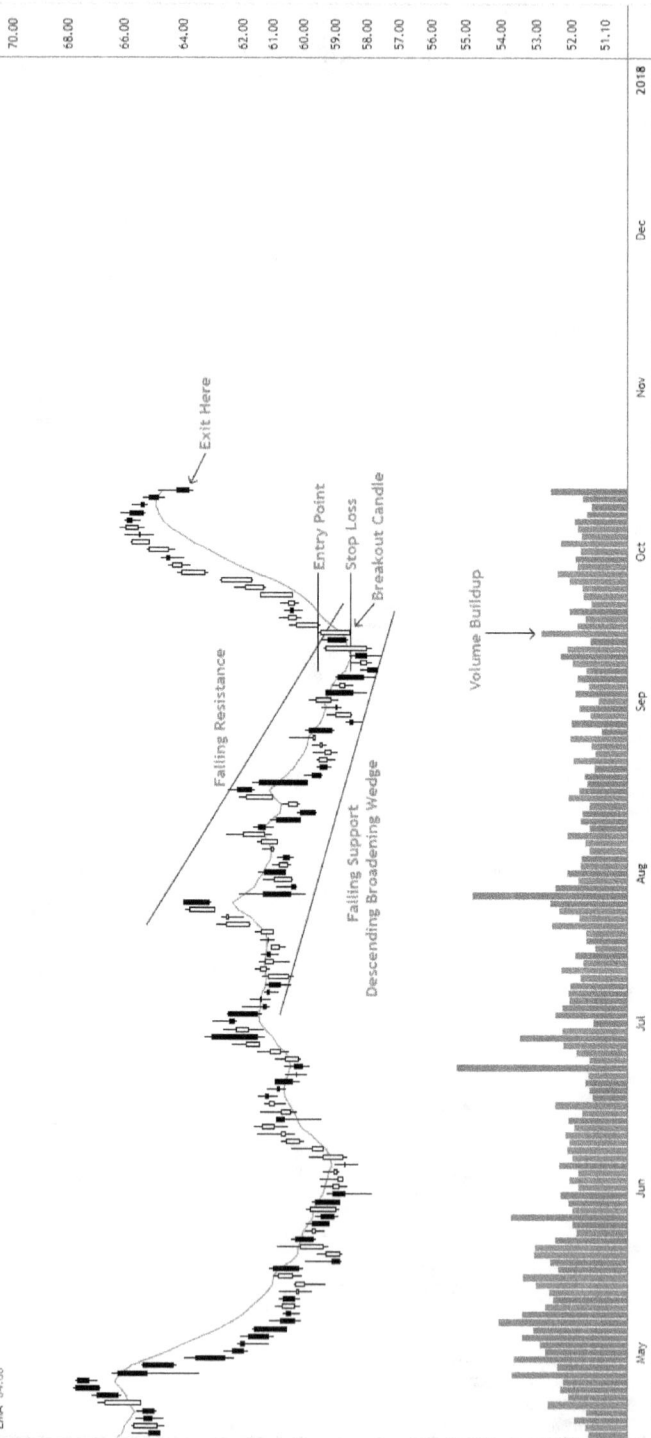

Image 12.111: Daily chart of Discover Financial Services showing us a built-in upside momentum from the breakout of bullish trend reversal pattern.

Ascending Broadening Wedge Reversal

A bearish ascending broadening wedge reversal pattern formed on the daily chart of Indraprastha Gas Ltd., from April 2017 to December 2017 as shown in image 12.112.

The stock was in a strong uptrend before the formation of a bearish ascending broadening wedge pattern and going through a series of white candles which indicates bullishness on the counter.

The breakdown of the pattern happened with a candle which was very strong. It was also supported by a decent volume build-up signifying downward pressure going forward.

Here, the short position is taken at below Rs 340 with a target of around Rs 264 (78 points below the entry area) and the stop is placed around Rs 360 (high of the breakdown candle).

In image 12.113, once the breakdown occurred, the stock price did not look back and kept coming down with strong bearish candles.

The price started falling from Rs 340 all the way down to Rs 264 within a very short duration. In this entire downfall we got to earn 22% returns against 6% risk.

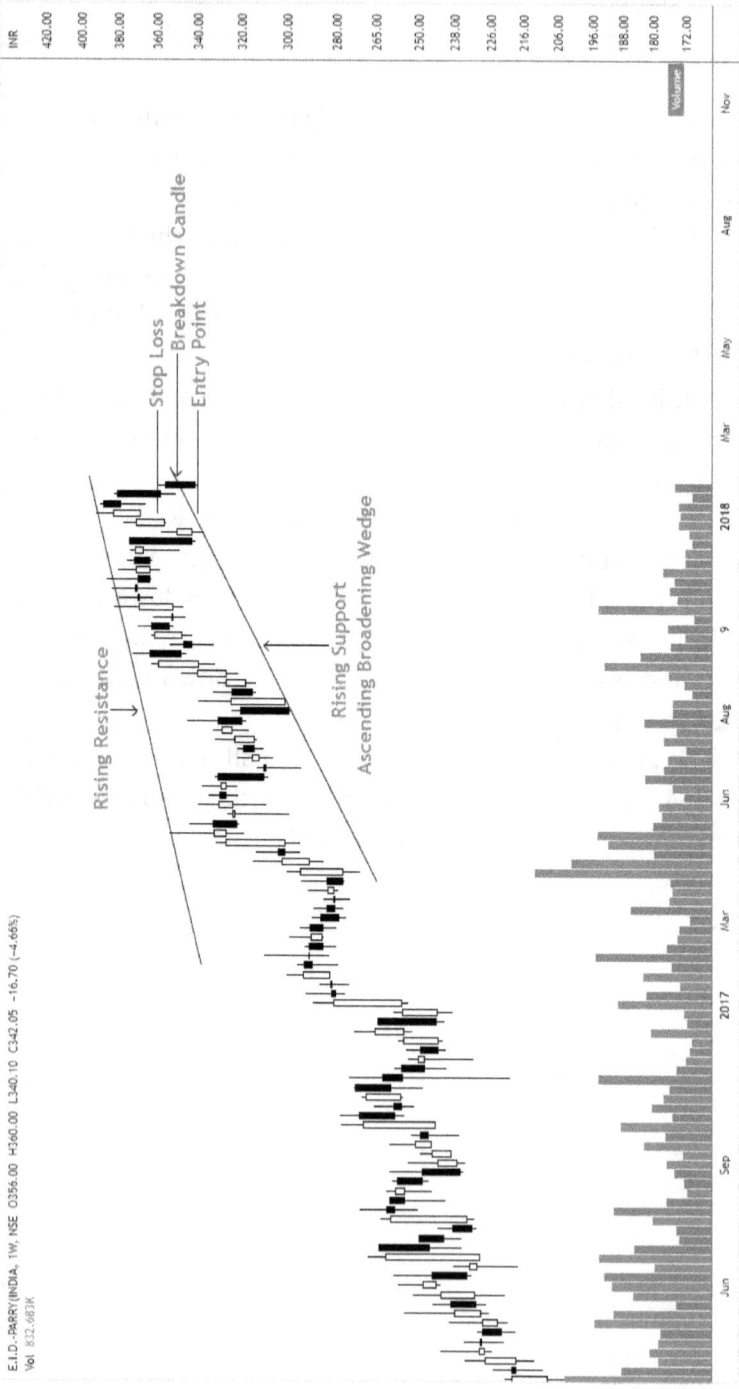

Image 12.112: Daily chart of Indraprastha Gas Ltd. (bearish ascending broadening wedge reversal pattern)

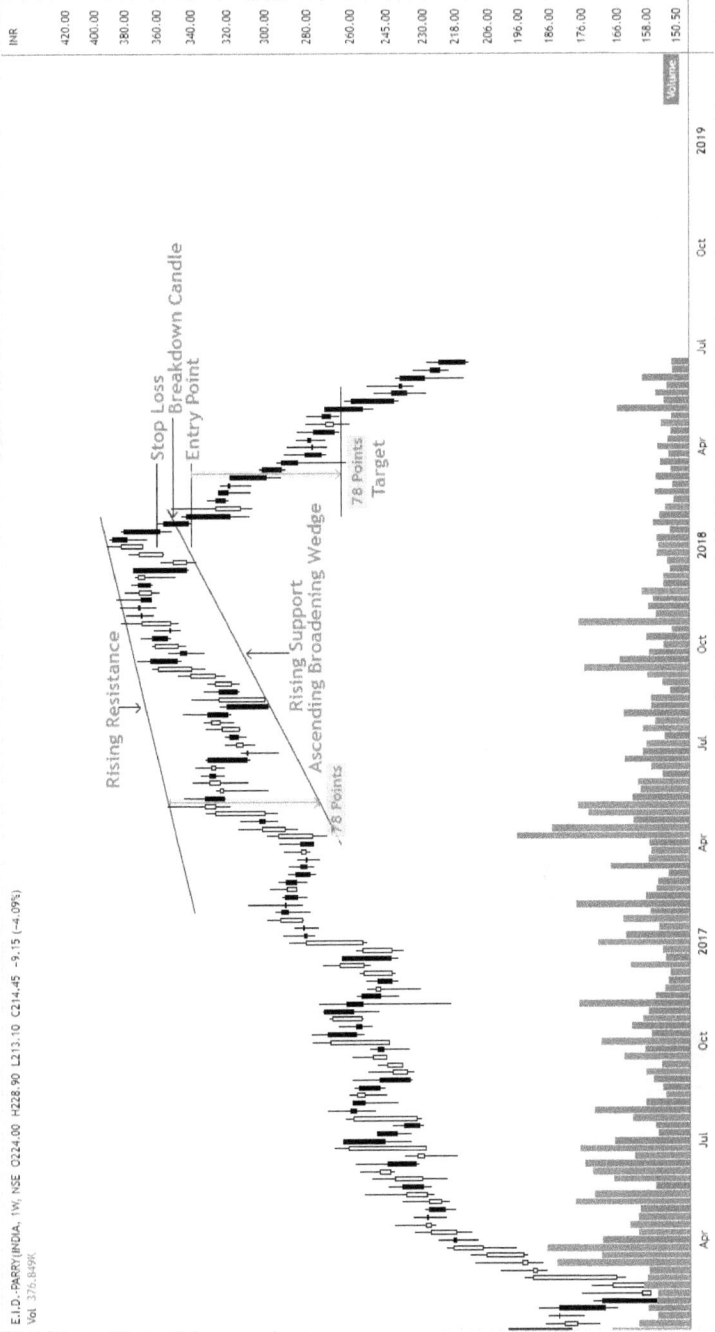

Image 12.113: Weekly chart of EID Parry(India) depicting one-way downside momentum after the breakout from bearish trend reversal pattern.

Conclusion

Congratulations on completing *Breakout Trading Made Easy*! This book has equipped you with the necessary knowledge and strategies to excel in breakout trading. Let's recap the main points and set you on the path to becoming a profitable breakout trader.

Reflect on Your Journey: Take a moment to appreciate your progress. You've learned about identifying breakout opportunities, assessing risk and reward, and executing precise trades. Remember, success in trading is an ongoing journey of learning and adaptation.

Discipline and Patience: Breakout trading requires discipline and patience. Stick to your plan, follow your rules, and don't let emotions cloud your judgment. Be patient, wait for the right setups and let the market situations unfold.

Risk Management: Protecting capital and sustaining profitability are crucial. Set clear risk parameters, determine appropriate position sizes, and use stop-loss orders effectively. Consistency in risk management is key for long-term success.

Adaptability: The markets are dynamic and ever-changing.

Continuously monitor market conditions, stay updated with economic news, and adjust your strategies accordingly. Flexibility and adaptability give you an edge.

Psychology Matters: Manage emotions, avoid impulsive decisions, and stay focused on your strategy. Understand that losses are part of trading and maintain a resilient mindset. Learn from mistakes and stay motivated.

Learn and Seek Growth: Every trade offers an opportunity for learning and growth. Review your trades, analyse patterns, and keep a trading journal. Seek feedback from mentors or fellow traders to accelerate your learning curve.

Build a Supportive Network: Surround yourself with a community of traders who share your passion. Engage in discussions, share ideas, and learn from each other's experiences. Collaboration can provide fresh perspectives and support.

Remember, breakout trading is not a guaranteed path to instant wealth. It requires dedication, continuous learning, and adaptability. Embrace the challenges, be patient, and trust your abilities. May your breakout trades be profitable, and may you achieve your financial goals through breakout trading.

Best wishes for your future success as a breakout trader!

Sunil Gurjar

JAICO PUBLISHING HOUSE

Elevate Your Life. Transform Your World.

ESTABLISHED IN 1946, Jaico Publishing House is home to world-transforming authors such as Sri Sri Paramahansa Yogananda, Osho, the Dalai Lama, Sri Sri Ravi Shankar, Sadhguru, Robin Sharma, Deepak Chopra, Jack Canfield, Eknath Easwaran, Devdutt Pattanaik, Khushwant Singh, John Maxwell, Brian Tracy, and Stephen Hawking.

Our late founder Mr. Jaman Shah first established Jaico as a book distribution company. Sensing that independence was around the corner, he aptly named his company Jaico ('Jai' means victory in Hindi). In order to service the significant demand for affordable books in a developing nation, Mr. Shah initiated Jaico's own publications. Jaico was India's first publisher of paperback books in the English language.

While self-help, religion and philosophy, mind/body/spirit, and business titles form the cornerstone of our non-fiction list, we publish an exciting range of travel, current affairs, biography, and popular science books as well. Our renewed focus on popular fiction is evident in our new titles by a host of fresh young talent from India and abroad. Jaico's recently established translations division translates selected English content into nine regional languages.

Jaico distributes its own titles. With its headquarters in Mumbai, Jaico has branches in Ahmedabad, Bangalore, Chennai, Delhi, Hyderabad, and Kolkata.

SINCE 1946

* 9 7 8 8 1 1 9 1 5 3 9 8 5 *